Rock Climbs
in
Lancashire
and the North West

ROCK CLIMBS
IN
LANCASHIRE & THE
NORTH-WEST

Phil Kelly
and
Dave Cronshaw

CICERONE PRESS

ISBN 1 85284 021 8

BARNOLDSWICK

1969: *Lancashire: A Guide to Rock Climbs*
Compiled by Les Ainsworth, edited by Phil Watkin.

1974: *Lancashire Updates I, II and III*
By Les Ainsworth, Dave Cronshaw, Bob Macmillan and Rob Meakin.

1975: *Rock Climbs in Lancashire and the North West*
By Les Ainsworth.

1979: *Rock Climbs in Lancashire and the North West: Supplement*
By Les Ainsworth, Dave Cronshaw and Al Evans.

1983: *Rock Climbs in Lancashire and the North West*
By Les Ainsworth

1986: *Rock Climbs in Lancashire and the North West: A Supplement*
By Dave Cronshaw and Phil Kelly

Typesetting by Synergy, Royal Oak Barn, Cartmel, Cumbria, LA11 6QB.
Published by Cicerone Press, 2 Police Square, Milnthorpe, Cumbria,
LA7 7QE.

Contents

Introduction

When considered as a whole, the Lancashire area and the climbing grounds therein are so very varied that to make a comparison between each separate area (of which there are nine) would become a task which borders closely on the impossible. Therefore there is a brief precis outlining the character of each area, under the relevant section headings.

This guide acts as a natural progression to the fine series of guides, brought out under the editorship of Les Ainsworth, over a period of twenty-five years. Few changes have been made to the format for this new edition; the gradings have seen a much-needed going over, the main reason being the total eradication of that infamous beast, the 'Lonsdale Hard VS', whilst a new approach has been made as to which crags to include. Many a boozy hour has been spent discussing the relative merits of crag 'x' and crag 'y', and to just how much emphasis should be put on selling each one. Now that the final product is out, all the crags which have been given the full works are certainly worth visiting; Wilton, Anglezarke, Hoghton, Chapel Head Scar are all crags of national importance and rate very highly on any climber's list of favourite crags. Several minor crags have been omitted, because some of them were so insubstantial as to be a complete waste of space, but the ones that are included have all got something to offer – solitude, freedom and adventure in an uncharted wilderness! The now common trade-off between rival guidebook areas has taken place again, with the Peak District taking the Tameside area off our hands (Hobson Moor specialists will mourn that development), and the boundary with Yorkshire being rationalized; Booth Dean Clough, Mytholm Steep, Crow Nest Wood Quarry and Horsehold Scout have all been swapped for Blackstone Edge which, given its close proximity to other crags in the area, is probably more at home in Lancashire. Two other 'new' crags have been included in this volume; Thorn Crag up in the Trough Of Bowland is a natural gritstone edge of great quality, and Craig Y Longridge, which saw an interim guide printed in the 1986 Lancashire supplement, and has come on leaps and bounds in the meantime.

About gradings: This is not the time or the place to get involved in the perpetual grading argument; we have produced as accurately-graded a guidebook as possible, under the following 'ideal' stipulations:

(a)   The technical grade is 'ideally' the grade of the single hardest move on a pitch, taking no other factors into account.

(b)   The adjectival grade 'ideally' goes hand in hand with the technical grade, taking a myriad of other factors into account, to give climbers an impression of how hard the route will feel in relation to the technical grade.

Got that... good, because the English grading system has been on the decline in recent years and can't work to its fullest and best potential whilst climbers are constantly cramming grades down into lower grade niches, in a misguided attempt to compete in what is not (and hopefully will never become) a competitive sport.

The familiar star rating system has been used to indicate the quality of routes: 3 stars indicates a route which must not be missed for the sheer ecstasy of moving on rock at that particular grade, while even one star routes are themselves exceptional enough to give a fair amount of enjoyment. That is not to say that routes without stars are unworthwhile. Closely coupled with the star ratings are the various superlatives enclosed in the text; 'don't touch it with a bargepole' would usually mean a route whose first ascensionist (a) signed a disclaimer, (b) is now a resident of the Moorside Home For Mental Misfits, or (c) both! Excellent on the other hand speaks for itself, and means just that. The now-common dagger symbol (†) has been utilised and implies that a route either hasn't had a repeat ascent, or that the first ascent cannot be confirmed (though the latter type has largely been written out of this book). The deadly black spot symbol brands a route unjustifiable at the time of writing, and it is quite hard to conceive a person ever wanting to do these routes!

Lastly, it is quite commonplace to finish off with a sentence declaring the area covered by the guidebook to be well and truly worked out and there being nothing left for the future, only to be proved wrong in the next spell of dry weather. To make such a rash statement about Lancashire would really be tempting fate; in a land which encompasses well over a hundred crags there are always gaps, surely. It may be true that the cake has nearly been eaten, but there's quite a bit of icing left, if you know where to look. Good luck!

Glossary

PR, PA, PB: the three contexts in which pegs are used; as runners, aid pegs, or for belays.

BR, BA, BB: similar to pegs, and are less likely to have been stolen, because the neanderthal gear-thief has not yet figured out how to get them out.

TR, TA, TB: same as the above two, but much prettier.

Dobs: doubtful or unsafe blocks.

Dyno: make a jump to gain the next holds; a Craig Y Longridge special!

The Crag Environment

Prepared by Bill Wright, BMC Access Officer

Climbing in Lancashire is unique. "Tell us summat we don't know lad" you may say if you regularly climb there. For a foreigner (Yorkshireman) however, it is a revealing place because the climbing is mostly man-made, unlike Yorkshire where it is made by God and probably includes the greatest concentration of quarry climbing anywhere.

Now, the creators of these outdoor walls were not always as clever at their design as the employees of Bendcrete and DR Climbing walls are today, though contrary to popular opinion, their intention was to provide stone for all sorts of purposes rather than reveal rock faces for Lancashire Rock Jocks to show off their skills (and latest pattern of lycra tights).

The point of this is that quarries, by their very definition, are often of a transient nature and in some cases have a limited lifespan: they may be subject to further quarrying or possible infill, or just become yet another set of foundations for the latest creation of Wimpey happy houses.

At for example, Trowbarrow, legal quarrying permission still exists, and for the company to maintain this 'live quarry' status they must:-

(a) Stop all glory seekers and lesser mortals entering the site.
(b) Regularly, Frank Bruno-like, rearrange the face so that they are seen to be keeping the 'live quarry' status, so this doesn't lapse.

The Health and Safety at Work Act and the Mines and Quarries Act don't take too kindly to quarry owners who allow anyone (climbers or otherwise) onto the designated sites. So when they politely tell you to "naff off", they are fulfilling an obligation which the law says they must do.

If then you decide to run the gauntlet of the wrath of the quarry management, bear in mind that you will probably be politely but firmly asked to leave, and if you refuse to do so, the local constabulary may take a less understanding view when they are called out. Diplomacy and courtesy will gain more in the long-term than a rude glory crusade. Other quarries (such as Withnell) are similarly affected, and it is a sad fact that during the happy life of this guide, some of the crags listed (mostly minor) will as a result radically alter or disappear altogether; may Britannia rest in peace, or whatever it was they buried it in!

At the time of writing though, the greater concern will be the likely change of ownership of a significant number of crags. Huge tracts of land are owned by Water Authorities and privatisation is going to affect climbing in Lancashire more than anywhere else; plans have already been discussed for the NWWA sale of the Wilton Quarries. The BMC are keeping a watching eye on the position so read the climbing mags to keep abreast of how it is likely to affect you and your local gem.

In view of this, at all crags if you encounter a landowner or the like who wants to know what you are doing, don't reply by telling him/her to "go jump in the lake" or similar as it isn't normally conducive to preserving the long-term access to the crag. Too many hours of patient discussion have been wasted due to tactless and downright rude outburst by climbers who, when approached, feel they have a God-given right to climb.

Dogs are one of the most common reasons for such friction. Your cuddly little Jekyll may be the most wonderful doggy in the whole world with the kids, but unfettered around livestock may very well be a canine Mr Hyde with the fundamental instinct to kill and maim. Keep your dog on a lead, or if you're likely to have to leave it alone, leave it watching the tinned dog food adverts on the telly at home.

Lancashire may not be particularly noted by climbers as the new World Centre of wildlife but at the north and in Cumbria there are crags (such as those on the Whitbarrow Escarpment and around Silverdale) where there is a wide variety of both flora and fauna which are protected by law. The simple rule is don't pick 'em, don't frighten 'em but do 'wise up' any one that you see who does.

In conclusion, future access problems will be avoided by climbers who LEARN and FOLLOW the COUNTRY CODE (as covered in the BMC booklet 'Tread Lightly', available at all good bookshops and by post from the BMC, etc., plug, plug.) By doing so they will not only greatly improve the possibility of continued access to the crags, but also make these 'unique' playgrounds much more pleasant places to climb.

Note: The inclusion of any crag in this guidebook is by no means a carte-blanche statement that access is available, as regards both climbing and rights of way, to members of the general public.

Acknowledgements

This guidebook has received assistance from every conceivable quarter. Right from the start when we had a noisy guidebook meeting in a crowded disco pub in Holcombe Brook, attended by around 30 climbers (doubtless more set off but got lost trying to find Holcombe Brook!) all eager to help, then later when the final guide team was assembled and the work spread out, offers of assistance still came in from other sources.

To thank all the people involved would be a Herculean task and doubtless some crucial names would be omitted. To all those who gave assistance – thank you. Some of the people who immediately spring to mind are; the area co-ordinators – Chris Hardy (the perfectionist), Bruce Goodwin (for taking on the Yorkies at the last minute), Jon Sparks, Al Phizacklea (can you believe the nation's security is in this man's hands?) and more recently Paul Cornforth – they are all the reasons for my near bankruptcy and shares in the Wiggins-Teape paper industry. To all the individual crag authors, whose names are too numerous to mention though their names lie at the head of their respective sections; thanks for the endless sessions of cleaning, checking, trundling and occasional new-routing. To the four artists in our employ; foreman Malc Baxter and his three henchmen, Mark Griffiths, Jim Whitham and Geoff Haigh. All four have turned out consistently excellent work that adds that extra touch of class to the book.

And to all and sundry; the people behind the scenes who generally gave vast amounts of assistance, and without whom the guide would never appear at all. To Geoff Hibbert, Paul Pritchard, Hank Pasquill, Ian Lonsdale, Bill Wright (a future convert to Lancashire climbing), White Scar, John Ryden, Brian Cropper and Ann Smith (for helping me to look on the brighter side of life when nothing seemed to be going right). Andy Moss stepped in at a late stage to help with the Wilton history, unintentionally uncovering a massive can of worms in the process! Thanks are also due to everyone who proffered comments and to all those who entered photographs for consideration. The photos we have chosen speak chapters about the differing facets of Lancashire climbing.

Lastly, there is a special thank-you extended to Les Ainsworth, who threw himself wholeheartedly into the task of publishing the then much-neglected crags and quarries in the area, way back in the 1960's. Les brought the crags well and truly up to date with a superb series of guidebooks, each one of which was the state-of-the-art at the time. It is good to know that this guide was typeset by Les's own firm (Synergy) and that he is still actively involved with the Lancashire guidebook.

Once again; thank-you one and all and see yawwl White Scar y'hear?

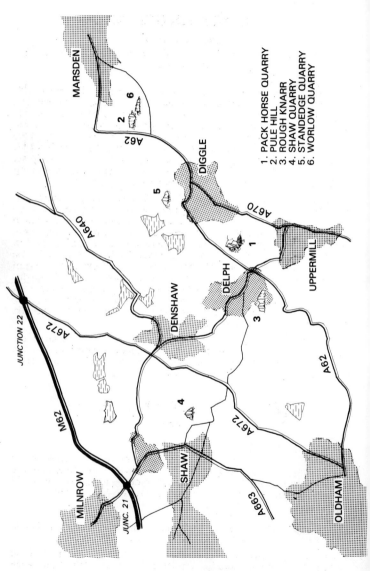

1. PACK HORSE QUARRY
2. PULE HILL
3. ROUGH KNARR
4. SHAW QUARRY
5. STANDEDGE QUARRY
6. WORLOW QUARRY

I. THE STANDEDGE AREA

Compiled by Chris Hardy
with assistance from Malc Baxter, Geoff Haigh, Bruce Goodwin,
Chris Booth and Carl Dawson

This neglected area comprises a series of quarries on the moorlands to the north-east of Oldham. The two major crags, Pule Hill and Shooter's Nab, have to an extent been spared of the quarrymen's activities giving climbs on both quarried and natural gritstone and are both unusual examples of quarry architecture. Both crags give excellent opportunities for a days climbing and merit a visit from afar; Pule Hill is an excellent venue for soloing, or for beginners. Shaw Quarry, once billed as an 'enigma to climbing', is becoming increasingly popular as an evening venue and justifiably so.

Although crags such as Pack Horse Quarry, Rough Knarr and Standedge Quarry compare favourably with minor crags in more popular areas, they have not been widely used since their inclusion in the previous edition of this guide and a decision was made to represent these crags in diagrammatic form – a decision mourned by some, but not by others! In such a selective guidebook, this portrays their true importance; they are certainly not worth a visit from a distance of greater than 10 miles (or is it 10 yards?). However, the 'majestic' Worlow Quarry has somehow eluded the purge; it probably won't next time! Once again, traditional names have been used for some of the routes in these latter four quarries and it is hoped that the true first ascensionists will not be offended.

As a final note, all puns, jokes etc. found within this section are unintentional and your suspicions are therefore confirmed – the cragsmen of Chew Valley are just jealous at us having acquired their best crags over the past ten years!

PACK HORSE QUARRY (SD 995 084)

By Geoff Haigh

APPROACH AND ACCESS
Approaching through Delph village from the north, drive down to the crossroads on the A62, then turn left and after ½ mile the tops of the quarries can just be seen on the right side of the road. Park by an old barn and follow the fence up the hillside into the quarries.

SITUATION AND CHARACTER
This quarry overlooks the A62 (Oldham – Huddersfield road) ¾ mile north-east of the centre of Delph.

There are in fact two quarries on this site. The one to the right of the fence is short, but suitable for problems. The quarry left of the fence

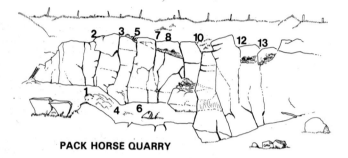

PACK HORSE QUARRY

is U-shaped and contains all the recorded routes. At the back there is a wall full of cracks, which ends at a corner, and to the right of this is a steep slab. All but one of the routes are on the back wall.

THE CLIMBS are described from LEFT to RIGHT.

1. **Keffer** Hard VS 5b
2. **Shaz** Diff
3. **Time Switch** Sev
4. **Grey Donkey** Hard VS 5a
5. **White Horse** VS 4c
6. **Ego Trip** E1 5a
7. **Dark Horse** VS 4c   ★
8. **Stallion** Hard VS 5a
9. **Roundabout** Hard Sev
4b. Start as for Dark Horse, but make a rising traverse leftwards to finish up Shaz.
10. **Mark** V Diff
11. **Times Passed** VS 4c   ★
12. **The Riffler** Hard Sev 4b   ★
13. **Slabdab** V Diff
To the right is a broken wall. At its left end is an alcove, with a crack.
14. **Kestrel Crack** Hard VS
5b. Climb the crack stepping left to a large foothold. Finish direct.

PULE HILL ROCKS (SE 032 108)

By Chris Hardy

SITUATION AND CHARACTER

The outcrop, visible from the road, stretches for approximately 900 yards along the top of Pule Hill; roughly 500 yards east of the Oldham – Huddersfield road (A62), where it runs down from Standedge Cutting into Marsden.

On the very left of the rocks, and to the left of a track leading up from the road, is an isolated mass – The Sentinel. Starting at, and extending rightwards from the track is the quarry, which is divided into three sections. From left to right these are: Northern Section, Leprosy Wall and Triple Wall.

After the quarry, well to the right and past a number of small buttresses, is The Flying Buttress (a natural archway of rock) and behind is the infamous Trog 'Ole. About 80 yards farther right, a large hemisphere-shaped hole in a small buttress above some natural steps is The Tomb, and 40 yards right again is The Apse which is obvious from its name. Fifty yards right, the last named feature is Square Buttress.

The rocks can be divided into two distinct types; the natural rocks and the quarried rocks. The outcrop has a clean rocky top, reaches a height of 40 feet, and gives both strenuous and delicate climbs on rough, sound gritstone. The routes hereabouts tend to be steep and unusually juggy, though the occasional 'hollow' flake adds to the excitement. The quarry attains a height of 50 feet with generally clean rock, which varies in quality from excellent to downright atrocious.

The hill is a favourite spot with hang-gliding enthusiasts, and strong winds often prevail, which accounts for the quick-drying nature of the rock. The rocks' close proximity to the road, sunny western aspect and numerous soloing possibilities make this an excellent place for an evening visit.

APPROACH AND ACCESS

From Oldham follow the A62 – Huddersfield road – to the top of Standedge Cutting at the crest of the Pennines. After a further quarter mile, the Great Western Hotel will be seen on the left. Park at a lay-by on the right-hand side of the road, ¾ of a mile beyond the hotel, 1½ miles before Marsden.

The rocks are the property of the National Trust and consequently the general public is allowed access, including to climb, provided the Trust's bye-laws are adhered to i.e. NO CLIMBING FENCES and NO LITTER.

HISTORY

The first real climber to leave his mark on the rocks seems to have been

George Bower, who scrambled here in the early 1920s. However, considering the natural attraction of the edge, it is surprising to find that its main development as a climbing ground came at a much later date.

Probably the first climbers to give the edge any real attention were the Chew Valley Cragsmen, prominent amongst them being Graham West and Roy Brown, who visited the rocks occasionally during the '40s and '50s.

In the summer of 1957 Tony Howard, Alwyn Whitehead and Brian Hodgkinson paid several visits and within a few weekends they had accounted for most of the routes on The Outcrop, although several of these had probably been climbed before. The base for their operations was the infamous cave behind The Flying Buttress, known as the Trog 'Ole, where many pleasant nights were spent.

In October 1960, the quarry was visited by members of the Rimmon M.C. and two routes were added, these being Tut by Brian Woods and Delilah by Tony Jones. In January of 1962, Malc Baxter of the Manchester Gritstone C.C. added The Ratcher and The Great Scoop, although the latter route may have been climbed earlier by Tony Howard. A few years later the Rimmon paid another visit, climbing most of the cracks on Leprosy Wall, but kept no records of first ascent details. Several years later Bob Whittaker and Brian Cropper reclimbed all of these cracks, and others, but chose to name and record only a selection for the 1976 Chew Valley guide.

In the late '60s, Krilt and Wellington were added by Bill Tweedale and in September 1969 and April 1970, Tony Howard and Bill Birch climbed, respectively, Odyssey, and the girdle of the quarry – Amazing Revelation.

The next major additions, climbed in March 1977, were Spellbound by Nick Colton and Godspell by Jim Campbell, with Con Carey seconding both routes. Within three days these two routes were repeated by Gabriel Regan, who thought he had just made the first ascents of both lines. The following year John Smith added The Bulger, although this may have been done before.

The period 1979-81 was largely dominated by Paul Cropper who found Midas Direct, Beyreyat Wall and Mega Factor, as well as free-climbing Delilah Direct Start together with the aid section on the last pitch of Amazing Revelation. Being a hybrid route and completely different in character, the resultant was named Gold Rush. Paul also climbed the previously overlooked Necronomicon in April 1980, taking full advantage of the bolt on Odyssey which had recently been replaced.

In 1981, Gary Gibson got a look in with Lethal Lemon and the vicious Blood Finger, as well as confusing issues by renaming variations on existing routes on the first wall of Triple Wall. Virtually all these variations had been climbed before and hence the original names have been restored.

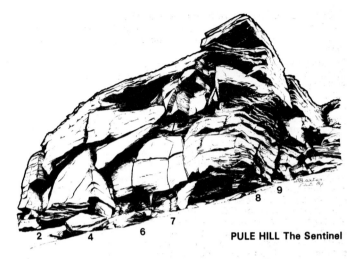

PULE HILL The Sentinel

THE CLIMBS are described from LEFT to RIGHT, beginning at some broken rocks 50 yards to the left of The Sentinel. On the right-hand side of these rocks, a wrinkled face has a short dog-legged crack at mid-height:

1. Forerunner 20ft Sev
The wrinkled face is climbed rightwards to finish up the arête.

THE SENTINEL

2. The Peeler 20ft Sev
At the left-hand end of The Sentinel is a steep crack which is climbed past a small overhang.

3. Overlapping Wall 20ft E1 ★ †
6b. Start 6 feet to the right of The Peeler at an obvious handhold and climb direct, passing the overlap with great difficulty.

4. No Traverse 20ft Hard Sev
4b. Start a few feet right of Overlapping Wall. Climb the short arête to finish up a crack.

5. Tony's Traverse 60ft Hard Sev ★
4b. Climb No Traverse until a semi-hand-traverse, above or below the overhang, leads rightwards for 20 feet. Move up and across to a comfortable stance (The Throne). Continue traversing around the arête to finish up a short wall.

6. No Exit 25ft VS ★
4c. Five feet to the right of No Traverse is a short finger-crack. Climb directly up the crack and steep wall above.

7. **Traverse Not**   25ft   Hard Sev   *
4c. Start 5 feet to the right of No Exit at an undercut, faint groove. Climb the fingertip layback and short crack to reach The Bed. Finish direct or slightly rightwards.

8. **Bed End**   35ft   V Diff   *
Start at the right-hand wall of The Sentinel, and below an easy chimney. Climb leftwards via a Z-shaped crack to reach The Throne, moving up and slightly leftwards to finish.

9. **Sentinel Wall**   20ft   Sev
From the base of Bed End, climb directly up the left-hand edge of the easy chimney.

Sixty yards to the right is the start of Pule Hill Quarry which is divided into three sections, beginning with: **NORTHERN SECTION**

At the left-hand end of this section and directly behind a grassy incline (the approach to the rocks) is a man-made wall halfway up the face. Starting below and 6 feet left of this is:

10. **Schmarren**   35ft   VS
4c. Start below a large sandy pocket and climb the wall direct.

11. **Skull Climb**   35ft   V Diff
Climb the crack to reach a cave on the left of the man-made wall, then move rightwards to finish up a groove.

12. **The Iliad**   35ft   VS
5a. Start 15 feet right of Skull Climb and climb directly up the wall via thin cracks and a wide horizontal break.

Thirty feet right is a corner capped by a triangular roof:

13. **Retreat**   25ft   Moderate
Move rightwards across the slab, then climb up to the overhang which is avoided on the left.

Immediately right, the buttress has a scoop in its centre.

14. **Midas**   30ft   VS
4c. Start below the scoop and trend leftwards past a short crack to finish up the arête.

15. **Midas Direct**   30ft   Hard VS   *
5a. Start as for Midas, then gain the scoop with difficulty and finish direct.

16. **Lethal Lemon**   30ft   E1   *
5a. The vague arête 5 feet right of Midas Direct is gained and followed direct.

17. **Geoff's Groove**   25ft   Moderate
Right of Lethal Lemon, climb the obvious V-shaped groove.

18. **Spellbound**   25ft
The severely undercut arête 5 feet right of Geoff's Groove is climbed with difficulty, especially now, as half of the route lies on the ground!

Next comes The Great Scoop which consists of two slab strips running up from left to right beneath a large overhang. The orange-coloured top slab overhangs the lower, which in turn overhangs the ground.

19. **The Great Scoop** 50ft VS   ★★
4c. The lower slab is traversed from left to right to gain a short corner, from where a long reach lands one beneath a huge overhang (possible belay). Finish up the steep wall to the right. The right-hand side of the lower slab can be gained direct, 5c, which would make a good introductory pitch to:

20. **Godspell** 30ft E2   ★★★
5b. From a belay on The Great Scoop, climb up to the centre of the large roof. Hand-traverse wildly leftwards until a foothold on the arête can be gained, then finish up the steep wall.

Fifteen feet right of The Great Scoop is a short overhanging crack leading to a sandy hole; Hard VS 5b. Four feet right again is:

21. **Annual Route** 30ft Sev
Gain a ledge at head-height, then layback the corner to reach an overhung ledge which is quitted by a wide crack on the left.

22. **The Bulger** 35ft VS
5b. Start 8 feet right of Annual Route. Climb the bulging wall to reach a ledge. Move right, then finish up Dedfer or its left-hand edge.

Twenty feet to the right and round the arête is:

23. **Dedfer** 30ft Sev
Climb the hanging corner, passing a ledge to finish up a V-shaped groove. The ledge can also be gained by the arête to the left of the corner, or by a long traverse past a bulge and starting from the slab of Annual Route.

24. **Blood Finger** 35ft Hard VS   ★
5c. Start just right of Dedfer and climb a short overhanging finger-crack, moving right on a ledge to finish up the wall on the right of a faint rib.

Fifteen feet to the right is a slab taken by:

25. **Sew** 45ft V Diff
Climb the right-hand edge of the slab to gain a ledge (possible belay). Traverse left for 10 feet and finish up the centre of the wall. The left-hand side of the same slab, (SO SEW), can be climbed at a similar standard.

26. **Wall and Flake** 45ft VS
5a. From 6 feet right of Sew, the cracked wall is taken leftwards past a small cleft to reach a ledge. Finish up the wide flake.

Eight feet right is a well-defined chimney which forms the boundary between Northern Section and:

LEPROSY WALL

27. **Tut** 50ft Hard Sev
Climb the chimney, then follow a short crack to gain a cave on the right.

Step up left under the overhang, then stride back right above the cave to a good foothold. Finish up the arête – exposed.

Twelve feet to the right of Tut are two large caves, one above the other. At the left-hand side of these is an obvious thin layback flake:

28. Krilt 45ft Hard VS
5a. Climb the left side of the cave to reach the layback flake. Take this and 'finish directly up the wall just left of a short wide crack'.

29. Aquarius 45ft VS
4c. Climb into the lower cave and pull out right to a short crack which leads to the upper cave. Move out left and finish up the short steep crack just right of Krilt.

30. Mega Factor 45ft Hard VS   *
5a. From 12 feet right of the cave, climb the wall to gain the right-hand side of the upper cave. Step left and finish direct up the clean wall.

31. Apollo 45ft VS
4c. Five feet right of Mega Factor, climb directly up the scarred wall, finishing up a short jamming crack and vague flake.

32. Venus 45ft VS
4c. Start 6 feet right of Apollo and climb a crack to gain an obvious niche. Exit left via a flake, and finish up the shattered wall.

33. Spacewalk 45ft VS
4c. Climb Venus to the niche and leave this by a thin crack on the right. Step right and finish direct.

34. Wellington 45ft VS
4c. Start 8 feet to the right of Spacewalk and climb the steep crack to below an ill-defined chimney, moving right past a 'wobble-block' to finish direct.

35. Sinbad 45ft VS
4c. Six feet right of Wellington, climb directly up the crack past a large sandy pocket.

36. Appendix 35ft VS
4c. Twenty feet right of Sinbad, a wide crack leads to a cave which is quitted by the right wall.

37. Sandman 35ft VS
4b. Start 5 feet right of Appendix and climb a short groove and crack which has a loose finish.

38. Beyreyat Wall 35ft Hard VS
4c. Start 7 feet right of Sandman and climb the wall which contains a sandy hole low down.

39. Boozers Way 30ft Hard Sev
From 5 feet right of Beyreyat Wall, climb cracks into a recess which in turn is vacated by a crack up its left edge.

40. Fusion Chimney 40ft E1
4c. At the right-hand end of Leprosy Wall is a revolting wide-angled corner...avoid it at all costs!

PULE HILL Leprosy Wall

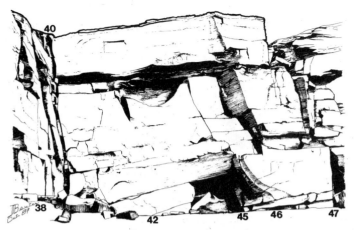

PULE HILL QUARRY Triple Wall Delilah Area

TRIPLE WALL

At right angles to Leprosy Wall is the first of these walls which has a huge sandy cave just above mid-height.

41. Necronomicon 55ft E3 (1BA) ★★
5c. Climb Fusion Chimney for 12 feet, then move right and climb a thin crack to gain the left-hand side of the large cave. Gain the bolt in the wall above and use it for aid, then free-climb to the top.

42. Odyssey 50ft A1/E1 ★
5b. Make a long reach across the crevasse to place the first peg and continue past a drill-hole (bong or wooden wedge) to the centre of the sandy cave. Exit from the left-hand side of this, as for Necronomicon.

43. Odyssey Variant 55ft E3 (1BA) ★
5c. Start 12 feet right of Odyssey and surmount the jutting nose using a convenient drill-hole. From a ledge, continue up the thin crack to reach the right-hand side of the sandy cave. Finish as for Necronomicon.

44. All Quiet on the Eastern Front 60ft E3 (1BA) †
5c. Links Odyssey and Odyssey Variant by a short traverse leftwards from the ledge.

45. Delilah 60ft E1 ★★
5b. Start just right of a large fallen block and thrash up the narrowing cleft to a ledge on the left. Gain, and then climb, the cracked corner on the right, traversing 10 feet right to finish up the centre of the wall.

46. Gold Rush 40ft E2 ★
6a. Eight feet right of Delilah, climb the scarred wall to a triangular 'flat'. Stand on this and finish diagonally to the right by a series of deceptively innocent-looking ledges.

47. Sampson 30ft   Hard VS   *
5b. Move up leftwards past a protruding piece of metal and finish up a thin bulging crackline.

To the right and set well back is the Second Wall of Triple Wall, taken by:

48. The Ratcher 25ft   VS   *
5a. Start from below and just right of a sandy gash. Move up then rightwards past a sharp fingerhold to reach a flat hold. Stand on this with difficulty, then go easily to the top.

49. The 8-Foot Kid 25ft   VS   *
5b. A counter-diagonal to The Ratcher, starting some 8 feet right at some well-worn, chipped holds.

At right angles to the previous routes is the Third Wall of Triple Wall. Ten feet feet from its right end is a deep chimney.

50. Brian's Route 30ft   Hard Sev
Start just left of the chimney and climb directly up the thin crack, followed by a jamming crack, to the top.

51. Sandy Cleft 30ft   V Diff
Climb straight up the chimney.

52. Green Ridge 25ft   Diff
Climb the wall right of Sandy Cleft, moving right to finish up the ridge.

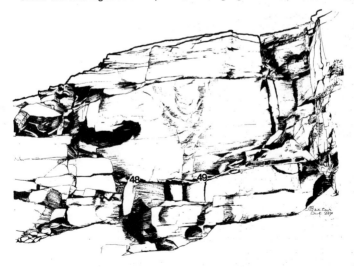

PULE HILL Triple Wall, The Ratcher Area

53. Amazing Revelation 420ft E1 5b(3 pegs for aid)
This girdles the quarry from left to right.
(1) 35ft. As for The Great Scoop and belay on the ramp.
(2) 45ft. Traverse round the prow into a corner, then cross the right wall past a sandy hollow to belay on Dedfer.
(3) 40ft. Make a long reach for a jug, then follow the undercut foot-ledge round the prow.
(4) 50ft. From the end of the ledge stride across the chimney and go up into the cave on Tut. Continue right to reach another cave and belay on an iron stanchion.
(5) 110ft. Follow the gently descending foot-ledge across the shattered wall for 35 feet, then step down to a jammed block and continue the traverse for another 20 feet to a yellow pocket. Go up the steep cracks to a rake just under the quarry top, then traverse right into a cave.
(6) 65ft. Escape right passing two more caves to loose blocks in the corner of Fusion Chimney. Using 3 pegs for aid, cross the wall and belay in the huge sandy cave.
(7) 75ft. Climb down right to join Delilah, then move right again to Gold Rush which is taken to the top, crux.

THE OUTCROP

Seventy yards right of the quarry, past lesser rocks, is a prominent buttress with a large hollow in its centre. On its left is a very short crack leading to a ledge:

54. Crude Crack 30ft Diff
Gain the ledge and avoid an escape by climbing the mediocre, shattered crack to the top.

55. Tariff Wall 30ft Hard VS
5b. Climb into the hollow, then move left to the arête and climb it finishing just right of Crude Crack.

56. The Token 25ft E1
5c. A direct finish from the hollow, via the overhang above.

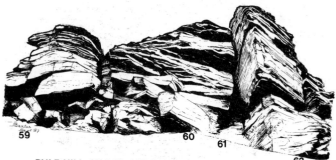

59   60   61   63

PULE HILL Wrinkled Wall Area

57. Godsend 30ft Hard Sev
4b. Ascend into the hollow, then leave it by moving up and out to the right until a good finishing hold is reached.

58. Dusky Doddle 25ft Hard V Diff
Climb directly up the face, starting 8 feet to the right of Godsend at a small overhang.

Twenty yards right is an obvious overhanging corner. To the left of this is an easier-looking wall, and left again is a roughly square buttress:

59. Atlas 30ft Hard Diff
Step off the sloping-topped block and ascend directly up the centre.

60. Whacker's Wall 35ft Hard Diff
Start just left of the overhanging corner. From a short groove, climb the wall and turn the second of two overhangs on the left.

61. Amen 35ft Hard V Diff   ★★
Climb straight up the overhanging corner-crack. The final 12 feet are very steep, but the holds are superb.

The right-hand wall of the corner terminates in an arête. On its right-hand side is a wrinkled face.

62. Sobeit 35ft VS   ★
4c. Move up and left to the arête, which is climbed directly on its right-hand side.

63. Wrinkled Wall 35ft Sev
4c. As for Sobeit, but avoid a move left by continuing direct up the wrinkled face and passing an overhung ledge.

Ten yards to the right and across the gap is **THE FLYING BUTTRESS**. Starting under the archway is:

65   **66 67**   **PULE HILL Flying Buttress Area**

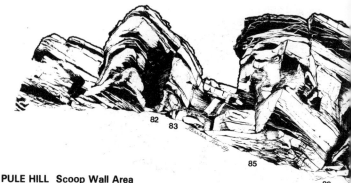

PULE HILL Scoop Wall Area

64. **Minotaur** 30ft Hard VS *
5a. Bridge up above the left entrance of the archway, then swing onto the outer face (exposed) and finish direct.

65. **Flying Buttress** 40ft Sev **
Start at the lowest point of the buttress. Climb a short wall and thin polished crack, then finish up the final wall on good holds. An excellent variation is to make an exposed traverse left to finish up the arête.

66. **Flying Arête** 40ft Hard V Diff
Five feet right, a disjointed route taking the arête of the buttress.

67. **Pilot Crack** 40ft Hard V Diff
Climb the wide crack on the right to the archway, then finish up the short overhanging corner by some unusual moves.

Seventy-five yards right and past some small buttresses (which give many good problems) is a steep wrinkled face known as **WINDY WALL**.

68. **Hangover Edge** 25ft Sev *
4b. Climb the overhanging left arête of Windy Wall on improving holds.

69. **Windy Wall** 25ft Sev *
A similar, though slightly easier climb up the face 5 feet to the right.

Across the gap on the right is a pleasant buttress with an obvious corner at its centre. The next climb starts 12 feet left of this corner:

70. **The Swinger** 40ft Hard V Diff
Go up the wall to the overhang, then hand-traverse left and finish up the edge of the buttress.

71. **Celtic Swinger** 30ft Hard VS
5a. Follow The Swinger to where that route traverses left, then finish directly over the shelving overhang.

87 88 89 90 91

72. Kletterschuhe Capers 40ft Sev ★
Take a fairly direct line up the wall 8 feet left of the corner, past a large block near the top and a slight deviation left at mid-height. The line can be straightened out at Hard VS 5a, BOO.

73. Coffin Corner 30ft V Diff ★
This climbs the obvious corner. Go up the chimney to The Coffin, then swing right to reach good holds and continue more easily.

74. Route 1 30ft Hard VS
4c. Climb the overhanging wall and arête just right of Coffin Corner.

75. Route 2 30ft VS
4c. Just right, climb the steep wall.

76. Blind Buttress 30ft Hard V Diff
Start just right of Route 2. Step off a slab onto the face which is climbed past two large 'eye-sockets'.

Higher up and to the right is a small cave – The Tomb. The wall on its right is climbed by:

77. Furly 'ard 25ft V Diff
Climb direct up the centre of the face passing several horizontal breaks to the top.

78. Overhanging Arête 25ft V Diff ★★
Just right, the undercut arête is tricky to start; the rest is pure delight.

The outer face of the buttress is known as **WINDOWSILL WALL** and on it are two routes:

79. Left Route 25ft Hard Sev
Climb the centre of the left half of the buttress.

80. **Right Wall**   25ft   Hard V Diff
Climb directly up the wall, right of centre.

Ten yards right, **WIZENED WALL** has a number of problems. Across to its right is a buttress containing The Apse – a large hole in its right wall.

81. **Apse Arête Indirect**   35ft   Hard V Diff   ★
Climb the arête left of The Apse gaining it from the left by a short traverse along an undercut ledge.

82. **Apse Crack**   20ft   V Diff
Climb the crack above the right-hand edge of The Apse roof.

83. **Apse Wall**   20ft   Hard V Diff
A barely independent line up the wall just right of Apse Crack.

84. **Eel**   25ft   V Diff
Opposite The Apse is a smaller cave with a block at its entrance. From the block, hand-traverse right on improving holds and finish up the wall.

Round to the right is a scooped arête giving:

85. **S.H.M.**   30ft   Hard V Diff   ★
Move right onto the arête, then go leftwards until a good hold enables a swing right to be made and so gain a ledge. Finish direct.

86. **Has Been**   30ft   V Diff
Go up the wall 5 feet right of the arête, then climb a short groove and finish up a crack.

87. **Ladder Ridge**   25ft   Moderate
Eight feet right, climb a series of step-like ledges and the scoop above.

88. **Deceit**   35ft   V Diff
Climb the chimney on the right, passing outside a large chockstone. Avoid walking off by traversing across the hanging wall, then finish up the arête.

89. **Flack**   35ft   E1   ★
5a. Start just right of Deceit and climb directly up the left-hand side of an arête, with a hard move to reach a conveniently-placed chipped hold.

90. **Scoop Wall**   30ft   VS   ★
4c. On the right-hand side of the arête, climb the wall via an obvious scoop which is hard to enter.

91. **Cloister Wall**   30ft   Sev
4b. A 10-foot high block leads to a platform. Climb the short arête to The Cloister (an unusual hole), which is passed with difficulty via the overhang on the left or, better, the bulging wall on the right.

92. **Suspension**   20ft   Sev
4c. Climb the severely undercut crack which contains two chockstones and has a gymnastic start.

93. **Cracked Ridge**   25ft   Hard V Diff
Climb the arête which bounds the wall on the right, then gain the slight scoop on the right with difficulty and follow it to the top.

PULE HILL Square Buttress

Fifty yards right, and past a series of short problem walls, is **SQUARE BUTTRESS**. Its left-hand wall is taken by:

94. **Bung** 25ft Hard VS ∗
5a. Climb directly up the left-hand side of the arête with a long stretch for a ledge at 20 feet. The arête can be climbed direct – **Problem Arête**, Hard VS 5c.

95. **Square Buttress** 25ft VS ∗
4c. Trend leftwards up the front face of the buttress to a wide horizontal pocket. The step into the 'eye' is awkward and is facilitated using a small right fingerhold. From the incut ledge climb the overhangs direct.

Right of Square Buttress are a few broken rocks and then:

96. **Last Ridge** 20ft Moderate
Climb straight up a broken ridge.

97. **The Last Fling** 20ft Sev
4c. The undercut nose to the right is climbed direct.

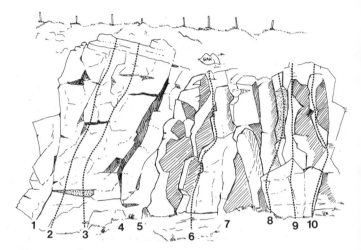

ROUGH KNARR (SD 981 071)

By Geoff Haigh

SITUATION AND CHARACTER

These quarries are situated between Delph and Scouthead near the
A62, above a minor road which runs parallel with the A62, and about
¾ mile west of the centre of Delph.

Although much of the crag is 'scruffy', the views into the Chew Valley
are incomparable. It is worth an evening visit.

APPROACH AND ACCESS

From the centre of Delph, follow the road (Stoneswood Road) by the
side of the library for about half a mile to a bend, from where the
quarries can be seen on the right. There appears to be no access
problem.

1. **Right Route** V Diff
2. **Golfers Groove** Sev
3. **The Printed Page** Hard Sev 4a
4. **The Open Book** Diff
5. **Delph** V Diff   ★
6. **Dobcross** Sev   ★
7. **Diggle** VS 4c   ★

8. **Denshaw** VS 4c   ★★
9. **Gardeners' World** V Diff
10. **Fireman's Lift** Sev
11. **Teacher's Pet** Sev
12. **Mason's Lodge** Sev
13. **Half Moon** VS 4b

SHAW QUARRY (SD 955 103)

By Bruce Goodwin

SITUATION AND CHARACTER

Known locally as Buckstones or Pingot Quarry, Shaw Quarry lies on the western slope of Crow Knoll, in the Crompton Fold area of Shaw. The quarry is of an open aspect and, being box-shaped, the sun touches all parts of the quarry at some time during the day.

The excellent climbing hereabouts has been ignored by all but the cognoscenti for many years, and it certainly deserves more attention. The rock is a fine-grained gritstone whose compact nature lends itself to small sharp(ish) holds. Well-developed crack systems are rare and thus the routes need modern protection and also the skill to use it. A few climbs have little or no protection – this is indicated in the text. Developments over the past few years have indicated that the quarry's reputation for loose rock is ill-founded. The Back and Right Walls take time to dry after rain, but the Left Wall dries rapidly. The quarry is described in three sections: the Left, Back and Right Walls. Belays above the Left Wall include stakes, nuts and Friends, the number and position of the stakes varying according to the whim and strength of local vandals. The belays on The Back Wall section are quite a way up the easy-angled slab above the routes. The belays for the Right Wall are assorted fence posts, well up and back.

Shaw Quarry lies in an area under conversion to a country park, thus special exhortations about behaviour and litter obviously apply.

APPROACH AND ACCESS

The quarry can be reached from the A663 (Shaw – Newhey road) by turning into Buckstones Road (B6197) about half a mile north of Shaw. If approaching from the M62, turn off at junction 21 from where the A640 leads into Newhey and the A663 leads out past The Jubilee public house. Buckstones Road lies half a mile ahead on the left. Follow this road until 200 yards past the Park Hotel, a cobbled track, before a church, leads left past Pingot Cottages. The lane ascends to a sharp left turn and the way into the quarry lies straight ahead. There is no access problem.

HISTORY

Old pegs greeted the first visits made by the Rimmon Club in 1962–63, which is when recorded ascents began. First off the mark was Bill Tweedale who made ascents of Tweedledum and its twin, and Parrot Crack. An evening visit saw Tony Nicholls solo the excellent Bugsy followed by Perganum and T.F.G. He was very pleased to complete the latter; the full route name is truly blasphemous and indicates Nicholls' thoughts as he pulled over the top to safety. Ginger Warburton added The Pretty Thing and Ginger. A traverse of the Left Wall was also reported, but Sting Girdle remains obscure.

Steve Bancroft, a Shaw resident at the time, climbed three routes in 1970, the best of which was probably Crozzle though Steve was forced to use a point of aid (dispensed with by Brian Cropper two years later). Phil Booth free-climbed The Pretty Thing with Bancroft and led ascents of Guano, Red Revolution and A Whiter Shade Of Pale. Bancroft continued his developments with a bold solo ascent of Cynic in 1974 and the following year John Hampson soloed Rattle. This phase of development ended in 1978 with Bancroft adding Cynical, which was then the hardest route on the crag, despite C. Johnstone and R.C. White having climbed both Curig's Corner and Flying Pig the previous year.

Fresh possibilities were noticed by Ian Conway in 1982 and he returned with Bruce Goodwin, Clive Morton, together with Nicholls and Hampson, supplemented at times by John Lord and John Vose. Another Shaw resident, Dougie Hall, also noticed gaps and began working through these, making most of his ascents solo. Pride of place at the time were the two peg cracks on The Back Wall, which Hampson free-climbed and named, only to find later that Hall had soloed both routes the previous year. Conway meanwhile cleaned and re-ascended Red Revolution and added The Gouk and the superb Phosphatic. Hampson boldly added Apology together with Pull And Go and Brandy amongst others. Nicholls led A Question Of Balance and Commitment whilst Goodwin 'Dodged It' and climbed a traverse of the right wall with Morton.

Conway moved north leaving two lines, and Hampson stepped in to lead the aptly named Sleeping Partner and Capital Offence, plus Red-Green Eliminate. Things started to slow, though Goodwin added Blusher and straightened out A Whiter Shade Of Pale in 1985. In a separate dimension, Dougie Hall returned and, with John Smith, climbed Flaked Maze up the wall right of Voting Age. Hall also soloed a very hard eliminate between Ginger and Brandy as well as adding his 'training routes' to The Back Wall.

LEFT WALL
All THE CLIMBS are described from LEFT to RIGHT. The first two routes are hard for their grade.

1. **Tweedledee** 20ft VS
5a. A hard layback gains a faint groove which leads to the top.

2. **Rattle** 20ft VS
5a. Climb to a small square-cut corner at 8 feet and finish direct.

3. **Blusher** 25ft Hard VS
5b. The faint blocky arête just left of A Whiter Shade of Pale leads to a short wall.

4. **A Whiter Shade of Pale** 25ft E1   *
5b. Climb the slab to a ledge. Follow the groove over the overhang to the top, taking care with protection.

5. **Crozzle** 35ft E1   *
5c. Climb up to a leaning shot-hole with a thin crack. Make hard moves past an old peg to stand on a small ledge. The top lies just above.

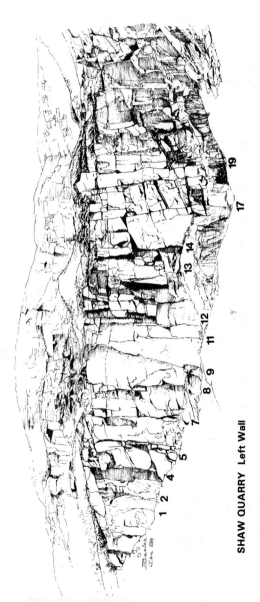

SHAW QUARRY Left Wall

6. **Perganum**   35ft   Hard VS   *
5a. Start as for Crozzle but continue up a corner just right to an awkward move to gain a 'Thank God' ledge just below the top. An easier start is possible by gaining the small corner from Numbug.

7. **Numbug**   40ft   E1
5b. Climb straight up to a butterfly-shaped overhang. Layaway and bridge, then reach for the top.

8. **Bugsy**   35ft   E1   **
5b. A groove on the blunt arête leads up and left to slabby ledges, then a short crack points the way to a little groove and strenuous pulls to the top. Sustained and thought-provoking.

9. **The Pretty Thing**   45ft   Hard VS   **
5b. The obvious diagonal crackline leads to a ledge at 20 feet. Reach up the wall, then step right to regain the line and hopefully the top. Excellent, steep and bold.

10. **Red-Green Eliminate**   40ft   E3   *
6a. Go up easily to a large ledge. Pull up the middle of the red/green wall, then go right to a large foothold. Move up and left to finish. Graded for side-runners, otherwise unprotected.

11. **T.F.G.**   40ft   Hard VS
5b. As for Red/Green Eliminate but continue and gain a small ledge in the groove above by a 'somehow' move. Finish direct or (harder) go out right then up.

Right is a slabby groove leading to an overhang.

12. **Apology**   40ft   E3
5b. Climb direct to the right-hand end of the large ledge of T.F.G. Step right to the groove (which can be reached direct, harder) and go up to its top. Pass the overhang on its left and continue in muscular fashion. Sustained and serious.

To the right is a large low ledge. A grassy mound slopes down rightward to a drop into some slutch.

13. **Pull and Go**   40ft   E1
5b. From the low ledge follow a steep thin crack to gain a ledge, then move up and go left to good holds. Continue steeply to the top. Graded for side-runners in Parrot Crack, otherwise none where it matters!

14. **Parrot Crack**   35ft   VS
4c. A short blocky groove leads to the ledge on Pull And Go from the right. The obvious corner crack leads steeply upwards from here.

The wall right of Parrot Crack has two good though unprotected routes:

15. **Cynical**   45ft   E4   *
6a. Climb the wall on its left side. A scoop-cum-groove leads above the overhang to the finishing wall.

16. **The Cynic**   45ft   E4   *
5c. Follow the wall on its right side, at a thin crack; the bulge is

overcome at an obvious shot-hole. Continue in the same line to reach the top.

17. **Ginger** 50ft Hard VS   ★★★
The classic route of the quarry; clean and continuously thought-provoking, easy for its grade.
5b. From the foot of Parrot Crack descend the grass rightwards. Traverse across to below a groove. Follow this weakness to a move right at an old peg, then continue past two mantels to a heathery finish. A direct start is possible from the slutch below the groove – ughh!

The next route goes well with Ginger. This route, and two more, start from a grassy terrace on the right.

18. **Brandy** 55ft E2   ★
An excellent climb; bold and poorly-protected.
5b. Gain the grassy terrace. From its left-hand end, step left to below a triangular overhang. Go up to and over this with difficulty, trending slightly right then direct to finish. The line may also be started direct from a slabby boulder.

An 'eliminate-eliminate' is possible between Ginger and Brandy; good moves at 6b.

19. **Red Revolution** 55ft E2   ★★
5c. Gain the grassy terrace. Above its left side is a bow-shaped depression which is followed to a bulge (strenuous). A pull or two then lead to the top. A good, sustained route.

20. **The Gouk** 50ft E2   ★
5c. A thin crack system above the right side of the grassy ledge provides the route.

21. **Tweedledum** 40ft VS   ★
4c. Go up right of an overhang on the arête. Climb a groove past 'old-timers' protection' to a roof. Pull out left to stand on a slabby block, then step right and finish direct. **Variation Start** (VS 4c ★): The groove left of the arête gives sustained climbing up to the slabby block.

22. **Ledge Way** 40ft Hard Sev
4b. Climb the broken corner on the right for 15 feet, step left then go back and up right. Continue over heather for belays. Usually wet with spray from the waterfall.

The waterfall provides a good ice pitch in winter conditions, as can the region between Avoidance and A Question of Balance.

THE BACK WALL
This is the area of rock right of the graffiti-covered slabs. The slabs themselves provide an easy descent from the next few routes. The peg-scarred cracks give two good, sustained and deceptively difficult routes:

23. Back in the Swing 35ft E2   ★
5c. The left-hand crackline.

24. Voting Age 35ft E2   ★
6a. The right-hand crackline gives excellent climbing.

25. Flaked Maze 35ft E4   ★ †
6b. Climb the wall past a peg runner with sling (sling not in place).

26. Late Finish 30ft E2
5b. Climb a thin crack to a small square-cut overhang. Go over this and continue up ledges in the same line. Bold and poorly-protected.

27. Avoidance 25ft V Diff
A line of unstable flakes and blocks lead from right to left starting just right of Late Finish. Probably best avoided!

The Back Wall may be girdled (the once-pegged section). These 'training routes' (quote "they are only training exercises 'cos a fall wouldn't kill you!") go at a variety of heights, and range from 5c upwards.

28. A Question of Balance 25ft E2   ★★
5c. The obvious corner leads to the overhang. Go over this and up to ledges and a block belay.

29. Commitment 30ft E1   ★
5c. Climb a wall below a slabby corner. Enter this, then gain a niche and follow a crack to good nut belays on the right.

30. Dodged It 35ft Hard VS
5a. Climb Commitment for a few feet and deviate right to a good ledge. From here, a delicate move gains the crack right of the niche, which is followed to a steep finish. Nut belay on left.

A poor unstable route has been climbed up the obvious corner system just right; **Rocker**, Hard VS 5a (†). Beware, the whole of the top corner block rocks!

RIGHT WALL
The obvious chimney above a green slab is the first route.

31. Guano 70ft E1
5b. Start below the line but go right into a wide groove. Go up to a bulge and step left onto the slab, then go up into the chimney which is vacated leftwards. **Direct Start** (5a); climb straight up stepped rock, pull over onto the slab and continue as for the parent route.

32. Phosphatic 70ft E2   ★★
5b. Follow Guano to the bulge, then go straight up to ledges and climb a shallow corner to reach a large ledge. Take the overhang on its left, then continue direct to the top. Spaced protection.

33. Grinder 30ft E2
5b. The corner on the right leads to a crack which has an awkward move to gain a ledge running across the wall. Finish as for Flying Pig.

34. Flying Pig 60ft VS
(1) 30ft 4c. Start 15 feet right. Follow steps up and left into a niche. Go over the bulge to move left onto a big ledge.

(2)   30ft 4c.   Climb the left-hand corner to the overhang, then pull out left into a groove and hence the top.

35.   **Too Close for Comfort**   65ft   Hard VS
(1)   35ft 5a.   Climb up stepped rock, right of Flying Pig. A difficult move, right of the niche, leads over a bulge. Delicately gain the ledge and belay.
(2)   30ft 4c.   Finish up Flying Pig, or up rightwards as for One Twin.

36.   **Curig's Corner**   65ft   VS
(1)   35ft 4b.   Climb stepped rock to gain a corner which leads to the ledge and belays.
(2)   30ft 4c.   Finish as for the previous route.

37.   **One Twin**   60ft   VS
(1)   30ft 4c.   Climb an overhang below a concave wall then, from ledges, follow the right side of this concavity to the ledge and nut belay.
(2)   30ft.   Climb easily up to steep grass, to fence post belays.

38.   **Twin Two**   55ft   VS
(1)   30ft 4c.   Gain the ledges below the concave wall at their right-hand end. Go up past an interestingly-shaped hole and move left to gain One Twin and the large ledge.
(2)   25ft.   Finish as for One Twin.

39.   **Quadramantel**   60ft   VS
5a. Climb up to the overhang on the right and pass it on its left to gain a sloping ledge. Follow a groove system until a way right leads to a grassy slope.

Just right is an obvious V-shaped groove below an open corner.

40.   **Sleeping Partner**   45ft   E2   *
5c. Climb up and left to the groove. A difficult move leads up to gain the corner which is followed to the top.

41.   **Capital Offence**   45ft   E1   *
5b. Gain and then follow thin parallel cracks over a bulge. Pull up, gain a niche, then the top.

42.   **Tripod**   30ft   Hard VS
5b. A crack in the wall left of Endymion may be reached in three ways: via ledges on its left, direct (hardest), or from the base of the next route.

43.   **Endymion**   20ft   VS
5a. At the right-hand end of the face is a steep groove. The arête on the right provides the route.

A traverse of the Right Wall, from right to left is:

44.   **Intuitive Momentum**   120ft   E1   **
(1)   60ft 5a.   Start as for Sleeping Partner. Go up and gain the wall right of the V-shaped groove. Swing rightwards into the top of the groove, then follow the horizontal break round to join Quadramantel. Go left and up to the large ledge. Walk to its far end. Nut belay. This pitch can be started from Endymion.
(2)   60ft 5b.   Step round onto the face and go across to ledges (Friend runner above). Descend one move, then go left and enter the base of

Guano's chimney. Reverse this route to a block, then go up and leftwards to an overhanging block. Swing round and climb up left using flakes to gain heather-covered ledges. Nut belay 20 feet farther across the path. Take great care to protect the second man.

SHOOTER'S NAB (SE 065 109)

By Chris Booth

SITUATION AND CHARACTER
Deer Hill Moss is home to Shooter's Nab. It is a substantial old working with many impressive features, tucked away on the hillside above a peaceful reservoir, and commanding excellent views all round. Indeed this is a superb venue, the only drawback being the obvious danger afforded by the high-velocity bullets from the firing range below the quarry.

APPROACH AND ACCESS
From Marsden take the B6107 towards Meltham for about 2½ miles to an unmetalled road on the right. Follow this round to Deer Hill End Road and continue along this, passing through two gates, to the reservoir. Park here and go through the gate, walk beside the reservoir for a hundred yards then climb the hillside on the left to gain the quarry. 10 – 15 minutes.

IT IS ESSENTIAL THAT PERMISSION TO CLIMB BE SOUGHT PRIOR TO APPROACHING THE CRAG. FROM THE PARKING PLACE, DRIVE FARTHER ROUND TO THE SHOOTING HOUSE AND SEEK PERMISSION.

HISTORY
The first climber to visit the crag was Richard Henry Isherwood, a member of the Rucksack Club, who soloed some of the obvious easy lines in the 1920s. His explorations remained unknown, but in 1951 he said that he had used nails and thought the crag had much to offer.

Graham West and Michael Roberts visited Shooter's in 1957 having spotted the crag from a passing train. They found no evidence of previous visits by climbers, and thought the crag to be untouched, even though Tony Howard and Alwyn Whitehead had made a brief recce and done routes a month earlier. The rifle range was in existence even then, and this effectively curtailed their explorations, limiting them to the Green Bowl. Despite the bullets flying around, they managed to climb four fine routes; Rifleman's Chimney, Elbow Jump, Bull's Eye Crack and Sweatyman. West returned with Clive Barker the following month and this time made ascents of The Light, Redeemer's Wall and Shin Skinner all in the Green Bowl area, plus three routes on Oval Buttress. The next recorded visit was a whole year later and it was West again who was responsible; he took Bryn Higgins along this time and they attempted Cream Cracker Crux, a route which deposited West from the crux at least five times into the mud below. Panic Knott was the other route to succumb that day, this time to Higgins.

1959 saw the arrival of the late Barry Kershaw, and the result was a bold lead of Magpie together with ascents of Chimp Crack, S. Bend and Cuticle Crack, the latter being one of his finger-jamming specialities. A lull then followed until the early '60s, when the Rimmon Club came to check the crag for the 1965 guidebook and ended by adding seven routes, including Trundle Groove and Wanderlust to Tony Howard, and Barney Rubble to 'Harpic Harold' Heald. The publication of the 1965 guidebook did little to attract people to the crag; the Peak District and the natural edges of Yorkshire were more attractive to most. This period of quiet gave John Stanger just the opportunity he needed; he now had a free hand to work through the lines still remaining. Over the next few years he solved Pisa, Plane Face, Orphic Power, Space Slab, The Shroud, Olympian and Lone Stone Buttress. The latter route then employed a peg for aid until Chris Hardy soloed the line free in 1980.

During a spectacular thunderstorm, Stanger attacked the most impressive of the quarry's features; the nine-foot roof capping the highest portion of The Rostrum. This route he christened Thunderball in direct reference to the huge claps of thunder as he hung free in space, dangling from the lip of the roof. From the roof he spotted an obvious traverse line leading leftwards round the arête and he was soon back undeterred, this time with John Earnshaw, to attempt the traverse. Stanger completed the route (Crescendo) and then belayed to bring up Earnshaw. Once on the hand-traverse, Earnshaw's strength rapidly decreased and eventually his arms gave out and he made a huge pendulum around the arête and into space; quite a climax.

John Hart climbed Eric the Cosmic Fiend in 1971 and then teamed up with Stanger for the Girdle Traverse. Stanger then led Stimrol with Julie and John Hart.

Ken Mercer and Brian Cropper put up Scoop Wall in 1974, then they switched leads for Brian to complete The Long Reach; a route which had to wait a decade for a second ascent. Things quietened down yet again and remained so until 1981 when Stanger discovered The Clingon, a route which had remained tucked away on a hidden buttress opposite Tickle Wall. The buttress is easily visible from the main crag, but looks fairly innocuous until one actually surveys it at close quarters.

One of the most important influences in Shooter's more recent history, Paul Cropper, was introduced to the crag in 1982. He immediately started to fill in the lines which Stanger had overlooked, and quickly polished off Cool Man's Wall and Slip Arête with Jeremy Daniels, followed closely by Light Fantastic and Surprise (originally named Scooping Surprise), the latter with Gary Gibson. Gary himself made a couple of contributions such as Yellowcake UF6 and a solo ascent of the obvious line right of Lone Stone Buttress; Lone Stone Groove.

During the summer of 1984, Chris Booth climbed the undercut arête on the buttress left of the Lone Stones, whilst the moors beneath the crag burned away, and named his magic little creation Smouldering Moors. The following year Paul Cropper led the right arête of Cuticle

Crack to give the serious Legs. Phil Kelly made a visit soon after and repeated some of the newer routes, and climbed Paddington. Later that year Chris Booth succeeded on the vague seam in the blank-looking wall left of Ricochet Wall, but only managed to complete the problematical moves at the expense of a strained tendon, hence the name; Born at a Price. His belayer on that route, Will Steel felt aggrieved at having to spend his time at college, working hard whilst others enjoyed themselves, and so that same day he led a direct line up the wall direct between Elbow Jump and Magpie, No Time to be 21.

THE CLIMBS are described from LEFT to RIGHT.

1. **Pisa** 25ft Sev
A fine route up the gently leaning wall. Start direct and move left to finish.

2. **Plane Face** 35ft Sev
Climb the steep face on holds unseen until reached.

3. **Orphic Power** 35ft VS
4c. Start around the arête to the right and make a difficult move over the overhang to reach pleasant slab climbing. Move left to finish.

FIRST BOWL
This is the huge V-shaped piece of moor on the right. The left arête of the 'V' is a hanging slab.

4. **Space Slab** 40ft VS   *
4c. The loose wall left of the slab. Step right onto the slab and climb it to the top.

Beyond the First Bowl is the **GREAT CAVE**.

5. **Zing** 35ft Hard V Diff
Trend right on small holds up the steep wall 10 feet right of the arête of the First Bowl.

6. **Fossil Crack** 40ft V Diff
The arête below the crack on the left of the Great Cave, then climb the crack to the top.

7. **Cuticle Crack** 30ft Hard VS   **
5b. Pull onto the large, undercut, pointed flake which projects down on the right of the Great Cave and follow the thin crack above.

8. **Legs** 30ft E4   *
6a. Start as for Cuticle Crack, but move out right just above the bulge to gain the arête. Finish up this.

9. **Dwarf** 30ft Hard V Diff
The damp corner to the right.

The ground now rises onto a small plateau.

10. **Giant** 20ft VS
4c. Climb directly up the centre of the wall facing Cuticle Crack.

11. **Tickle Wall** 20ft Severe
Start just right of Giant and climb up trending rightwards, to finish just

left of the arête. The arête itself can be climbed direct at 4c.

Approximately 50 yards distant and opposite the right arête of Tickle Wall is what appears to be a small buttress. Approaching this from its right side, a large roof becomes apparent. This is climbed by a fine route:

12. The Clingon 40ft E2   *
6a. Start below the crack which splits the roof. Climb up to it, then cross the roof (hard move on the lip) and finish up the short cracks.

Round the arête from Tickle Wall, the long low right wall has some fine problems, best (re)discovered for oneself. The wall ends at another bay; **THE BLACK BOWL**.

13. The Shroud 25ft Hard Sev   †
4b. Climb up to an old bolt-hole, then finish up a hanging flake with care.

14. Cream Cracker Crux 40ft VS
5a. Climb to a large pocket at the back of the bay, then go up a leftward-trending rib to reach the top.

15. Peek Freen 35ft VS
4b. The thin crack in the right wall of the bay.

16. Ginger 30ft V Diff
The arête on the right.

Moving right, the next bay is known as the **SOUP BOWL**.

17. Blue Peter 35ft Hard Sev
4b. The obvious narrow chimney in the right corner.

18. Black Crack 35ft Sev
Climb to a grassy ledge 10 feet right of the corner, then take the overhanging crack to the top.

Forward of this and facing Marsden is a natural edge; **OVAL BUTTRESS**.

19. Paddington 25ft Hard VS
5c. The short problem wall left of If Looks Could Kill leads, via a one-finger hole, to the break then take the easier upper wall.

20. Silly Way 25ft VS
5a. The wall just left of If Looks Could Kill.

21. If Looks Could Kill 30ft Hard Sev   *
4b. The thin groove/crack in the centre of the buttress and the rippley wall above.

22. One Two Wall 30ft VS
4c. The wall right of the crack is undercut, and hard to start.

Thirty feet to the right is another natural buttress with a hanging arête.

23. Demerera   25ft   Diff
The centre of the wall left of the arête.

24. Smouldering Moors   30ft   E3   *
6a. The hanging arête is climbed on its right side to a small ledge, then easier moves lead to the top.

25. Tipperary   25ft   Diff
Go up the corner, traverse left then up to finish.

Right again is a square buttress which contains an old peg at 15 feet. This is **LONE STONE BUTTRESS**.

26. The Wigan   20ft   E1
5c. Climb the left arête of the square buttress to the overlap and make a long reach to the top.

27. Lone Stone Buttress   20ft   E1   *
5c. Climb direct to the old peg (small hole) and pass it with difficulty to reach the top.

28. Lone Stone Groove   20ft   E2
6a. The undercut groove on the right.

GREEN BOWL
Farther right is a huge overhanging buttress named The Rostrum. The continuous section of rock which contains this is the Green Bowl, and here are the best climbs in the quarry. The first routes start on the rock which is set back to the left of The Rostrum.

29. Pocket Route   65ft   V Diff
The first broken groove, with a choice of starts.

30. Panic Knott   65ft   Sev   *
The fine groove on the right.

31. S. Bend   80ft   Sev
Take the obvious chimney, then climb the arête and hand-traverse into Panic Knott. Follow this to a horizontal crack which leads round a small overhang.

32. Gabriole   65ft   VS   *
4b. Climb the undercut diagonal crack which slopes up to the right. Step left and go up the wall to a platform and an easy exit.

33. Shin Skinner   60ft   Hard Sev
4b. Follow the curving crack on the right to gain the platform and thus an easy finish.

34. Wanderlust   75ft   VS   *
(1) 50ft 4b. Climb the groove on laybacks, then traverse left below the overhang to a grassy bay.
(2) 25ft 4c. Move left and step across on to the arête, then move round on to the face of the buttress and finish up the centre.

35. Eric the Cosmic Fiend   65ft   Hard VS   *
5b. From the grassy bay on Wanderlust, move back right and climb the thin bottomless crack. A spacy route.

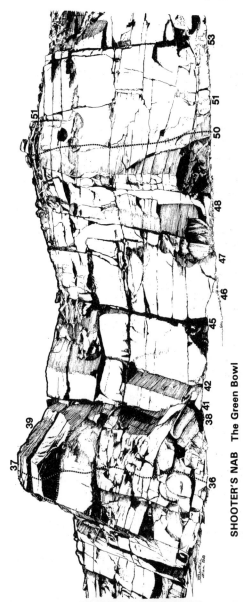

SHOOTER'S NAB   The Green Bowl

36. **Crescendo**   80ft   E1   ***
5c. Climb the intricate wall directly under the roof of The Rostrum, to gain the base of an old bolt ladder. Climb the wall just right of this by a confusing sequence to reach the roof. Hand-traverse sensationally left around the arête to a welcome foothold and finish direct.

37. **Thunderball**   80ft   E1/A2   **
5c/A2. A direct finish to Crescendo, tackling the monster roof above on bolts, with exhilarating moves on the lip.

38. **Sweatyman**   75ft   Hard VS   ***
(1) 35ft 5a.   Pull strenuously out of the recess on the right and climb cracks to a 'proud' shelf.
(2) 40ft 5a.   From the middle of the ledge gain the horizontal break above, then traverse left to the edge. Ascend the slab and traverse to the outermost point of the overhang, then stomach-traverse through the gap in the overhang and finish up the front.

39. **Cool Man's Wall**   65ft   VS   **
4c. Climb Sweatyman to the proud shelf, then make a long reach to the horizontal break above and enter a scoop. Finish direct.

40. **Rifleman's Chimney**   65ft   Hard Sev
4b. The chimney on the right.

41. **Slip Arête**   70ft   E2   **
5b. The prominent arête on the right is climbed until level with a large break. Move right into the crack of Magpie and climb this for a few feet, then go back left to finish up the arête.

42. **Elbow Jump**   85ft   VS
4c. Climb the corner on the right to below the overhang, then elbow-traverse right to gain a ledge. Move back above the overhang and finish direct.

43. **No Time to be 21**   65ft   E3   †
6a. Climb the wall between Elbow Jump and Magpie, direct. A long reach comes in useful above the break.

44. **Magpie**   65ft   Hard VS   **
5a. Start by the arête and rise diagonally left to an overhanging corner crack. Follow this to the top.

45. **Bull's Eye Crack**   65ft   V Diff
The broken chimney just right.

46. **Yellowcake Uf6**   65ft   VS
4c. Climb the slab and cracks to the top.

47. **Redeemer's Wall**   65ft   Hard Sev
4a. Ten feet right is a wall of weathered pockets. Climb these direct, taking care with the rock.

48. **The Cuspidor**   75ft   VS
4b. Start just left of the arête and ascend to a flake. Move right and follow the arête until a move left can be made to finish.

49. **Tind**   70ft   Hard VS   *
5a. Climb the undercut crack right of the arête to a hard move onto the arête itself. Finish up this.

50. Born at a Price 70ft E4   ** †
6b. Start below a hole and climb up past this to a good break below a vague seam in the upper wall. Follow the pegged-out pockets above by baffling moves, to an easier finish.

51. Ricochet Wall 70ft E1   ***
The obvious route of the wall; classic. Low in its grade.
5b. Climb the vague groove (poor protection) to its top, then traverse left to gain a crack which can be followed to the top.

52. Scot's Wall 70ft E1
5c. On the right is a thin slanting crack. Follow this to the break and move right to a second crack. Exit via this.

53. The Light 65ft VS   *
4c. The long crack on the right, which splits 15 feet from the top. Hard to start.

54. Light Fantastic 50ft Hard VS   *
5b. Climb the wall to the right, passing a hole. Traverse right at the break and finish direct.

The next buttress has a slabby front.

55. Second Thoughts 40ft Sev
4b. From a yellow block climb the left edge until it is possible to move right on small holds, then climb the scoop and cracks above.

56. Ball Bearings 40ft Hard VS   *
5a. Start to the right, below a small overhang with three cracks above. Climb up to and pass the overhang, then trend right to the top.

57. Surprise 40ft E2   *
5c. Climb directly up to a shallow scoop and enter this with difficulty. Exit via the slab above.

58. Barney Rubble 40ft VS
4c. The dirty corner crack, exiting right at the chockstone.

59. Stimrol 40ft E1   **
5b. The fine arête to the right, passing an old iron spike at half-height.

60. The Long Reach 35ft E3   *
6b. Climb the groove right of the arête to a ledge. Make a hard move up the thin crack above to gain a good hold on the left, then finish direct.

61. Chimp Crack 35ft VS   *
5a. The zigzag crack on the right (old wooden wedge) leads to a terrace, then the thin rightward-slanting crack above.

62. Olympian 30ft Hard VS
5c. A route in two halves. Climb the wall 15 feet right, then walk right and climb the scoop with a good hold in its centre. Beware though, the finishing hold is often full of grit!

The final feature is **SQUARE BUTTRESS**.

63. Fairy Arête 35ft VS
4c. The left arête, with an easy start and a thin finish.

64. Trundle Groove 30ft Hard V Diff
4a. The groove to a ledge, then finish up the wall.

65. Scoop Wall 30ft VS
4c. The flake on the right. Finish direct.

66. Final Corner 30ft Hard V Diff
The cracks in the centre of the buttress, finishing up a groove.

67. Girdle Traverse 320ft Hard VS (1 point of aid) †
(1) 70ft 5a. Start at the grassy ledge on Chimp Crack and traverse left at a lower level to another grassy ledge. Continue round the arête into the corner of Barney Rubble, and climb this to reach a large chockstone (runner). Step onto the bulging slab and descend this to belay on Second Thoughts.
(2) 30ft 4c. The leader can use the rope around a notch to move across the wall round the left arête. Continue along an obvious traverse line to a grassy ledge and belay. The second man can then lower from a sling on the notch, and climb up to the traverse line.
(3) 60ft 5a. Go to the top of The Light and descend its double crack until level with a hand-traverse across Ricochet Wall. Follow this and belay on the arête of The Cuspidor.
(4) 70ft 4b. Follow the ledges across to Bull's Eye Crack, then drop down slightly and cross Magpie's wall to belay in Rifleman's Chimney.
(5) 60ft 5a. Go along Sweatyman's ledge, then drop down and traverse under The Rostrum to a junction with Wanderlust. Follow this to a belay.
(6) 30ft 4b. Round the edge on the left, then semi-hand-traverse to the corner and finish on a ledge at the same level.

STANDEDGE QUARRY (SE 012 103)

By Geoff Haigh

SITUATION AND CHARACTER
The quarry is easily visible just above and to the north of the A62, Oldham to Huddersfield road, and is directly below the Pennine Way.

The quarry consists of two bands of gritstone. The upper band being harder and much less friable than the lower one. The result is an obvious overhang which runs the length of the quarry. However the lower band is loose, giving all the routes a serious air. The traverse below the overhang is not technically difficult for those who like stomach-traverses on sandy ledges over earthy blocks.

APPROACH AND ACCESS
From the car park and tea van just past the Floating Light Inn, follow the track of the Pennine Way northwards until the old quarry track is met on the right. The quarry is about 10 minutes walk from the car park, tea van and pub! No access problems have arisen so far.

1. Pennine Arête Diff
The obvious arête.

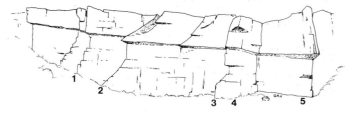

STANDEDGE QUARRY

Thirty feet left is a small wall with two cracks:

2. **Short Line** Sev
4a. The right crack.

3. **Thin Line** Hard Sev 4b

MAIN QUARRY

4. **Wall and Crack** Sev
5. **Firefrost** V Diff
6. **Watching the Detectives** VS 4b
7. **The Flake of the Floating Light** Sev
8. **Footless Oasis** VS 4b

WORLOW QUARRY – Lower Pule Quarry (SE 307 103)
By Chris Hardy

APPROACH
Approaching from Oldham on the Huddersfield (A62) road; a few hundred yards beyond the Great Western Hotel, Mount Road on the right (and just before the Eagle's Nest Hotel) is followed for half a mile. A track on the left marks the way up to the quarry.

HISTORY
The first recorded routes in this small quarry were climbed in 1978 by Al Pierce, Nadim Siddiqui and Paul Cropper. The crag was further exploited one day in May 1982 by Dave Cronshaw and Bob Whittaker, accompanied by Les Ainsworth. Four new routes fell (and were fallen off), amongst which Albatross, Eagle and Red Wing perhaps combined with the more recent (1985) additions – The Bengal Badger and Peach Party by Chris Booth and Will Steel – may provide an evening's entertainment for the jaded connoisseur.

THE CLIMBS are described from LEFT to RIGHT.

MAIN BAY

An obvious feature of this, the largest of the two bays, is an unclimbed corner complete with a gravity-defying block at 20 feet. To its left, three climbs have been recorded; left to right, these are: **The Slab** (20ft Diff), the centre of an easy-angled slab, **Bengal Badger** (25ft E2 5c), a faint groove starting midway up the wall; **Swallow Dive** (30ft VS 4b), a well-defined groove and crack system . The wall to the right of the unclimbed corner contains the following routes:

1. Albatross 40ft Hard VS   *
5b. Climb up to a roof, then move leftwards up a ramp to reach good footholds. Finish by a thin crack just to the right of the repulsive corner. A more direct version is **Shrew to a Kill** (E1 5b).

2. Eagle 40ft E1   *
5b. As for Albatross to the roof, then surmount this via a thin crack to a ledge and finish direct.

3. Red Wing 40ft VS   *
4c. To the right again, a prominent crack is climbed direct.

SMALL BAY: Around the arête from Red Wing, a crack (starting at 10 feet), ledge and short corner form the substance of **Raven** (30ft Hard Sev). Finishing up the right-hand arête of the short corner is **Hot Pants** (Hard VS 5b).

The remainder of the routes, described from left to right, start with **Rook** (25ft Sev), a wide chimney/crack 15 feet right of the arête. Right again, an attractive 20-foot wall gives a fingery problem, **Peach Party** (E2 6a). The short corner in the angle of the bay, climbed by three mantelshelves, is **The Corner** (20ft Diff). On the wall right of The Corner are several cracklines. The second of these is **One More Move** (25ft Sev) and 5 feet right is the obvious jamming crack of **Needles and Pins** (25ft Sev). The niche and thin crack right again, **Thin Line Dynamite** (25ft Hard Sev) completes the excitement!

MINOR CRAGS

NAB END (SE 031 118)

This quarry lies just to the north of Pule Hill and is visible from the road. A memorable V Diff, climbed by Terry Carr and Mandy White in July 1983, was named in personal response to the political climate at that time: Various Obscenities Directed at Margaret Thatcher!

II. ROCHDALE/TODMORDEN AREA

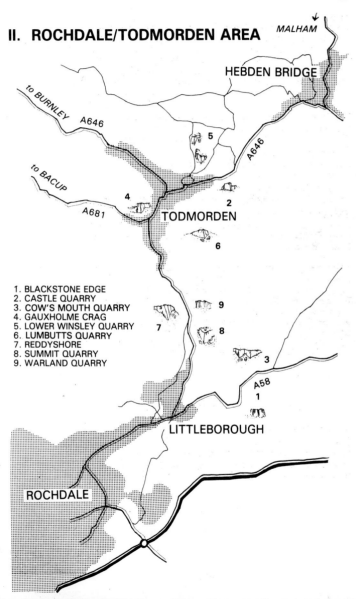

MALHAM

HEBDEN BRIDGE

to BURNLEY A646

to BACUP

A681

TODMORDEN

A646

1. BLACKSTONE EDGE
2. CASTLE QUARRY
3. COW'S MOUTH QUARRY
4. GAUXHOLME CRAG
5. LOWER WINSLEY QUARRY
6. LUMBUTTS QUARRY
7. REDDYSHORE
8. SUMMIT QUARRY
9. WARLAND QUARRY

A58

LITTLEBOROUGH

ROCHDALE

II. ROCHDALE – TODMORDEN AREA

By Bruce Goodwin
With thanks for assistance to Ian Conway, Tony Nicholls,
and Bob Whittaker.

The Rochdale – Todmorden area is a region of contrasts, with high rolling moors cut deep by narrow, steep-sided valleys. Crags stand proud or are hidden away in man-made quarry holes: cliffs cool and sombre contrasting with those of a sunnier aspect.

There are many crags of regional importance but none of national importance in the area and so solitude is almost guaranteed as one enjoys routes conventional, esoteric, good or excellent. The area contains crags of natural grit and many quarries, and they all give steep arêtes, walls, cracks and slabs – in short, a wealth of experience awaiting collection.

BLACKSTONE EDGE (SD 973 167)

SITUATION AND CHARACTER
The outcrop known to climbers as Blackstone Edge lies on the west flank of the ridge which runs from north to south and which gives the edge its name. The edge faces north-west and commands a fine view over Hollingworth Lake, Chelburn Moor and Littleborough. The rock is a dark coloured and compact natural gritstone, providing climbs of all grades, of up to 40-feet. The pity is that there is not more of it, but some excellent routes make it certainly worth an afternoon or an evening visit.

The Pennine Way, a 'Roman' road and other popular paths ensure that the area is well used by walkers and ramblers.

APPROACH AND ACCESS
From the White House (see approach to Cow's Mouth Quarry), walk downhill to join a footpath (Pennine Way) that leads up left to Broadhead Drain. Follow this drainage channel across the 'Roman' road until below the crag it is possible to cross the moor direct, to reach the rocks.

The car park at the foot of the Roman road is an alternative starting point, though either approach takes about 20 minutes. An hourly bus service (Rochdale – Halifax) runs past the White House.

HISTORY
Some climbing was recorded on Blackstone Edge as far back as 1827, this date being carved in the upper walls of South Chimney, though whether the ascent was completed is not known.

Modern records of first ascents began with the publication of Laycock's 'Some Gritstone Climbs' in 1913. The easier routes existed then, but little more was done and as late as 1957 'Climbs on Gritstone' (volume 3) only added Central Groove – although Pendulum Swing also existed by then. Cornflake was aided later and Mangler added in 1960. Pendulum Swing Direct was ascended in 1962 and this period also saw Manibus Et Pedibusque climbed with 'opposed tension' techniques, it is said, and Little Miss Id was climbed by Richard McHardy.

Accounts of new routes and aid reductions, etc. are vague but the Solvé club were active here as well as at the nearby quarries at Summit and Cow's Mouth, and they should probably be credited with ascending most of the routes. Tryche dates from this time (with a peg for aid), and later, in 1986, Bruce Goodwin made an involuntary ascent of Central Groove which was covered in crusty, wind-packed snow-ice. Cornflake had been free-climbed by the end of the decade, though who was first to succeed is not known, and then the crag was put on 'hold' for the nearby Cow's Mouth attracted (and still attracts) more climbers, with its superior number of routes to enjoy.

In 1977, Goodwin, together with fellow members of the Black and Tan M.C. began a purge on the lines. All the existing routes received repeat ascents and Dennis Carr, with a hint of self mockery, climbed Pots. This was so named because he had soloed Quietus (Stanage) a few days earlier, and was still wondering...

The famous A.N. Other was rumoured to have made lead ascents of Tryche and Manibus Et Pedibusque by the early 1980s, and the length of some of the locals' noses were seen to grow by the minute! 1983, however, saw Goodwin climb a complementary route to Little Miss Id; Master Ego and Tony Nicholls' search for a third pebble was the reason for the naming of No Sign of Three. Recent attention has focused on the roof left of Little Miss Id; this hard (and rather artificial) problem has been top-roped by several parties, and can only be a matter of time before it succumbs to a forceful leader.

THE CLIMBS are described from RIGHT to LEFT. A short face right of the first climb gives pleasant problems.

1. **Pendulum Swing** 30ft VS
4c. Climb a crack to an overhang then move left and finish up a chimney.

2. **Pendulum Swing Direct** 25ft Hard VS
5a. The wall left of the crack leads with difficulty to the chimney.

Rounding the arête on the left a shallow groove left of an obvious pocket gives:

3. **No Sign of Three** 35ft E2   ∗
5c. Climb cracks to a horizontal break. Move left and go up to the groove which, in turn, leads to a ledge. Finish via the weakness above.

4. **Twin Cracks** 35ft Hard Diff – V Diff   ∗
The left-hand crack is easier than the right-hand, or they can be combined.

5. South Chimney 35ft Diff
The obvious chimney contains numerous interesting inscriptions.

6. Pots 35ft E2
5c. Climb the thin crack left of the chimney, which leads to a horizontal break. Move left for a few feet and climb up and back right to 'one of those' finishes.

7. Tryche 35ft E4   ★★ †
6a. The wall on the left is climbed to a pocket (runner) from where a move up leads to the final (crux) move. Bold.

8. Little Miss Id 40ft E1   ★★★
5c. The blunt arête left of Tryche leads to an overhang. Step onto this from the right and gain a ledge. Finish up the left-hand side of the short wall. **Variations**: a) Climb the wall left of the usual start to the roof, step right and finish as usual. b) From the large ledge, finish rightwards – hard (6a).

9. Master Ego 40ft E2
5c. The left arête leads to the overhang, pass it on its left to gain the ledge and finish as for Little Miss Id. Low in the grade.

A wide chimney/recess on the left has cracks at either side. The right-hand one is:

10. Central Groove 30ft Sev
The steep start soon eases to a pleasant upper section.

11. Central Crack 30ft V Diff
The left-hand crack is a bold climb. An eliminate line is possible between the two cracks at 5a.

12. Cornflake 35ft E2
5c. The corner left of Central Crack gains a horizontal break; the flake above can be gained with difficulty and this leads steeply to the top. Care needed with protection.

13. The Mangler 35ft VS   ★
5a. The obvious overhanging crack provides a good testing pitch.

The overhanging corner on the left has a hard start (4c) to gain the cave of the next route.

14. North Chimney 40ft Mod
Gain the cave from the left and leave it on the right. A variation (**Nor Nor' Chimney**, V Diff) leaves the cave leftwards over a chockstone.

15. Manibus Et Pedibusque 40ft E3   †
6a. A difficult traverse across the wall left of Nor' Nor' Chimney leads to a finish up the arête. A route with a controversial history!

The left end of the crag has a widening crack in its upper section.

16. Slim Jim 25ft VS
5a. A lower wall leads to the foot of the crack. After a bold move the crack eases.

The boulders well right of the crag (near the trig. point) provide pleasant bouldering in restful seclusion.

CASTLE QUARRY (SD 953 246)

By Bruce Goodwin and Bob Whittaker

SITUATION AND CHARACTER

Castle Quarry (or Lobb Mill Delf) stands above the Rochdale canal some 2 miles east of Todmorden. It is a steep, steep crag being bowl-shaped with overhangs everywhere. The routes weave their way through this steep country, rather than attacking it frontally. The rock is surprisingly sound considering the appearance and atmosphere of the crag.

APPROACH AND ACCESS

The quarry is owned by Mr Driver of Bank Side Farm (the second house on the right on Hough Lane – see below). He asks that all climbers seek his permission before approaching the crag. Permission is normally given, but anyone ignoring this request will be asked to leave.

The crag is approached from Hough Lane (park near the viaduct on the main road). A path leads rightwards below the first house on the right and gains the cliff in 60 yards.

HISTORY

The Prow was the first route put up on this impressive (and oppressive) cliff, in 1966, and was perpetrated by Bob Whittaker and Ian Butterworth. This pair returned in 1969 to add Crossbow and then Whittaker returned again with Allan Austin and Mike Bebbington, for Austin to lead Viking and Warrior.

Nothing more was added until 1977 when once again Whittaker paid a visit, this time with Ralph Pickering, to add Carlite and Misty, and then things rested yet again until Geoff Haigh and Geoff Hamridding climbed Hooded Raider, Prophylaxis and Stealer of Souls in 1981. The hardest route was added later that same year when Dave Cronshaw and Les Ainsworth claimed Saxon and then the same pair, followed by John Ryden, found Norseman to which Ian Conway and Tony Nicholls added a near relative, Dane in 1982.

There are several lines left to go here, all of which encroach onto impressive territory, though only further developments and the passage of time will tell whether Castle Quarry has the potential of its near-neighbour Heptonstall Quarry.

THE ROUTES are described from LEFT to RIGHT.

1. **Crossbow** 35ft VS
4c. Climb the short corner with difficulty, then ledges slightly rightwards to a steep wall just left of the corner. Surmount the overhang direct onto the wall and then a mantel gains the top.

2. **Carlite** 35ft Sev
Swing over a prow a few feet right, and climb up into the corner above. Traverse left across the steep wall to finish up its left edge.

3. **Misty** 40ft VS
4b. Follow Carlite to the traverse, then gain the groove in the right wall and follow this to the top.

Twenty feet right, past the prow is a flat platform in a corner below huge roofs. Here starts:-

4. **The Prow** 45ft V Diff
Climb diagonally left to the nose and follow the groove above to the top.

To the right is a large cracked slab.

5. **Hooded Raider** 60ft VS
(1) 35ft 4b. Start from the left edge of the slab and climb the first jagged crack to a roof, then move right to a break and surmount this to a belay.
(2) 25ft 4b. Climb the ramp on the left to finish up a short, wide crack.

6. **Prophylaxis** 60ft VS
(1) 35ft 4c. Climb the second jagged crack to the belay of Hooded Raider.
(2) 25ft 4b. Directly above is a wide chimney at the top of the crag. Aim for this and then climb the corner on the left.

7. **Stealer of Souls** 60ft VS
(1) 35ft 4c. As for Prophylaxis pitch one.
(2) 25ft 4c. Continue direct and up the wide chimney. Exit out right.

To the right is a very impressive steep buttress which is guarded by several overhangs, and which strongly resembles parts of Heptonstall. This is **MEDIAEVAL WALL**, and here are found the best and hardest routes in the quarry.

8. **Saxon** 75ft E2   ★★
5c. Start from the lowest point on the wall at its left side and climb a flake and shallow groove, then make a hard mantel to gain a standing position on a small triangular foothold on the left (PR above). Follow the obvious right-leading crack, then move left round the roof and continue straight up to grass ledges. Peg belay by the grassy ledges.

9. **Dane** 100ft E1
5b. Climb Saxon for a 20 feet, then follow the obvious right-slanting ledge for 15 feet to its end. Mantel onto the sloping ledge above, then traverse back left and finish up Saxon. (Peg belay).

10. **Longship** 110ft E1   ★
5b. Start 30 yards right at a higher level, just left of an overhanging corner. Follow the obvious ramp left to a shallow cave, then step back round the nose on the left and continue in the same line to grass ledges overlooking Saxon.

11. **Viking** 100ft VS
(1) 45ft 4c. Start at the same point and climb an overhanging crack just left of the corner for 15 feet to ledges. Move left for 10 feet to a

cave, then up to a second cave and belay.
(2) 55ft 4c. From the left side of the cave climb a steep crack, then the wide crack above to a ledge and climb right and up to the top.

12. **Warrior** 90ft VS
(1) 40ft 4c. Climb the overhanging corner, then move right over blocks and back left to a sloping ledge and belay.
(2) 50ft 4c. From the right side of the ledge climb onto the slab above, then trend right to an obvious wide crack and finish up Viking.

13. **Norseman** 65ft Hard Sev
(1) 40ft 4a. Twelve yards farther right is a shallow groove leading to a V-shaped niche. Climb this to a large ledge on the right.
(2) 25ft. Move left and climb up obvious cracks. Loose.

COW'S MOUTH QUARRY (SD 962 195)

SITUATION AND CHARACTER
Cow's Mouth Quarry is probably the most pleasant of the many crags in the Rochdale Area. It stands beside the Pennine Way where that route travels a gravelled track maintained by the NWWA. For the running climber this gives an extra dimension as there are various reservoir circuits of between 3½ and 10 miles roundabouts. Another advantageous feature of Cow's Mouth is the excellent views; one can appreciate the panorama even more when the blue-gaiter-and-orange-cagoule brigade stroll by on the Pennine Way. They always seem to carry huge packs and wear waterproofs, whatever the weather and from their expressions it looks more like they are walking the Penitent's Way, not the Pennine Way!

The crag is made of good, solid gritstone, and although quarried there is also a small area of natural rock. On the whole the crag dries rapidly, and because it faces west, it catches the sun.

APPROACH AND ACCESS
There are no access restrictions in force here. The quarry can be reached from the A58 (Littleborough – Ripponden section); an each-way, hourly bus service passes the White House pub, or park cars on the parking area on the downhill side of the pub. Walk up the hill past the pub and up a slight rise to iron gates on the left. Follow the track, passing the reservoir, and round to gain the quarry in around 20 minutes. The White House also serves as an access point for White House Quarry and Blackstone Edge (q.v.).

HISTORY
The quarry's pre-historical phase saw the creation of such routes as Cornette, the excellent Route One, Seasier, Curving Chimney and Flipper. Documentation, however, began with the activities of the Solvé Club. Their best efforts include Route Right, Dessers, Groovin', Sandy

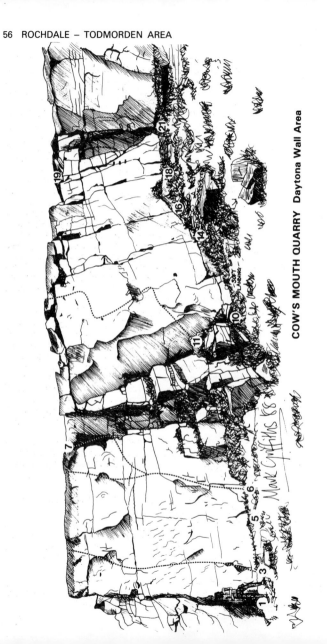

COW'S MOUTH QUARRY Daytona Wall Area

Crack and most of the routes right of Flipper. One of the Solvé members, Paul Horan, put up three good routes in the shape of Overhanging Crack, Z Crack and The Bijou. Les Towers bolted across Daytona Wall and in 1964 'Ras' Taylor rawlpugged and wood-screwed his way up Screwy, later free-climbed by Bob Whittaker in 1966. As the decade drew to a close, Carl Fletcher added the changeable Carl's Mark.

The early 70s saw different groups taking an interest in the quarry. Bruce Goodwin soloed some of the easier routes, and in 1972 members of the Black and Tan M.C. soloed Groundhog and Los Endos. In 1973 Whittaker, with Richard Sawicki, added Slab Crossing, Happy Wanderer and the good Overlapper. The late 1970s saw Al Evans add Pavanne, Romeo Error and the superb Daytona Wall. The latter route caused some controversy at the time, with allegations of resting and dubious tactics being rife; it later transpired that Evans had, in fact, done the route completely free and once the dust had settled a magnificent route remained. 1977 saw Screepain named though it was not to be climbed for nine years! A premature attempt by Goodwin ended with his recumbent form on the scree below, nursing two cracked ribs! The line was top-roped later and soloed by Andrew Eaton in 1987. In 1978 Clive Morton and John Vose traversed rightwards from Pavanne to Los Endos and later in the year Brian Cropper and Ian Lonsdale free-climbed Three Little Piggies; a fierce little crack climb that has been the bane of many an able climber.

The 1980s opened with a hard problem from John Ellis – The Don, and then the impending Lancashire guide of 1983 brought a rush of activity from Bob Whittaker who added sixteen routes, the best of which were King B, Slabmaster, Lapper, Space Invader, Wallin', The Hand Traverse and Golden Slipper (which took in the Morton/Vose traverse of 1978, and was freed by Chris Hardy on a solo excursion in 1983). Phil Kelly soloed the direct start to Daytona Wall in 1984 and Andrew Unsworth did the same to Romeo Error. Shortly afterwards Dougie Hall top-roped the direct finish to Daytona which even now, remains unled. As a pre-guidebook flourish, Whittaker returned yet again to his old stamping ground, still hungry for new rock, and climbed Deadline.

THE ROUTES are described from LEFT to RIGHT commencing with the obvious slab. The smaller upper quarried area (Bivouac Wall) has a 4c/5a traverse and some problems, as has the short wall at right angles to the base of the slab.

1. **Cornette** 30ft Hard Diff
The corner crack bounding the slab on its left. At the ledge take the arête above on its left-hand side; disjointed.

2. **Deadline** 30ft VS *
4c. An eliminate line between Cornette and Route One starting from the large foothold of the latter. A hard move gains the break and a pocket on the top wall leads on to a thin horizontal crack and a difficult rounded finish.

3. **Route One** 30ft Hard Sev **
4b. From a large foothold just right of Cornette, step up delicately and climb to the break. Climb the groove above to finish.

4. **King B**   30ft   Hard VS   *
5b. An eliminate line just right again, leading over a bulge and finishing up the second groove in the upper wall.

5. **Route Two**   50ft   VS   **
4c. Boulder up to a shallow groove then step up to the break. Finish up the next groove.

There is a shallow groove near the right end of the slab.

6. **Slabmaster**   30ft   VS
4c. Climb the groove, mantel onto a ledge and continue up the wall passing two slots, or go left from the first slot and pull up steeply to join Route Two: 5a.

7. **Route Right**   30ft   Hard Sev
4b. Climb to the ledge of Slabmaster then trend right to a short finishing chimney. The chimney may be gained direct at V Diff.

8. **Happy Wanderer**   40ft   VS
4c. A 'find-your-own-way' route climbing diagonally from the left to gain the chimney of Route Right.

9. **Slab Crossing**   40ft   Hard Sev   *
4b. Follow Route Right to the horizontal break then follow the break left to finish up Cornette. Slightly harder if the break is hand-traversed.

A low-level traverse of the slab is 5a. To the right, a corner runs the full height of the crag. This is:

10. **Right Corner**   40ft   Hard V Diff
Follow the corner, exiting right at the capstone.

The red wall right again has been eyed by many and tried by a few, though with no success as yet. Around the blunt arête is a good hard route.

11. **Daytona Wall**   35ft   E3   ***
6a. Start at a flake on the left. Traverse right and then up to a bolt runner and footledge. Pass the bolt on its left to a hole and move right to another then finish direct.

12. **Direct Start**   6a
Boulder up the thin crack system to join the route at its bolt runner.

13. **Direct Finish**   6b   Not led
From the bolt runner, gain the hole and continue direct to the top.

Right is a steep wall, split by many cracks.

14. **Overlapper**   30ft   Hard VS   **
5a. Climb the first crack to a little groove. Step left and finish direct.

15. **Lapper**   30ft   Hard VS   *
5a. Start as for Overlapper but continue up the groove to the top or,

from the horizontal break, traverse right to finish up Dessers.

An eliminate line is possible up the narrow wall between Overlapper and Dessers at E2 5c.

16. **Dessers** 30ft VS
5a. The crack right of Overlapper has a hard start.

17. **Sard** 25ft Hard VS   ★
5a. Climb the wall just right of Dessers.

18. **Seazy** 25ft Hard Sev
4c. The third crack leads with difficulty past a niche. Finish direct.

19. **Seasier** 25ft Hard V Diff
4a. Follow a left-slanting break then finish direct. A direct start is 5a.

20. **Niche Direct** 25ft Hard Sev
4b. Gain the triangular niche on the right, and leave it by a thin crack.

21. **Cracked Wall Chimney** 20ft Diff
The corner chimney.

22. **Space Invader** 65ft VS
A girdle of this part of the crag.
5a. Traverse left from Cracked Wall Chimney, past the niche of Seazy and downward to join Dessers. Climb this to the hand-traverse into Overlapper and finish as for that route.

23. **Cow's Cheek** 25ft Sev
4a. From the chimney go right past a nose to a ledge. A mantel leads to a finish rightwards.

24. **Calf** 20ft V Diff
The crack on the right leads to a wider crack above.

25. **Cow's Rib** 25ft Diff   ★
The obvious rib down and right of Calf.

26. **Cow's Hide** 25ft Sev
4a. Layback up, just right of the rib to gain a thin crack and the top.

27. **The 'Udder' Way** 25ft Sev
4a. From a ledge on Cow's Hide, finish rightwards.

The steep wall on the right has the remains of an ancient bolt route. It also has a free route which has repelled attempts by various notables. One such star said after having a 'bash' that it was harder than the route 'Masterclass' at Pen Trwyn. Others (cynics?) say it would get E4 in the Peak, or 5b at Brownstones!

28. **Three Little Piggies** 20ft E3   ★
6b. The impending wall leads to a thin crack and a relenting finish.

At the right end of the wall is a faint arête with flakes above.

29. **Carl's Mark** 20ft E2
5c. Gain a ledge on the arête and continue steeply up the flakes to finish. This route has changed quite dramatically in the past, and will no doubt change again as the holds alter or disappear; serious.

30. **Bob's Mark** 20ft Hard Sev
4b. Climb the overhanging corner on the right with a stiff move to gain a ledge, then finish up the crack on the left.

31. **Mark Bob** 25ft Sev
The crack a few feet right, then the centre of the wall above.

The quarry drops to a lower level. High up, just right of the arête is a bore-hole; the next route starts directly below this.

32. **Bore** 35ft VS
4b. Start below the bore-hole. The wall leads to a ledge then climb just right of the bore to finish just left of the arête.

An easy way down; **Intro** (Moderate) follows. Right of this is a prow.

33. **Flake Crack** 20ft Diff
Climb the flake to a ledge on the left of the prow.

34. **Scruff** 25ft V Diff
A groove on the right, with a jammed block at its base, leads to a square-cut groove and finish.

35. **Scruffy** 25ft Diff
The steep wall right of the groove.

To the right is a square-cut overhang at 10 feet. The groove left of this is:

36. **Groove** 30ft Sev
Go up to a ledge and follow the groove to a second ledge. Traverse left for six feet and climb the wall.

37. **Wallin'** 20ft VS ★
5b. An eliminate line up the wall beneath the overhang and over it to the top; a good problem.

38. **Groovin'** 30ft Hard Sev ★
4a. From a slabby boulder go up the groove to reach a ledge and then finish as for Groove.

39. **The Romeo Error** 30ft Hard VS
5c. The first move on Groovin' leads to a six-foot traverse right to below a sloping ledge. Move up onto this ledge and step delicately up to the break. Sneak off left or finish direct. A direct start is possible, direct to the sloping ledge; 6a.

40. **Screwy** 30ft E1 ★
5c. Baffling moves up the slick slab, just right of a line of wood screws, to the break. PR in situ above, finish direct. De Bono protection.

41. **Groundhog** 30ft Hard VS ★
5b. A good series of moves up the wall a few feet left of Sandy Crack, with a runner in that route.

42. **Sandy Crack** 25ft VS
5a. The crack left of the chimney, stepping right to finish.

43. **The Hand Traverse** 35ft VS
4c. Climb Sandy Crack to the break then traverse left.

44. **Curving Chimney** 25ft Hard Diff
The obvious chimney; a traditional squirm leads to an interesting finish.

45. **Jumping Jive** 25ft Hard VS
5b. Gain the large ledge on the right of the chimney and climb the wall just right of the cleft dynamically or reachily to the top. Tall leaders will be able to place runners.

46. **Pavanne** 25ft Hard VS
5a. Gain the large ledge by a neat mantel (or an ungainly belly-flop) and step up and right to join Overhanging Crack.

47. **Overhanging Crack** 25ft VS   *
4c. The obvious crack on the right gives sustained climbing.

48. **Z Crack** 35ft VS   ***
5a. Obvious by it's name. From the second crack finish straight up or (harder) by moving left to gain a little groove and thus the top. Excellent.

49. **The Don** 35ft E1
6a. The wall right of Z Crack, direct on small holds.

50. **Los Endos** 25ft Hard VS
5a. The arête on the right has a problem start on its left-hand side, though it can also be gained from the right; slightly easier.

51. **Golden Slipper** 50ft E1   *
5c. Climb Romeo Error to the ledge in the centre of the slab. Traverse right with difficulty to ledges on Sandy Crack (poorly protected). Continue right to gain ledges right of the chimney and follow Pavanne into Overhanging Crack. Climb this and cross into Z Crack. Finish as for Z Crack, or traverse right to finish up Los Endos.

The wall right of the arête provides a fine collection of routes that, though short, give worthwhile climbing on mainly natural rock.

52. **Screepain** 20ft E2
6a. From the scree, climb up to a horizontal slot and continue direct to the top. Sustained, unprotected and with an atrocious landing.

53. **Flipper** 20ft Sev   *
4b. Start right of the arête and step up to a footledge. Go over an overlap and climb daintily to the top.

54. **Flopper** 20ft VS
4b. Start at a horizontal flake below a shallow groove. Go up and trend left to finish.

55. **Flapper** 20ft VS
4c. From footholds climb the flakes above which lead steeply upward.

56. **Flook** 25ft Hard VS   *
5b. Climb the wall 10 feet left of the right arête of the wall. Steep moves

COW'S MOUTH QUARRY The Bijou Area

lead past a fingerhold to finish.

57. Flak 20ft E1
5c. The sloping, rounded horizontally-flaked arête is followed closely to an appallingly rounded finish; very frustrating.

58. Flooper 25ft Diff
The shallow corner on the arête leads up and right, then left to finish over a prominent nose. There are a number of easy scrambles and a couple of problems between Flooper and the obvious overhang on the right. The overhang itself is:

59. The Bijou 30ft Hard VS   ★★★
5a. The large flake/roof is approached from its right. An awkward and fearful move on the lip of the roof, over and into the slot above, leads to an easing finish over another prow.

59a. The Bijou – The Variation 25ft Hard Sev
4a. Where The Bijou goes left across the roof, continue direct over the breaks, pleasant.

GAUXHOLME CRAG (SD 927 231)

By Bob Whittaker

SITUATION AND CHARACTER
The crag overlooks the Bacup – Todmorden road (A681) about 200 yards from its junction with the A6033 Todmorden – Littleborough road. Its position is a climber's dream – in the 'garden' of the cottage to its left – who wouldn't want their own crag? The crag is about 80 feet high, of dark gritstone with an obvious roof near its top.

APPROACH AND ACCESS
Access is with the permission of the owner who lives in the cottage adjacent to the crag. This has readily been given in the past but this may change for, at the time of writing in December '87, the cottage is up for sale. A problem, unique in climbing, is also found here; standing on the TV aerial attached to the crag will bring strong protests from an old lady across the road – it makes her picture go awry!

The climbs take the centre of the main face. A bracket is bolted to the wall and a ramp drops down leftwards to the ground.

1. **Pillar Face** 80ft VS (1 nut for aid)
(1) 50ft 4c. Go up the ramp to the overhang and over this with a nut for aid to the ledges above. Move diagonally left to belay under the roof.
(2) 30ft 4a. Traverse right around the arête. A slabby corner leads to the top.

2. **Wood's Route** 80ft VS/A2
(1) 50ft 4c. As for Pillar Face.
(2) 30ft A2. Artificial climbing over the roof on bolts and screws.

LOWER WINSLEY QUARRY (SD 946 263)

By Bruce Goodwin and Bob Whittaker

SITUATION AND CHARACTER
Lower Winsley is a typically small delf situated on the edge of the moors above Todmorden. This south-facing quarry is of good gritstone in a very pleasant setting.

ACCESS AND APPROACH
Access is officially banned as the local farmer is concerned about pollution to his water supply. His son, who has recently taken over the running of the farm, whilst still 'anti-climbing' for the same reasons, is more appreciative of our case, thus things may change in the future. Until then, it would be wise to respect their wishes so as not to affect future access negotiations.

The quarry is reached from the Todmorden – Hebden Bridge road via Cross Stone Road, which leads up onto the moor until after about 1½ miles, a very sharp bend left is reached. The quarry is 50 yards right of this bend and is just visible from the road.

HISTORY
All the climbs were put up by Les Ainsworth, Dave Cronshaw, and John Ryden on three snatched visits during the summer of 1982.

The crag is divided into two sections; the left slightly broken, the right steep and compact. At the right end is a wall at right-angles with a wide crack/chimney, this is:-

1. **Soot Juggler** 25ft Hard Sev
4a. The crack/chimney is climbed up its left side until the arête on the left can be gained and followed to the top.

2. **Blackface** 25ft VS
5a. Start 12 feet left and climb the thin crack to a grassy ledge, then finish more easily up the wall above.

Left is an easy grassy descent, and left of this is the main buttress.

3. **Win** 25ft Sev
Start at the right side of the buttress at a small letterbox and climb straight up to the top.

4. **Roman Letocetum** 25ft Diff
Start 4 feet left of Bystander and climb the slab at its centre.

5. **Bystander** 30ft Hard VS
5a. Follow the obvious right-slanting fault which is the main feature of the wall, then finish through a niche.

6. **The Watch** 30ft VS
4b. As for Bystander until a move left leads to ledges and an easier finish.

Thirty feet left is a thin crack with a small inverted-triangular niche, above a 'hollow' in the ground.

7. **Stopwatch** 30ft VS
4b. Climb the thin crack with difficulty to a ledge. Step round the arête and finish up the wide crack on the left.

To the left is a grassy break, then comes the final short buttress.

8. **Winsley Slab** 25ft Sev
Climb the obvious flake-cum-slab, veering slightly right to gain the upper slab and then the top.

8a. **Direct Finish** 4a. At the obvious roof above the first slab pull over and climb direct to the top.

9. **First Come** 25ft Sev
Start 12 feet left at the back of a small bay. Climb up and slightly left through a break by an awkward mantel to the top.

LUMBUTTS QUARRY (SD 955 223)

SITUATION AND CHARACTER
The various quarry faces that collectively constitute Lumbutts Quarry lie along Langfield Edge, which faces north-east, overlooking the village of Lumbutts.

Excellent views and restful seclusion make Lumbutts a pleasant place to climb, although its northeasterly aspect dictates that good weather is required to fully enjoy the routes here. The main quarry is impressive at first sight, but a closer inspection shows otherwise. Perhaps the evolution of a new breed of 'railway navvy' could make this section climbable (or the development of the portable JCB). There are a few routes here, but the best climbing is found on the three buttresses at the left end of the edge, past the Main Wall. Even here there is a little loose rock, but this is usually obvious and is usually noted in the text. For the middle grade climber there is much to enjoy at Lumbutts – a 'curate's egg' of a crag.

APPROACH AND ACCESS
There are no access problems here; there is a right of way leading from the Shepherd's Rest up to the edge, linking with a network of footpaths, including the Pennine Way.

The Shepherd's Rest can be reached from the A6033 Todmorden – Littleborough road from Walsden. Follow the Lumbutts and Mankin-holes signs, always bearing right until the pub is reached after two miles; park opposite. A gate gives access to a footpath leading up the hill and along the base of the rocks. The pub can also be approached from Spring Side, about 1½ miles on the Hebden Bridge side of Todmorden; a lane opposite the Rose and Crown pub crosses the canal and leads up to Lumbutts village, and the Shepherd's Rest lies a mile farther on. The crag is reached after a pleasantly brisk 20-minute walk.

HISTORY
As usual, the earliest climbers to visit Lumbutts obviously kept quiet about their discoveries, as when John Taylor and Geoff Bradshaw ascended the first recorded route (Desperado) in 1966, the bolt route existed even then! Fifteen years after Desperado, Bob Whittaker and friends visited the crag and a wave of intense development began. Bob put up the most of the easier routes and of the hardest, the best were probably Rojim, Bob's Crack, The Hunter, Deliverance, Tired Digits, Cuckoo's Nest and Rings Of Saturn which is still unrepeated at the time of writing. Ron's Crack was the work of Ron Blunt, then in 1982 Dave Cronshaw, with Whittaker and Les Ainsworth, climbed Warp and Warp Factor and the following year Tony Nicholls soloed Nican.

In 1986 Gordon Mason added a good direct finish to The Hunter and also put up a complementary route – The Killer. Desperado was re-gardened and in its new and unprotected state it was found to be a little harder than its previous Hard VS 4c grade – take a look at the new grade to see what we mean! In the Hidden Wall area, Bruce Goodwin added Goma and the excellent Alibob whilst Andrew Eaton showed good technique on Digital Abuse then Goodwin, as a final flourish, ascended the overhanging crack system left of Bolt Route, well named Power Surge.

ALL THE CLIMBS are described from RIGHT to LEFT. The unfortunately named Main Quarry is the large expanse of rock first seen from the approach path. The best climbing is found well left of this region. The Pillar is a good reference point and Hidden Wall is up the grass slope to its right. There are some climbs in the Main Quarry, starting at the Solar Slabs area; this is part-way along the main cliff, being somewhat lower and set at an angle. An obvious wide crack just right of the right arête of Solar Slab is the first route described.

SOLAR SLAB AREA

1. **Rings Of Saturn**   40ft   E1   †
5c. Climb the wide crack.

The slab round to the left has a ledge running across it and two cracklines.

2. **Lazer Beam**   50ft   Hard VS
5b. Gain the ledge and traverse right past both cracks to finish just left of the arête.

3. **Star Wars**   45ft   VS
4c. The right-hand crack is gained from the ledge.

4. **Quasar 40ft**   Sev
From the grass ledge follow the right-leaning crack and finish over ledges.

5. **Black Hole**   40ft   V Diff
The curving corner a few feet left.

Thirty yards left is a crack in a steep slab with a grass ledge.

6. **Split Pin**   40ft   VS
4b. The crack is gained from the left and leads to a difficult finish.

7. **Bungalow**   40ft   VS
5a. Above Split Pin, and slightly to the left, is a roof which leads leftwards to a corner. Follow this to a ledge and move right to finish up a slabby corner.

8. **Wishbone**   45ft   VS
5a. Climb out of a shallow corner and up to a ledge, then continue up a crack on the left.

HIDDEN WALL AREA

The Hidden Wall area is split in to two sections, separated by a grassy mound. The right-hand area has a series of steep corners, arêtes and cracks, whilst as a contrast the left-hand side contains mostly slab routes, though with some steeper walls. At the right side of the right-hand area lies a corner with a steep slab.

9. **R.P.**   25ft   Diff
Climb the series of steps in the shallow groove to the top.

10. **Recessed Slab**   25ft   VS
4b. The right-slanting corner, left of R.P.

11. **Flash Harry**   30ft   VS
4c. Start as for Recessed Slab, then climb the twin cracks in the groove on the left.

12. **Daz**   30ft   VS
4c. Follow Flash Harry to the overhang, then layback left round this and finish up an arête.

13. **The Warp** 35ft VS *
5a. The steep groove and flake around to the left.

14. **Bob's Crack** 35ft VS *
4c. The obvious crack 6 feet left.

The loose corner on the left is best ignored. To its left is:

15. **Ron's Crack** 30ft Hard VS *
5b. Climb the crack which bends left and has a niche in it, to a hard finish. Sustained.

16. **Warp Factor** 30ft Hard VS *
5c. The thin crack a few feet left of Ron's Crack.

17. **Armstretcher** 25ft Hard Sev
4b. Climb the corner just left, traversing left to finish up the arête.

18. **Silk Cut** 25ft Sev
The next arête, on its left.

19. **Crumble Corner** 20ft Diff
The next corner.

20. **Tired Digits** 20ft Hard VS *
5b. The arête on the left leads steeply to an awkward upper section.

21. **Cold Digits** 20ft Diff
The last corner.

22. **Digit** 20ft VS
4c. The thin crack in the steep wall just left.

SLAB AREA
The Slab area is over the quarry rise. The slab has has a block at its lowest point. Here starts:

23. **Alibob** 30ft E1 **
6a. Gain sloping holds, move up and right then delicately step up to the break and the top. Good.

24. **Rojim** 25ft VS *
4c. Climb the slab rightwards to gain a crack/groove, then climb left of the two 'pods' to finish.

25. **Goma** 20ft Hard VS
5b. A shallow groove on the left gives a hard start which, thankfully, relents on the upper wall. Low in the grade.

Left is a large ledge at ⅔ height. Two crack systems gain this ledge; the right-hand one is **Dry** (V Diff) and the left-hand is **Damp** (Diff). Traverse off to finish both of them. **Waterslide** (Hard Sev 4c) is the oft-wet corner whilst the flake left of the arête is **Flakey** (Sev). The slab at the end of this section has a corner with a jamming crack (**Sandman** V Diff) whilst the rib on the left is **Blunt Rib** (Sev).

THE PILLAR
This buttress gives routes of up to 65 feet long. The climbs are usually

solid and any loose rock is obvious. The far right-hand side of the buttress has a slabby wall and some grass.

26. **Nican** 35ft Hard VS
5a. Gain a grass ledge then step left and climb a slab, finishing rightwards; serious.

27. **Desperado** 65ft E4
5c. The shallow corner just right of the pillar proper gives unprotected climbing to a ledge (Loose block and poor protection in arrival). Follow a left-slanting weakness to a large situ peg below The Hunter's direct finish. Either climb this to finish, or skulk off left.

28 **The Hunter** 65ft Hard VS
5a. From Desperado, follow a ramp left to a flakey crack. Go left and up to a corner which leads to the terrace. The wall above the huge situ peg gives a steep and airy finish (5a).

29. **The Killer** 65ft Hard VS   *
5a. Start left of the arête. Go right over an overlap to join The Hunter at the Flakey crack. Climb this then traverse right and ascend slightly leftwards to a large ledge and the huge situ peg. Finish as for the above route or traverse right for 10 feet and pass a bulge rightwards to an easing finish (4c).

30. **True Grit** 40ft VS
4c. Follow a bore hole to a ledge and continue steeply to the grass terrace. A corner above can provide a finish, if desired.

The path passes beneath an orange/brown wall. Above a step in the path are some thin cracks.

31. **Digital Abuse** 30ft E2
6a. Climb the wall, more or less direct, just left of the cracks; fingery!

There is a chimney at the left end of the wall, ten feet right is:

32. **Deliverance** 30ft Hard VS
5b. Gain the niche 10 feet above the ground with difficulty, then continue up the crack above.

33. **Cuckoo's Nest** 25ft E1
5c. From the chimney go up and right to a crack, then the top. Hard.

Twenty yards farther left is a buttress with 'W.Kershaw' chiselled into the rock.

34. **Convoy** 30ft Hard Sev
4a. Climb to a ledge and follow a ramp leftwards to the top.

A block about 20 yards from the cliff gives some worthwhile problems. The steep face on the left has a line of rusting ironmongery running its height – **Bolt Route** (A1). The central weakness of the wall is:

35. **Power Surge** 40ft E3   **
5c. Start with difficulty and gain the niche (hard) then go left and up to

a second niche. Exit this and go left and finish direct. There is a belay stake to the left.

36. **Bull's Horns** 40ft V Diff
The corner at the left end of the wall leads to a ledge, then finish through the 'bull's horns' above.

REDDYSHORE SCOUT (SD 942 197)

SITUATION AND CHARACTER
Reddyshore Scout is the series of buttresses that lies on the eastern rim of the moorland plateau overlooking the river Roch and the Rochdale canal, some 2½ miles north of Littleborough.

This collection of steep buttresses is in an imposing and exposed position, further enhanced by the angle of the slope beneath. The sense of exposure that this situation engenders gives it that 'big crag' feel and ensures that seconds must belay to the rock. The excellent routes here are usually on sound rock, and where there is loose rock it is noted in the text, and does not interfere, usually, with the quality of the climbing.

The crags face east thus they are in the shade by the afternoon and consequently are at their best during fine weather. The routes dry reasonably quickly. The black wall of Fence Buttress, from Tattersall's Lament to Hidden Gem contains a fine collection of routes well worth seeking out.

APPROACH AND ACCESS
The crags are reached from Calderbrook Road, which leads off the A6033 Littleborough – Todmorden road at the toll house (an obvious and interesting octagonal building clearly placed on the Littleborough side of the junction). From this road, 2 tracks lead to the crags; one along the top of the cliff, the other below the grass slope. The upper track is gated, the lower track begins near a ventilation shaft for the Summit railway tunnel. Park off the road and walk to the crag in 5 – 10 minutes. Access is unrestricted.

HISTORY
The first routes date from 1959, when Rochdale guru Bob Whittaker with Bill Hardacre put up Layback Corner. They also added Tattersall's Lament in 1961 and added a brace of routes the following year; the excellent Blind Panic dating from this time. Two more routes were climbed in 1964, before a consolidation period set in. This ended when Jed O'Neill demonstrated that Galileo was wrong by pulling off a large block whilst attempting a new route; the block fell and so did Jed, though somehow he contrived to reach the ground after the block! Jed's injuries were severe and the crag immediately gained a reputation for loose rock and nothing more was added until 1978 when

Whittaker once again took an interest in the crag. With his two long-time partners Gordon Mason and Ralph Pickering, he climbed Bitter Friends, Beautiful Dreamer, Chasing Dreams and Hidden Gem, which were all fine routes and which brought the crag back to the forefront of development amongst the Rochdale and Todmorden climbers.

Whittaker was back the following year to add War Dance and Test Piece, which both employed a little aid, though Test Piece was free-climbed solo, by Ian Carr in 1983 and Whittaker himself reduced the aid on War Dance to a single nut in 1986.

A new face appeared on the scene in 1979, when Ian Lonsdale paid a swift visit with Whittaker, just after Brian Cropper's wedding; the pair celebrated the day by adding Travellin' Man and Wedding Day and for the occasion they both wore their penguin suits and their EBs had been specially cleaned! Others involved in the development of the crag at this time were Tom Miller and Frank Shaw (who together added Midnight Express), Harry Taylor, Geoff Hainridding and Sid Siddiqui. Geoff Haigh stayed long enough to add Peeler and Nailbiter, and Derek Wright developed Tower Buttress.

The pace now slowed, and little was done until 1984 when Brian Cropper climbed Go For Broke and then in 1987, Ralph Pickering claimed Pig Farmer and Gordon Mason added the bold Sceptre.

PIT BUTTRESS
The usual point of arrival at the crag is Fence Buttress. Pit Buttress lies 100 yards left. THE CLIMBS are described from LEFT to RIGHT.

1. **Pig Farmer** 35ft VS
4c. Climb the corner to the overhang. Continue, moving left as required.

1a. **Sceptre** 35ft E1   †
5b. Climb the arête on its right-hand side to gain a groove. Finish up this. Reachy and poorly protected.

FENCE BUTTRESS
A stream runs down the hillside, and a small face on its right has a broken gully to its right. At the base of this face is:

1b. **Intro Wall** 25ft Sev
Climb the groove, step left then finish up the crack left of the arête.

2. **Sidestep** 25ft V Diff
As for Intro Wall but step right and finish up the arête.

3. **Night Time** 20ft V Diff
Start just right. Go over an overhang and finish up a corner.

4. **Test Piece** 30ft E1   ★★
5c. Climb the scoop and gain the horizontal break. Go left to the cracked arête and follow this which smooths out higher up. ⌐

5. **Piece Green** 35ft VS
5a. The initial difficult scoop of Test Piece leads to a finish up Green Slabs.

6. **Green Slabs**   40ft   VS
4c. Climb the corner on the right, step right then back left onto a slab. From the overhung corner above, swing right to another slab and finish direct.

7. **Tailor Made**   45ft   VS
A V-shaped groove 6 feet right leads to a ledge. A traverse left below an overhang leads to another grassy ledge and the slab above leads to the top.

8. **War Dance**   50ft   Hard VS   (1 nut for aid)
5b. The arête on the right contains a groove with a small roof 10 feet below the top of the crag. Climb to the groove and continue to the roof. Use one NA to pass this and finish direct.

Right again is a broken chimney with a grassy ledge beneath.

9. **Diagonal**   60ft   V Diff
Climb the groove to the grassy ledge. Semi hand-traverse left and follow the fault to finish up a slab.

10. **Green Piece**   50ft   V Diff
Gain and climb the chimney.

11. **Midnight Express**   50ft   Hard VS
5b. Climb the left wall of the chimney for 25 feet (possible belay). Hand traverse left to a small square-cut groove on the arête and go up this to the top.

The right wall of the chimney forms a pinnacle. To its right is a grass ledge twenty feet above the ground.

12. **Dropover**   50ft   V Diff
Climb cracks on the left to gain the grass ledge. The crack in the left wall leads to a loose(ish) finish.

13. **Travellin' Man**   50ft   VS
Climb the face just right of Dropover to the ledge, then follow the right-slanting crack above.

Right again is a fence and right of this is a blocky groove-cum-crack.

14. **Central Crack**   60ft   VS   *
Follow the block-filled crack, step left and follow the crack above to finish up a little corner.

15. **Worthy Venture**   60ft   Sev
Climb the ramp on the right until a swing left leads to a V-shaped groove, up which a finish can be made.

16. **Wedding Day**   60ft   VS   *
The ramp, wall and overhanging crack lead to a ledge (possible belay). The centre of the slab on the right provides a finish.

17. **Go For Broke**   60ft   E1
5b. The short groove right of Wedding Day is gained direct.

The rock now becomes grassy and broken for 20 yards and then recovers to become a fine wall with an excellent selection of routes.

The prominent arête has a corner and a cracked wall on its left.

18. Layback Corner 40ft V Diff
The corner to an exit onto easy ledges.

19. Tattersall's Lament 40ft Sev   ★★
Follow Layback Corner then gain the crack in the right wall and continue direct.

20. Blind Panic 45ft VS   ★★★
4c. Gain the arête from the block (or direct – 5a), and proceed coolly to the top. Poor protection.

21. Bitter Friends 55ft E1   ★★★
5b. The shallow groove and cracks a few feet right of the arête.

22. Beautiful Dreamer 55ft Hard VS   ★★
5b. The overhanging crack 10 feet right, then the thin crack above.

The right-hand end of the wall has a crack left of some square-cut overhangs.

23. Chasing Dreams 55ft Hard VS   ★★
5b. Go left under the roof to the crack. Climb to the break and follow the thin crack above.

24. Hidden Gem 40ft Sev   ★★
The deep corner on the right leads to the top of a flake. Go up the crack above to a large ledge and step left to a slabby finish.

25. Peeler 25ft Sev
Follow the groove farther right.

26. Happy Wanderer 80ft VS
5a. From the break on Chasing Dreams, traverse left to finish up Bitter Friends.

27. Wild Goose 150ft Hard VS   ★
A girdle traverse of Fence Buttress giving some good climbing.
(1) 65ft 5a. Follow Happy Wanderer, but continue the traverse to belay on Travellin' Man's ledge.
(2) 35ft 5a. Gain the arête then hand-traverse left below the overhang and continue to a belay on the pinnacle of Dropover.
(3) 50ft 5a. A fault leads across the steep wall to finish up the top slab of Green Slabs.

TOWER BUTTRESS

The large buttress on the right has a shaley base. The sounder rock above provides routes which, although relatively easy, can provide problems with route-finding. The buttress is currently neglected and is becoming overgrown. The buttress consists of two bands of loose shale supporting a band of more solid rock. On top of these three bands are set two slabs. The right slab is parallel to the lower bands, whilst the left slab slopes back and up into the hillside. Both slabs end at a ledge, above which lies a 15-foot wall leading to the top of the buttress. The top of the left slab is split by an obvious irregular crack. The left edge of the buttress has a crack which provides:

28. **Smoker's Satisfaction** 45ft V Diff
Follow grassy ledges to gain the crack and a ledge above. A platform leads to a crack on the left and a loose finish.

29. **Piecer** 40ft V Diff
Climb cracks 6 feet left of Smoker's Satisfaction, then a corner above leads to a ledge then a scramble right leads to the finish as above.

30. **Reiver** 45ft V Diff
Two grooves 10 feet right of Smoker's Satisfaction lead to rightward-leading steps and a short crack leading to a ledge. Just right of the arête is a hidden chimney which provides a finish.

Twenty feet below and right is a rotting cave, and a grassy ledge leads across the face. A grassy bay fifteen feet right of the cave is the start of the next route.

31. **Farrier** 60ft V Diff
Go up steeply to a slab. A groove at its left-hand side trends right to short cracks, the left-hand of which leads to a ledge and a crack above to finish.

32. **Hand Loom Weaver** 60ft V Diff
A second bay twenty feet right has a wall which is climbed to a nose of natural rock. Pass this on the left and follow the slab above to join Farrier at its two cracks. Finish up the right-hand crack.

33. **1878** 60ft V Diff
Follow Hand Loom Weaver to the nose. Pass this on the right and climb the slab above to a ledge at the right of the buttress. Go left to a gangway and up left to a crack which leads, with care, to the finish of Hand Loom Weaver.

CHIMNEY BUTTRESS
This buttress has had an obvious rockfall on its left side.

34. **Nailbiter** 40ft VS
4b. The obvious broken groove slants right.

35. **Loggerheads** 40ft VS
4c. The left-hand of two cracks, passing some overhangs en route.

36. **Weekend Wonder** 40ft VS
4c. The right-hand crack, past a flake to the top.

SUMMIT QUARRY (SD 948 196)

SITUATION AND CHARACTER
The quarry is set on the moor above and east of the A6033 Littleborough – Todmorden road. The various sections of the quarry provide good climbing on rock that is generally sound but, as with all quarries, some rock is suspect – this is usually obvious and the text draws attention to any loose rock where necessary. The variety of climbs is such that cracks, slabs (steep), and fingery walls are all to be found here. Unfortunately some parts do dry slowly after rain so a visit

is more profitable after a day or two of dry(ish) weather. Canal Buttress is situated above the Rochdale Canal and lies beside the footpath that leads to the main quarry.

A re-gardening of two sections of the main crag has shown that this cliff – although less popular than Cow's Mouth – has arguably more to offer. Many of the climbs are excellent and as it approaches maturity, this quarry is well worth a visit.

APPROACH AND ACCESS
Access is not currently a problem as there is a public footpath up to and alongside the quarry. The farmer whose land the quarry lies on is anxious that any litter be removed and that activities are such as to give no danger to his sheep (!) Unfortunately one of his sheepdogs was injured recently when it collided with a belay stake, necessitating expensive vet's fees. Thus some belay stakes are 'hidden' and a good eye for alternatives may be necessary. Fortunately Mr. Fielding does not object to climbing, so please be polite and friendly when he passes by, as he often does on his rounds.

The best approach is from the Summit Inn, about 2 miles north of Littleborough. Park in the pub car park and follow the cobbled lane down beside the inn and cross the canal. Turn left and follow the track to a concrete section, hairpinning off right. A stile crosses a fence on the left and the path beyond is followed to the shaly bank and Canal Buttress. The path continues and contours right alongside a sheeptrod and up to another stile. The narrow defile that leads into the quarry lies ahead. This pleasant approach takes about 20 minutes. Summit may also be approached from Cow's Mouth, or may be used to approach that crag. A line of pylons across the moor indicates the line to be followed. The popular round of the three crags (Summit, Cow's Mouth and Blackstone Edge) can also be started (or finished) here.

HISTORY
Recorded development began with the activities of the Solvé Club; in the early to mid-1960s they regularly visited the crags roundabouts and were responsible for the majority of earlier routes on both Summit and Cow's Mouth. Perhaps the best routes to come from the Solvé's era were Twixt, The Crab, Layback Crack, the Cnig's routes, the bold Grave's End and the very hard Who Dun It? Good routes were also added to the right-hand end of the quarry in the shape of Split Leg Corner, Hot and Cold. Among the more active members of the Solvé Club, who climbed most of the routes between them, were S. Halliwell, Paul Horan, Mike Quinn, Ian Butterworth and J. Lothian. Horan was probably responsible for The Crab, Twixt and Layback Crack, with S. Halliwell, as well as the Cnig's routes and Who Dun It?

The early 70s saw different groups in action. Bruce Goodwin soloed some routes on the Wall Of Grooves area in 1971, while John Hampson and Steve Cunnis climbed The Shroud by its Turin Finish, these two being named by Bob Whittaker who made the second ascents of the lower section and Andy Eaton who followed the Turin Finish in 1985, thinking it to be a first ascent. Goodwin soloed Alexander The Great in mistake for Cnig's Direct, and the routes on the far right walls were added by Goodwin and other members of the Black and Tan M.C., including Central Corner on Canal Buttress.

In 1974 Bob Whittaker climbed Hangman and Sunstroke, but afterwards efforts dwindled, and new routing went out of fashion, the only other route of any significance being Windy Wall which was soloed by Clive Morton in 1977.

Nothing further was done until 1981 when a pre-guide charge was led by Bob Whittaker. With Ralph Pickering he developed Canal Buttress and added The Coffin and Free Spirit, as well as climbing most of the easier routes in the quarry, usually solo, whilst Ron Blunt, Gordon Mason, Derek Walker and Pickering also added a few titbits.

In 1983 Goodwin and Tony Nicholls put up Clueless Groove on Pylon Buttress but left the remaining possibilities for new routes elsewhere and it was not until 1985 that the rest of Pylon Buttress saw any further development. Goodwin returned with friends and they added First Circle and Sunny Day. Nicholls climbed Groundbait which he named because he hit the deck from 25-feet!, and John Ellis traversed The Chud. The Pool Area of the main crag also received a vigorous cleaning; Clive Morton cleaned and re-ascended Hot, while Mason did the same to Cold and also soloed Shorty. Goodwin continued his ongoing route-fever with Sinking Feeling, Comfortable and a new finish to Split Leg Corner. Nicholls soloed Yes later that year, and Ellis spotted Hawkeye, then Goodwin Split and Ellis showed us his Personality. Hampson returned and added a technical and bold route in the shape of The Laying Away and thus the crag rests.

ALL THE CLIMBS are described from LEFT to RIGHT.

CANAL BUTTRESS
There is a belay stake in place at the time of writing.

1. **Short Crack** 20ft VS
The crack up the left-hand side wall.

2. **Fluted Arête** 25ft VS
4c. The arête, climbed on its right side.

3. **Fluted Wall** 25ft VS
5a. The wall and overhang, finishing up a groove.

4. **Central Corner** 25ft V Diff
The obvious corner is followed, mainly on its right side.

5. **Cracked Wall** 20ft VS
5a. The wall on the right leads to a niche, the wall right of this leads to the top.

MAIN QUARRY
The Main Quarry has an outlying section 40 yards to its left, over a grassy ridge. There is occasionally a pool below it. This section is

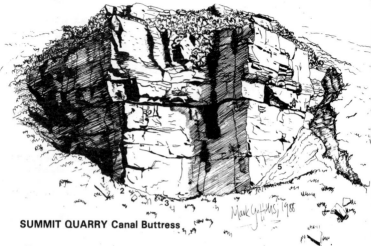

SUMMIT QUARRY Canal Buttress

called:
PYLON BUTTRESS; Belays are about 70 feet back and left of a large block just above the crag.

6. **Clueless Groove** 20ft VS
4c. The obvious corner system at the left of the face.

7. **First Circle** 35ft E2   *
5c. Start 10 feet right of Clueless Groove. Gain a little slab at the bolt holes and follow a thin crack to the break. The flake/block and thin crack lead to the top.

The smooth wall to the right has a line of bolt holes, then the ground starts to rise.

8. **Groundbait** 35ft E2   *
5c. Follow the slanting line up right, PR. Go up to the break and continue up the headwall just left of the obvious yellow scar.

9. **Sunny Day** 30ft Hard VS
5b. Start just left of grassy cracks. Gain a ledge at 10 feet then continue to the break and on, passing a ledge to gain the top. Stake belay (not obvious).

10. **The Chud** 70ft E1   ***
A traverse of the obvious break from right to left.
5b. Climb a little corner right of Sunny Day and traverse left into Clueless Groove, finishing up (or down) that route. Exciting!

ALCOVE AREA
The Main Quarry proper has a little wall, left of a square-cut arête:

11. **Wall Climb** 20ft V Diff
Climb the centre of the short wall; stiff moves for the grade.

12. **Twixt** 20ft VS ★
5a. The square arête is climbed on its left side. Good.

13. **Windy Wall** 20ft VS ★
5b. The right side of the arête has a hard start.

14. **Double Mantle** 25ft Sev
Climb the ledges on the right, finishing up the final crack of The Crab.

15. **The Crab** 30ft VS
4c. Climb the two converging cracks from an alcove, to a move left onto
a ledge. Finish up the crack above.

16. **Creepy Crab** 35ft VS
4c. Follow The Crab to the large ledge then traverse right to another
ledge and finish via a mantel.

17. **Layback Crack** 30ft VS ★★
5a. The steep ramp is climbed to hard moves round the overhang to
finish.

18. **Starters** 30ft Diff ★
The obvious stepped corner; an awkward problem.

CEMETERY WALL
The steepening, slabby wall right of Starters provides excellent
climbing, the routes being generally better protected than they may
appear.

19. **The Coffin** 45ft VS
4c. Follow a rightward curving groove just right of the arête to a big
ledge on the left (on Starters). The thin crack in the left wall provides
the finish.

20. **The Shroud** 45ft E2 ★
5c. A good mantelshelf is reached direct or from lower on the right. Go
delicately up to a ledge and a little groove. The steep wall is the scene
of a tense, fingery climax.

21. **The Shroud: Turin Finish** E2 ★★
5c. From the little groove go left to the arête, pull up and finish on its
left side. Care with protection.

22. **Grave's End** 45ft E1 ★★★
5b. A groove slants right; climb up to it and move left to footholds.
Step up delicately into the scoop and follow this to a finish up the wall,
or step right to finish up Order.

23. **The Laying Away** 45ft E2 ★★
5c. Start as for Grave's End. Continue up the groove (hard) to gain a
standing position (small nut in slot on the right). Make some exacting
moves to gain the blunt arête above, then a jug and mantel and a finish
'made to Order'. A few feet right is a deep groove:

24. Order 45ft Hard Sev   *
4a. Follow the groove to ledges, and then a shallow corner which leads to the top wall.

25. Free Spirit 45ft Hard VS
5b. From the groove of Order, climb the wall on the right to a ledge (on Disorder). The thin crack above leads via reachy moves to a finish just right of the overhangs. A side runner in Disorder is necessary for this grade, otherwise E2.

26. Disorder 45ft Sev   **
4a. The next groove on the right leads diagonally leftwards to neatly rectify itself and become Order.

Right again is a curving flake in the wall.

27. Cnig's Direct 45ft VS
4c. Climb the groove to the flake and pull over this direct, follow ledges to finish.

28. Cnig's Underhang 40ft VS
4b. Climb to the flake as for Cnig's Direct but follow this rightwards to ledges. A crack on the right leads to the top.

On the right is a sloping ledge a few feet above the ground. A small overhang lies just above, split by a triangular notch.

29. Alexander The Great 40ft Hard VS   *
5b. Gain the left end of the sloping ledge and follow the indefinite crackline above, which leads delicately to the overlap. Pass this on its left and go left to join Cnig's Direct.

30. Brightspark 40ft VS
4b. A groove above the right-hand end of the sloping ledge leads to the notch in the overhang; climb through this to finish up the crack on the right.

31. Laser Beam 40ft Sev
Start as for Bright Spark, but follow a line left of the arête, passing a mantel to a cracking finish.

A wide ledge on the right forms the base of a large open alcove. The roof above is currently unstable and some rockfall has occurred. The routes hereabouts wisely dodge past this upper section.

32. Delicatessen 35ft V Diff
Go up to the left end of the large ledge, finish leftwards or up the corner above.

33. Take Away 35ft Diff
Gain the ledge at its centre then the deep corner on the right leads to a finish rightwards.

34. Pickwick 30ft Diff
Climb up to the right end of the ledge and take the shallow corner on

the right.

35. Swordfish 40ft Hard Sev
4b. Start right of Pickwick, at an overhanging corner. Climb up and left to the arête. Gain a ledge above then follow the right hand side of the sharp arête above to finish.

36. Squid 40ft V Diff
Follow Swordfish to the ledge then finish up a square-cut corner on the right.

There is an obvious steep slab at a lower level on the right.

37. Sunstroke 30ft V Diff
Climb up left of the arête, unprotected.

38. Who Dun It? 25ft E1 ★
6a. The chiselled holds on the slab lead to a very hard move (or a leap sideways to safety) and then the top. Use of the left arête makes the 'tick' easier; 5c. No protection is available whichever route one chooses.

The steep wall on the right is becoming overgrown.

39. Derek Did It 25ft V Diff
Start just left of the twin cracks and climb up to a groove, finish up this.

40. Knuclist 20ft VS
4c. The undercut groove on the right, with two cracks.

41. Hangman 25ft E1 †
5b. The square-cut groove in the arête to the right; still unrepeated since the demise of what would appear to be a crucial flake.

42. The Noose 25ft Hard VS
5a. From the large ledge on the right, reach a hole in the left wall and finish direct over the block overhangs above.

43. Gardener's Nightmare 25ft VS ●
Gain the large ledge and follow cracks in a green and earthy manner. Eminently forgettable!

Past a dirty chimney lies a steep pillar, just left of a square-cut corner on the arête.

44. Th'way 25ft VS
4c. Climb the pillar to the horizontal break, follow the wall above slightly left to the top.

WAY OUT WALL is the short compact wall right of the arête almost opposite the quarry entrance. Climbing here is good and the routes here are often sustained.

45. Epicoff 25ft Mild Severe
4a. Climb the groove left of the arête to the overhang then step right into a crack and follow this to the top.

46. Giggle Pin 25ft VS ★
5a. Climb the blunt arête to join Epicoff. Climb down that route to

beneath the overhang then stand up in the horizontal crack, step right and follow the little arête.

47. Slight Wall 20ft VS ⁎
5a. Climb the wall/arête just right of Giggle Pin stepping right to finish up a crack.

48. Way Out 25ft VS
5a. Up the wall 6 feet right to a sloping ledge, then the thin crack on the left.

49. Combination 30ft VS ⁎
5a. Start as for Way Out, but traverse left to finish up Epicoff.

A small corner a few feet right is the start for the next two routes.

50. Exit 20ft Hard VS ⁎
5a. Climb the corner and the thin crack above, past a mantel.

51. L.M.J. 20ft Hard Sev
4b. Climb the corner then move right to a grassy groove which leads to the top.

WALL OF GROOVES
Right again is a grassy area, offering an easy descent route. The rock soon improves and transforms into a wall gradually increasing in height as it approaches the pool. Just right of the grass is a steep black wall.

52. Black Wall 25ft Hard Sev
4a. Follow the left edge of the wall.

53. Tidemark 25ft Sev
4a. The right end of the wall, starting under a left-leaning overhang.

54. Kebab 25ft Sev
4a. The first groove 10 feet right.

55. Babke 25ft V Diff
The next break and corner.

56. Play it Again Sam 25ft Sev
The thin crack and right slanting groove, 5 feet right.

57. Hart to Hart 25ft V Diff
Farther right is a heart chiselled into the rock. Start here and climb to a grassy ledge and then take the corner above.

58. Sam 25ft Hard V Diff
The crack and corner 5 feet right.

59. Mas 25ft V Diff
The crack and corner on the right, starting on a higher grass ledge.

Right of the grass ledge is a hanging flake:

60. Casablanca 30ft Hard VS
5b. Follow the left-slanting crack through some small overhangs and finish up a jamming crack above.

61. Buttertoe Wall 30ft Hard Sev ⁎

4a. Climb the crack and hanging flake direct. Strenuous.

POOL AREA: The Wall of Grooves area now merges into the Pool Area. The first route starts just left of the pool.

62. **Latentest** 30ft Hard VS
5a. Climb a thin crack to gain a ledge then finish up the corner above. Poor protection.

63. **Split** 2ft E1 *
5c. Above the left end of the pool is a ledge with a bolt above; climb up to the ledge and finish direct. Harder for the short.

64. **Personality** 40ft E2 **
6a. Gain the ledge as for Split, then traverse right using bolt holes to make a series of hard and reachy moves up and right to a ledge (well nigh impossible for the short). The headwall is something of a relief. An early failure means an early bath!

Above the right side of the pool is a corner. Left of this is a leftward-slanting crackline. There is a stake belay hidden in a clump of rushes, in line with Hot and Cold wall.

65. **Sinking Feeling** 30ft E2 *
"A fall would give that sinking feeling!"
5c. Step down to a ledge just above the water and follow the crackline above to a large ledge, then follow the continuation crack to finish.

66. **Split Leg Corner** 30ft Hard VS
5a. The obvious corner leads to a large ledge. From here either finish direct or via the crack on the left. Or, traverse left and climb ledges.

67. **Hawkeye** 30ft E2 **
5c. Climb the wall a few feet right of Split Leg Corner. Care with protection.

68. **Hot** 25ft Hard VS *
5a. The diagonal leads leftwards to a little groove and a mantel to finish.

69. **Comfortable** 25ft Hard VS *
5b. The wall right of Hot gives a testing route. Care with protection.

70. **Cold** 25ft Hard VS
5b. The next crack on the right; poorly protected.

71. **Shorty** 20ft VS
5a. The wall just right again.

The last routes lie on the short wall at right angles to Pool Wall. There are no belays, though a braced, sitting belay is possible in a dip a little farther back. This is not as insecure as it sounds, but most climbers prefer to solo the routes.

72. **Gardener** 20ft Hard Sev
4b. Start at the left side, reach a mantel, and thus an easier finish.

73. **It's Slippy** 20ft Hard VS
5a. The groove on the right leads with difficulty over an overhang, then climb direct to the top.

74. Pull Hard 20ft VS
4c. Pull strenuously up the wall on the right to gain and follow a little corner.

75. `Yes 20ft VS
4c. A slabby arête leading to a finishing wall.

76. Maybe 20ft Hard Sev
Start on the right of the slab and climb up left to join and finish up Yes.

77. The Pit Girdle 150ft Hard VS
Start at the left-hand side of the Main Crag.
(1) 80ft 5a. Start as for Wall Climb, at half-height follow the line leading right to the arête, then go across to The Crab. Traverse right as for Creepy Crab and continue into Layback Crack. Make a worrying hand-traverse to reach Starters, PB (not in situ, so it may be preferable to continue).
(2) 70ft 5a. Move delicately down and right onto the slab and follow a line of holds to join Order and Disorder. This line continues further, past the Cnig's routes and a jamming crack on their right which provides a finish.

WARLAND QUARRY (SD948 201)
by Bruce Goodwin

SITUATION AND CHARACTER
This pleasant little quarry is situated east of the A6033 some 2½ miles from Littleborough. It is clearly visible from the Littleborough – Todmorden road, on the hillside almost opposite the Bird I'Th Hand pub.

All the routes are on solid gritstone (there being thankfully no climbing on the upper tier). Although the routes are short, they are all worthwhile, with Grinning Arête a minor crag classic. The climbing is on two tiers; the Main Tier has a loose upper tier above it and set back, and the Lower Wall lying hidden in a small hollow in the hillside. A useful addition to the area.

APPROACH AND ACCESS
The attitude of the crag's owner towards climbing is unknown, so a low profile is recommended. To reach the quarry, leave the A6033 at Warland Gate End, which lies almost opposite the Bird I'Th Hand pub. Follow this lane across the Rochdale canal and left up a hill. A sharp turn right at some houses leads to a steep hill. This can be followed to a parking place, opposite a corrugated iron cottage. A gate below the cottage leads onto a track which contours past sheds and leads into the quarry. A direct start is possible; cross the canal and go over a fence right of the house. A track leads up from here into the quarry. This approach often renders the hardest moves of the day, as a guard dog living by the house and sometimes unleashed needs an impromptu body-swerve for success.

HISTORY

The line of rusting bolts (almost mandatory in Pennine quarries) on the lower wall and peg remains in what is now Laughing Crack provide a small insight into the activities of previous unknown climbers. The routes recorded here were the work of the present writer and Tony Nicholls on two days in 1983 and of Nicholls and John Lord in 1984. The best routes of '83 were undoubtedly Grinning Arête and Last Laugh by Nicholls, and Sickly Smile and Laughing Crack by Goodwin. The girdle was also good. On the lower wall, Maiden Over and Trent Bridge fell to Nicholls whilst John Lord put up his first new routes with Lord's and Old Trafford.

MAIN TIER: The climbs here are described from right to left, using the obvious arête as a reference point. Right of this is a large ledge. All belays (Friends, nuts etc) are at the foot of the upper tier.

1. **Sickly Smile**   30ft   E1
5b. Climb a slabby crack, slanting up to the left end of the ledge. The groove above leads to the top. Bold

2. **Grinning Arête**   45ft   Hard VS   ★★
5a. Climb Laughing Crack for 10 feet then move right to the arête and follow it to the top.

3. **Laughing Crack**   40ft   VS   ★
5a. Take the thin crack left of the arête to finish up it.

4. **Smiler**   35ft   VS
5a. The wall left of Laughing Crack joining Chuckle Corner at half-height.

5. **Chuckle Corner**   35ft   VS
4b. The wall below a leaning corner; follow these and move right to finish up the arête.

6. **Last Laugh**   35ft   E1   ★
5b. A ledge/block at 12 feet is gained via the wall on its left. Pull up and out left over a bulge to finish.

7. **Side Smirk**   30ft   Hard VS
5b. Climb the overhanging groove left of Last Laugh to a grassy ledge. Go up to another ledge then diagonally left into a groove with difficulty. Up this to the top, a disjointed line.

A girdle starting from the large ledge right of the arête is:

8. **Laugh A Minute**   70ft   VS   ★
5a. Gain the ledge then follow the horizontal crack to the arête. Continue into Chuckle Corner then semi-hand-traverse to finish on the grass slope.

LOWER WALL: Below the main part of the quarry is a short wall of smooth gritstone. A bolt ladder runs up its right-hand side.

9. **Maiden Over**   25ft   E1
5b. The blunt arête right of the bolt ladder; unprotected.

10. **Old Trafford** 25ft VS
4c. The right-hand crack of a pair is followed closely.

11. **Lords** 25ft VS
4b. The left-hand crack of the pair.

12. **Trent Bridge** 20ft Hard VS
5b. The crack at the left side of the wall.

MINOR CRAGS

CLIVIGER (SD 881 271)
The hillside south-west of the A646 Todmorden – Burnley road has
many buttresses and exposed rock faces. Most of this is unstable or
would require extensive navvying before becoming climbable.

CROSS STONE QUARRY (SD 951 248)
APPROACHES
This quarry, which is marked on some maps as Foot Delf, is situated
overlooking the Todmorden – Hebden Bridge road (A6033), about one
and a half miles from the centre of Todmorden. From Todmorden go
to the Bus Shed and turn left up Pheonix Street (just by the Shannon
and Chesapeake pub). Continue past a railway bridge, then turn right
and at the end where the road turns left, go right then left onto a dirt
track. Pass some houses and follow the track right into the quarry.

HISTORY
All the routes here were ascended in June of 1981 with Bob Whittaker
climbing most of the routes at the left-hand end of the crag with Geoff
Hamridding (who in turn added Bird Lime Corner), or Derek Wright;
Wright himself added the routes to the right of the prow.

THE ROUTES are described from LEFT to RIGHT.

The first overhanging corner on the left is **Stretcher Case** (Hard Sev 4a)
and the arête on its right has a crack, taken by **Vulcan** (VS 4c). **Vulcan's
Variant** (VS 4c) climbs Vulcan but quits it leftwards at a ledge, to gain
and follow a crack and slab. The hanging flake on the right is **Endless
Flight** (VS 5a ★), the obvious **Bird Lime Corner** (VS 4b ★) leads to a
ledge then left across the wall whilst **Broken Lance** (E1 5b ★) gains the
ledge via an arête and scoop.

To the right of the large square prow is a steep gully. **Recess Crack**
(Sev) follows a crack just to its right and a crack system just above a
pinnacle is **Black Crack** (Hard Sev 4a) with **Crumbling Corner** (Hard VS
5a) just to its right.

The next, slabby wall is seamed with cracks. The first of these is
Redshift (VS 4c), then follows **Whiteshift** (VS 4c) up the chimney/crack,
finishing on the left. **Nightshift** (VS 4b) takes the thin crack just right,

again finishing on the left. **Landshift** takes the broken crack to a wider crack finish. The corner on the right is **Gates of Eden** (VS 4c) whilst 10 feet right, cracks and ledges go for **The Jugular** (Hard Sev 4a).

SHORE QUARRY (SD 922 171)
This quarry lies above the public footpath that leads from the right turn before the King William pub in Shore, Littleborough. There are many vegetated routes in the easier grades and as a beginners crag it could have value. The harder and more substantial routes are at the left-hand side; a wide crack provides **Shore Crack** (Mild Severe), the wall left of the crack is **Wall and Crack** (VS 4b) whilst the thin crack line above a niche, widening in the overhanging upper section, is **Shore Buttress** (Hard VS 5a ∗). Left again is **Domino Theory** (VS 5a) which goes up the wall to a broken groove and carefully to the top.

WHITE HOUSE QUARRY (Blackstone Edge Delf − SD 964 174)
A bouldering ground of mainly local interest. Useful for an hour or so's workout, but could become popular and more important if cleaned!

WINTER CLIMBING IN CLIVIGER GORGE
(SD 880 273) MAIN AREA, (SD 890 268) WATER SLIDES
By Jeff Hope
The Cliviger crags lie on the opposite side of the valley from the bouldering mecca, Kebs, on Bridestones Moor. Its loose and vegetated character discourages all but the most Fowlerish of climbers, but it is a popular winter climbing ground when the conditions are right. The numerous gullies and water courses which split this sprawling crag give steep and in the main, non serious 'ice-bouldering' possibilities, with three or four longer routes up the slabby hanging gullies of the central section, below the obvious broad grass terrace.

For the main area, park in a lay-by on the left soon after passing through the village. A short walk in the Todmorden direction leads to an unmetalled road on the right, which swings round and passes under the railway line. From beyond this the routes can be seen to the left, past a wooded area. Right of the wooded area, a number of gully lines give shorter pitches.

For the two water slides, continue towards Todmorden for about ¾ mile, to a point where the road crosses a stream. From the large lay-by on the right follow the stream into the gorge. The first pitch lies only a few minutes from the road. The second pitch (which comes into condition more often) lies about 175 yards farther up the gorge.

Short pitches begin to form after 3 to 4 days of hard frost. A longer period of frost, such as that which occurred in 1986, aided by a snow cover on the terrace, is needed to produce the build-up needed for the longer routes. When these conditions do occur, the resultant pitches rival those on such popular Lakeland crags as Helvellyn and Great End.

The main section of the crag is the central area; an obvious feature to the left of this area is the large hanging icicle which forms an overhang 40 feet from the base of the gully. When complete this gives a testing grade IV problem with pleasant slabby climbing on thin ice above the overhang. To the right, a large triangular grassy mound cuts into the base of the buttress. Beyond this is a deeper gully with a few short pitches. The next route lies slightly right again, taking a less well-defined line up a series of steep steps. At its base hangs a steep icicle-fringed wall (35 feet) and the gully eases off afterwards, only to rear up into a final bulging section near the top: Grade III, though ice build-up does not always make this route easier! Farther right a vague, slabby gully gives similar sustained climbing (grade III) for 130 feet.

Ice climbing in the area is not complete without sampling Todmorden's answer to inner-city bouldering: on the edge of the town and behind the local swimming baths, 3 to 4 days of hard frost will freeze two waterfalls hidden in dense vegetation. The second pitch is about 35-feet high and is steep and well worth a visit – a closely guarded secret for some time!

III. THE ROSSENDALE VALLEY AREA

Compiled by Bruce Goodwin
with assistance from Al Cameron, Phil Kelly, John Mason
and Bob Whittaker

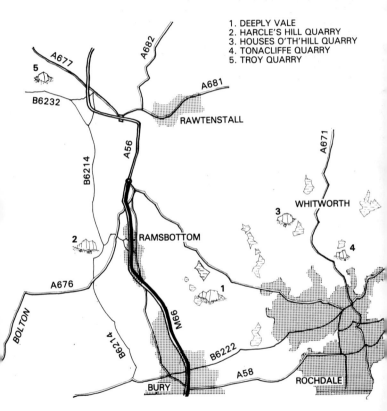

1. DEEPLY VALE
2. HARCLE'S HILL QUARRY
3. HOUSES O'TH'HILL QUARRY
4. TONACLIFFE QUARRY
5. TROY QUARRY

The Rossendale Valley and its environs contains many quarries of different characters and qualities; most quarries in the area are unworthy of more than the merest passing mention, but the remainder – the ones that are described here – are all good quality, enjoyable climbing grounds.

The most extensive quarry in the area is probably Troy Quarry, above the Haslingden Grane Road, which still contains a little loose rock but is sound on the whole, and the climbing is good. Deeply Vale on the other hand is a small buttress just outside Bury, and although only of limited size the climbing here is excellent and varied. Tonacliffe Quarry offers a little bouldering in an accessible position between Rochdale and Whitworth, and Harcle's Hill Quarry, lying on the back slopes of Holcombe Hill, is worth a visit if only to construct a realistic appraisal of the remaining crags. Brittania Quarry was unveiled in the 1986 supplement, and this led to many visits and much praise as to the climbing therein. It now transpires that Brittania is soon to be lost to climbers as tipping has recently taken place, and quarrying is about to recommence.

Houses O'Th' Hill Quarry has seen very little traffic since the 1983 guide, and no new routes have been ascended there, whilst all the other crags have some extra routes to offer. All the crags now described in the area are of quarried gritstone, except for Brittania which is a good-quality flagstone, and rock from which actually supports Nelson's Column! The rock at Troy tends to be more broken than the rest because of its more recent working, whereas Deeply Vale and Harcle's Hill are classic quarry architecture; steep walls split by large open corners and sharp arêtes.

DEEPLY VALE (SD 823 149)
By Phil Kelly

APPROACH AND ACCESS
Deeply Vale is an enjoyable little buttress of good quality quarried gritstone which is easily accessible, being situated only about 4 to 5 miles from Bury town centre. Follow the A556 (Walmsley Road) north out of the centre for about 2½ miles until, after a short rise, a church tower appears on the left. Turn right at the traffic lights at the crest of the rise (Walmsley Old Road) and follow this for about half a mile to the Mason's Arms pub. Turn right here (Bentley Lane) and go under the motorway bridge, to a parking spot 100 yards farther down on the left. Follow the left-hand continuation track ahead, up a hill, to a junction; turn right and follow a metalled lane, going left and rising up to a second junction. Turn left here and after 200 yards, go right along a tree-lined track to a gate at it's end. Go over the gate and down right, past the reservoir, and after 75 yards the crag will be seen set back a little on the right.

SITUATION AND CHARACTER
The crag is one solid buttress of excellent, quarried gritstone; a series of arêtes and corners, between which lie steep, slabby walls, punctuated at times by good solid cracklines, and the huge roof of Mein Kampf in the centre. 'The Vale' is a popular place amongst local climbers, especially on warm summer evenings.

HISTORY

The first known recorded routes here were the work of Mick Pooler and friends. During the early 1960s they added such routes as The Crack, Central Arête, Slab Dab (with a little aid), and the strenuous Scoop and Traverse. Besides these, they made aided ascents of Twilight Cracks (which Al Evans free-climbed in 1979 and re-named Leftless) and the big roofs of Mein Kampf. Mick attempted to climb the central corner of the crag but was repulsed, and the following day one of his friends who had been waiting in the wings, stepped in to snatch Renegade Corner. Mick's vengeance was swift, and his prize was the excellent Ha'penny Arête, which originally escaped right to finish up the upper crack of Inflexion and was then the hardest route on the crag! Mick left proof of his ascent on the ledge just below the top, and the rush was soon on for the second ascent and the ha'penny prize!

Two routes were added during 1981; Dave Cronshaw and Les Ainsworth climbed the bold Night Out and Derek Kenyon, the disappearing crackline left of Renegade Corner (Zanadu) which was originally slightly undergraded; it turned out to be his first extreme lead! Phil Kelly began filling in the remaining gaps and added Victim of Changes in 1982 – after failing to top rope the line, and Watership Down. He also free-climbed the direct start to Inflexion which nobody thought would be possible. The remaining aid on the crag necessitated the importing of Mark Leach to rid Mein Kampf of it's indiscretions. Mark's ascent, in July 1982 of this 8-foot roof problem, retained one rest point at the top peg, which was freed two months later by Kelly and Mark Griffiths.

HOOK BUTTRESS

THE CLIMBS are described from RIGHT to LEFT starting at an arête just right of a large wall set with an iron hook at 15 feet.

1. **'Go with Noakes'** 25ft Hard Sev
4b. Climb the right side of the short arête to a ledge move right to an obvious handhold then direct up the steep wall to a loose finish.

2. **Arête and Slab** 25ft V Diff   *
The left side of the arête to a small ledge then step left and climb the centre of a steep slab.

3. **Deep End** 25ft V Diff
Don't do this route! From the corner, traverse the higher breaks left to finish just right of the arête. Yukk!

4. **Inflexion** 40ft E2
5c. The wall is split by a clean diagonal fault line, follow this left to bulging cracks 6 feet right of the arête. Finish up these by hard moves, crux.

5. **Inflexion Direct** 20ft E3   *
6a. The steep hanging cracks left of the hook join Inflexion after 20 feet.

6. **Watership Down** 35ft E2
5c. Mantel onto the traverse line of Inflexion and boldly climb the thin wall above to the bad break of Deep End, finish up that route.

DEEPLY VALE

Mark Griffiths 1988

7. Ha'penny Arête 35ft E1 ★★★
5a. The square-cut arête left of the iron loop. Superb climbing, with the crux at the top.

8. Scoop and Traverse 40ft VS ★★
5a. Start in a short corner groove 10 feet left of Ha'penny Arête, climb this awkwardly onto a ramp and up to a horizontal break. Traverse right below the overhangs to finish on the arête.

9. Evening Visit 30ft VS
4c. Thin initial moves up the narrow slab left of Scoop and Traverse lead to the overhangs; go over these to finish.

CENTRAL AREA
On the wall to the left is an obvious right-slanting crack.

10. Crack Variation 40ft Hard Sev
4a. The wall right of The Crack.

11. The Crack 40ft V Diff ★
The flake crack offers enjoyable climbing up rock which is becoming rapidly more suspect!

Around the arête is an excellent wall with an overlap at half-height.

12. Central Arête 40ft VS ★
4c. Climb the large, central arête starting on its left-hand side.

13. Slab Dab 40ft VS ★★★
4b. Just left of the arête, climb cracks to a hard move over an overlap, then finish up the wall above on good holds.

14. Victim of Changes 40ft E2 ★
5c. Start just right of Renegade Corner and climb old bolt holes up the steep wall to the overlap, PR. Surmount the overlap and continue up the slab above.

15. Renegade Corner 40ft VS ★★
4b. The deep central corner of the crag, laybacking past a small

overhang at 10 feet.

16. Zanadu 40ft E2
5c. The right-slanting fault in the green wall left of Renegade Corner, to its end, then direct up the wall. 3 PRs (not in situ).

17. Leftless 30ft E2
5c. The peg-scarred crack just right of the cave.

18. Mein Kampf 40ft E3 ★★★
5c. THE route of Deeply Vale. Start in the back corner of the cave and climb to a BR. Stretch out and gain the lip of the first roof, BR. Attain a standing position on the protruding block on the right, (Friend in break on right), and balance up to PR. Pull up and left then continue left to finish up the arête. Excellent.

19. Night Out 25ft Hard VS ★
5b. Start just right of Nod's Nightmare and climb pockets boldly up and right to gain the exposed upper arête of Mein Kampf, finish up this.

20. Nod's Nightmare 20ft VS
4c. The corner on the left side of the main overhang.

21. Back Seat Rock 'n' Roll 25ft VS
4c. Climb up and leftwards from the start of Nod's Nightmare to join and finish up Crystal Climb.

22. Crystal Climb 25ft Sev
Climb the fault in the wall 8 feet left of Nod's Nightmare.

23. Second Wall Climb 25ft Hard Sev
4b. A direct line up the wall left of Crystal Climb, finishing leftwards to the arête.

END WALLS: Farther left the crag starts to diminish further in height, but there remains a series of arêtes, walls, corners and slabs which all provide good enjoyment should you wish to seek them out. All the obvious lines have been done. A low-level traverse of most of the crag is possible, starting at the left end and continuing rightwards with hard moves to get to Ha'penny Arête.

24. Girdle Traverse 150ft E2 †
(1) 40ft 5c. Climb Inflexion and cross to the top of Ha'penny Arête. Reverse the hand-traverse of Scoop and Traverse and belay.
(2) 60ft 4b. Move down slightly and cross The Crack to Central Arête, then climb this to below the top overhangs and traverse into Renegade Corner, belay on the ledge, NB.

(3) 50ft 5a. Reverse the corner until a thin crack leads across and up to a hand-traverse on Mein Kampf. Go round the arête and finish up Crystal Climb.

HARCLE'S HILL QUARRY (SD 779 169)

By Phil Kelly

APPROACH

This quarry is situated 5 miles north of Bury, just above Ramsbottom, and half a mile from the prominent local landmark of Peel Tower. From Bury, take the B6214 north for 4 miles to a junction at Holcombe Brook (Hare and Hounds pub opposite). Continue up the steep continuation of the B6214 (Lumb Carr Road) for nearly a mile to the Shoulder of Mutton pub on the right. Opposite the pub is a bridleway marked Moor Road; take this, past a cattlegrid, to a fork in the track. Go left here and follow the track up and round into the quarry. It is possible to drive cars right up into the quarry, otherwise, if you can't afford a new sump, they should be left in the pub car park.

SITUATION AND CHARACTER

There are in fact two quarries on this site; the first (smaller) one has some boulder problems, whilst all the routes described lie in the second (larger) quarry. Climbing here, on the whole, can only be described as mediocre, and mostly for the connoisseur of loose finishes on vegetated rock, but one or two routes are worth seeking out.

THE ROUTES are described from LEFT to RIGHT with the first on the small buttress on the left-hand side.

HISTORY

Harcle's Hill was first explored by Dave Cronshaw and Phil Warner in 1977, with Warner soloing first ascents of Black Maria and the awkward Court Jester, and following Cronshaw up The Judge, Jailbreak and the clean arête of Blue Lamp. They both decided to leave the remaining possibilities to the next unfortunate souls to stumble blindly on the crag. This next bunch were members of the newly erected Bury Mountaineering Club (the MOB), and between them they accounted for all the other routes. Phil Kelly began with a solo ascent of Bastille Day which was then a much easier proposition, but has since lost many holds, whilst Paul Dewhurst added Late Night Mob and Another Late Night. Paul's brother Mick led Sovereign with Colin Buckley and Bob Spencer, and Pete Wolstenholme climbed Hammerhead. Kelly continued the explorations when the other's enthusiasm waned and soloed Caress Of Steel after top roping, and put up The Golden Moment with one rest point which he eliminated the following night, one day ahead of Dave Whittles, who seconded him on the original ascent. Kelly also laid siege to the overhanging sentry box to the right on a top rope and eventually managed a lead ascent to give The Atomic Rooster.

1. **Black Maria** 20ft V Diff
The centre of the first buttress on the left.

2. **Left Chimney** 20ft Moderate
The loose (as most routes here are!) chimney just right.

3. **Lord Foul's Bane** 25ft VS
5b. A difficult boulder problem start up the centre of the next buttress leads to easier climbing above the break.

4. **White Maria** 25ft Hard Sev
4a. The short crack right of Lord Foul's Bane to the break, step left to join and finish up that route.

5. **Time Bandits** 25ft V Diff
An unfortunate line which should never have been climbed in the first place, it takes a non-descript line up the choss right of White Maria.

On the right side of the bay is a jutting nose overlooking a step in the quarry floor. On the left of the nose is a shallow corner.

6. **Court Jester** 30ft Hard Sev
4a. Climb the corner and ledges above.

7. **Caress of Steel** 40ft E2   **
5b. Start right of the nose and climb the wall just right of the arête to an overlap, swing left around the nose to gain easy ledges and a slabby finish.

8. **Whoops Apocalypse** 40ft Sev
4a. A great route embodying a certain esoteric charisma; the large open corner 15 feet right of the nose.

9. **The Judge** 45ft VS
4b. Gain the shelf in the wall on the right, and climb twin cracks to a niche, finish easily.

10. **Blue Lamp** 45ft Hard VS   *
5a. The sharp arête passing two peg runners. Good climbing.

The next two routes accept the challenge of the forbidding main wall of the quarry, but unfortunately the climbing ceases after 35 feet and degenerates into a vertical scree slope. A rope hung over this section allows the climber to escape.

11. **Jailbreak** 45ft VS
4c. Climb the groove 10 feet right of the arête for 20 feet, then step right into another crack and follow this to the top.

12. **On the Wings of Freedom** 40ft Hard VS
5a. Climb straight up to cracks right of Jailbreak and follow these to the bad breaks.

13. **Halucinogenics** 45ft E1   †
5a. You've got to be out of your trees to lead this one! Right of the

corner is a sentry box in a steep 'wall'. Gain the sentry box and climb it, carefully!

14. Late Night Mob 35ft V Diff
The arête just right, starting over a nose.

15. Windbreak 35ft Sev
Climb the centre of the wall and finish up a jamming crack.

16. Another Late Night 30ft V Diff
The slab right of Windbreak.

On the right wall of the gully is a steep wall. This turns into the quarry again and has a step at ground level. Starting from the step is:-

17. Hammerhead 35ft VS
4c. Climb the thin crack in the wall to ledges, then finish over these (PR).

18. Cinderella Man 35ft Hard VS
5a. Climb direct up the slab via a thin crack to a flake, either step right and finish easily over grass (preferable) or finish direct above the flake.

19. Sovereign 25ft Sev
4a. Gain and climb the groove-line on the right side of the slab.

20. Krsna Consciousness 35ft VS
4c. Start further right, in the base of the pit. Climb a series of ledges to a move right to gain a finger crack. Follow this to a grassy finish.

BASTILLE DAY BUTTRESS
Bastille Day Buttress is the overhanging sandy-looking wall on the right as one enters the quarry. For safety reasons it would be prudent to hang a rope down the top few feet of the routes Bastille Day and Atomic Rooster to help overcome the loose finish.

21. Bronze Medal 30ft Hard Sev   †
4b. The left arête of the buttress.

22. The Golden Moment 35ft E3   *
5c. Moves left from the first good holds on Bastille Day, to a sloping jug, then climb the thin crack above (crux), with a move left to join and finish up the arête.

23. Bastille Day 30ft E1
5b. Climb cracks 15 feet right of the arête to a ledge then move up a crack to follow a line of ledges on the right to a loose finish.

24. Atomic Rooster 35ft E4   * †
6b. Six feet right of Bastille Day is an overhanging sentry box, starting at 15 feet. Gain and climb this feature, grunting and groaning all the way.

HOUSES O'TH'HILL QUARRY (SD 876 175)

SITUATION AND CHARACTER
This quarry is situated only 2½ miles north-west of Rochdale, above Spring Mill Reservoir in Whitworth.

The crag is literally a box-shaped hole in the ground, with a shorter wall above and to one side of the main quarry. The climbs are on sound rock, although the usual care applicable to quarried rock should be observed. The crag is very sheltered, and it is at its best during the warmer periods. Some tipping has taken place in the past though this in no way affects the climbing, but the crag has been used little over the past couple of years, and some vegetation is starting to return.

APPROACH AND ACCESS
The quarry is on land owned by the NWWA, and no access problems have been encountered.

Two approaches are possible from the junction in Hall Street which is just off the A671 in Whitworth (almost opposite the Dog and Partridge). The junction is just past Whitworth Comprehensive School.
  (1) Turn left and go through Wall Bank Estate to a parking place near a mill. Walk up by the wall above the mill for 50 yards, cross it then a track leads across flat open ground to a rise which leads to the quarry.
  (2) Turn right and go up until a tight left-hand hairpin leads to a narrow lane. The lane ends at an open space near a farm and two houses; Park here. The quarry lies over the wall right of the houses. This approach is quickest if on foot – 10 minutes.

HISTORY
The quarry was first visited in the late 1960s when its thick mantle of turf and loose rock presented quite a problem in those far-off days of on-sight leads and 'get up it somehow' techniques. Two corners were climbed by persons unknown, and it is possible that these are the two routes now known as Cross Bred and The Lamb. This experience was so off-putting that the climbers forgot about the quarry completely and the crag was left alone, although the wall just left of the main quarry had been noted by many as a possibility. In 1980 Bob Whittaker and his team put up Return to the Fold which remains the hardest route to date. Bob then introduced Ian Conway, Bruce Goodwin, Clive Morton, Mark Leach and others, and this team (armed with pickaxes, spades, brushes and furtling sticks) rapidly demolished the loose outer skin of rock, soon to begin climbing new routes on the clean, sound rock beneath. Within four months most of the routes were done; Conway produced most of the Hard VS's, except for Lonk (Bruce) and Pulpy Kidney (Clive). These three shared the other routes between them and Mark Leach (then only a young proto-starlet) soloed some hard problems on the left wall.

THE ROUTES are described from RIGHT to LEFT starting at a corner, just right of a green wall, capped by an overhang.

1. Scragg End 25ft VS
4b. Climb the corner to a ledge on the right, then ascend the wall just right of a crack.

2. The Shepherd 35ft Hard VS   ★★
5b. Climb the green wall, or the corner, to the overhang. Follow the left-most crack over the overhang and continue to the top.

3. Crossbred 35ft V Diff
From the foot of The Shepherd go left to grass, then climb the corner to just above the overhang. Traverse right and up to a ledge and then the top.

4. The Lamb 30ft Diff
From the foot of The Shepherd go left to grass and then ascend the corner.

5. Docked 40ft V Diff
Start lower down in a groove behind an elderberry tree. Climb the groove and step right, then climb up to the obvious crack and follow this to a dirty finish (or traverse right just below the top and finish as The Lamb).

The next climb starts from the floor of the quarry, left of a dirty corner and below an overhang at 20 feet.

6. Pulpy Kidney 55ft Hard VS
5a. Start below the overhang. Climb the wall to the overhang, then over this at the obvious weakness to gain a large ledge (on the girdle). Climb a crack to a ledge on the right arête, and up into a short corner that leads to the top. An inferior variation using corners to the right and then finishing at the same point has been climbed.

7. Lurcher 55ft VS
4c. Start as for Pulpy Kidney, but move left to a slight crack, and up this to an overhung niche. Exit from this to the girdle ledges and then finish up the corner above.

8. Elastrator 55ft VS   ★★
4c. Gain a little rib just left of the quarry corner, and follow thin cracks to the girdle ledges. The wider crack above leads to the top.

9. Come By 55ft VS   ★
4c. Starts at the obvious overhanging corner. Climb into the corner, then move left under the roof, gain the front and ascend to a good ledge. Move right to a small corner and follow this to an overhanging niche. An awkward move leads out of the niche and the top is then in reach.

10. Tess 55ft VS
4c. Climb a short crack and face to join Come By. The large corner leads past a tilted block to a steep slab and crack on the left. Up the slab to the bulge and over this to the top.

11. Rough Fell 55ft VS
4c. Start 10 feet left. An overhung groove leads to a crack system which

leads to the girdle. From here follow a groove leading to a V-shaped groove with a crack in it and follow this to the top.

At the left of the wall is a small cave at 8 feet.

12. Spring Bite 55ft VS
4c. Climb the crack to the right side of the cave, go right to a small groove and up to the girdle ledge. Climb up onto a large yellow block, then gain the triangular niche on the right and climb more or less direct to the top.

13. Mutton Swing 55ft VS
4b. Climb up and left of the cave, then move right and follow cracks and a cracked slab to a large overhung niche. Swing left and up to the top.

The large overhung corner has been climbed below and above the overhang, but a detached block held together by faith or by skyhooks has deterred attempts at a complete ascent so far. The next route starts 10 feet left at a block.

14. Dales Bred 70ft Hard VS *
5a. Climb into a corner and then gain a flat nose on the right. Continue up the wall to a roof, then over this and up left into a corner with a crack. Climb this until another crack on the left leads to the top (cave).

15. Teeswater 70ft Hard VS *
5a. From the block on Dales Bred, climb into the first corner and gain a ledge below an overhang. Climb the crack/groove to good ledges. Ascend to a crack which leads to an overhang and surmount this with the help of a thin crack on the left. Finish direct, just right of a sandy cave.

16. Masham 70ft VS
(1) 45ft 4c. Start 15 feet left. Climb into the right of the large recess, then follow the wall to a good ledge overlooking the grassy corner (nut belays).
(2) 25ft 4c. Follow the corner to an overhang, and pull over this to large sandy holds, then move easily to the top.

17. Asparagus Tarzan 60ft Hard VS
5a. Climb the wall to a small corner. Up this to the large ledge of the girdle. Move left to a crack, and climb this past a large white-scarred block to a shallow sandy cave. Finish over the left side of the cave.

18. Reeperbahn Equaliser 60ft Hard VS
5b. The upper wall has an obvious, short, overhanging crack in it. Follow a line up the wall to below the crack. Follow the crack to bold and exhilarating moves up the wall to a horizontal fault. A cracked wall leads to the top.

19. Cloven Hoof 60ft Sev
The obvious chimney. Climb a short ramp to a corner and up to a large ledge below the chimney. Climb the chimney and gain the recess. Move right for 10 feet and finish up the wall as for Reeperbahn Equaliser.

20. **Acid Flush**   65ft   VS
4c. Climb the big corner to the crack and follow this to the overhanging vertical slot. Continue direct to the recess, then traverse right (care needed to protect second) and finish as Reeperbahn Equaliser.

The crag continues round to the left, and the next routes start underneath the black, cracked, overhanging wall.

21. **Cast Horn**   60ft   Diff
Follow ledges up and right to gain a large clean ledge. A long, dirty traverse left leads to a corner above Derbyshire Gritstone and a finish.

22. **Muddy Hoof**   50ft   VS
4b. The corner leads to a dirty move into the traverse of Cast Horn which is then followed to join Cast Horn.

23. **Derbyshire Gritstone**   45ft   Hard VS   *
5a. Start just left of the corner. Climb the cracked wall to the overhang, then continue up the crackline to a large sloping ledge (strenuous). Belay in the little corner (several nuts) or proceed to stakes on the top.

24. **Lonk**   45ft   Hard VS   *
5b. Climb a corner on the left, to the left of a hole. Move right and up a steep rib, then pull up and climb past the large battered flake to gain a jamming crack and then the large sloping ledge. Belay as Derbyshire Gritstone.

25. **Underbelly**   45ft   VS
4c. Follow Lonk to the hole, then climb the corner to the roof, swing boldly out 6 feet left and go up to a ledge. Move up past a flake to gain a ledge with a large block and then the top.

26. **Pot Belly**   30ft   V Diff
The grassy groove left of Underbelly.

27. **Belly Flop**   30ft   V Diff
A line on the left of the wall some 25 feet farther left.

At this point the quarry turns left again, and a steep crack is seen on the wall.

28. **Return to the Fold**   25ft   E1
5b. Gain the crack and follow it strenuously to a nasty finish.

29. **Sheep Trod**   180ft   VS
A traverse of the quarry from right to left, starting at the foot of The Shepherd.
(1) 120ft 4c. Go left onto grass, then left again to a large ledge system which is followed across the walls crossing the 'dangerous' overhang between Muttons Swing and Dales Bred at foot level. Continue across ledges, then up to a belay (nuts) on a ledge overlooking the grassy corner rake in the centre of the back wall.
(2) 60ft 4c. Move up slightly and follow the obvious ledge across the wall until a move down leads across to Cloven Hoof. Go across into

the overhanging slot of Acid Flush. Make an awkward move out left onto a large sloping ledge (care needed to protect second) and follow the earthy traverse of Cast Horn to belay as for Derbyshire Gritstone.

TONACLIFFE QUARRY (SD 883 166)

SITUATION AND CHARACTER
Tonacliffe Quarry is situated on the western edge of Roshy Hill, overlooking the Whitworth Valley just north of Healey. It reaches 30 feet in places and is a quarried gritstone; the rock is reasonable although the ravages of the past few winters have caused some rockfall — There is some dubious rock, but this is obvious and doesn't usually interfere with the climbs, or the enjoyment thereof. It is a well used crag, being popular for evening or 'short day' visits.

APPROACH AND ACCESS
There is no access problem but care must be taken if approaching by car as thoughtless parking will give offence to the local householders.

The quarry is reached from Rochdale by following the A671 until ½ mile north of Healey Corner. Tonacliffe Road leads off right and in turn Highpeak Lane turns off right ½ mile further on. The steep hill is followed to where it eases off into a level green track which leads back left. Considerate parking is available a little farther on, near the 'public footpath' sign. The green track leads to the quarry in about 200 yards.

HISTORY
The original pioneers of the quarry are unknown, except that Derek Clutterbuck has climbed here for many years and still lives below the crag. Many of the problems are 'traditional', though many should have Derek's name tagged to them. Derek used to visit the quarry regularly and solo Layaway Wall (some say nightly in summer) to prove to himself that he could still do the business.

Modern recorded development began in 1970 when Bob Whittaker and Ralph Pickering visited the crag, climbing The Corner and Overhanging Crack. Then they left the quarry to Clutterbuck and no new climbs were ascended until 1978 when news of a prospective supplement guide spurred Whittaker and Pickering into another visit, this time in the company of Gordon Mason. This trio climbed about twenty new routes, including Hand Jam Crack, Little Cameo, Hidden Corner, Groovin and Escort. Other climbers were involved around this time — Harry Taylor, Ron Blunt and Carl Fletcher all helped out from time to time.

The pre-guidebook rush saw Whittaker climbing Paper Tiger and Diamond Solitaire in 1980, though Les Hardman broke Bob's monopoly in 1981 when he added Wazzock.

A young Mark Leach added Icarus Ascending in 1981, and some weeks later tried to repeat the route; somewhat cockily he only tied the rope round his waist and set off, only placing one runner. Unfortunately he slipped near the top and took a 20-foot fall, narrowly missing the deck; Ouch! Later Clive Morton cleaned and re-climbed Central Pillar and in 1985, shortly after bigger things in the Peak District, Andrew Eaton climbed the sharpish arête just right to produce a fingery little route, well-named Apprentice's Edge.

The quarry is best considered in two sections; when entering the quarry the Main Bay is seen first, with the left-hand section making up another bay. With startling originality these have been named from left to right as Bay One and Bay Two. The first climbs start at the extreme left end of Bay One. THE CLIMBS are described from LEFT to RIGHT.

BAY ONE: The first climbs are unstable due to rockfall, but they are included here for completeness.

1. Andy's Arête 25ft VS
Climbs to the big ledge and finish up the arête.

2. Nean 25ft VS
Climb to the big ledge. The crack up the wall leads to the top.

3. Escort 25ft Sev ✱
Up the wall a few feet right of Snout.

4. Cavalier 25ft Hard Sev
4a. Just right a triangular niche leads to an overhang, then right to finish up an arête.

5. Groovin' 25ft Diff
A groove containing jammed blocks.

6. Wazzock 25ft Sev
The wall on the right is climbed direct.

7. Retreat 25ft Sev
Climb the crack to gain a groove with difficulty.

8. The Arête 25ft Hard Sev
Climb the crack as for Retreat (or direct) then move right and climb the square-cut groove on the arête.

9. Lux 30ft Hard Sev
4b. Start below the arête and climb up to a ledge on the right then step left and climb direct to the arête.

10. Little Cameo 30ft VS ✱✱
4c. Start right of the arête, gain the large ledge and follow the wall above, just left of centre.

11. Fallout 30ft Hard Sev ✱
The open corner right of Little Cameo provides the substance of this route.

12. Central Pillar 30ft Hard VS ✱
5a. The 'pillar' is gained direct over an overhang then the narrow wall leads to the top.

13. The Apprentice's Edge 30ft E2
5c. Takes the arête of Central Pillar on its right-hand side; fingery. Graded for runners in Overhanging Crack.

14.   Overhanging Crack   30ft   Hard VS   ★★
5a. The obvious cracks around the arête give a sustained route.

15.   The Corner   30ft   VS   ★
4c. The obvious corner gives a good route.

16.   Shortie   30ft   Hard Sev
4b. The crack a few feet right of the corner leads to strenuous pulls and then the top.

17.   Flicker   25ft   Sev
The wall just left of The Chimney.

18.   The Chimney   20ft   Diff
The obvious chimney.

19.   Beginners' Route   20ft   Diff
The wall right of the chimney, finishing left of a pointed block.

20.   Starters' Route   20ft   Diff
The wall right again finishing right of the pointed block.

BAY TWO
A disjointed route climbs left of Hand Jam Crack,**Done Before** 4c/5a depending on line.

21.   Hand Jam Crack   20ft   VS   ★★★
4c. The obvious crack taking an overhang en-route. Good.

22.   Paper Tiger   20ft   Hard VS
5b. A boulder problem start leads to the wall right of Hand Jam Crack.

23.   Layaway Wall   20ft   VS   ★★
5a. Start at the right arête, move up then left to the middle of the wall and go over the overhang using flakes and thence the top. Sustained.

24.   After The Ordeal   20ft   Hard VS   ★★★
5b. Follow Layaway Wall to the end of its block then go up the smooth wall above via a shallow scoop.

25.   Diamond Solitaire   35ft   VS
4c. Start as for Layaway Wall. Climb the arête to a hand-traverse line. This leads left to a finish up Hand Jam Crack.

26.   Icarus Ascending   25ft   E1
5c. Start as above but continue up the arête on its left-hand side.

Layaway Wall may also be reached by a direct start (5c), and the wall may be traversed with hands below the overhang (5b). There is also a low level traverse at 6a.

27.   Hidden Corner   25ft   Sev   ★
The V-groove and corner groove.

28.   Star Of Sirius   25ft   VS
4b. The smooth wall a few feet right leads to a finish up Hidden Corner.

29.   The Groove   25ft   Diff
Right again is a loose groove leading to a blocky finish.

There is an obvious overhang on the right, this appears to be held up by faith, fresh air or invisible skyhooks. There are in fact four routes up this piece of rock but you don't have to believe it! Nor do you have to do them so it's best to pass on to the wall lying at right-angles, it has two cracks which give:-

30.   Back Wall Left   30ft   Hard Sev
The left crack, moving right to finish as for the next route.

31.   Back Wall Right   25ft   Hard Sev
The right crack leads to a break and either finish up large ledges or traverse off.

32.   Pop   20ft   V Diff
The end of the wall has a short crack.

33.   The Ceiling   5a
A good roof problem. The roof has 'loose' painted beneath it!!

34.   Girdle Traverse   150ft   Hard Sev
A girdle traverse starting as for Diamond Solitaire or Layaway wall gives 5a(ish) climbing across to the arête left of Hand Jam Crack. Various ways can be followed to The Corner; high (5c) or low (5a) leads to the ledge of Little Cameo. Go around the arête and follow the break to finish down (or up) Cavalier.

TROY QUARRY (SD 763 235)

By Al Cameron and John Mason

SITUATION AND CHARACTER

Troy Quarry overlooks Haslingden Grane about 1½ miles north-west of Haslingden. The quarry is composed of fine grained grit with many cleavage lines due to the quarry working methods. It is of open aspect, and the South and West facing walls dry out rapidly after rain. The rock is (generally) sound and the protection usually good. Belay stakes are in place on the West Face but are limited on the South Face. However, a new fence (please don't damage this) with solid posts provide safe but distant belay points. On the North Face it is advisable to belay to a rope hung over the top, again anchored to the fence, as the exits of the climbs here should be viewed with some trepidation. In sunny weather the place is a sun trap.

APPROACH

From Haslingden follow the Grane Road (B6263) towards Blackburn, past the Duke of Wellington Inn for 200 yards to a lane on the right which is signposted 'Thirteen Stone Hill'. Follow this lane past some cottages to a gate by some garages. Park on the right before these garages. Continue along the quarry track for 200 yards, then turn right along another track to a large concrete building in the quarry itself. The South Face lies directly behind this building, but to reach the North Face, turn left in front of the building and cross the ditch by a boulder bridge, and continue for 75 yards to the rock.

HISTORY

John Ryden and John Grundy visited Troy sometime in the early 70's and it is believed they led a number of routes which were left unrecorded. They led their routes on-sight and found the climbing 'distinctly worrying', and finally gave up in disgust, the quarry being abandoned and the routes forgotten

The second wave of development began in 1980 when Ian Conway, Tony Nicholls and Mark Leach began to explore the possibilities. Bruce Goodwin and Clive Morton also became involved and all concerned recognized the need to trundle rock in order to rid the rock of any detritus, and reach the sounder rock beneath. All the climbers had excellent sport, with six people levering on a monster custom-built crowbar, whilst others gingerly abseiled down the sides of a six foot roof, above what was later to become Nicholls' Slow Motion. The climbers' relative attitudes to the necessary 'heavy-duty' cleaning was obvious – Mark had a distinct aversion to the excavations whilst Ian revelled in the mining though was worried if he was discovered and made to do the gardening at home! Many of the route names resulted from the climbers' condition at the time of the first ascent, hence Jaundice Crack refers to Bruce's yellow colouration as he pulled over the dusty top. Bruce also named Dusky, which he climbed roped-solo in the dark. Towards the top the weight increased and as he struggled on the lip he pulled on the rope which came loose, with his clogger clipped in upside-down! Mark was later to take a spectacular flier during the second ascent of Two Dabs, when the top fell off in his hands. Tess is named after Ian's dog, while Jussy and The Flea refer to Tony's children; Clive's family are represented by The Bairn and Wor Lass. Literature and television documentaries deeply affected Ian, when they gave a gripping account of Huntington's Chorea.

The honours were virtually equal, and many of the best routes were climbed during the period 1981 – 83; Pink Edge, Tower Of Orthank, Huntington's Chorea and the superb Rapunzle. Mark's major contribution was One Step Further which still remains the hardest route in the quarry. The team quickly exhausted most of the possibilities and when the impetus provided by the imminent publication of the third edition of the guidebook was gone, they left the quarry and forgot about it for some time.

Local stars Pete Cain and Greg Rimmer paid a short visit and added two routes to the North Face (Frazer and Dad's Army) and thus instigated a further minor phase of exploration; Mark Leach and Mick Johnston climbed the wall left of Tess to give Rock Lobster, whilst Bruce took off again and added Sounder, and then newcomers Al Cameron and John Mason found four routes, the best of which is probably the fine Shadowfax. Dave Etherington joined them and forced the direct finish to Bruce's Sounder and found a couple of minor routes to add to the crag's repertoire. Dave was also responsible for the demise of Slow Motion, (which Nichols had climbed in 1980); the 30-foot column which formed the route bit the dust with little encouragement. The groove-line which remains has still not been re-ascended – a small loose roof giving cause for concern.

THE CLIMBS on the SOUTH and WEST FACES are described from RIGHT to LEFT on entering the quarry, those on the NORTH FACE being dealt with from LEFT to RIGHT as one would normally approach them.

THE WEST FACE
The first route is just left of the obvious descent, to the left of the fence.

1. **Stilton** 20ft VS
4c. The right arête of the groove.

2. **Open Sesame** 25ft V Diff
The obvious chimney/grooves.

3. **Little Sneak** 30ft VS
4c. Climb cracks in the wall on the left to a niche and a mantel. Finish just left of the arête.

4. **One Way Street** 30ft Sev
The corner is climbed direct.

5. **No Right Turn** 35ft VS
4c. Follow the thin crack left of One Way Street, strenuously.

6. **Lema** 30ft Hard VS
5c. Climb the arête with difficulty to an easier finish.

7. **Nova** 30ft Hard VS
5c. Boulder up the centre of the slab and finish direct.

8. **Bob The Gob** 40ft VS
4c. The groove, then the crack in the red wall.

9. **Mucky Pups** 40ft Hard VS
5a. The overhanging corner off-width with a crack in it's back.

10. **Shadowfax** 40ft E2   ★★
5c. Climb the arête without using the routes on either side; an eliminate line with sustained climbing.

11. **Rapunzle** 40ft Hard VS   ★★
5a. Climb thin cracks to gain the barred window. Finish in the same line.

12. **Stacked Deck** 40ft VS   ★★
4c. The fine crack and flake line 6 feet left.

13. **Updraught Corner** 40ft Sev
The corner on the left is followed to a groove, and the top.

14. **Jaundice Crack** 40ft Hard VS
5b. Climb the crack left of Updraught Corner direct to the top.

15. **Right Siamese Twin** 40ft Sev
Climb a blunt rib to below the wide crack, then follow this moving up and right at the top of the crack to ledges.

16. **Left Siamese Twin** 40ft VS
4b. Start as for Right Siamese Twin but move left to the thin crack and climb this to a steep move into a corner. Finish easily.

17. **Cracked Wall** 40ft VS
4c. The B-shaped crack is followed direct.

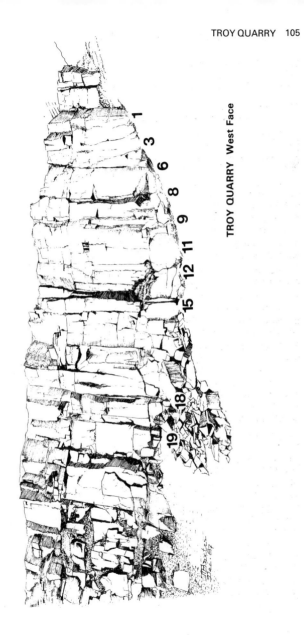

TROY QUARRY West Face

18. Troy Groove 40ft VS
4b. Climb the groove to a tricky move to gain ledges at 25 feet. Finish up the corner.

19. Gopher 40ft Hard VS
5a. Up the flake/crack to the ledge then make an awkward move off the ledge into the corner crack. Finish direct.

THE SOUTH FACE
The South Face and West Face are separated by the loose bay. Described from RIGHT to LEFT, the South Face overlooks the pool.

20. Little 'un 25ft Sev
Climb the crack and arête to grassy ledges and an escape on the right.

Further left is some unstable rock then a fine little wall.

21. Solo Wall 20ft VS
5a. Gain the obvious ledge in the left corner of the bay. Trend slightly right then straight up. Unprotected.

22. Grand National 30ft VS
4c. Climb the greyish corner 10 feet left to an easier finish.

23. Aldanite 35ft Hard VS
5a. The crack and shallow groove on the left provide difficult climbing to the large ledges.

24. Tess 40ft Hard VS
5b. Start below a blunt arête with a square cut groove in it. Climb the crack, move right into the groove and follow it to the top.

25. Rock Lobster 40ft E3   ★★
6a. The wall just left of Tess.

26. Sounder 40ft Hard VS   ★★
5a. Climb the crack to the ledge. There are three finishes:
(a) **Direct** E2 5c. Straight up the headwall.
(b) **Right-hand** HVS 5b. Hand-traverse right and finish up the arête.
(c) **Left-Hand** HVS 5a. Finish up Questionable Stability.

27. Questionable Stability 40ft VS
4c. The overhanging corner crack.

A narrow buttress is prominent at the right end of the pool. A corner crack on its right gives the next route.

28. Loose Living 45ft Sev
The corner crack leads steeply to a chimney, from where a steep move leads to the top.

29. Pink Edge 45ft Hard VS   ★★
5b. From the right edge of the buttress climb up left to a square cut groove then continue to a ledge and another groove. A strenuous pull on flat holds leads to the top.

TROY QUARRY South Face

30. Tower of Orthank 50ft E1   ★★
5b. Climb the groove at the left edge of the buttress to a cutaway at half-height. Layback the obvious crack and finish direct. Reach an advantage.

31. Pillar Cracks 45ft VS
4c. A crack system on the left leads to a short groove at the top of the wall.

32. Jussy 45ft Hard VS   ★
5a. The corner between the buttress and the long wall is followed direct.

33. Two Dabs 45ft E2
5c. An eliminate line. Climb Jussy then move left to a crackline and up this with two dabs right to the top.

34. The Flea 45ft E2   ★
5c. Climb the corner on the left to a niche, then exit via a crack.

35. Grane Wall 45ft E1   ★★
5b. Start just left of a sandy recess and follow the wall to a small overlap, then up the fine crack above.

36. Huntington's Chorea 45ft E2   ★
5c. Climb the wall to a hard mantel at mid-height, then continue with difficulty.

37. Distemper 50ft Hard VS
4c. Climb the groove/crack system on the loose rock. Escape from the vegetated cave any way you can!

38. Deep Throat 50ft VS
4c. The obvious overhanging chimney on the left. Finish left at the top.

39. Fallen Friend 50ft E2   ★
5c. The wall on the left is climbed direct to a bottomless groove, go up this moving left at the top.

40. Curlew 45ft Hard VS
5b. Climb the cracked wall just right of an obvious V-groove, moving right for a runner at 15 feet.

41. Dovetail 40ft E1
5b. Climb the V-shaped groove to an overhang and the top.

42. Grooved Arête 40ft VS
4c. Start under the groove, then climb up to the square cut groove and ascend this to below the overhang. Surmount this on the left on flat holds to reach a block and the top.

43. Troy Corner 30ft V Diff
Twin cracks are followed to a V-chimney and the top.

44. Troy Wall 35ft VS
4c. Follow Troy Corner to the horizontal fault, move left to a steep groove and follow this to the top.

45. Annic 30ft Hard VS
5a. Climb the short corner then move right to a crack in the upper wall. Finish up this.

Around the arête to the left is a broken blocky corner with a sentry box. left of this is:

46. **Pisa** 30ft E1
5b. Climb the wall trending right at the top.

47. **Dusky** 30ft VS
5a. Climb the short right angled corner then finish direct.

48. **Conian** 30ft Hard VS   ⋆
5a. Climb the shallow corner, step left and climb the wall above.

49. **Nilsar** 30ft VS
5a. The crack system 6 feet left.

50. **Ventnor** 30ft E2
6a. Start 6 feet left at an obvious foothold and follow an indefinite crack over a bulge to good holds on slabby rock, finish direct.

51. **Deception** 30ft Hard VS
5b. The steep crack and wall immediately left of the slabby scoop.

Between the South and North faces is **LITTLE BUTTRESS** which rises almost out of the pool.

52. **Wor Lass** 25ft VS
4b. The right-hand crackline.

53. **The Bairn** 25ft Hard Sev
4a. The left-hand groove/crackline.

NORTH FACE
Climbs here are described from LEFT to RIGHT as approached from the 'bridge'.

54. **Don't Look Down** 45ft E1
5b. The wall 3 feet right of the corner. Sustained.

55. **Whoops Apocalypse** 45ft Hard VS
5a. The groove left of the arête.

56. **Penwood Forge Mill** 50ft Hard VS
5a. Climb the prominent corner past an overhang to reach a large ledge. Finish on the right.

57. **Sunsalve** 50ft E1
5b. The thin crack in the wall right of the corner.

58. **One Step Further** 55ft E5   ⋆ †
6b. Traverse left from the foot of Anxiety to a niche. Gain the thin crack and use this and the arête to reach the top, sustained. There is also a direct start at 6a.

59. **Anxiety** 50ft Hard VS   ⋆
5a. The steep corner crack.

60. **What I'd Give for a Friend** 50ft Hard VS
5a. Climb to a V-shaped slot and then the cracks above.

61. **Pike** 40ft Hard VS
5a. The next deep corner crack right is climbed by finger jams and bridging.

62. **Captain Mainwaring**   40ft   Hard VS   ★★
5a. The arête on the right is climbed mainly on the right.

63. **Fraser**   40ft   Hard VS
5a. Forty feet right, climb the groove and wall.

64. **Dad's Army**   35ft   VS
4c. The groove and crack on the right.

THE PINNACLE
This is the finger of rock which is obvious on entering the quarry. It has several climbs, the most notable being the 5a crack on the south side, and the 5c crack on the north side which leads out of an alcove to a horizontal fault and the top.

GIRDLE TRAVERSE
65. **The Triumvirate**   140ft   E2   ★
(1) 80ft 5a. Climb Annic then follow a line right to the corner, and continue to the arête. Cross Dovetail, then move right and up to gain the top of the chimney of Deep Throat. Descend this to a step right, then right again to a belay in the deep corner of Distemper.
(2) 60ft 5c. Move right onto a footledge and cross to a crack (on Grane Wall) and then down to the niche on The Flea. Continue at this level to Jussy. Move up the crack system of Pillar Cracks to the second groove, step around the corner on good handholds onto the Tower of Orthank and continue to the ledge on Pink Edge and finish up this route.

MINOR CRAGS

ASHWORTH MOOR QUARRY (SD 824 159)
A pleasant quarry situated above Croston Close Bottoms. It is about ¾ mile west of the A680 Rochdale – Edenfield road. The quarry is reached by a track (parking) from the main road, in a dip about 600 yards on the Edenfield side of the New Inn. The track leads to a derelict mill on the left, the stream is crossed and a path leads left and upwards into the quarry.

A spacious grass ledge at the foot of the crag gives easy access to the routes and problems. There is little for the 'hard man' here as most of the routes are up to about VS. The lines are obvious and the protection usually good. Climbing has taken place here for upwards of 35 years and it has always been a place where one finds ones own way; usually in pleasant solitude.

BRITTANIA QUARRY (SD 880 199)
A crag that has modulated from minor to major and now (and this is probably the final resolution) back to minor again. Recent blasting has blown the best routes of the upper tier into the hole containing the best routes in the quarry. Thus there is little left and the place is best disregarded for the foreseeable future.

DOCKY DAM (SD 854 151)

Geographically in Rochdale, this newly discovered crag is included here for its proximity to the Bury — Rossendale crags. It is situated in woods above the old mill lodge after which it is named. The routes are on the right hand end of the quarried face and all are steep and strenuous. Because the crag is in trees, it is fairly green, although this algal covering does not interfere with the climbing and it is often in condition when other crags are not. However it is mainly of local interest and value. The routes were ascended by B. Goodwin, A. Nicholls and C. Morton in 1984.

Follow the A680 Rochdale — Edenfield road to Norden. In a dip is the Bridge Inn, Greenbooth Lane is opposite and leads left past a cleared site then back right until the mill lodge is reached. A lay-by on the right provides parking and a footpath leads across a field to a footbridge. Cross this and the quarry lies ahead in the trees.

At the right-hand side of the quarry is a corner; this is **Fluebrush** (Hard Sev) and is dirty. The wall on the right has three routes. **Sparkler** (HVS 5a) climbs the short wide crack at the right hand side of the wall, just left is **Diploma** (VS 5a ⋆) which takes the crack system and wall. **Touch Right** (HVS 5b) takes the steep crack to touch Diploma then moves left and up to finish. Left of Fluebrush is an obvious ledge, **Shelf and Wall** (HVS 5a ⋆) gains the ledge at a weakness and leaves it to the right. Further left is a small tree near a cracked corner, **In and Out** (VS 4c) follows this line.

HIGHER LENCH (SD 824 216)

At the top of Lench Road, between Rawtenstall and Bacup a small bulging buttress has some impressive looking cracks but the rock looks appalling! Routes have been climbed in the past, though no details are available.

MUSBURY TOR (SD 772 208)

Small outcrops on the moor above Helmshore may offer bouldering possibilities, but it is nothing to write home about.

PEEL QUARRY (SD 779 165)

Below the local monument Peel Tower, just below the crest of Holcombe Hill. A small 25-foot buttress offers numerous problems on sound rock. The crag has been visited regularly in the past and all the lines have been climbed. Routes in the vicinity of the central pillar are especially enjoyable at around VS.

IV. THE BOLTON AREA

Compiled by Phil Kelly
with assistance from Tim Lowe, Dave Sanderson, Geoff Hibbert
and Andy Moss

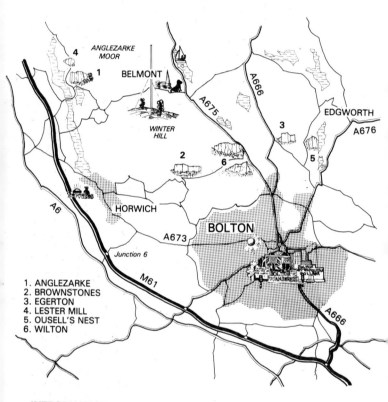

1. ANGLEZARKE
2. BROWNSTONES
3. EGERTON
4. LESTER MILL
5. OUSELL'S NEST
6. WILTON

INTRODUCTION

The Bolton area and the crags encompassed therein are considered the epicentre of climbing amongst the Lancashire quarries, and the role they play in bonding the local climbing fraternity together is second to none, Tetleys excepted.

Of the nine major crags in this area, Brownstones has perhaps the longest and most consistent history, and has been visited regularly by local cragsters since early this century, and by travelling to this quarry, other possible crags were discovered and exploited. The quarryman's working methods dictated the character of today's quarry faces; modern day explosives completely devastate the mother rock leaving loose and unclimbable rubble, though the explosives used in the last century were by no means as powerful and damage was not quite so severe. The early climbers took advantage of this by (logically) attacking the more vulnerable lines of weakness, which at the time were not quite the same sound character as they are today; climbed from the bottom up and on sight in the main, cleaning en-route. Today, thousands of passing pairs of boots have gradually cleaned the routes of detritus, and the routes are generally solid.

All the quarries are gritstones of varying textures. The best quality is found in the Wilton Massif and at Brownstones, or in the slightly more brittle Anglezarke Quarry. Egerton and Ousell's Nest also contain much good rock and there is much to be done in both of them.

ANGLEZARKE QUARRY (SD 621 162)

By Tim Lowe

SITUATION AND CHARACTER
Anglezarke is one of the larger quarries in the Lancashire area. It is sited on Anglezarke Moor, close to the reservoir, and just across the road lies Lester Mill Quarry. Despite being tree-filled, it is a suntrap and the routes tend to dry relatively quickly after rain. The rock is a sandy gritstone and is generally sound though it can tend towards brittle in some parts. Care should be taken when climbing on Coal Measure Crag however, as the stone fall from the upper band is more frequent than on the Eigerwand. Some rock above the Terror Cotta area should also be treated with respect.

APPROACH
The quarry lies on Anglezarke Moor, between the M61 and Winter Hill. To reach it from the M61 (junction 6) follow the A6027 until the A673 (Bolton – Horwich road) is reached, and then turn left. About 1 mile past Horwich, turn right at the Millstone Inn and follow a narrow road to a motorway bridge. Turn right just before this bridge and continue to the Yew Tree Inn. Take the right fork here and follow this past a sharp left-hand bend, to where it branches left and right. Turn left and follow the road into an extensive car park. On foot now, scramble up to the rear end of the parking area to gain a road (the right-hand branch of the road) with the quarry lying opposite.

HISTORY
> *'...and Anglezark Quarry near the Yew Tree Inn, Horwich, has a few climbs and one of the most imposing buttresses on gritstone, the Golden Tower, up which runs a continuous and magnificent virgin crack. Alas the rock in this quarry is*

> *fairly green and can only be described as extremely dangerous.'*
>
> Walter Unsworth, 'The English Outcrops' 1964

Walt Unsworth and Bev Heslop first discovered Anglezarke Quarry late in the 1950's and ascended the first recorded routes here. Walt and Bev attacked the lines of least resistance first and climbed a few of the easier routes on Triple Bob Buttress as well as one on Grey Buttress (Pedestal Route), they also attempted what was later to become Foxes Corner and made ascents of Plain Bob and Tocsin Wall (the hardest route in the quarry at the time) late in the 50's. Glister wall was soon to follow, which was led by Bev though both climbers were amazed to find a peg in situ, which confirmed their suspicions − that other climbers had visited the quarry previously and that routes had been climbed though left unrecorded. This pair also managed to entice other climbers into the quarry but loose quarry climbing was neither in vogue or appealing, and so the quarry was forgotten until Les Ainsworth began research into what was to become the first edition of the Lancashire guidebook. Walt took on the task of writing the Anglezarke section in the early 60's and in order to develop the crag, invited others along. Walt introduced Arthur Hassall, Gra Whittaker and Stu Thomas to the quarry, and this team (supplemented at times by others) were the main protagonists of the first major wave of development. Gra climbed Whittaker's Almanac, Thomas added his Wall Climb and Ian Aldred climbed his Original.

Attention though swapped to Grey Buttress (actually a misnomer, but it was so called because on their first visit, peering through the mist, Walt and Bev thought it to be grey!) and the atrocious prevailing conditions accounted for the route name Storm which was climbed by Arthur and Stu, whilst Arthur also led Elder Groove, the name being both a reference to the tree and also a pun on his own age!

Things were beginning to hot up a bit now with many more climbers 'getting a look in'; Les Ainsworth was always hungry for new routes and started to visit the quarry on a regular basis, soon adding a stiff problem and then extending it even further to create Traumatic Eversion, on which he employed one point of aid, later freed by Dave Knighton.

Left Wall received its first routes in the early sixties when Les climbed a fine crackline which he named Wedge and Gra Whittaker raced up Quickstep, not daring to hesitate unless all his points of contact fell to the ground! Whittaker then teamed up with John Whittle to create the changeable Metamorphosis, or an earlier version of Metamorphosis, because their route changed with every ascent for the first six months or so of its existence. Les, meanwhile, became attracted by the curious finger of rock which pointed outwards from the area of rock just right of Glister Wall, and very soon he had exhausted every possible entry to and exit from this; The Finger, Finger Chimney and The Thumb, then Hassal led the stiff Wedding March just right again, in reference to Stu's impending marriage. John Whittle co-opted Roger Tweedy into the fray and together this pair climbed one of the more popular routes in the quarry today, the excellent corner groove of Samarkand, Whittle had also added Fleabite a few weeks earlier.

By this time, news of the 'continuous and magnificent' virgin crack had begun to spread and had even reached Yorkshire. At least one Yorkie team had actually run the gauntlet of border guards and managed to reach the crag undetected. Arthur and Gra had attempted the route, unsuccessfully apart from the first pitch, a few weeks earlier and had meant to return for a second bout. Les heard of the Yorkie's 'ascent' and set off on a second ascent bid with Ian Cowell; Les led the first pitch, and Ian the second, though moving slightly right (with two aid pegs) near the top. Soon after, Ian moved from the area and then Les discovered that the Yorkshire team's ascent had only been a top-rope affair. The forcing of the Golden Tower marked the end of the first major wave of development in the quarry.

When the explorations restarted in the early seventies, the next 'last great problem' was a short wall on the Left Wall Area, leading to a short V-shaped groove, which was tried by many people, all of them unsuccessful until Stu Thomas forced the line with a couple of aid pegs and Terror Cotta was born. It gained immediate fame a couple of years later when a picture of the first ascent was used to illustrate the front cover of the 1975 guidebook to the area. Later it was suggested that Hank Pasquill had made a secretive, unrecorded ascent of the line, naming it Ten Pound Bail. Prior to Thomas's ascent of Terror Cotta, Hassall had been slowly badgering away farther left, climbing Many Happy Returns and Birthday Crack, while Thomas himself led Bay Horse with a bit of aid.

The magnificent lines on Coal Measure Crag had lain virtually untouched for some time, until Dave Cronshaw and friends began the long, protracted navvying needed to gain access to safe belays above the routes. Many weekends were spent digging an escape path along the bottom of the shale, though this path has been neglected in recent years and has now fallen into a state of disrepair. It was Pasquill, however, who started the ball rolling by free-climbing Sheppey and then Ian Lonsdale and Mick Bullough climbed an alternative start (Moscow Mule) which had previously been climbed with aid from a skyhook by Martin Selby. Moscow Mule itself has recently been incorporated into the start of Age of Reason, climbed in 1987 by Mark Liptrot.

Dave and Les attacked Coal Measure Crag proper, climbing Gritstone Rain in 1978, followed soon after by Kaibab, then Dave soloed Soot Juggler on Grey Buttress, and turned his thoughts to free-climbing Bill Chevrest's aided girdle traverse of Golden Tower, which he succeeded on that July. 1980 arrived and saw Mark Liptrot and Dick Toon open up Waterfall Buttress (now called Falkland Walls since the waterfall dried up; with a little help from Lonsdale!) with Grond, with Cronshaw and Lonsdale following hot on their heels with Rockin' Horse and the ever-popular Tangerine Trip, which is still one of the most widely used routes in the quarry today. Just round the corner, Dave led John Ryden up Bellringer and Ding Dong, whilst Ian free-climbed Bay Horse with Nigel Bonnet.

In 1982, Liptrot took on the modern day development of the quarry, and he kicked off with a solo ascent of Vishnu Direct Start and a free ascent of its 'sister' route, Havasupai, which he renamed Obiwan. The three peg runners Mark used on his ascent of the latter, were later removed by an irate local, who thought they were unnecessary, and were put to more use on the Eiger; the route had to wait five years for a pegless ascent, again by Liptrot, who re-re-renamed it The Lean Mean Fightin' Machine. The following year saw Mark open up the steep wall right of Supai Corner when he made ascents of Shibb and New Jerusalem, both three-star routes, the latter being substantially less serious if you have a Friend 4! Over on the Golden Tower area, Liptrot broke out left from Glister Wall, with minimal protection to create the bold Give Thanks. The boldness took on another dimension in 1986 when Andy Gridley climbed a direct start to this route (Milk Syringe) which utilised a glued-in R.P. (now stolen) for protection on its desperate crux moves.

The wall left of the Tower saw Bernie Bradbury climb Please Lock Me Away and the next year, Gary Gibson paid a return visit (having climbed Ain't Nothing To It in February 1982) and stole a line from under the nose of Tim Lowe. Tim had lightly cleaned the wall right of Please Lock Me Away and was about to equip the line, when Gary stepped in and forced the line, now curiously named Septic Think Tank. The second ascent of this route was something of a shocker for Tim, when he made it to the peg runner, only to find that the peg was a desperate clip, having a small eye and only clippable in one direction. The next year Liptrot was back, firstly to add The Absent Minded Professor, and also to break out left from Please Lock Me Away, to join Klondyke and named the line King Of Kings. Mark returned later and gave the route an independent finish, and Ian MacMullan made the direct connection up the crack as a direct start, but did not climb the whole route. Well aware that his crown was in jeopardy, Liptrot pulled out all the stops and made the connection of direct start and direct finish, which was the hardest route in the quarry at the time, only surpassed when Paul Pritchard climbed the impressive wall right of New Jerusalem; Karma Mechanic.

GREY BUTTRESS
Identified by some fallen blocks and its distinctive red colour (!); some belay stakes are in place at the top, well back. All THE ROUTES are described from RIGHT to LEFT, i.e. anticlockwise.

1. **Just William**   30ft   Hard V Diff   *
The prominent crack at the right end of the long low wall. Dirty finish.

2. **Soot Juggler**   35ft   Hard VS
5b. Start 9 feet left at an obvious sentry box and follow a direct line to the top.

3. **Thomas's Wall Climb**   30ft   Hard Sev
4a. Start slightly left of the large tree which grows above the centre of the wall, and climb a blunt rib to a ledge at 8 feet, then move up and right to finish through the obvious break.

4. **Years from Now**   30ft   E2   *
5c. Start left of a tree-filled corner at an obvious finger crack in the

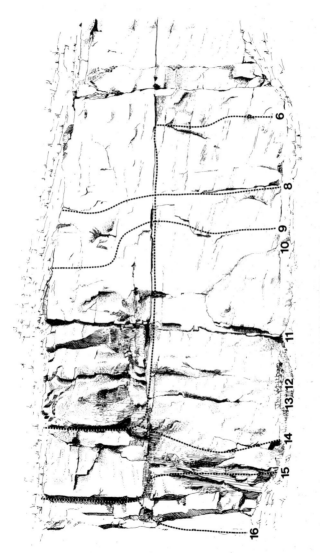

ANGLEZARKE QUARRY Grey Buttress

arête. Climb this for 15 feet, then move left and climb the wall direct over an overlap.

5. Whittaker's Almanac   25ft   Sev
The steep corner groove on the left. Finish direct or on the left.

6. Traumatic Eversion   130ft   E1   **
A girdle. Start 4 feet left of the arête, at a small ledge about 7 feet off the ground: Master's Ledge.
(1) 60ft 5c.   Mantel onto the ledge, then climb straight up using flake holds on the left to gain a small ledge below the horizontal break. Step up and hand-traverse left along the break for 12 feet to Sheppey, then continue for another 15 feet until it is possible to step down onto a pedestal belay.
(2) 70ft 4b.   Up a little, then easily left and finish up the deep corner of Elder Groove.

7. Sparrow   45ft   E4   †
6b. Start on the vague pillar just right of Sheppey, and climb up and right to PR (on Traumatic Eversion). Go directly over the small overlap to a tree belay.

8. Sheppey   55ft   E2
6a. A few feet left is a steep crack which has been heavily pegged. Climb this past a small ledge to a ledge above the horizontal break, then finish up the corner on the left.

9. Age of Reason   60ft   E6   * †
6b. Start just left of Sheppey, and climb a blind flake to the break. Place runners in the corner and a sling on the sapling, then swing out left to holds which lead to a pocket and PR. Finish direct.

10. Storm   55ft   VS   **
4c. Climb the prominent pedestal flake then a fine crack-line to a large ledge. Step round to the left and through the break in the overhangs to a good stance. Finish up the groove above.

11. Sunbeam   50ft   VS
4b. A direct line up the crack which bounds the pedestal flake on its left, then after the overhang finish up the final groove of Storm. The route contains very little independent climbing.

12. Kaibab   65ft   Hard VS
5b. The weakness 5 feet left of the prominent flake, finishing direct.

13. Turkish Delight   50ft   VS
5b. Start just left of Kaibab, climb its parallel groove system to a ledge then traverse left to finish up Elder Groove.

14. Elder Groove   55ft   Hard Sev   *
4b. Start 8 feet left and climb a blunt nose diagonally left to a ledge. Then climb the vertical corner crack with a tree in it.

15. Pedestal Route   50ft   Hard Diff
The pedestal lies beneath a large tree at the top of the crag. Climb a groove and rib, then step left onto a broad flat pedestal. Climb the short crack above and go left into a V-shaped groove, which is followed to a tree at the top.

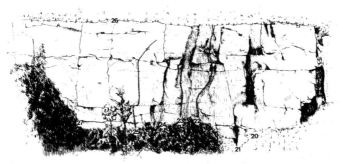

ANGLEZARKE QUARRY Coal Measure Crag

16. **Slab Start**   Hard V Diff
Climb the slab on the left of the pedestal to reach the upper ledge.

17. **Rope Thief**   35ft   Hard Sev
4b. Fifteen feet left is a short corner groove almost directly below a sapling at the top of the crag. Climb this and the shallow groove above. PR in horizontal break.

18. **William the Conqueror**   40ft   Hard Sev
4b. The conspicuous shallow corner groove 6 feet left.

COAL MEASURE CRAG
The long, high wall left of Grey Buttress contains many splendid lines, but the top section is guarded by a band of shale which prevents safe access to any belays. A path was once cut along the top of the rock, but this has been reclaimed by the constantly-falling shale, so it may be advisable to belay to a rope hung from the top.

19. **The Rapidity of Sleep**   60ft   E1
6a. The thin crack and wall 10 feet right of Flake Out, traversing into that route 10 feet from the top to finish.

20. **Flake Out**   55ft   VS
4c. A resurrection of the old route Great Flake (which now lies almost buried under shale) climbing the obvious break behind the fallen flake.

21. **The Lean Mean Fightin' Machine**   60 ft   E4   ★★
6a. A superb, finger-tearing line up the thin diagonal crackline veering left from the top of the flake, just left of Flake Out. Finish up Vishno, to BB. Abseil off.

22. **Vishnu**   60ft   VS   ★★
4c. Start at the base of the deep corner and climb the flake on the right to finish up an S-shaped groove. Bolt belay at the top of the groove, abseil off. A **Direct Start** exists (E1 5c), which climbs the thin crack 10 feet right of the original start.

23. **The Taciturn Boy**   60t   E4   †
6b. Left of Vishnu is a deep corner. Climb the cracked left arête of this corner.

24. **Gritstone Rain**   60ft   Hard VS   ★★
5b. Start just left of the arête and climb up to a ledge at 15 feet. Then climb the groove above to a large ledge and exit from this up a short corner. Bolt belay about 3 feet right of corner on the ledge.

25. **The Karma Mechanic**   60ft   E6   ★★★ †
The steep wall left of Gritstone Rain.
6c. Start at a short diagonal crack, and climb to a thin break at 15 feet (PR). Move right and dyno for a large hold. Mantel onto this hold and climb the wall above, passing two PRs. Bolt belay on the right, AO.

26. **Shibb**   65ft   E3   ★★★
6b. The obvious crackline 15 feet left of Gritstone Rain.

27. **New Jerusalem**   65ft   E4   ★★★
6a. The next obvious crack feature. Peg runner.

28. **Supai Corner**   50ft   VS
4b. The corner which limits the main wall of Coal Measure Crag on its left.

29. **Bright Angel Corner**   45ft   VS   ★★
4c. Climb the next corner, 3 feet left, starting from the left.

30. **Anasazi Arête**   40ft   E2   ★
5b. From the top of the scree slope climb up and right to the blunt arête, then continue on large holds to a ledge at 25 feet. Climb the left-hand side of the arête (crux) to a BB just below the top, AO.

31. **Son of Dicktrot**   40ft   E2   †
5c. The narrow wall and thin crack just left of Anasazi Arête, to the BB of that route. AO.

32. **Zoroaster**   35ft   VS
4b. Climb the corner formed by two flakes, just right of an obvious bush.

33. **The Changeing**   50ft   E1   †
5b. A lead version of the old route Torroweap Overlook; climb the 'stuck-on' flake just left of the obvious bush. A hanging rope is essential for a belay, AO.

34. **Whiter Shade of Shale**   35ft   Hard VS
The left crack in the back of the square recess. Abseil descent.

35. **Tapeats**   25ft   Hard Sev
4a. Start 3 feet left of left arête of the recess and climb direct to the top of the pedestal. Abseil descent.

LOW WALL
The short wall between Coal Measure Crag and Beginner's Buttress.

36. **Midgebite Wall**   20ft   VS
5a. The wall 15 feet right of Fleabite.

37. **Fleabite**   20ft   Hard VS
5a. Start immediately right of a deep groove in the low wall. Climb to

a ledge, traverse left and step up onto a very sloping undercut ledge. Using the crack above, pull onto the overhang and go up to a dirty finish.

GOLDEN TOWER AREA
The Golden Tower is obvious. Sixty yards to its right is the easy-angled **Beginner's Buttress**; a good way down.

38. Yapi 20ft Hard Sev
4b. The slanting corner which bounds Beginner's Buttress on its left.

39. First Night 25ft Hard Sev
4b. Climb the thin crackline just left of the obvious arête to a ledge, then finish up the flake on the left, or climb the wall direct (harder).

40. Night Before 30ft V Diff
The indistinct chimney left of Beginner's Buttress, guarded by a pedestal.

41. Stag Party 30ft Hard Sev   *
4a. Twin cracks on the left lead to a ledge, (THE BRIDAL SUITE) then climb the right wall to the top.

42. Wedding March 35ft VS   *
4c. Climb the fine crack to the left end of the Bridal Suite. Continue up the crack or use the left wall and crack.

43. Finger Chimney 45ft Hard VS   *
5a. Farther left a prominent finger sticks out at 15 feet. Climb the hanging chimney on the right of this, mount the finger, then step right over the chimney to a small ledge and finish direct.

44. The Finger 25ft VS
4b. Climb the Finger from the left and mantel onto its end, then straight up by a crack.

45. The Thumb 30ft Sev
Starting on the left climb to the Finger, step left and finish up a short blocky crack.

46. Glister Wall 35ft Sev   **
Climb the centre of the broken wall on the right of the Tower. Not all that easy.

47. Give Thanks 65ft E3
5c. Start as for Glister Wall, but step left into the thin groove in the wall and climb this to finish just right of Samarkand. A direct start (**Milk Syringe** E5 6b) somehow climbs the lower wall direct past two old bolt holes, to join Give Thanks at its groove.

48. Samarkand 65ft VS   ***
4c. The crack which limits the Tower on its right. Finish by sloping rocks on the right, or continue direct.

49. Fool's Gold 70ft Hard VS   *
Takes the awesome hanging crack in the front face of the Golden Tower, then finishes up the bold right arête.
(1) 30ft 5b. Climb to the ledge at mid-height on the Tower, by a hanging groove near its right edge.
(2) 40ft 4c. Climb the right arête. Very bold!

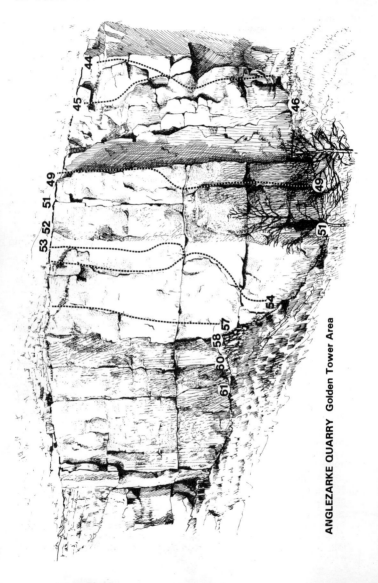

ANGLEZARKE QUARRY Golden Tower Area

50. Agrajag 80ft E3
6a. Start just left of Fool's Gold and climb the thin crack (runner in Golden Tower) and wall above on spaced holds (PR) to the belay ledge of Golden Tower; finish up that route.

51. The Golden Tower 80ft E2 ★★★
A fine route at the lower limit of its grade. It is described here in two pitches though it is probably better done in one runout.
(1) 40ft 5a. Start in the small cave at the left edge of the Tower and follow the jamming crack just right of the arête to a ledge. Step right here to NB.
(2) 40ft 5c. Climb the crack which splits the wall above. Well protected.

52. Gates of Perception 80ft E4 ★★★
6a. Follow Golden Tower to the ledge then climb the crack just right of the left arête by a series of layback and finger jamming moves; a sustained pitch.

53. Septic Think Tank 60ft E5 ★★★
6b. Follow Please Lock me Away to the break of Lucky Strike. Move right (PR) and boldly attack the wall just left of the arête, on spaced finger edges, to a lo..o..ng reach to a poor peg runner. Climb the wall above finishing just left of the arête. Fail to clip the peg at your peril!

54. Please Lock me Away 55ft E5 ★★
6b. Climb up to the left-hand end of the undercut flake and follow it rightwards (PR) to the break. Climb the crack above, finishing over some doubtful rock.

55. King of Kings 65ft E6 ★★★
6b. Start as for Please Lock me Away but at the flake climb the hairline crack above, direct to the break. Move slightly rightwards and continue up the technical wall finishing direct. Three PRs. A very sustained route.

56. The Nausea 85ft E4 †
6b. Climb Klondyke to the overlap then move out right onto the wall and traverse across to finish as for Septic Think Tank.

57. Klondyke 60ft E3 ★★
6a. Halfway up the earthy slope on the left of the Tower is a previously pegged crack. Thin finger jams lead to a good resting ledge. Layback up to the overlap, PR, and make some trying moves to finish.

58. Dirty Corner 50ft VS
4c. The pedestal corner further left. Traverse off to the right at the top.

59. Lucky Strike 200ft E2 ★★
A girdle of the Golden Tower Area, starting from the pedestal on Dirty Corner.
(1) 80ft 5b. Climb onto the pedestal and traverse right to gain the first ledge on Klondyke. Follow the horizontal break right, around the arête to the front of the Tower. NB as for Golden Tower.
(2) 40ft 4c. Traverse right to the arête and continue into Samarkand.
(3) 80ft 5a. Go across to the Finger, move round this to gain Wedding March. Descend and make a hard move to reach a willow tree and finish up Beginner's Buttress.

ANGLEZARKE QUARRY Falkland Walls

60. **Helical Happiness** 50ft Hard VS
5a. Start at the left side of the pedestal and follow the crack to the top.

61. **Gilt Complex** 50ft Hard VS
5b. The crack on the left. Very sustained.

62. **A Series of Boring Mantelshelves** 30ft Sev
Twenty-five yards left is a short, solid buttress. Start on the left and climb the nose. Steep grass finish.

FALKLAND WALLS
Twenty yards farther left is the steep back wall of the quarry. Diversion of the old waterfall has meant that there are now some worthwhile climbs on this part of the quarry, though drainage over parts of the wall can sometimes pose a problem on some climbs.

63. **Rockin' Horse** 45ft E2
5c. Start at the base of a blocky ramp 20 feet left of the right limit of the wall, and follow a direct line into the very shallow pod, then continue up a crack to the top.

The next route was described in the 1983 guide as Grond, though that route actually lies farther left and was called Superb. This position has now been rectified, except that no first ascent claim exists for 'Grond II' and it may not have been climbed!

64. **Grond II** 45ft Hard VS   †
5a. The obvious block-filled crack 8 feet left.

65. **The Absent Minded Professor** 55ft E3   †
5c. Start just right of Tangerine Trip. Climb a thin crack which joins that

Right: Dave Peace and Mick Ryan on 'Golden Tower' - Anglezarke Quarry. Photo: Peace collection

Rob Smitton on 'Bend of The Rainbow', Craig y Longridge.

route at the break at 25 feet. Swing left and climb the wall, moving back right at the top.

66.   Tangerine Trip   55ft   E3   ***
An excellent and strenuous route which stays dry even when most of the quarry is wet.
5c. Follow the obvious right-slanting crack in the overhanging wall to the break, move right and climb to a bolt belay. Abseil off. Traditionalists, or those who enjoy the scree climbing encountered on Coal Measure Crag, may prefer to eschew the use of the bolt and ascend the horrible shale to finish (as on the first ascent).

67.   Hunter, Killer   50ft   Hard VS
5a. Start as for Tangerine Trip and climb the slightly left-slanting crack.

68.   Falkland Groove   50ft   VS   *
4c. The broken groove 8 feet left provides a good climb which should improve with traffic. Gain the sloping block at the base of the groove with difficulty, then continue up the groove and step left near its top to a foothold on the arête. Move back left and finish via the deep cleft.

69.   Corned Beef Dictator   50ft   E1
5a. The obvious deep chimney on the left and continuation groove above. First ascent: David Bellamy!

70.   Grond   55ft   Hard VS   **
5a. Start 3 feet left and ascend a corner crack for 25 feet, then move left to an obvious notch on the arête. Climb straight up the arête to finish. Previously known as 'Superb' in the last guide.

At present there is only one route on the left of the Falkland Walls, this is:

71.   Hermes   60ft   VS
4c. Start 3 feet left of the arête and climb cracks to an obvious sentry box at mid-height, then continue direct to the top.

TRIPLE BOB BUTTRESS AREA
After the above wall there are two small buttresses and then an impressive grey buttress 40 yards left and at right angles to it. This marks the right side of the Triple Bob Area, which extends to a complete break in the rock on the left where there is an easy descent path. The Triple Bobs themselves are 3 perched blocks about 20 feet left of the grey buttress.

72.   Gold Digger   45ft   VS
4c. Climb the thin crack just right of the right arête of the grey buttress and finish just left of the arête.

73.   Tinkerbell   50ft   Hard V Diff
Start on the right side of the Triple Bobs and climb an easy groove to a large ledge at mid-height. Step left onto a slab, then climb this and the thin crack above to a finishing mantel.

74. **Triple Bob Major**   60ft   Hard Diff
The stability of the Bobs is open to doubt. Either climb the blocks, or the crack on their left, or a combination of both. In any case arrive at a large grass ledge at 30 feet; cross it and climb another 30 feet of easier rocks to the top.

75. **Tocsin Wall**   25ft   VS
5a. The steep little wall left of the Triple Bobs is climbed to an easy finish.

76. **Bellringer**   50ft   Hard VS   *
5b. Climb the obvious thin crack which splits the wall left of the corner.

77. **Ding Dong**   50ft   Hard VS
5b. Immediately left, on the arête is an orange groove. Climb this, moving awkwardly over bulges to ledges, then directly to the top.

78. **Tintinabulation**   60ft   VS   **
4c. A line up the shattered wall on the left. Starts from a distinctive pedestal, then climb the wide crack for a few feet until it is possible to move right via an obvious foothold to another crack. Up and right past dobs to the ledge above. Finish direct or step left and then finish.

78a. **Direct Start**
Climb the right edge of the lower chimney crack to meet the original route.

79. **For Whom the Bell Tolls**   50ft   VS
4b. Start just right of Plain Bob. Gain the obvious mantel on the right and then continue to the top via a groove in the wall left of a crack.

80. **Plain Bob**   50ft   Sev   **
4a. A few feet right of the easy way down is a pillar of firm rock. Climb the right face of this to the top, then go easily to a curving crack and follow this to the top.

81. **Plain Bob Variant**   50ft   VS
4b. The layback crack on the left of the pillar.

82. **Unappealing**   50ft   Moderate
Left of the last climb a series of small ledges lead eventually to the top.

LEFT WALL AREA
Between the Triple Bob and Left Wall Areas is the largest break in the quarry, and the best way down on this side.

83. **Foxes Corner**   30ft   V Diff
The dirty, broken groove and deep set chimney above.

84. **Edipol!**   40ft   Hard Sev   *
4a. Start below a crack on the left, and surmount the overhang using a large hold on the left (strenuous), then continue up the crack above to a ledge. Traverse the ledge to the right and climb the edge of the wall above.

85. **Bossa Nova**   45ft   VS
4b. The obvious corner on the left. Traverse right to finish.

86. Bay Horse 50ft E1
5b. The first big crack left of the easy way down. Climb for a few feet, then using a subsidiary crack on the left continue until a hard move can be made onto a small ledge. To finish either, go right using a flake and mantel onto a pointed block, or, climb the shattered headwall.

87. Rock Lobster 35ft E2
5c. The left side of the arête left of Bay Horse, gained from a few feet up that route.

88. Skin Game 40ft E3 *
6a. Climb the wall left of Rock Lobster, passing a thin crack and a dodgy PR. The top wall feels bold.

89. Terra Firma 50ft Hard VS
5b. Really a variation start to Cotton Terror, taking the thin crack 10 feet right of Terror Cotta.

90. Cotton Terror 55ft E1 **
5a. Start as for Terror Cotta, then step right immediately to a thin flake crack and ascend this to a small ledge, and then up the grooved wall to a large ledge below the top, PR. Finish straight up or traverse right from the peg, to BB on Rock Lobster. Abseil off.

91. Land 55ft E4 †
The open corner right of Terror Cotta.
6a. Climb the open corner direct (peg clipped on Terror Cotta) and go straight over the capping roof.

92. Terror Cotta 70ft Hard VS ***
5a. On the left is a big yellow wall with some jutting overhangs above. Start in a short yellow corner and climb up and left onto a platform. Swing left around the arête, onto a blank wall and go up (PR) on friable rock to the overhangs. Make a difficult pull into the groove above and finish up this.

93. Terrorific 65ft E4 *
6a. A direct start to Terror Cotta. Start 10 feet left, below a crescent-shaped hold; climb directly past this feature and move right to join Terror Cotta and finish up that route.

94. Mission Impossible 100t E2
A high-level girdle of Terror Cotta's Wall; climb this route quickly – it may self destruct at any moment.
5b. From the break on Terror Cotta traverse left beneath the roofs to finish up Zarke.

95. High Revver 150ft E1 *
An interesting girdle of the main section of Left Wall.
(1) 75ft 5b. Follow Terror Cotta to the platform, then step onto the front wall and traverse horizontally to Double Trip (PR). Continue traversing in a more strenuous manner to the crackline of First Finale. Up this past a situ PR to the overhang, then arrange protection and semi-hand-traverse left along the break into the corner of Birthday Crack (PB).
(2) 75ft 4c. Step up and move onto the left wall, continue to an ancient PR, then step down and move out to the arête. Swing round

onto Metamorphosis' wall and follow the obvious horizontal break left past Punchline to finish just right of the broken corner at the left of the wall.

96. Double Trip 60ft E2 ***
5b. Start in the centre of the yellow wall, 3 feet left of a V-shaped groove in the top overhang. Climb the snappy wall past 2 PRs to the overhang (PR on right) and from the break beneath the roof, yawn out across the roof to reach a good hold just over the lip and pull boldly onto the upper wall, finishing slightly left.

97. Liptrip 70ft E3
6a. Climb the wall just left of Double Trip to the break, traverse right and finish over the roof right of that route.

98. First Finale 60ft E2 *
5b. Climb the thin broken crack 5 feet left, to an overlap and finish up the shattered groove above.

99. Zarke 65ft Hard VS **
5a. Start as for First Finale. Mantel onto a sloping ledge to reach an overlap at 12 feet, then move left and up to a small ledge. Move left onto a large ledge, and from the right of this climb up to another ledge. Make an exposed crossing of the wall on the right until possible to finish straight up through an obvious break. **Evil Digits** (E2 6c †) is a direct start.

100. Fingertip Control 50ft E4 **
5c. Takes an almost direct line up the bold wall just left of First Finale with a long reach to gain a good hold and the crux leaving it to gain the break, way, way above the protection; serious.

101. Birthday Crack 55ft VS
4b. The corner on the left, traverse out left along the obvious break to finish.

102. Many Happy Returns 50ft E1
5a. Climb the crack in the middle of the wall on the left.

103. Ain't Nothing to It 45ft E3 **
5c. Climb the crack left of Many Happy Returns to its end (PR), then reach up the arête (crux) to good holds and finish direct or to the left.

104. Dancing on the Valentine 40ft E2
5c. Climb Metamorphosis to the first ledge and climb the wall above direct, just left of the arête.

105. Metamorphosis 55ft VS **
4b. The big, black wall with a flake on it, left of the yellow wall. Start at the right arête and go up until the top of the flake can be reached. Climb past another small ledge and trend slightly right to finish.

106. Transformation 50ft VS *
4c. The thin crack on the left. Loose finish.

107. Punchline 50ft E1 *
5b. Start just right of a small niche. Climb the wall until almost level with the porthole, then go diagonally right to the porthole. Finish on the left.

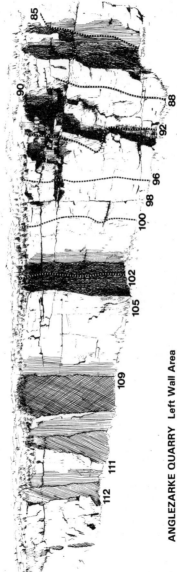

ANGLEZARKE QUARRY Left Wall Area

108. Punch Up 45ft VS
5a. Climb straight up past the niche.

109. Coconino 35ft Hard Diff
The deep corner on the left.

110. Snorter 35ft VS
5a. The left side of the wall left of Coconino.

111. Telegraph Arête 30ft Hard Sev
4b. Left, past some suspect rock, is a steep arête with a telegraph pole above it, climb the left edge.

112. Quickstep 20ft Sev
The next arête at an easier angle, but still loose.

113. Pandooi 30ft E3   †
6a. The wall just right of Shorty, step left beneath the overhang and finish direct.

114. Shorty 30ft E2   *
5b. Climb the left-slanting weakness 8 feet left of the arête. Where the cracks end move up to a break and then go right to finish.

115. Nowhere Man 25ft E1
5b. The wall 9 feet left.

116. Sleeper Bay 25ft V Diff
Left again is a bay with an old railway sleeper sticking out near the top. Up the dirty rocks to the sleeper.

117. Mark 30ft VS
4c. Climb the crackline to join Wedge at three quarters height.

118. Wedge 30ft Hard Sev   **
4a. The steep crack 25 feet left of the corner.

119. Elaine 30ft Hard VS
5c. The boulder problem wall and crack just left of Wedge.

120. Nightmare 25ft Hard Sev   *
4b. The prominent inverted Y-crack just right of the left arête of the wall.

121. Mini 20ft Diff
The short crack at the left edge of the same wall.

122. Writer's Cramp 40ft Sev
This is the low-level traverse of the wall which contains the last 4 climbs. Start in the right corner and traverse left along an obvious line until you run out of rock.

123. Because 20ft Hard Sev
4a. Farther left is a depression with a wall above it, further identified by a block at its top. The climb takes the blunt arête on the right of the wall.

124. Meanwhile 20ft Sev
The wall has 4 cracks. This is the right one.

125. Whittaker's Original 20ft Hard Sev   **
4a. The second crack.

126. **After The Blitz**   20ft   VS
4b. The wall direct from the small platform.

127. **Alldred's Original**   20ft   V Diff
The third crack, just left of the fallen block. Hard to start.

128. **Side Step**   20ft   Hard Sev
The fourth crack is less well defined. Climb to a bulge which is avoided by a long step left, and escape by a narrow ledge.

129. **Get This One in the Guide it's a Gem**   20ft   VS
4b. The wall just left is climbed direct.

130. **Original Wall Traverse**   60ft   Sev
Traverse the wall at mid-height, from right to left.

131. **Last Post**   20ft   V Diff
A conspicuous isolated buttress on the left has an iron spike in it. Either climb the front arête, or (harder), the side by the spike.

BROWNSTONES QUARRY (SD 681 124)

By Denis Gleeson with acknowledgements to previous writer Ian Lonsdale

SITUATION AND CHARACTER
Brownstones is situated some 4 miles from the centre of Bolton and lies conveniently next to Scout Road, within a stones-throw of ample car parking. The quarry is a fellstone grit of similar nature to (though a finer texture than) Wilton. It is generally clean, with the exception of the tops section of the Back Wall.

APPROACH
Approaching from Bolton follow the Blackburn signs (A666), about ½ a mile from the town centre is a fork in the road. Take the left-hand fork (Blackburn Road carries straight on) and follow Halliwell Road to where it crosses the ring road (Ainsworth Arms pub on corner). Continue straight on up Smithills Deane Road to a crossroads (approximately 1 mile) and turn left here. The quarry is now visible on the right after about ¼ mile, set back slightly from the road. Alternatively, if approaching from the Wilton Quarries, Brownstones lies approximately 1½ miles farther along Scout Road.

HISTORY
The first record of climbing in Brownstones Quarry was published in the journal of the L.C.& C.C. in the spring of 1947 and was written by Eric Parr. This original guide included 47 problems, many of which are still bouldering 'classics' of today. Notable routes which date from this period include Godwit Groove and Crossbill Crack, now known as Parr's Crack and Layback to the modern devotees, and both still retain the potential to shock jaded rock-jocks in early season.
The early guide was revised in 1948 and between that date and the publication of the first definitive Lancashire guidebook in the late 60s,

development was spasmodic; during the intervening years all the original problems became known by other names, probably caused by the lack of an available guidebook.

When it finally arrived, the Rocksport guide listed 67 routes, along with their technical grades (a new innovation in the area and following the example of Pete Crew's Cloggy guide, interestingly the example did not spread to other crags for many years!). Digitation by Hank Pasquill became a masterpiece of delicacy, just left of Ashpit Slab whilst Var, Knar and Impo surely rank as some of the hardest additions of a talented 'Bolton team' in the 60s. Pasquill never quite forgot about the place though and added Rusty Wall in time to make the pink supplement of 1979, and in the early 80s he 'big-booted' his way up Hank's Wall to create a superb technical problem. In 1987 Mark Leach pointed the way to the future with a desperately hard crack-line on the Back Wall (Thunder) which had previously been tried by many able climbers.

Considerable development over the past few years has definitely brought Brownstones up to the minute in terms of both difficulty and quality, and considerably potential still remains...

POOL AREA

1. **Pondule**   2. The small arête on the right of the pool.

2. **Ponder**   4b. The crack just left.

3. **Pond Traverse**   5c. An excellent traverse. Start at the arête right of the pond and traverse the pond walls from right to left. Can be extended right round as far as Hernia.

4. **Riddle**   5c. From Piddle, traverse right for 10 feet and climb the wall above.

5. **Middle**   5c. Traverse right a few feet from Piddle and finish direct.

6. **Piddle**   5c. Climb the wall just right of the right-angled corner of the Pool Walls.

7. **The Corner**   5a. Traverse left from Pondule into the corner and finish up this.

8. **Splosh**   5c. The thin crack 8 feet left of the corner.

9. **Splish**   5a. Twin cracks in the wall on the left.

10. **Splash**   5b. The third crack past the corner.

11. **Wet Foot**   5a. A direct line 3 feet right of Watery Arête.

12. **Watery Arête**   4c. The left arête of the pond has a slippery start.

13. **Slab Variant**   2. The corner, slab and arête in sequence.

14. **Wet Corner**   3a. Straight up the initial corner of Slab Variant.

15. **Muddy Arête**   4b. The arête above fallen blocks.

16. **Muddy Wall**   4c. Climb the wall 5 feet left.

17. **Chockablock Corner**   3b. Up the corner which contains a jamming flake.

18. **The Mantelshelf** 2. Mantel onto a little platform, then climb the wall.

19. **Two Step** 4b. The wall on the left has 3 small ledges. Follow these right and finish on The Mantelshelf. 5c if the top is not used.

20. **Two Step Left-Hand** 5b. As Two Step but go left not right.

21. **Verdi Wall** 5a. Climb the short wall at a crack.

22. **Verdinand** 6a. The shallow groove in the wall left of the crack; use of the jug on the arête being illegal.

23. **Verdi Corner** 4a. The corner crack.

24. **Verdi Ramp** 4b. Left up the obvious scoop.

25. **Moss Wall** There are at least 4 ways up the wall on the left (4b to 5c).

26. **The Crack** 3a. The obvious crack.

27. **Slimer** 5b. The wall on the left.

28. **Hernia** 5a. The left end of the wall.

LONG BACK WALL
This is the long steep wall to the left of the easy descent route. The first route starts at a pedestal on the right. Unfortunately the routes here are somewhat neglected; the wall has its own fair share of vicious test-pieces and is similar in character to Craig Y Longridge, though not quite so steep and with heavily vegetated tops.

29. **Dave's Route** 5b. The corrugated wall is climbed via a crack-stepped wall.

30. **Hank** 5c. The stepped wall on the left (marked 15A).

31. **Black Wall** 5c. The steep crack (marked 19B).

32. **Rusty Wall** 6c. The wall on shallow pockets just right of Stop Butt.

33. **Stop Butt** 5c. Marked (16) on the wall.

34. **Butt End** 6a. From Knep climb the wall on the right.

35. **Knep** 5c. Marked (16a).

36. **Dave's Other Route** 5b. The crack with a small sentry box.

37. **The Slanter** 5c. Climbs twin cracks.

38. **Thunder** 6c. Desperate climbing up the thin crack in the wall right of Feintline.

39. **Feintline** 6a. The crack 4 feet right of Heartline.

40. **Heartline** 6a. Marked (16b).

41. **Hardline** 6a. The thin crack 10 feet left.

42. **Var** 5c. Marked (17).

43. **Lifeline** 6a. The feint crack 3 feet left.

44. **Knah** 5c. Marked (18).

45. **Traverse** 6b. Start 20 feet left of Knah and traverse right into that

route via an undercut flake. The traverse can be continued to Var.

46. **Impo** 6a. The big slanting crack is climbed to a niche.

47. **Crackle** 5a. The broken wall on the right of an overhang is climbed from right to left.

48. **Hangover** A1. The corner and roof.

49. **The Key** 5c. The crack on the left, marked (21).

50. **The Lock** 5c. The crack just left.

51. **Finger Crack** 5c. Climbs the green corner direct.

52. **Y Front** 4a. The right end of the wall, well marked.

53. **Tom** 5a. The middle of the steep wall.

54. **Jerry** 5a. The left side of the wall.

At this point a path leads round an arête at a higher level.

55. **Butch** 6a. A short problem whose fall potential is quite unnerving; climb the wall just right of the arête, stepping in from the left.

56. **Little Man** 4a. The first crack left of the arête.

57. **Crooked Crack** 4b. The next crack.

58. **Way Down** 4a. Marked (27).

59. **Vertigo** 4a. The next crack, which is marked (28).

60. **Inferno** 4c. Twin cracks and then a wall to finish.

61. **Dragnet** 4c. The next crack.

62. **Haskit** 5c. The forked cracks in the wall just left.

63. **Layback** 5a. Start just left of the forked cracks of Haskit and climb into a short niche and thus the top. Marked (32).

64. **Hank's Wall** 6c. A strict problem climbing the wall between Layback and Parr's Crack, avoiding holds on both those routes.

65. **Parr's Crack** 5c. The next crack and slight groove.

66. **Parabola** 5b. Follow the flake leftwards to its end, then arc back right across the wall on small holds to the top of Parr's Crack.

67. **Parabola Direct** 6a. Climb direct to the left end of the flake, and take the crack above by hard moves.

68. **The Chimney** 4c. The wide chimney crack at the corner.

69. **Wibble** 5a. The corner itself.

70. **Nexus** 4c. Excellent steep climbing up the wall on the left on good holds.

A pumpy low-level traverse is possible from Tom to Nexus (and further), in both directions; 6a.

ASH PIT SLABS
This is the name given to the rock to the left of the arête, and at a higher level.

71.   **Ash Pit Slab**   3a. Up the clean arête by a series of ledges.

72.   **Digitation**   5c. The centre of the slab left of Ash Pit Slab, with plenty of "you can't use that" and sometimes a sandy finish.

73.   **Ash Pit Traverse**   4c. From the ledge on Ash Pit Slab go left and gain the sloping slab below the overhang. At its end step down (crux) and continue left to easier ground.

74.   **Fraud**   5a. The slab between Digitation and Analog, using chipped holds.

75.   **Fraudulent Slip**   6a. As for Fraud but no chipped holds. Will someone please decide which holds are actually chipped and which aren't?

76.   **Analog**   4c. The next crack, just right of an overlap.

77.   **Directissima**   5c. The wall on the left, going over a small overlap. This route is getting much trickier as it gets more polished; a classic teaser.

78.   **Degree Crack**   5a. The crack on the left edge of the overlap, marked (43).

79.   **Scraper**   5b. Marked (44).

80.   **Hopper**   4c. Marked (45).

81.   **Corn Mantel**   5a. Marked (46).

82.   **Unjust**   6a. The blunt nose either using two small chipped holds or by a long reach for a poor pinch. Lonsdale rules apply to this problem.

83.   **Arur**   4b. The dirty crack right of the nose.

84.   **The Nose**   3c. Climb over the jutting prow from the left.

85.   **Rambler**   3a. Climb the little slab to a ledge, then right up the scoop above.

86.   **Climber and Rambler**   4a. Up the crack on the left to join Rambler.

87.   **Wall Climb**   5c. The wall on the left. Desperate if holds on the two adjacent routes are strictly avoided.

88.   **Noddy's Crack**   5c. The thin crack.

89.   **Apple**   4b. Dirty rock left of the wall.

90.   **The Thrutch**   3a. The isolated problem wall left of the main rocks.

BOTTOM END CLIMBS
The quarry rises slightly at this point, and the first routes are around the obvious sharp prow of rock.

91.   **Delicatessen**   4b. The small slab at the right side of the prow.

92.   **The Prow**   4c. The sharply-pointed prow is climbed on the left.

93.   **Halt**   4a. The crack left of the prow.

94.   **Blurt**   5a. Climb the blunt nose strenuously.

95.   **Blurt Variant**   5b. Start at a crack on the left and make a hard move, then move right to finish up Blurt.

96. Fineline 5c. The crack is climbed direct to the top avoiding the obvious easy cop-out leftwards.

97. Diane 3c. Climb the awkward corner.

98. Dezertion 6b. The undercut arête just left of the corner; short but very sharp!

99. Dezerit 5b. Around the arête is an undercut crack and tiny niche; Dezerit takes these.

100. Boopers 6a. The wall on the left, direct.

101. Beano 5c. The left arête is climbed via an awkward crack, and avoiding the large jug on the arête. Finish awkwardly.

102. Bitto 5c. Start up the left side of the wall and climb the thin horizontal crack to finish up Dezertion.

103. Grass Groove 2. The crack on the left.

104. Dezis Wall 4c. Start from a block and climb the wall direct.

105. Slab Direct 4a. Climb the exact centre of the slab to a ledge and broken wall above.

106. Tiptoe 4b. Traverse the slab from right to left (top must not be used) and continue to the far corner.

107. Short Corner 3a. The corner on the left.

108. Green Wall 5b. From a block 8ft left of the corner, climb the wall above.

109. Bunnies Dilemma 2. The broken, slanting groove on the wall left of the slab.

110. Obscenity 5b. From the foot of Bunnies Dilemma climb the wall of the slab.

111. Pocket Hole Wall 3b. Pass the pocket to reach the rib.

112. The Pock 5a. Traverse the wall low from Bunnies Dilemma to Pocket Hole Wall.

113. Magic Circle 4b. An eliminate line, but in horizontal format. Around the rib is a tiny amphitheatre of slabby rock. Starting at the right edge of this, traverse left without using the top for hands, to finish at the left arête; good fun.

114. Test Piece 5a. The clean overhanging block left of Magic Circle. Grasp the top and mantel, numerous variations being possible (backwards, etc).

115. Somersault 4c. Go directly over the jutting roof.

116. End Wall 3a. Up the final wall right of the crack.

117. End Crack 3a. Climb the crack direct.

118. Layback 3c. A short layback crack where the rocks end.

EGERTON QUARRY (SD 719 143)

By Geoff Hibbert and Mick Bullough

SITUATION AND CHARACTER

Egerton Quarry is considered by many to be a dark and esoteric crag, to be avoided at all costs. Those who do venture here, however, will find several routes which are the match of anything in the area in terms of quality.

In the past, copious vegetation and inaccurate route descriptions have meant that it was virtually impossible to locate some of the routes. This situation has now been rectified by extensive gardening and the painting of the initials of some routes at their base.

APPROACH AND ACCESS

Egerton Quarry is situated approximately four miles north of Bolton just off the A666 Bolton – Blackburn road. To reach the quarry, turn right off the A666 at the Egerton war memorial and continue along Darwen Road for about ¼ mile, until the Dunscar Arms is passed on the right. Turn left up the next side road (Arnold Road) and left again at The Flag public house. A steep hill is then ascended until the last houses on the left have been passed. Cars may be parked at the white gate on the left. The easiest way to enter the quarry is to follow the path past the white gate, which leads through undergrowth to a flat area next to Graffiti Wall and – farther along – to an archway leading into the quarry proper.

HISTORY

Sometime in the early 1970s, Hank Pasquill and friends visited Egerton Quarry (easily visible across the valley from Wilton, their usual haunt) and climbed a handful of routes. Records were not kept, however, and little is known of their activities. The first definite record of a first ascent belongs to Jim Fogg who paid a short visit a couple of years after Hank, and climbed Thin Crack. News of a potential guidebook supplement provided the necessary impetus, and the crag was rediscovered by Tony Preston in 1975. Tony climbed Dickies Meadow on the area of rock just right of Wood Buttress proper, a significant route, but something of a flanking attack, leaving the remaining possibilities for later.

Nigel Holmes, who was soon to become one of the prime movers in the race to develop the quarry, added Red Prow Original later in '75, and made the mistake of telling Dave Knighton about the place. Knighton was soon in the thick of things, ever hungry for new rock and new adventures – and there were plenty of those! Together, Knighton and Holmes spent many days in January 1976 clearing away the recent snows and loose rock from, and climbing, Amphitheatre Terrace, Windchill and Dust at Dusk, Holmes having previously climbed the perfect jamming crack of White Out with 'Shad' Makin.

The early part of 1976 saw Knighton and Holmes emerging from within the dark recesses behind the Red Prow, and they were drawn ever closer to the steep, almost virgin walls of Wood Buttress. First to fall was Zoot Chute round to the left of the wall, and then the race was on again, though this time with Ian Lonsdale to see who would get the first free ascent of Gallows Pole (won by Knighton). Ten Minutes Before The Worm was also climbed about this time and is still popular today, as was Esmerelda which is still distinctly unpopular. Wednesday Corner and Insipidity have suffered the same fate as Esmerelda and have only seen a handful of repeats so far.

Lonsdale smarted for some time after losing the race for Gallows Pole, but made up for it by following the Pilgrim's Progress and adding Chalk Lightning Crack, which Knighton had already top-roped, in preparation for a lead ascent. All these routes were documented in the 'pink' supplement of 1979, together with a couple of more minor routes, though as is common the post-guidebook period saw a rush for the obvious gaps; Dave Cronshaw climbed Cherry Bomb with Bob McMillan, and Holmes added two routes to the understandably-neglected Lonely Wall – Initiation and Nasty Little Lonely. Holmes then introduced a friend to the crag, Dai Lampard, and the development of the crag seemed to become some kind of a tortured obsession with these two. Ascents of Niff-Niff the Guinea Pig and Each Way Nudger were soon on the cards, soon to be followed by the cryptically named Nobody Wept For Alec Trench; a route that has taken some notable scalps in the past few years. Later that year Mick Johnson and his brother Ian fired off left from Ten Minutes Before the Worm and followed the left arête, a gem of a pitch which they named I shot Jason King. This route was somewhat superceded in 1987 when Mark Liptrot top-roped and then soloed the arête direct; an astoundingly serious route, smugly entitled I'm Alright Jack.

1984 saw Paul Pritchard and Phil Kelly take a day's holiday from their beloved Wilton, taking great delight in such an expanse of unclimbed rock, and climbing three new routes; Gnat Attack, Rhythm of the Heat and a poor route up the left arête of Lonsdale's Neighbourhood Threat. Pritchard returned a few weeks later with Andy Gridley to climb Gnat Attack by a slightly more direct line, though this created an even poorer alternative!

Geoff Hibbert now began his protracted campaign to fill in the remaining gaps in the quarry; during 1985 he climbed One Minute To Midnight and the cryptically-named No Screws in Skem (both with Nigel Holmes), and a diagonal traverse across Wood Buttress, The Disappearing Chip Buttie Traverse (with Mick Bradshaw), whilst some unknown climbers made ammends for the deliberate mistake in the 1983 guidebook by following the line shown as Niff-Niff on the diagram; the resultant route is now suitably called Naff-Naff (The Route).

In 1986 Hibbert really set about the quarry with a vengeance, desperate for new routes, but before he could get a look in that year, Màrk Liptrot had climbed two lines up the buttress just left of Esmerelda: Eleventh Hour and Mumbled Prayer, and these were soon followed by Dicktrot II: The Movie. Geoff restarted his campaign with Lucky Heather ("a baby brother to Alec Trench") and Mental Mantel, which was dried with a blow-torch before the ascent. A few weeks later he again demonstrated a penchant for routes bordering on the lunatic when – after climbing Don't Stop Believing on sight – he forced a direct line over the compelling rock formation on top of Red Prow, Acme Surplus Overhang. As a complete contrast to Acme Surplus, and following a few day's attempts, Christmas Eve 1986 saw Geoff finally succeed on the sickle-shaped feature in the smooth wall just right of Zoot Chute, which had provisionally been named the 'Egerton Exam' and had seen many attempts from the very able John Monks some years earlier. This route – The Reaper – is still unrepeated at the time of writing, though not without attempts by some very strong teams.

As a climax to the work into this guide, Hibbert explored the Phantom Zone area, adding a couple of heart-stoppers, and developed the wall below Amphitheatre Terrace, climbing several short but worthwhile problems; Fathomathon, Bob Bandits and Brittle Fingers.

GRAFFITI WALL
This is the wall, shattered in its upper reaches, on the war memorial side of the road. The first route of any note is situated behind the pool at the left side of some derelict sheds.

1. **Pilgrim's Progress** 50ft VS   *
4c. Start just right of an arête, on a small grass ledge. Up the wall to a situ wire sling below the final overhang, then swing left round the arête and finish diagonally left.

The walls further left offer good bouldering and a good sustained low-level traverse at 6a, but no routes have been recorded.

BRIDGE AREA
This comprises the rock under and on both sides of the bridge. The right wall is described first.

2. **Broken Toe** 30ft Hard VS
5a. Climbs the obvious thin crack in the middle of the red wall.

3. **Thin Crack** 30ft Hard Sev
4b. The obvious overhanging crack past an iron spike.

4. **Markova** 30ft Sev
The crack on the left, finishing right.

5. **Cleft Climb** 30ft Hard Sev
4a. Climb the cleft, finishing right up the climbing wall.

6. **Bridge Crack** 40ft VS
4c. Climb the obvious jamming crack to the roof, then traverse left to finish.

7. **Twilight Crack** 30ft Sev
The crack 15 feet left.

8. **Just Out** 30ft Sev
The blunt arête just left.

9. **Ludwig** 30ft V Diff
The obvious stepped line on the wall to the left.

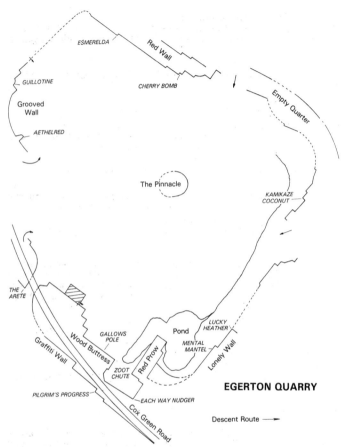

The next routes start on the left wall facing Thin Crack.

10. **Colgy** 30ft Hard Sev
4b. The crack just left of The Arête.

11. **The Arête** 20ft VS
5b. The problem arête on the right.

12. **Wide Crack** 25ft V Diff
The crack on the right.

13. **The Nose** 25ft VS
4c. Climb direct to an old 'telephone thing', then step right to finish.

14. **Hydrophobia** 35ft Hard VS
5a. Twenty-five feet right of The Nose past a red scar is a black wall. Start just right of a crack and climb the wall direct, trending right to finish.

15. **Rabid** 35ft Hard VS
5a. Start 15 feet right, below an iron spike. Climb leftwards past this to finish as for Hydrophobia.

16. **No Screws in Skem** 35ft E1   †
5b. Climbs the wall direct from the iron spike.

17. **Black Dog** 35ft E1   *
5c. Start 10 feet right by a crack on the arête. Climb this for 20 feet, then move left and finish up the thin crack above.

18. **The Beauty of Poison** 35ft E1   †
5a. The shattered crack immediately right of Black Dog.

19. **Ceremony** 35ft VS   **
4c. Start 10 feet right at the right side of a small overlap, and climb the thin crack direct to the top past hidden jugs. Worthwhile.

20. **Green Thoughts** 30ft Hard Sev
4a. Climb the crack 8 feet right, passing a red scar at mid-height.

WOOD BUTTRESS AREA
This is undoubtedly the best section of rock in the quarry, and is somewhat reminiscent of Chimney Buttress at Wilton. It is the large buttress about 40 yards left of the far side of the bridge, which starts at a much lower level. However the first route starts at the higher level, by an iron spike in the ground.

21. **Neighbourhood Threat** 35ft Hard VS
5a. Step left onto the wall and climb the cleaned flake (PR).

The next route starts at a lower level.

22. **Shakey Flakes** 20ft Sev
Climb the right side of the short wall below and right of Neighbourhood Threat.

23. **Dicktrot** 25ft E1
5c. Climb the thin crack on the left to a pod finish.

A contrived line (**Temptation: 6b**) is possible between Dickies Meadow and the right arête at 6b, whilst the right arête itself has been climbed on its right-hand side with runners in Neighbourhood Threat; **The Lamb Lies Down on Broadway (E4 6a)**.

24. **Dickies Meadow** 55ft Hard Sev
4a. Climbs the obvious corner, just left of the arête.

25. **Insipidity** 50ft VS   *
4c. Up the short corner on the left, then step left and climb the impressive corner groove, moving left to the arête to finish.

26. **One Minute to Midnight** 50ft E3   * †
5c. Climbs the technical lower arête, left of Insipidity, to the ledge then follows the slightly easier (but less well protected) upper arête to the

top.

27. Wednesday Corner 50ft VS   *
4b. Climb the long corner groove, moving right at the top to finish.

28. Bag of Bones 50ft Hard VS
4c. The obvious crackline which starts from ledges just left of Wednesday Corner.

29. Naff-Naff (The Route) 55ft E2   †
5b. Climbs the crack between Bag of Bones and Niff Niff.

30. Niff-Niff the Guinea Pig 55ft E2
5b. Climb the wall/crack just right of Gallows Pole.

31. Gallows Pole 55ft Hard VS   **
5a. Start directly beneath a wooden sleeper which overlaps the top of the crag, and follow a vague crackline to finish just left of the pole.

32. The Disappearing Chip Buttie Traverse 95ft E1   **
A rising right to left traverse across Wood Buttress.
5b. Start just left of Wednesday Corner, move up and traverse diagonally left to a PR, continue towards a second PR (in God Save the Queen), move left and climb up for a few feet to an exit left along a stiff finger traverse into Ten Minutes Before the Worm. Finish as that route.

33. God Save the Queen 55ft Hard VS   *
5a. Start 12 feet further left and follow a crackline to the top.

34. Ten Minutes Before the Worm 65ft VS   *
4c. Follow God Save the Queen for 15 feet, then follow an obvious line of ledges which lead to a niche. Move past a PR to the arête, then back right to finish. A direct start is possible at 5b.

35. I'm Alright Jack 60ft E5   ** †
6a. Excellent climbing up the terminal left arête of the buttress, easing in its upper reaches. The initial crux section can be avoided by gaining the arête via a leftwards traverse from Ten Minutes Before the Worm, at 15 feet; I Shot Jason King (E2 5b).

36. The Reaper 50ft E5   *** †
6c. Another excellent route climbing the wall right of Zoot Chute direct to a PR, move right to gain a vague groove then desperate moves up the thin slab above lead to a welcome ledge, and a finish up Zoot Chute, PR.

37. Zoot Chute 50ft VS   *
4b. Climb the recessed slab and the wall above (PR).

38. Windchill 35ft Hard Sev
4b. Climb the short corner on the left, then step right to a green groove, and up this to an awkward exit.

39. Amphitheatre Terrace 70ft V Diff
The obvious terrace which splits the back wall from right to left.

40. Life During Wartime 60ft Hard VS
5b. Follow Amphitheatre Terrace to the grassy bay (old PR), then climb up and right on large holds until a traverse right can be made to the

base of a thin crack. Finish up this.

41. **Bob Bandits** 25ft E2
5b. Climb the obvious off-width crack in the wall left of the start of Amphitheatre Terrace.

42. **Fathomathon** 25ft E2
5b. Start just left and climb the wall to a good though doubtful jug, then make an 'all-out-mega-span' and climb direct to join Amphitheatre Terrace.

43. **Brittle-Fingers** 40ft E1
5b. Left again, climb the crack to gain the bottomless groove. Pass this and finish up the arête above on its left-hand side.

44. **Each Way Nudger** 40ft E3   **
6b. The overhung corner on the left. Desperate bridging moves lead to a long, blind reach over a bulge and then to easier ground.

45. **Dust at Dusk** 40ft Sev
Climb the left corner at the back of the amphitheatre.

46. **White Out** 40ft Hard Sev   **
4b. The wide crack on the left.

RED PROW
This is the obvious sandy prow of rock with a pool on three sides, and a 'roadrunner-style' pinnacle on its top.

47. **Ice Cool Acid Test** 45ft E4   ***
6a. Superb wall climbing to the left of White Out. Climb the middle of the wall to a large ledge at 10 feet, then traverse left for a few feet and climb straight up the exposed wall, passing a peg at ⅔ height.

48. **Nobody Wept for Alec Trench** 45ft E5   ***
6a. Undoubtedly the centrepiece of the quarry, and one of the finest arêtes on gritstone. Ascend the striking arête starting on the right, past 2 PRs of dubious worth, to a thrilling finish on sloping holds.

49. **Chalk Lightning Crack** 50ft E2   ***
5b. A classic thrutch-and-grope up the off-width crack splitting the buttress. Good protection but still a thought-provoking lead.

50. **Don't Stop Believing** 50ft E2   †
5c. Start just left of Chalk Lightning and climb a short wall to a crack. Up this to a sloping mantelshelf (crux) and break above (Friends). Attack the wall above, trending right at the top.

51. **Gnat Attack** 40ft VS   †
4c. Gain and climb the left-hand of two hanging grooves, either direct, or from easy rock on the left.

52. **Rhythm of the Heat** 25ft E1   †
5c. Situated above the ledge on the end of the prow; climb easily up stepped rock just left of Gnat Attack onto the ledge, then take the dogleg crack in the wall above, continuing direct where the crack sneaks off left.

53. **Acme Surplus Overhang** 20ft E2   †
A route which completely encompasses the full spectrum of fear.

5a. The roadrunner-pinnacle type roof on the top of Red Prow; to second is not to have lived!

54. **Stringbiff** 120ft VS †
4c. Climb the two left arêtes on the end of the Red Prow, to finish up the easy ramp left of the previous route.

55. **Red Prow Original** 70ft VS
4b. Situated round the back of the Red Prow. When the pool is full the start can be reached by abseil. Start in the corner and climb a rib to a thin crack, then follow this to a ledge. Step right and up the crack above to a ledge and large blocks, then finish easily up a ramp on the left.

LONELY WALL
Farther left, around the back of the pool, begins another long wall, with much rock that is obviously less than perfect. One or two of the routes are well worth doing, however.

56. **Initiation** 45ft Hard VS *
5b. Climb the obvious crack which splits the smooth, grey wall on the right.

57. **Mental Mantel** 55ft E2 †
5b. Left of Initiation is an obvious clean slab; climb this to a difficult mantelshelf onto sloping ledges. Step left, around the corner and finish up the short jamming crack just right of the corner.

58. **Nasty Little Lonely** 60ft Hard VS
4b. From the left side of Lonely Wall climb the loose pillars just right of a smooth red wall. Pass a PR to a disintegrating ledge, then an obvious traverse left leads to a fine finish up a groove. Serious.

59. **Lucky Heather** 30ft E3 ** †
5c. A baby brother to Alec Trench, but if possible less well protected! It consists of a series of boulder-problem type moves up the left side of the left arête of the wall, to a (heather) gripping finish.

60. **Cholera** 25ft Hard VS * †
5a. Thirty yards left of Lucky Heather and climb the off-width crack to a sloping mantelshelf finish.

EMPTY QUARTER
One hundred yards left of Lucky Heather, past an easy descent slope, the rock arcs back left; the Empty Quarter is formed by two tiers of rock – the Upper Tier is only suitable for bouldering, whilst the Lower Tier offers some good climbing.

LOWER TIER

61. **Kamikaze Coconut** 30ft Hard Sev
4b. The prominent corner near the right side of the wall.

62. **Space Between my Ears** 40ft Hard Sev
4a. The conspicuous arête 35 feet left. Climb the crack on the right of the arête, then finish on the left using a large detached flake.

63. **Return of the Native** 30ft E1
5c. A problem start at the right of the wall, just left of a black streak,

leads to easier ground above.

64. Phantom Zone 30ft E2   ★★
5c. The steep Phantom wall of the Empty Quarter is climbed up the middle via a hairline crack to reach good finger jams at mid-height, with the crux layback to finish.

65. Phantom Zone – Left-Hand 35ft E3   ★★
6a. Climb Phantom Zone to an obvious traverse line leftwards. Play the piano leftwards until a C-major chord enables vertical progress to be made.

UPPER TIER

66. Cancer 30ft VS   †
Climbs the wall above Phantom Zone, to finish up the chimney.

67. Dribbles 35ft Hard VS   †
5b. The thin crack by the blue paint streaks, to finish on poor rock.

RED WALL
Back in the floor of the quarry, the rock which stretches left into the corner is called Red Wall. This begins as a series of impressive arêtes and corners:

68. Red Shift 40ft VS
4c. Start just right of the blunt arête, by a block and climb the shallow groove. Finish via a flake on the left.

69. Cherry Bomb 45ft VS   ★★★
4c. An excellent route, climbing the blatantly obvious corner capped by an overhang.

70. Satin Sapphire 45ft E3   ★★
5c. The fine arête to the left of Cherry Bomb is climbed in its entirety; a serious and sustained route of great quality.

71. Malvinas 50ft Hard Sev
4b. Start 50 feet left of Satin Sapphire, and climb the wall into the obvious leaning corner.

72. Desert Dust 50ft Hard Sev
4b. Twenty-five feet right of 'Phantom' is a corner, climb this until a wide crack is reached and finish up this.

73. Dizzy the Desert Snake 50ft Hard VS
5a. Start 15 feet right of 'Phantom'. Use a jug on the left to gain access to a crackline and follow this to a large platform. Finish up the crack on the right.

74. Why Climb Right? 50ft Hard V Diff
The slabby wall between 'Chopper' and 'Phantom' daubed on the rock. Start in the middle of the rubble cone and mantel at 7 feet, then traverse right to finish.

75. Esmeralda 50ft Hard VS
5a. Fifteen yards left are some obvious cracks in a red wall. Climb the right crack and finish up a short corner. Belays well back.

Left of Esmeralda is a second wide crack, and then three obvious lines up a steep wall:

76. The Eleventh Hour 60ft E3   †
6a. The right-hand line.

77. Mumbled Prayer 60ft E5   †
6a. The central line.

78. Dicktrot II – The Movie 60ft E3   †
5c. The left-hand line.

GROOVED WALL
The final section of rock arcs back towards the Bridge Area. For the most part the rock is of poor quality, however at the right side are two very prominent corners.

79. Sham '69 50ft VS   ★★
4c. Climbs the obvious corner by excellent hand jams, just left of the grey gravel banking.

80. That's Life 50ft Hard VS
5a. The next corner on the left.

81. Guillotine 50ft E1   ★★
5b. Jam the V-shaped groove up to the wedged block.

82. Trumpton 45ft Sev
Start 40 feet right of where the crag ends, at a corner with a crack/chimney in it. Climb the crack, then step left over the slab and finish up the corner with a small tree at its top.

83. The Creaking Fossil 45ft Hard VS   †
4c. Climb the wall right of Aethelred to an overlap, over this to finish

84. Aethelred 45ft E2   ★
5b. Climb the unprotectable arête just left of Trumpton.

LESTER MILL QUARRY (SD 619 164)

By Dave Sanderson

SITUATION AND CHARACTER
The quarry is on the opposite side of the Rivington – White Coppice road to Anglezarke Quarry and is a working of the same rock series, but at a lower level. As this quarry was worked up until the 1930's and does not see a lot of activity, some suspect rock is present, but this is localised and should improve with traffic. Special care should be taken with Cheese Buttress, The Set Back and the Upper Tier.

APPROACH
The approach is as for Anglezarke Quarry, except that from the water board car parks on the steep hill, a path leads through a kissing gate at the bottom end, and down towards the reservoir. The path passes the quarry entrance (on the right) and Introductory Bay is the first rock to be encountered, and by following the path, Evil Wall is soon encountered.

HISTORY

Lester Mill Quarry ceased to be worked in the 1930's and previous to this stone was taken (along with Anglezarke) to pave the city of Salford. The quarry's name derives from Robert Lester, who once owned a small mill that stood nearby and in fact this quarry and Anglezarke were collectively known as Lester's Mill Quarries.

Much of the early development is still locked securely away in the memories of the participants and consequently is not available to the general climbing public. Some of what is known follows, but the early history is very sketchy and much of it is 'clutching at straws'; further details of the early history would be welcomed, but in the meantime we can only apologise if mistakes are made.

The earliest known route is the classic arête of Lester Rib which was climbed in the early 1960's and was part of the first wave of development led by John Bennison, Arthur Hassall, Walt Unsworth and Bev Heslop. During this period an educational report known as the Newsom Report was published and as most of the aforementioned climbers were teachers, they were soon acting on its recommendations in taking pupils out of the classrooms to give 'instruction through experience', and one of their early routes was called Newsom Slab.

John was working at Southland's School and visited the quarry one afternoon a week with his students and added such routes as Southland's Scoop, Introductory Crack, Caerphilly, Small Oak Crack, Lester Corner. Arthur climbed Blossom with one peg and Stilton and Cheddar were both pegged by unknown climbers.

Later, towards the end of the decade (and into the next), Les Ainsworth and Brian Cropper were active and the Upper Buttress was developed. The first route on Evil Wall was Dooms Day which was climbed by Graham Rigby and Bernie Bradbury and then next came Pagan and Dave Walsh's Heretic, up the right-hand side of the wall. The main section of the wall remained untouched however, mainly due to its oft-wet character, though this problem was soon to be resolved; in 1982 Ian Lonsdale persuaded the N.W.W.A. to divert the drainage away from the face, and so the stream was directed elsewhere. The result was a complete success and the wall dried out totally, paving the way for Ian and Dave Cronshaw to make incursions onto the wall the following year, to produce a series of excellent routes. Dave added a direct start to Mixed Veg with John Ryden, Brian Cropper having free-climbed the original route solo, about two years previously and also added The Rurper. Dave continued with The Beast, Return To Fantasy and Non-Stop Screamer (with various seconds) and Ian climbed Evil Crystal with Dave Knighton which was given the much-feared grade of 5b by Lonsdale.

INTRODUCTORY BAY

This can be identified at first sight by a sharp arête at the base of a conical-shaped banking and the leaning wall of Stilton.

1. **Introductory Crack** 35ft V Diff
Where the rocks first gain a respectable height is a broken crack, follow this and the rib above.

2.   Southland's Scoop   50ft   Sev
A deep scoop 15 feet left. Climb to a big grass ledge, then up the wall, working right into a broken crack to the top. Or climb direct to the top from the scoop at Hard Severe.

3.   Stilton   40ft   Hard VS
5b. The crack 10 feet left of the scoop, to the ledge, then finish up the short wall above.

4.   Blue Stilton   50ft   E1
5c. Start as for Stilton and traverse the thin peg-marked crack leftwards into Double Gloucester. Finish as for that route.

5.   Double Gloucester   40ft   Hard VS
5a. Climb the crack in the leaning wall 6 feet left to reach the large ledge, then finish as Stilton.

6.   Caerphilly   40ft   VS
4b. The broken groove on the left to an obvious dob, then right to the ledge and finish as Stilton.

7.   Flake Wall   50ft   VS   ★
4c. This is the short wall at right angles to the previous climbs, and facing the quarry entrance. Start at the left arête and go slightly right to gain a detached flake above a horizontal crack. Go right then left to gain a ledge (on Blossom). Climb the steep wall above. PRs.

8.   Flakey Pastry   30ft   VS
4c. A direct line up the wall just right of Flake Wall's start. Unprotected.

9.   Blossom   45ft   Hard VS
5a. The gully on the left. From a ledge climb the right wall of the gully.

LESTER BUTTRESS
This is the next buttress, at the other side of the conical banking. A small ledge at 10 feet running out from the banking marks the start to the first route.

10.   Jughandle Wall   20ft   VS
4b. Climb up the centre of the small wall just left of the grassy banking.

11.   Small Oak Crack   30ft   Hard Sev
A wide crack with jammed blocks and an oak tree at its top, just beyond the grassy hummock.

12.   Lester Corner   25ft   V Diff
Start as for Lester Rib, but go right using a flake, into the corner and up this to a grass ledge. Scrappy.

13.   Sleeping Geenie   45ft   VS
4c. Climb Lester Corner to the flake, then go directly up the overhanging wall to a niche and then finish up the slabby wall above.

14.   Lester Rib   50ft   Hard V Diff   ★
At the end of the wall climb the rib and short corner above.

15.   Lester Eliminate   45ft   VS   ★
4c. Start just round the rib and climb past two overhangs into a hanging crack which leads to the top.

16. **Wirebrush Crack** 35ft VS
4c. The crackline 10 feet left.

17. **Newsom Slab** 30ft Hard Sev   *
4b. At right-angles is a steep, grey slab. Use the thin finger crack to climb the slab until a step right can be made. Step up then go left on good finishing holds.

CHEESE BUTTRESS
Left of Newsom Slab is a short break, before the next buttress, which is split by a large ledge at 20 feet, with an obvious flake on its left.

18. **Pinnacle Route** 40ft Sev
Climb the flake by its left edge and then the short wall above to finish.

19. **Left Twin Groove** 40ft V Diff
The right-hand groove next to the flake.

20. **Right Twin Groove** 40ft Sev
The left-hand groove, then step left and up a short crack to finish.

21. **Whip Me! Whip Me!** 30ft V Diff
From the top of the grass-covered rubble cone, just around the next corner, climb the broken crack. An experience in unbridled masochism.

22. **Klink** 40ft Hard Sev
4a. This route takes the major crack which starts at the bottom left side of the cone. Top is loose.

23. **Lancashire Crumbly** 45ft Hard Sev
4a. Start 4 feet left and climb the slab via a scoop direct to a ledge. Step right and climb the upper crack of Klink to a ledge, then finish up an arête.

24. **Cheese Spread** 50ft Sev
Up the centre of the wall on the left to the second ledge, then traverse right 12 feet from the top to a poor finish, as for Klink.

25. **Wensleydale** 50ft Sev
The corner direct.

26. **Bat Out of Hell** 45ft VS
4c. Start just left of the corner, and finish up the obvious slanting chimney above.

27. **Delta Dawn** 50ft VS
4b. Start at the next crack left and trend left, then back right to a flake and finish as for Bat Out of Hell.

28. **Big Eyed Beans from Venus** 40ft VS
4c. Fifteen feet left of the corner is a slanting chimney groove at the top. Starting at 'TG' chipped on the rock, climb direct to this groove, then to the top.

29. **Forte Dicks** 40ft E2   †
5c. Start at a crack just left of where 'TG' is chipped in the rock. Climb the crack to a ledge and then climb direct to the top using the

continuation crack in the wall. From the top ledge, finish up a short crack.

30. Neon Shuffle 25ft   VS
4c. The left arête direct.

THE SET BACK
This is the name given to the area of rock on the left, which is set back a little.

31. P.C.2 25ft   Hard VS   ★
5b. The thin crack 8 feet left of the arête, direct.

32. Fool's Paradise 25ft   Sev
The major groove 5 feet left which contains a loose spike. Climb 15 feet to a ledge, then finish up a short wall.

33. The Other Man's Alternative 30ft   Sev
Climb the next crack to a ledge. Traverse 10 feet right and finish up a short corner.

34. Juggernaut 30ft   VS
4b. Climb a pedestal and wall to a break, then ascend the buttress above via a niche on the face and finish direct. Poor protection on the crux.

35. Hit by a Lorry 45ft   Hard Sev
4a. Climb to the break on Juggernaut, then traverse 15 feet left and finish up a loose corner.

36. Resolute Roc 30ft   VS   ★
4b. The flake crack 8 feet left is followed to a break, then climb the steep wall above using a crack to finish.

37. Moorland Tooth Highway 25ft   Hard Sev
4a. Climb the crack on the right of a detached tooth to a break, then finish up the corner. Loose.

38. Gully Climb 35ft   V Diff
Climb the corner on the left of the previous route, trending leftwards.

39. Mythical Madonna 35ft   VS   ★
4c. Left is a prominent rib with a large block on it. Climb the corner crack on the right side of this (loose) to a hard finish direct up a crack in the nose.

40. Las Vegas Turnaround
On the other side of the rib is a crack. Climb this and the corner on its left.

41. Red Leicester 35ft   Hard Sev
4a. The steep crack in the narrow wall just left.

42. Lead Penguin 35ft   Hard Sev
The next arête direct, PR (not in situ).

The wall immediately left contains the next routes:

43. The Blimp 35ft   Hard VS
5a. The thin crack 4 feet left of the arête.

44. Mirror Man 30ft Hard VS
5a. Climbs the wall just left of The Blimp, on small flakes.

45. Woolly Bully 30ft Hard V Diff
From the corner a flake crack leads easily right. Loose.

On the left is an orange wall containing a very prominent flake crack at its left-hand end. This flake crack is taken by Brian's Route.

46. Black Betrayal 40ft Hard Sev
The thinner flake crack 6 feet right of Brian's Route, finishing as for that route.

47. Brian's Route 35ft VS
The prominent wide flake crack.

UPPER RIGHT TIER
This wall is the upper tier of Evil Wall. The first route takes the blunt arête immediately left of Brian's Route.

48. Blue Tile 35ft Hard VS
5a. Start up the arête just left, then climb to a small ledge and finish up the arête (PR – not in situ).

49. Walk Up 30ft Sev
Climb the flake just left, and finish direct.

50. 10 Metre Crack 35ft VS
Six feet left is an open corner with a thin flake crack in it. Climb the flake to the top.

51. On Reflection 35ft VS
4c. Start at the arête, eight feet left, where the path begins to narrow, and climb it direct to a poor finish.

52. Kentaxnip 35ft VS
5a. Climb the next corner to a ledge and dob at half-height, then up the groove to the top.

53. Barnstorm 35ft VS
4c. The next arête direct (PR).

54. Grit Salad Surgery 40ft Hard VS
5b. Up the flake just left of the arête, then traverse left and up the overhang to the top.

EVIL WALL
In the middle of the quarry below the Upper Right Tier, is a huge shattered wall at a much lower level, which is named Evil Wall. At the right corner is:

55. The Corner 50ft Hard Sev
The corner with a tree at mid-height.

56.   Heretic   70ft   Hard VS   ★
5b. Follow The Corner, then step left just below the tree and ascend a crack to a ledge. Continue direct up the wall on small holds (PR).

57.   Pagan   70ft   E1   ★
5b. Start 10 feet left of Heretic. Move round the overhang on good holds and up to a situ PR, then continue to a higher horizontal break and traverse left to a good resting ledge. Up right to another ledge and climb a crack to the top of a huge flake. The thin crack above leads with increasing difficulty (PR) to the top.

58.   Mixed Veg   80ft   Hard VS
5b. Just right of an overhanging groove is a block overhang. Climb this using a thin crack, to a ledge on the left. Move up to a second ledge, then step left and climb the corner crack above to finish. **Direct Start** (Hard VS 5b): Climb the overhanging groove direct to the corner.

59.   Evil Crystal   70ft   E1   ★
Start 20 feet left, below a niche/cave. Better done in one pitch.
(1)   30ft 5b.   Up the flake crack until it peters out, and continue to a poor stance in a cave.
(2)   40ft 4c.   Follow the crack on the left to a ledge, then up the wall (PR) and climb flakes to the top.

60.   The Beast   85ft   E3   ★★
6a. Start just left of Evil Crystal. Climb up to the overhang and traverse left to a small ledge. Gain the niche above with difficulty and finish direct to a small tree.

61.   Escharchado   70ft   E3   ★
5c. Fifteen feet left is a flake crack. Climb this to a break at half height, then climb the groove above to a small overhang 10 feet from the top. Move up and left to finish. Two situ PRs.

62.   Non-Stop Screamer   75ft   E2   ★
5b. Start 20 feet left of Escharchado and climb blocks and a thin crack to gain a groove. Follow the groove to a sloping ledge on the left and finish up a short wall.

63.   The Rurper   80ft   Hard A2   †
Just right of Return to Fantasy is an old ring peg below an overhang. Start here and follow a thin crackline to the overhang. Peg over this and then the wall above (13 pegs, 3 rurps).

64.   Return to Fantasy   70ft   E2   ★
5c. Start in the corner on the left with a sloping ledge at 15 feet. Climb the corner to the ledge and gain the crack above. Follow this with increasing difficulty to the top.

65.   Dooms Day   75ft   VS   ★
5a. The route takes the obvious large corner which rises from the large sloping ledge. Gain the ledge (possible belay) and climb the corner. At the very top, exit left. Descend by abseil from BB rather than face the horrible scramble off right.

66.   Gorgonzola   30ft   VS

4c. Climb the crackline just right of Jane's Route to finish up a short corner.

67.   **Jane's Route**   35ft   E1
5b. At the extreme left of Evil Wall is a small buttress with a prow-shaped overhang in its centre, start below this. Climb the crack below the overhang to a sapling, then pull up to good holds. Finish direct. PR.

On the left side of the next bay are some short easy climbs and a traverse.

OUSELL'S NEST (SD 731 142)

By Geoff Hibbert

APPROACH AND ACCESS
The easiest approach is from the A666 at Dunscar war memorial. Follow the B6472 towards Bromley Cross and turn left past Bromley Cross railway station (on Bolton – Blackburn line), immediately before a railway bridge. Follow this road (Chapeltown Road) for ¾ of a mile to Prospect Hill Cottages on the left. Turn right here and down to a parking area. On foot now, follow the path down from the car park and down into the quarry

SITUATION AND CHARACTER
The quarry offers good climbing in a very pleasant situation. The pool at the base of the crag disappears during summer and this makes access much easier. When walking across lush green fields to the rock face, an obvious boiler-plate slab will be seen on the extreme right, bounding the main wall on the left by a grassy corner. The first route starts 15 feet left of this corner.

HISTORY
Ancient pegs greeted Carl Dawson and John Spencer when they 'discovered' Ousell's Nest on New Year's Day in 1968. John returned later with Steve Jones and this pair ascended and named Hogmanay Slab, though it is now obvious that Jim Fogg and many others had in fact climbed it prior to this pair. Jones himself had paid an earlier, forgotten visit to the crag and had climbed a line over on the right-hand side of the crag called The Peeler, though no details are available. Spencer teamed up with Phil Bond that April and climbed a route which they named Freak-Out, though this is now known as Metropolis.

In May, Spencer and Dawson finally managed to entice the Wilton lads over to Ousell's, telling them tales of 75-foot overhanging walls, clean grooves and soaring arêtes. Amongst that team was Hank Pasquill, who left a calling card in the shape of The Crucifix, which retains its two points of aid to this day. Ian Lonsdale climbed Resurrection over on the right-hand extremity of the main wall, whilst 'Little Sid' Siddiqui cleaned the wall just to its left, which Nick Colton inadvertently pinched and called Sorry Sid. Dave Grimshaw climbed Please Ring the Plumber later that year and his brother Pete added two routes in the shape of Earwig and Anarchy. Sid meanwhile followed Paul Cropper up Angel Delight and thus things remained until Geoff Hibbert began to explore the untapped potential of the crag in 1985.

Beginning with Wiggerley Worm, Geoff began to systematically work through all the remaining gaps, in May adding Pigeon Toad Orange Peel, then the 'big cherry' at the crag and later succeeded on Prayer Battery, with Mick Bradshaw, though Dave Williams joined in the fun for a direct line up Hogmanay Slab, entitled Chasing Rainbows.

In 1986, Mark Liptrot paid a short visit and happened to encounter Hibbert at the crag. Eliciting some information from Geoff, he later used it for his own gain (naughty). Firstly he repeated Pigeon Toad Orange Peel, describing it as 'hard', then he broke out left from that route to create the fine and aptly-named A Thief in the Night. His other routes included Exile and The Kingdom, Mr & Mrs Liptrot go to the Seaside and a girdle of the left-hand section of the main wall – The Hollow Men.

MAIN WALL
THE ROUTES on the Main Wall are described from RIGHT to LEFT.

1. **Captain Hookleg**   35ft   Hard VS
5a. Climb direct past the tree stump and follow thin crack above to big ledges.

2. **Resurrection**   35ft   Hard VS   *
5a. Climbs the obvious crack just left of a tree stump in the rock 8 feet above the ground.

3. **Sorry Sid**   35ft   Hard VS
5a. Start 10 feet left in an overhung niche and climb direct, stepping right at three-quarters-height, then finish direct.

4. **Angel's Kiss**   35ft   E2
5a. The unprotected off-width crack 3 feet left.

5. **Wiggerley Worm**   35ft   Hard VS
5a. Start a few feet right of Please Ring the Plumber, at an obvious crack, and climb this.

6. **Please Ring the Plumber**   30ft   VS
4c. The often-damp groove just right of the point at which the trees finish.

7. **The Red Rose**   30ft   E2
5b. A few feet left, climb twin cracks to the wide upper crack. Layback this to the top.

8. Lace 30ft Hard VS
5a. Ten feet left, past a blank slab is a crack. Climb this in its entirety.

9. Gauntlet Route 35ft E3 **★★**
5c. Left again is a deceptively-easy looking groove; climb this and the overhanging crack above to finish on good jugs. Strenuous.

10. The Prayer Battery 35ft E3
5c. Climb the groove just left of Gauntlet Route, past suspect blocks (exciting).

11. The Angel of Death 35ft Hard VS **★**
5a. Climbs the clean groove, which is gained by an awkward start and step right.

12. Angel Delight 35ft Hard VS
5b. Start as for The Angel of Death but continue direct.

13. Mr & Mrs Liptrot Go to the Seaside 35ft E4
6a. Climb the wall and crackline just left of Angel Delight. A crucial hold has fallen off the lower section, though the route can now be started from Angel Delight. Very sustained.

14. Pigeon Toad Orange Peel 50ft E5 **★★★**
6a. The thin crack in the overhanging wall is climbed to the overlap by a series of increasingly technical and strenuous moves. Finish on the left.

15. A Thief in the Night 40ft E4 **★★**
6b. This aptly-named route climbs the crackline just left of Pigeon Toad Orange Peel. Start as for that route and gain the crack on the left (PR) and follow it to the top.

16. The Crucifix 35ft E2 (2 pegs for aid) **★ †**
5c. This route takes the three bands of overhangs at its right side. Start 30 feet left of Angel Delight, just right of a blank groove which leads to the first small roof. Use 2 PA's in a faint crackline to gain a hold on the left, then swing round on this and layback round the first roof. Make a hard move to pass the second roof, then gain the small ledge above and finish direct. Good thread belay.

17. Exile and the Kingdom 40ft E4 **★★ †**
6b. The hanging corner left of The Crucifix.

18. The Last Supper 40ft Hard VS
5a. Start 20 feet left at the base of a blocky groove that splits the overhangs. Pull over the overhang and move left to gain a good hold over the second roof, then traverse left into a shallow groove and step left into a grassy corner which is followed to the top.

19. Gemime Puddleduck 55ft E1
Start as for The Last Supper, but continue straight up the blocky groove until above the large roof on the right a traverse right can be made above the overhang to a flake. Up the flake, then step right and finish up the rib.

20. The Hollow Men 90ft E3
6a. A high left-to-right traverse of the wall. Starting up Gemime

Puddleduck and finishing up Angel Delight.

21. Knight of the Bath 50ft VS   *
4b. Start 15 feet left and climb a small corner, then traverse right across the smooth groove of The Last Supper into a block-filled groove and finish up this.

POOL AREA
The remainder of the routes start on the back wall, which is at right angles to the Main Wall, and is bounded on its right by an obvious steep slab and then a grassy break. In summer it may be possible to walk to the foot of these routes, but in wetter times it will be necessary to reach the dry land at the base of the slab either by descending a route or by abseiling. THESE ROUTES are described from LEFT to RIGHT, starting with :

22. Earwig 35ft Hard VS
5a. The obvious arête left of the pond.

23. Napoleon Solo 35ft E3
6a. The wall and thin crack just right of Earwig; crux low down but unprotected.

24. Anarchy 35ft VS
4b. The crackline splitting the wall on the right, on excellent hand-jams.

25. Artificial Insinuation 35ft VS
4b. The cracks 10 feet right.

26. Larceny 25ft Sev
Climb the obvious corner on the right and finish up the left wall.

27. Hogmanay Slab 30ft V Diff   **
Pleasant climbing up the left-hand side of the slab on good holds.

28. Chasing Rainbows 35ft E2   †
5b. Climb directly up the slab just right of Hogmanay Slab with increasing difficulty.

29. Metropolis 35ft VS
4b. Five yards right is an obvious crackline sloping from right to left. Follow this to a groove, then climb this and pull round the arête on the left to finish.

30. Flat Battery 40ft VS
A disappointing route. Twenty feet right of Metropolis is a loose rib, climb this and finish up the slab above.

THE WILTON MASSIF (SD 69 13)
By Phil Kelly

APPROACH
The complex of four quarries which makes up the 'Wilton Massif' lies only three miles North of Bolton on the A675 Bolton – Preston road. From Bolton, follow this road until the Wilton Arms pub is reached on the left. A small car park is available here for access to Wilton One

Right: John Ryden climbing 'East Lancs Rib' - Roundbarn Quarry.
Photo: Dave Cronshaw

which lies directly behind the pub and is reached by scrambling up the path behind the car park. To reach the remaining three quarries, continue up the A675 for half a mile to a sharp left turn (Scout Road) and follow this steeply to a small parking area on the right 300 yards up. Walking up the road from here, three metal gates are reached. These give access to Wilton Three on the right, the middle leads to Wilton Two, and the left gate to No. Four.

SITUATION AND CHARACTER
Collectively the four quarries are the biggest rock playground in the area, and the number of high-quality routes here is astonishing. Indeed, there are many classic climbs hereabouts, comparable to the best anywhere. Every climber will find something to whet his (or her) appetite, be it the easier angled walls of Three, the technical testpieces of Two, or the longer, more serious routes of One. Climbing in No. Four quarry has never really been in vogue, although many of the climbs are well worth seeking out. Do not be put off; a few minutes with a wirebrush will do wonders, and the climbs should stay clean with more traffic.

Two of the quarries are shared with the Bolton's two gun clubs and the interim agreement over climbing and shooting times still stands; Wiltons One and Four are completely free of the 'lone rangers', whilst in quarries Two and Three, members of Bolton Gun Club and Bolton Rifle And Pistol Club have preference over climbers at the following times;

	Wilton Two	**Wilton Three**
Wednesday	2.30 pm – sunset	10.30 am – sunset
Friday	2.30 pm – sunset	10.30 am – sunset
Saturday	midday – sunset	10.30 am – 5.30 pm
Sunday	10.00 am – sunset	sunrise – 1.30 pm

This is by no means a perfect agreement, though it is an amicable one, which the BMC fought hard for. **If one is asked to leave during shooting hours, then do so.** The gun clubs are bound by these times and may not shoot at any other times.

IN CASE OF ACCIDENTS
The access gates to quarries Two and Three can be opened with keys from a) Taylor's Farm, across the road from the Wilton Arms and obvious by its large green silo, and b) from the Wilton Arms itself. If speed is essential it is probably more prudent to head for the farm as this is manned constantly; the pub isn't.

THE ROUTES in all four quarries are described from LEFT to RIGHT.

HISTORY
All works of a historical nature are an amalgam of hard facts,

Left: Dave Kenyon soloing 'Rhododendron Buttress' with Simon Webster and Kev Glass on 'War of Attrition' - Hoghton Quarry.
Photo: Dave Peace

half-remembered stories, (drink induced?) exaggeration, opinion and the odd fib. This one is no exception.

It seems possible that climbers were visiting the quarries regularly by the late 1940s, as nearby Brownstones was proving popular and had a guide to it as early as 1947 (Lancashire Caving and Climbing Club journal). The first recorded Wilton route however was by Rowland Edwards and Ray Cook (Slim) in 1959; Belly Wedge Chimney was climbed on their first visit to Wilton Three and was named after an incident as Ray followed – 'he weighed about sixteen stone but he could climb as well as the next man.' During the next few years Edwards made many more visits and picked off most of the easier routes and natural lines to be had in that quarry, either climbing solo or with his wife Betty, or with Ray. The Groove (originally called Slim's Chimney), Slime Chimney, Forked Cracks and Parallel Cracks all fell by the end of 1960. Rappel Wall, 40 Foot Corner and the Eeny, Meeny, Miney, Mo routes followed the next year.

Aid climbing was also popular and in 1962 Edwards found a way up Constable's Overhang using home-made knife blades as, at that time, the crack was so thin. The route was named after a policeman who ambled into the quarry and accused the team of having stolen a motorbike which lay at the foot of the buttress; he was eventually convinced of their innocence, though what brought the motorbike or one of Bolton's finest to the crag still remains a mystery! The year also saw other excellent routes in the quarry – Canopy, Shivers Arête (believed not led until Hank Pasquill's ascent in the late 60s), Canine Crucifixion (originally called S.A.S. and free-climbed by Les Ainsworth later) and Central Crack (solo), all of which continue to be popular into the late 1980s. Betty's Wall was a family effort with dad leading, mum seconding and baby Mark asleep in a cot below the crag. The route, however, became known as Bettas Wall and remained so until the 1983 guide set the record straight.

Edwards next cast his pioneering eye over Wilton Two, ascending Falling Crack (some aid), Throsher and the tough Saturday Crack amongst others. 1962 was concluded with a girdle traverse of Wilton Three with his brother Joe following; a bit of free-climbing, a little aid, and even a tyrolean traverse!

The following year new sport was to be found, and Wilton One became a popular venue. The huge, jutting monolith known as the Prow was the focus of attention and soon it had enough routes to warrant its own guide. Edwards was again the main new-router, responsible for Dawn (pegged), Eliminate, Rambling Route, Bird Chimney and the finger-eating Flywalk (no hints, find out for yourself). Mick Pooler added the fine Christeena up the Prow's narrow front face which is not as hard as it at first seems, though it has been known to defeat the odd Himalayan leader of men. Mick later returned and managed the first half of Dawn free as a problem, so his friends threw a rope up to him in the niche so he could continue to complete the ascent.

1964 saw some tentative moves away from the Prow; Blackout was climbed by Dave Brodigan, John Nuttall and Ray Evans – a little aid was employed on a bitterly cold day with Nuttall complaining he was so cold that he was going to 'black-out' on the stance. After this initial taste of new-routing, Evans began to produce new leads of his own, many of them requiring the bold approach which characterised his later routes on the big Welsh cliffs: Frightful Fred covers impressive ground for a V.S., and was climbed by a 15-year old Evans followed by Nuttall and was originally a four-pitch route! Ray climbed Patience after two days had been spent falling off (what was then) the tension traverse, and added Manglewurzle Rib, which, even nowadays, attracts few takers. Eccle's Escalator and Western Terrace were both climbed in partnership with Ken Powell and were slightly easier than Ray's other routes, though they both provided good value, with the former route becoming popular as a two-day, bivouac route.

Competition existed even in these far off days; Ken Powell and Bob Hampson managing to pinch the much-fancied line of 999 from Evans, although it proved necessary for them to use the Great Slab finish – much vegetation covered the quarries and John Hartley had not yet arrived to clean it off. As the year drew to a close, Edwards signed off with Remembrance Corner, his last route before moving to Wales. Evans concluded with the short but fine Slanting Slab and the fine but bold Slipshod, which finally receives its rightful extreme grade in this guide.

The next area to receive attention was the steep, impressive Chimney Buttress: the first route, Leucocyte Left-Hand, added by Evans and Ken Powell was a good, steep Hard VS, made somewhat harder when Chris Williams laybacked the large flake into submission late in 1979. It would be wrong to think that Evans now had the place to himself, for, while beavering away and adding Green Wall, Kurma and Triptophane to the Allotment, Peanuts and the superb Cameo to the Prow, Les Ainsworth was busy with Ron Atkinson producing Jean, Ruby and Twazack. Evans showed a little lateral thinking however, turning right halfway up Dandelion Groove and continuing another few-hundred feet to produce what remains the crag's longest route, the Grey and White Girdle.

1966 was the year of World Cup success for England, Chi-Chi the giant pandas' first meeting with An-An, and the production of the first readily available guide to the Wilton – written by Ray Evans and distributed free by Bowden Black at his shop in Bolton. Like all good guides though, it was immediately out of date with its own author adding Wambat Chimney almost before it was out.

By this time the quarries contained many good routes; the early work of Edwards, the bold lines of Evans, and others, but a golden age was about to dawn and a new light would light the way. Hank Pasquill arrived on the scene – 'looked like a puppet with the strings cut' noted one observer, but what a talent. In 1967 Hank met Ray Evans and together they pegged Wilton Wall. Before long however, Hank was leading new routes of his own, and hard free routes at that. His first was Leucocyte Right-Hand, cleaned of its loose rock from below with a long pole! Others quickly followed; Willow Arête – stolen from the young Ian Lonsdale who had cleaned off some holds then replaced the sods hoping to complete the route later – Central Route which had stopped all-comers previously, proved easy, and routes such as Virgin's Dilemma and Cheat added further to his growing reputation.

Hank really confirmed his arrival with a stunning, on-sight lead of Christine Arête. A number of years later he repeated the routes in an old pair of Mountain boots; not as an act of bravado, but because his EB's were 'shot at' and he couldn't afford new ones. Impressive stuff though.

Ray chipped in with Knuckleduster and Les Ainsworth added the fierce Wipe Out with John Mason (looking at it now it seems a good name), Flimnap the Pirate and a free ascent of Ann (with John McGonagle), but by 1968 Hank was really starting to motor. Three major routes followed: Paradox, climbed with Ray, who was heard to remark 'you've really left me behind this time', Max – named after the pet dog from the Wilton Arms – climbed a very steep line left of Wambat Chimney, and White Slabs Bunt which remained unrepeated by anyone other than Hank for several years. Again it is worth reminding modern rock-jocks that the poor peg runners on climbs at this time were placed en route and the nice, sharp-edged mantelshelf ledges were often hidden under a botanists paradise.

The first Lancashire guide appeared in mid 1969 as did the annual crop of new routes. Almost inevitably it was Pasquill in the lead, with a willing and able group of seconds including Jim Fogg, 'Penk' Penketh and Dave Hollows. Hollows deserves particular mention as he was (and is) a bold, gifted climber in his own right, barely less able than Hank himself, and the only person at the time, making repeats of Pasquill's major lines. Routes such as In Memoriam, Nothing Fantastic, Master Spy, Thin Air, Roll Over (gained from the right, the direct start was added later by Ian Lonsdale), and Loopy all date from this time. Some of them were outrageously technical – Master Spy still rates 6b, whilst others were obviously bold; Thin Air was protected by a dubious knife blade, placed with the aid of tension from Hank's famous, home-made 'Wilton Hook', and has seen only a handful of ascents, entirely by idiots and/or the top locals of the day.

The pace of exploration slowed into the mid-seventies, although Dave Cronshaw and Les Ainsworth remained active, producing Merchant Crack, La Rue and a host of minor routes. Pasquill's golden age had really come to an end, though free ascents of Wilton Wall (1977) and Falling Crack showed he could still do the business, but by free-climbing Constable's Overhang he demonstrated that, spirit willing, he could still out-climb the best.

Things were not to remain quiet for long though; Ian Lonsdale, who had already been around for quite some time, began to get new route fever. Strange practices such as clearing away loose rock and soil from prospective new routes, and drying the fingers with chalk rather than on the shirt-lap, had started to become accepted. Armed with new ideas and an obsessive determination Lonsdale set about areas of unclimbed rock and old aid routes to produce a series of often good and popular climbs. Regatta De Blanc, Tweeker (free), Dracula, Supercrack (Obituary free) and Vampire (free) all proved popular, as did his free ascent of Spike. Other Lonsdale creations saw less traffic, some (Ummagumma for instance) because of bad rock, others such as Isle of White, because they were obviously too bold. Other notable additions were made by Dave Knighton, including a free ascent of Josser and by Geoff Mann. Geoff was a late convert to climbing, who produced a very hard, free version of The Shakes, renaming it K.P. after Hank's newly-born daughter Katy.

During the late seventies and early eighties the idea of training for climbing was gaining favour and the gifted amateur started to feel pressure from the athlete. The first of the manic trainers to make an impression were the two Johns – Hartley and Monks. Hartley used his fitness gained from weights, karate and innumerable hours spent bouldering, aided by his willingness to garden tons of overlying sods and rubble, to create a series of often excellent routes, usually of a highly technical nature. John attracted some criticism because of the extent of his cleaning, and his willingness to preplace pegs (or in the odd case, bolts) near to the crux of a prospective route, but time has now shown he was only a couple of years ahead of his time. He found this method of cleaning and preparation, followed by an un-practiced ascent preferable to the 'multiple top-rope, wire-the-move' method, and his routes are all well worth doing if you are up to them; The Devil's Alternative takes in one of Wilton's hardesty moves, whilst Sleepwalk and Astradyne have dozens of suitors each summer. Pigs on the Wing and Iron Orchid are musts for any aspiring hero.

Anyone climbing with John Monks was in for a hard time; always just one more route. Left to his own devices he would solo literally hundreds of feet of extreme rock and train, train, train. Often climbing new routes with Hartley, he also produced a good few of his own: Ego Trip (a free version of the aid route Stet climbed with Tony Preston) being a fine hard companion to K.P. Away in Wilton Four he soloed a number of mean crack climbs, none more impressive than Joseph Holt at 6c, free-climbing the aid routes ascended by an unknown pair of climbers known as the 'Wilton Sanction' in the early 70's.

All this activity and 'big number' routes attracted the occasional foreign visitor. New Zealander Roland Foster popped over in 1983 to add Join the Army, get Yourself Killed, Two PVC Girls go Slap Happy and Shaggy Mamba which links Cronshaw's old route Black Mamba (free-climbed earlier in the year by Dougie Hall) to one of Pasquill's 'come-back' routes, Shaggy Dog, climbed the previous year. Hank turned his re-kindled enthusiasm on the glaringly obvious arête between Paradox and Leucocyte on Chimney Buttress. He had partial success, climbing the upper half, and Jerry Peel managed the lower section. Dougie Hall later put the two pieces together to produce a hard and as yet unrepeated route.

Another personnel change was due at the end of 1983. John Hartley signed off his string of first ascents with Counter Intelligence, an opposing line to the classic Master Spy. Hartley and Monks' purple patch came to an end, Monks took up running (2½ hours for his first marathon!) and for the first time in years youth began to get a look in.

By the middle of the 1980s it seemed that all the major lines had been climbed, and Mark Leach's ascent of Against All Odds in 1984 seemed to confirm that all the 'last great problems' had been ticked. This route had previously been documented as 'S-Groove, not led' and had been tried on a rope by Pasquill in the early 70s and again by Hank and Jerry

Peel ten years later, amongst others, no-one could pass the obvious good hold under his own steam though. The line proved too good to leave however and 1983 saw renewed interest – John Hartley placed a bolt runner and various climbers attempted to lead it. The following year Mark succeeded without the bolt runner though using side runners in adjacent routes to safeguard the crux move – he still brushed his hair on the floor more than once!

Paul Pritchard's stickman-like form had been seen around the quarries for a couple of years, and indeed he had joined Phil Kelly on the occasional new route; Jimmy Mac (named after Phil's boss on the bins) and Plenty of Zzzzs which continues Ray Evans' Grey and White Girdle for a couple of hundred feet. Over the next two years Pritchard set about the place with a vengeance; virtually every unclimbed few feet of rock got a seeing-to, and a host of new routes appeared ranging from the appalling to the excellent, from dead-safe boulder problems to protectionless chop-routes. The number of high grade routes rose by the week; The Soot Monkey, Eliminator (direct), The Pretentious Gallery, Boy Racer and Cleansweep being Paul's pick of 1985, with a long awaited futuristic free ascent of Black Pitch (Run Wild, Run Free) from Mark Leach taking pride of place. The following year saw the first routes to be graded E7, Pritchard having become confident enough to string together 6b moves at a most disconcerting height above both the ground and protection (of which there often wasn't any). Perimeter Walk, climbed solo after practice takes a thin green wall in the less popular Allotment area, with Kelly clearing away a landing strip on the ground as Paul climbed. Strawberry Kiss, however, climbs the blank space up the wall just right of White Slabs Bunt with only marginal protection, which ensures that neither of these two routes will become polished.

So, what of the future? Did the class of '86 leave any pickings for the climbers of the 1990s? Precious few, one suspects if the rock-hungry Pritchard could only find a twenty-foot bolt-protected problem before leaving to make his fame and fortune in Wales. Other routes will no doubt be found by those with active imaginations, but thankfully there is still one 'last great problem': a free ascent of Triffid Wall would be a fine addition to these, the finest quarries in the world. Any takers?

WILTON ONE (SD 699 134)

Wilton One is the largest of the four quarries and, for help in identifying routes, is split up into nine very different and contrasting sections. From left to right as one surveys the crag these are The Allotment, The Pitface, Chimney Buttress, The Prow, Opposite Wall, White Slabs, Grey Wall, Red Wall, and The Graveyard.

THE ALLOTMENT

This lies at the far south (Bolton) end of the quarry. At first this area is scrappy and unclean, though it improves as the crag increases in height farther right. The fenced off area at the far end of the quarry is on private land and no climbing must take place in that area.

1. **The Deep** 25ft Hard VS
Climb the green groove in the buttress just right of the fence.

Forty feet right of the fence is a small buttress with a blunt rib.

2. **The Shark** 20ft Sev
Climbs the vague groove.

3. **The Fin** 20ft VS
4c. Climb the left edge of the blunt rib to a hard finish.

4. **Barbara Ann** 35ft Hard VS
5b. Thirty-five yards right of the fence is a narrow buttress. Follow the central crack by 2 hard mantels, trending left, then step right over the overhang to finish.

5. **Rhonda** 35ft A2
The thin crack 4 feet right, just before a short rise in the quarry floor. The next buttress lies at a higher level, behind a clump of willow trees.

6. **Grassy** 35ft Hard VS
5a. The vague crack line 10 feet from the left of the buttress.

7. **Willow Wall** 55ft Hard Sev
4a. Climb the most obvious crackline in the centre of the wall, to the large ledge. Traverse right and finish up the short wall behind.

8. **Asleep for Years** 50ft VS
4b. The twin cracks 4 feet right. At the terrace step right and finish up the short wall.

9. **Falling Wall** 50ft E1
5b. A scrappy line up the green wall left of Willow Arête.

10. **Willow Arête** 45ft E1 ★
5b. The right arête of the buttress. Start just left of the arête and climb up easily for 20 feet, then move right to the arête and follow this to the large ledge. Finish up the short wall behind.

11. **Kurma** 55ft VS
4b. Start in the deep corner just right of the willows. Climb the corner to the horizontal fault, the traverse to the left arête to reach a large ledge, and finish up the wall behind.

12. **Adidas** 60ft Hard VS
5a. The crack which starts about 12 feet right of the deep corner is followed to the horizontal break, then traverse left, use an iron spike and finish up the corner.

13. **Puma** 45ft E3 ★★
5c. Start at twin cracks 25 feet right of the corner, where the ground level falls slightly. Climb up to the break, step slightly left, then surmount the overhang and continue to the top.

14.   The Foot of an Oncoming Mexican   45ft   E4   *
6a. Free climbs the old aid route Needles and Pins; 6 feet right of Puma, with 2PRs. Step right at the break and up the headwall.

15.   Zapling   45ft   E3   *
6a. Power up the hanging flake left of Merchant Crack, gained from that route.

16.   Merchant Crack   35ft   Hard VS
5a. Start 9 feet right and climb a short, shallow corner and then the continuation crack to the horizontal break. Step right to finish.

17.   Perimeter Walk   30ft   E7   †
6b. An unprotected problem taking the challenge of the narrow slab right of Merchant Crack, with the crux high up.

18.   Flimnap the Pirate   30ft   VS   *
4c. The slim corner groove round to the right of Perimeter Walk.

19.   Reeling in the Years   35ft   VS
4c. Four feet right is a thin crack; climb this for 20 feet, move right, then step back left to finish.

20.   Baby Arête   25ft   Hard VS
5a. The short arête on the right, and just left of the vegetated corner of Grotty Muckden, is climbed on it's right-hand side.

21.   Grotty Muckden   25ft   V Diff
The second large corner past the clump of willow trees is somewhat overgrown. Climb it to a muddy landing.

22.   Triptophane   80ft   Hard Sev   *
4a. A good route involving bold climbing up the wall right of Grotty Muckden. Start in the corner and follow an obvious line of holds up and rightwards across the wall, culminating in a couple of thought provoking moves to reach the break. Go right along the break to finish up a short corner.

23.   Rope 'n' Rubber   60ft   E2   †
5c. The left-hand side of the wall right of Grotty Muckden.

24.   Pot Pourri   60ft   VS
4c. Start 10 feet right of Grotty Muckden and climb directly to a vague groove and the break above. Finish direct; unprotected.

25.   Lady Grinning Soul   65ft   Hard VS
5a. Start 7 feet left of Valine and climb up and right to gain a crack. Move left and up to join Triptophane. Finish up that route.

26.   Valine   50ft   VS
4c. Climb the obvious crackline 20 feet right of the corner, until it is possible to step left to gain the horizontal fault. Finish as Pot Pourri.

27.   Land   50ft   VS
4b. Move right onto the wall from 20 feet up Valine, traverse right for 6 feet then finish straight up past the break.

28.   Boy Racer   50ft   E6   †
6b. Boldly and delicately attack the wall left of Proline and finish just right of Land. Crux low down but still scary and committing.

29. Proline 50ft E1
5b. Twenty feet right of Valine are twin cracks at the foot of a grassy cone. Climb these stepping left at the break to finish as for Boy Racer.

30. First Cut 45ft Hard VS *
5a. Start from the ledge left of Green Wall and go up to a large pocket, then continue up the wall above.

31. Green Wall 50ft VS *
4b. Start at the top of the grassy cone and climb up to a small pocket, then step right and follow a shallow corner to the horizontal break. Move right along this and finish on the left.

32. The Pretentious Gallery 50ft E6 ** †
Technical dinkie pulling up the wall left of Dinah.
6b. Start just right of Green Wall and climb delicately up and right to a PR. Keep left of the peg and gain the overlap and second PR by some tricky moves. Finish either up the centre of the upper wall or up the left arête.

33. Dinah 50ft E1
5b. The block-filled crack at the right side of the grassy cone.

34. Eliminator 50ft E3 *
5c. A stiff unprotected problem direct up the wall right of Dinah, at the upper limit of its grade. The initial crux section can be avoided by gaining the line from 15 feet up Dinah (E1 5b).

35. Ruby 55ft VS
4c. Right again the quarry floor rises, and just left of an overhang is a crack. Climb this for 25 feet, until it is possible to traverse right and finish up Jean.

36. Insertion 50ft Hard VS
5b. Get your leg over the roof between Ruby and Jean and continue direct to the break. Finish up Ruby.

37. Jean 50ft VS *
4c. Gain the undercut groove just right, either direct, or by a traverse from the left side of the overhang. Follow the groove to the horizontal fault, then finish up the short broken groove on the right.

38. Gravitational Experiment 50ft E4
6b. Climb the steep thin cracks right of Jean, direct.

39. Crow's Nest 45ft E1
5b. Right again is a pod at 30 feet. Start below this and climb diagonally right (PR) to a large ledge. Step back left and enter the pod with difficulty, then continue to the top.

40. Headbutt Wall 40ft E4 †
6a. Start a few feet right and climb a problem wall to the ledge. Pass the PR above by tricky moves (use of the arête is illegal).

41. Eccle's Escalator 45ft Severe
Gain the ledge at the right side of the wall from the right, then follow a series of undercut ledges on the left. Steep!

The block-filled chimney on the right **(Christmas Chimney)** provides an excellent easy descent for the routes hereabouts.

42. Lime Street 180ft Sev
A high-level traverse of The Allotment area along the obvious dirty horizontal break. From the top of Eccle's Escalator, follow the break leftwards until about 12 feet from Grotty Muckden, a finish can be made rightwards up a short groove. Belay at will, but make sure you've made it out first. An alternative traverse, (**Ordinary Route**, E1 5b) starts up Jean and traverses left at half height, along cleaned holds to finish down (!) Pot Pourri. Good pendulum possibilities for the second!.

THE PITFACE
This is the area of more broken rock which stretches right to Chimney Buttress. Despite the appearance of some sections, there are a number of very good routes here.

43. The Power of the Mekon 30ft E1   *
5b. Just left of Grovel is a cleaned wall. Climb this by an exquisite series of moves on rugosities.

44. Grovel 30ft Sev
The loose, grassy groove 25 yards right of Christmas Chimney.

45. Regatta de Blanc 30ft VS   **
4c. Start just right of Grovel, climb rightwards then back left on good rugosities to a ledge, finish easily from here.

46. Streaker 30ft VS
4c. The narrow rib on the right.

47. Georgina 35ft Sev
The obvious slanting crack.

48. Jaws 35ft Hard VS   *
Just when you thought it was safe...
5a. The block-filled crack 4 feet farther right.

49. The Mouth 60ft VS
4c. Climb Jaws for 20 feet until it is possible to reach a ledge on the right. Mantel onto this, then traverse right to a large ledge and finish over an overhang. **Variation Finish:** The hanging corner above the mantel.

50. Ummagumma 50ft Hard VS   †
5b. Right again is an undercut slab whose left edge is formed by an awesome off-width crack; climb the crack by whatever means you see fit, to a scoop on the left and finish easily up this.

51. The Devil's Alternative 55ft E4
6b. Start 8 feet left of Deodand and gain the overhang guarding the undercut slab direct, PR. Make an evil mantel onto the slab above, PR, and climb the wall using two shallow grooves. Traverse right to a BB on Silently Screaming.

52. Deodand 45ft E1   *
5b. The corner at the right side of the undercut slab, passing an overhang at 15 feet.

53. Silently Screaming 45ft E3   *
6a. Climbs the arête right of Deodand. Start in the short corner right of the arête and climb up for a few feet until a traverse left can be made

to the arête. Move up to PR and continue past a second PR to a BB on the ledge, AO.

54 Transfiguration 30ft Hard V Diff
The orange scar on the right.

55. It 25ft E1
5c. The boulder problem up the wall left of This, past a bucket.

56. This 20ft VS
4c. The short flake just right proves strenuous.

57. T'other 20ft VS
5b. Climb the narrow wall on the right.

From the top of the mound in the centre of The Pitface an easy descent route **(That)** leads diagonally right.

58. The Pit and the Pendulum 50ft E5   ★★ †
6c. Start 6 feet right of the shallow corner up and right of T'other and climb a steep crack to a sloping ledge. With feet on the ledge (PR) move right into a bald groove and up, hopefully to the break; BB above, AO.

59. Erythrocyte 45ft VS
4c. Start 10 feet right of The Pit and the Pendulum and climb the groove above to a loose finish over blocks (better to step left before the rubble to BB on previous route).

60. Sleepwalk 50ft E4   ★★
6a. Climb the slab on the right to a ledge, then move right and follow the thin dog-legged crack above to the horizontal break. BB above, AO.

61. Astradyne 45ft E4   ★★
6b. Climb the bulging crack splitting the next wall, 10 feet left of the corner to a ledge. PB on left. A strenuous effort! Abseil descent.

62. Houses of the Holy 50ft VS
4c. Climb the off-putting corner on the right for 20 feet then follow the crack which branches to the left.

CHIMNEY BUTTRESS
This is the steep imposing buttress to the left of and slightly set back from The Prow's Outside Face. All the routes are strenuous and sustained, but well worth the effort.

63. Paradox 70ft E2   ★★
5b. Climb a diagonal crack just left of the left arête of the buttress, to a niche. Take the continuation crack above to its end. Hand traverse right to finish easily up the arête. A direct finish is possible but detracts from the route's quality.

64. Paracyte 60ft E5   ★★
6b. A direct line up the arête to the right, utilising the iron loop for protection. 2PRs in the break at half height.

65. Leucocyte Left-Hand 60ft E2   ★★
5c. Climb directly up to the iron loop and move right to gain a ledge. Move up left into a niche from where a couple of hard moves lead to easier ground and the top.

66. Leucocyte Right-Hand 60ft VS ★★
4c. From the large ledge on the Left-Hand, move up into the short corner on the right and climb it and the crack above exiting on the right.

67. The Hacker 60ft E4 ★
6a. Ten feet right of the arête is an obvious small ledge at 10 feet; gain this and pass it with difficulty to the overlap. Go over this and up to the break of Steeplejack. Climb the headwall boldly, trending left at the top. It is possible to traverse right to finish up Central Route, just above the overlap (E3 6a).

68. Central Route 60ft E1 ★★★
5b. Fifteen feet right of Paracyte is a large ledge at 15 feet. Gain this and climb the crack above to PR. Move right (5c direct) and up to jugs, trend up and back left to the crack and finish up this.

69. Max 60ft E3 ★★
5c. Eight feet right again, climb a thin crack to a shallow cave at 30 feet. Climb into the overhanging niche above and exit from this by a hard move. Follow the continuation crack to the top.

70. Wambat Chimney 65ft E2 ★
5b. Seven feet right of Max, follow a crack for 10 feet to PR and TR. Go up and leftwards to a rest below a tantalising flared chimney. Struggle up this to easy ledges on the right.

71. The Soot Monkey 65ft E6 †
6c. Start 8 feet right of Wambat Chimney and climb a hard, boulder problem wall to a PR. Move up and right through a slight bulge, then trend back left to the joke PR just right of Wambat's chimney. Make a scary move up and right to the break of Cleansweep (PR). From a standing position on this break, go left to a rest on the right arête of Wambat before moving back right to a strenuous finish.

72. Loopy 45ft E4 ★★★
6a. The ground starts to rise up towards a corner bounding the right-hand end of Chimney Buttress. Midway up the slope, is a steep crack running up to a small monolith near the top of the crag. Follow the crack (PR) to a semi-rest below the monolith. From here there is a choice of three finishes; a) Move up left into the hanging groove but break out left onto the slab and climb it diagonally leftwards, b) move up left into the groove and fight up it, (more in keeping with the crack below), c) swing right into the green groove on the right of the monolith and follow it to the top; easier but a poor alternative.

73. Cleansweep 90ft E4 ★★★
Free-climbs the old aided girdle traverse, Big Dipper.
6a. From the second PR on Loopy, go left around the nose and traverse the fault line past 2 PRs into Wambat Chimney; finish up this. Can also be done starting up The Corner and gaining Loopy at 30 feet by a short traverse, PR.

74. Friends 40ft Hard VS
4c. Climb The Corner for a few feet then step left and gain a niche. Finish directly through this.

75. The Corner 35ft VS ★★
4c. The corner which limits Chimney Buttress on its right gives good

climbing.

76. Steeplejack 160ft E1 ★★
5c. Climb the thin crack 6 feet left of Loopy to a ledge, then traverse leftwards along ledges into Wambat Chimney. Step down and left into Max and thus into Central Route. Climb this to just over the overlap and foot traverse left to finish up Leucocyte Left-Hand.

There is a low-level traverse of Chimney Buttress stretching from Paracyte to The Corner at 6b. If so desired the horizontal excitement can be extended by continuing right round at the same level, to finish at Scimitar; 6b. One of the best low-level traverses known to man.

OUTSIDE FACE OF THE PROW
The Prow is the obvious centrepiece of Wilton One: a huge monolith thrusting out from the mother rock and detached on three sides. Its outside face is about 60 feet high and tends to green after wet weather. The Inside Face is about 45 feet high and perfect clean rock. In sunny weather the Inside Face is something of a suntrap.

77. Peanuts 70ft Hard VS ★
(1) 30ft 4c. Start just right of The Corner. Climb up and right to good holds on the arête, swing round this and make an awkward mantle onto the belay ledge of Fingernail.
(2) 40ft 5a. Step back left and up to a ledge (PR). Attain a standing position on this then either finish rightwards or via a ramp on the left.

78. Horrocks' Route 55ft VS
(1) 25ft 4b. Right again is an overhung corner. From the base of this move up until the arête can be gained and followed to a large belay ledge.
(2) 30ft 4a. Climb the short corner above the belay, then climb easily to the top. **Horrock's Route Direct** (E1 5b) climbs the overhung corner direct and finishes up the thin cracks just left of the belay.

79. Fingernail 70ft Sev ★★
(1) 35ft 4a. Ten feet right of the arête is an iron hook set in the wall at 10 feet. Climb up to it by the crack on its left, then continue up and leftwards to a spacious belay ledge and an in-situ PB.
(2) 35ft. Step right around the short arête onto a steep slab, climb diagonally right to an obvious weakness, and follow this to the top.

80. Orange Peel 70ft Sev
As for Fingernail but at the hook step right, then climb the steep wall via a crack and finish easily.

81. Flingle Bunt 65ft VS ★★
Halfway up Eastern Terrace is a shallow, wide-angled groove. Start directly below this.
4c. Climb up slightly right into a short groove and climb ledges to gain Eastern Terrace. Enter the shallow groove above and follow it boldly to the top.

82. Spider Crack 65ft Hard VS
5a. Just right is another right-leading overhang. Layback round this and continue straight up to the terrace, then climb the deep crack above.

83. **Jubilee Climb** 60ft E2
5c. Start just right of Spider Crack and climb direct to Eastern Terrace.
Follow the thin crack left of Spider Crack to finish.

84. **Eastern Terrace** 85ft Moderate
The obvious line of ledges which splits the buttress diagonally from
right to left.

85. **Lazy Friday** 60ft E3   ★★
A bold proposition up the blank slab left of Cameo, with the crux just
where you don't want it: at the top!
5b. Climb Cameo for 25 feet then move out left and climb a shallow
corner to a PR. Go up and right to finish direct up the wall on small
holds, avoiding easier possibilities on the left.

86. **Cameo** 60ft E1   ★★★
First done with 2PRs, one of which was a bent over bicycle spoke! The
pegs have long since gone leaving a superb route.
5a. Start 5 feet right of Eastern Terrace and climb past breaks to a ledge
below a thin crack. Follow the crack past a tiny groove to easier ground
to finish.

87. **Pathetique** 60ft E5   †
6b. The rugositied wall right of Cameo direct, finishing up a thin crack,
a runner low down in Cameo provides 'protection'.

88. **Wedgewood** 60ft Hard VS
5a. Start 8 feet right, below a shallow groove at the top of the wall
(Christeena). Climb the wall direct to a small overlap (poor NRs), pass
this carefully and go left for 8 feet to a crack, exit via this.

89. **Christeena** 45ft VS   ★★
4c. Gain the large ledge on the end of The Prow. Move up left to a jug
(PR) and mantel onto this. Step left into a groove (intimidating tho'
straightforward) and finish easily up this.

INSIDE FACE OF THE PROW

90. **Christine Arête** 45ft E3   ★★
5c. The striking left arête of the Inside Face. Side runners.

91. **Dawn** 45ft Hard VS   ★★
5b. Six feet right of the arête is a wide crack; climb this to a break and
niche. Go up and right into a small alcove, then make hard moves to
the top. A harder alternative is the shallow groove on the left above
the break (E2 5c).

92. **Innominate** 45ft E3   ★
6b. Start just right, and climb a very thin crack, then traverse right along
the undercut flake to finish up the crack just left of the corner of Ann.

93. **Eliminate** 60ft VS   ★★
4c. Climb the short groove 15 feet right of the arête to a ledge, then
traverse right along the breaks until it is possible to finish easily up the
ridge of Rambling Route.

94. **Ann** 45ft E1   ★★
5b. Right of Eliminate is a short arête, climb the peg crack on its right
to a ledge then follow the steep groove above using both cracks, or

(harder) just layback the right crack.

95.   Cheat   45ft   E2   **★★**
5b. Start 5 feet right of Ann and climb a blind crack with a long stretch to reach the break of Eliminate. Step right and take the line of unnatural holds up the wall above. Designer climbing at its best.

96.   Rambling Route   40ft   V Diff
Further right is a very short chimney, followed by a groove. Climb the chimney by laybacking or bridging, then from the ledge finish up the groove or the ridge on the left.

97.   Bird Chimney   35ft   Sev   **★**
Right again is a wide chimney which turns into a groove. Follow this to the top, or (more usual) finish on the left.

98.   Flywalk   40ft   Hard Sev   **★★**
4a. Follow the line of holds leading left across the next wall from the corner, to a rocking block. Finish up the crack and over a small overhang. A direct start is possible (5c), whilst the problem just left, moving right into Flywalk is 6b.

99.   Flytrap   25ft   Hard VS
5a. The corner in which Flywalk starts, exiting right at the top.

100.   Veteran Cosmic Rocker   20ft   E4   **†**
6c. The flying arête right of Flytrap, started on the left and finished on the right past a series of dynamic pinch moves.

101.   Scimitar   20ft   Diff
The crescent-shaped crack rising right into the corner.

The gently rising gangway, known as **Max's Dilemma**, is the descent route.

102.   Girdle of the Prow   205ft   E1
(1)   30ft 4c.   As for Peanuts pitch 1.
(2)   100ft 4b.   Traverse easily right (many variations possible) to belay on the large ledge on the end of The Prow.
(3)   55ft 5c.   Swing right, around the arête and into Dawn. Place a high side runner and traverse right along the obvious break (crux) to join Ann at her ledge, NB.
(4)   20ft 4a.   Follow the traverse of Eliminate and finish up that route.

OPPOSITE WALL
This is the wall opposite the Inside Face of The Prow.

103.   Baby's Bottom   20ft   Hard Sev
4b. The small rib at the left of the wall; started by a mantel.

104.   Stegosaurus   40ft   V Diff
The broken crack 15 feet right.

105.   Nappy Rash   40ft   Hard VS
Climb Stegosaurus for a few feet, then move right and climb direct to the top. The direct start is E1 6a.

106.   Spec Crack   45ft   Diff
The left slanting groove directly opposite Eliminate.

107. **Jimmy Nip** 45ft E3 ★
6a. Between The Prow and White Slabs is a buttress on its own, split by a deep crack. Climb this to the break, then step right to finish.

108. **Titanosaurus** 40ft E4
6b. The thin crack in the small buttress 35 feet right. A grassy descent route is available down the slope on the right.

The next section of rock is **WHITE SLABS** which runs up to the obvious corner groove of Remembrance Corner.

109. **White Crack** 20ft V Diff
At the start of White Slabs is a crack starting at half height Climb the wall beneath this, and finish up it.

110. **Goon** 50ft Hard VS
5a. The next crack, with its crux at the top.

111. **Crater Traitor** 65ft E5
6a. Very bold climbing up the wall right of Goon. Climb a vague groove which gets progressively harder, to a RURP runner at 35 feet. Wobble up and right past this to a PR and climb the wall on the left (crux) to the break. BB above, AO. Bicycle clips essential!

112. **Red Flowers are Red** 65ft E2
5b. Another serious route, though at a more amenable grade. Climb the wall just left of Dandelion Groove direct via some small pod-shaped depressions.

113. **Dandelion Groove** 65ft Sev
The first groove on White Slabs is gained easily from the left, then followed to the top.

114. **Prickpocket** 65ft Hard VS
5a. Just right is an obvious crack in the top wall. Climb directly up the lower wall to gain and finish up this crack.

115. **Manglewurzle Rib** 90ft Hard VS
(1) 35ft 4b. The crack below the rib on the right is entered from the left and climbed past a PR at 15 feet to a small grass ledge. PB not in place
(2) 55ft 5a. Go right to the rib, then take the crack on the right to the top.

116. **Isle of White** 80ft E4 ★★★
6a. Take the unprotected wall left of White Slabs Bunt to the break, then continue direct to an obvious undercut; pass this, then trend rightwards to finish over the overhang as for W.S.B.

117. **White Slabs Bunt** 85ft E3 ★★★
6a. Start 15 feet left of Remembrance Corner, below an overlap at 20 feet. Climb to the overlap (2PRs), pass it on the left and up to the girdle break. Step right, PR, and climb the flake crack above (The Bunt) to two exposed mantels which give access to a shallow scoop. Pass the

capping roof via a crack. **White Lightnin'** E5 6b (†), is a short variant climbing direct from the second PR to the break.

118. Strawberry Kiss 85ft E7 ⋆⋆ †
"A perverse amalgam of natural difficulty and obscene boldness, combined to create a deadly cocktail of pleasure. A problem guaranteed to leave a bitter aftertaste." Take a skyhook.
6b. Climb the thin crack just left of the corner to the break. Arrange protection in the flake of White Slabs Bunt and from the break, launch up the committing wall above past sustained fingery climbing to a move left at a thin crack, and thus relief!

119. Remembrance Corner 70ft VS
4c. The prominent corner groove running the full height of the crag, passing a tree at 50 feet.

GREY WALL
The next section, to the sandy cave at half-height where the wall becomes predominantly red, is known as Grey Wall. It is split diagonally from right to left by Western Terrace and several routes either end on or start from this terrace. To the right of the Terrace is The Pit.

120. So Be It 75ft E3 ⋆⋆
5c. Just round the arête are two thin cracks. Climb the left hand one to the break then the sentry box above. Exit via Western Terrace.

121. Supercrack 80ft E3 ⋆⋆
5c. Follow the right-hand crack to the break, step left and continue up the continuation crack above.

122. Life in the Fast Lane 70ft E2
5c. From the metal spike on Patience, gain the bad break above and go over the overhangs direct to gain the Terrace. Leave the Terrace slightly rightwards to a loose finish.

123. In Memoriam 80ft E1
5b. Climb Patience to the metal spike, and gain the bad break above. Surmount the overhangs rightwards to a thin crack. Climb this and escape right onto Western Terrace.

124. Patience 75ft Hard VS ⋆⋆
(1) 45ft 5a. Climb to a large metal spike at the left of Grey Wall, then traverse right to a PB in a corner/niche.
(2) 30ft 4b. Up to a ledge, then step left onto a ramp and finish straight up.

125. Impatience 70ft E2
5b. Start below the centre of the traverse of Patience and climb a slim groove to the traverse, then move right as Patience. Climb the wall above to a groove, and then up this to a small ledge. Step left and finish up the wall above.

126. Dracula 40ft E1 ⋆
5b. Climb the stepped, overhanging groove below the iron spike on Niche Indirect, and continue past the spike and a PR to a niche and climb the wall on the right to finish at the foot of Vampire.

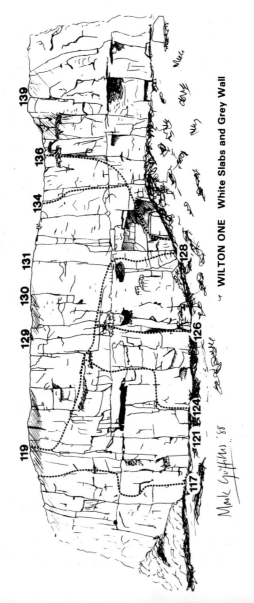

WILTON ONE   White Slabs and Grey Wall

Mark Griffiths '88

127. Niche Indirect 65ft E1 †
5c. Climb the short corner 12 feet right of the niche on Patience, then traverse left past the metal spike and finish as Patience.

128. Western Terrace 120ft Hard V Diff
The obvious diagonal break splitting Grey Wall from right to left. Exposed in its upper reaches.
(1) 80ft. Climb a short ramp to gain the terrace proper, then traverse easily left and up the small steps to a grassy bay (PB).
(2) 40ft. Continue left at the same height, step down, then finish up the right arête of Remembrance Corner, in a fine position.

UPPER GREY WALL
The next three routes start from Western Terrace and climb the walls above.

129. Vampire 30ft E3
6a. From the obvious step in Western Terrace, where Dracula ends, climb the crack above into a small niche. Leave this to gain the top by hard moves.

130. Spike 35ft E4 **
6a. Start 10 feet right of Vampire, at a line leading up and right to two niches in the wall. Follow it to the first niche (PR) and pass a second PR by hard reaches to a second niche and third PR. Finish up the crack above.

131. Run Wild, Run Free 40ft E6 *** †
6b. The steep crack above the ramp of Western Terrace. A serious start to the left of the crack gains the crack after a few feet; Follow this with much difficulty; bold crux at 20 feet.

132. Ego Trip 40ft E5 ***
6b. The twin cracks above and slightly right of the initial ramp of Western Terrace give a fine route.

GREY WALL – THE PIT

133. K.P. 55ft E5 ***
6b. The thin crack right of Ego Trip, rising out of a shattered sentry box. Initially gained by a rising traverse from the belay of Frightful Fred.

134. Josser 55ft E5 *
6a. From the large ledge on Frightful Fred climb a vague groove to a small overlap on the right. Pass this and fight up the crack above to a second overlap; move left under this overlap and finish direct. Strenuous, sustained and not well protected.

135. Welcome to the Pleasuredome 55ft E5 ** †
Bold and forceful climbing up the steep wall right of Josser.
6b. From the belay ledge, climb direct, passing a tiny overlap (crux) and PR, and onto the exposed wall above. Trend leftwards (PR) at the top. Significantly harder for the short.

136. Frightful Fred 85ft VS **
A good introduction to the climbing in this part of Wilton, providing plenty of variety, with nothing too difficult. Not for the faint-hearted!
(1) 25ft 4c. Up the wide chimney at the left of The Pit, then move

right onto a large ledge, PB.
(2) 60ft 4c. From the right of the series of ledges, mantel onto the lowest of 2 ledges on the left wall of a shallow groove and move up to a PR, then swing up to a ledge on the right. Then either, climb the right of a slab to a triangular ledge and make an awkward step left to finish, or, step awkwardly round to the left and climb the wall on the left by a series of ledges, then traverse back and finish over several small ledges. The latter is harder, but a very artificial line.

137. Jimmy Mac, Bin Man Extraordinaire 65ft E2
(1) 25ft 6a. The thin crack just left of Bohemian is unworthwhile.
(2) 40ft 4c. As for Frightful Fred, then continue straight up the groove over several small ledges to the top.

138. Bohemian 70ft Hard VS
5b. The crackline just right leads up through a hanging groove to the top.

139. Adrenalin 85ft E4   *
(1) 30ft 4b. Climb the broken crack which starts 10ft left of the large sandy cave, on poor rock to a belay at the left of the cave
(2) 55ft 6a. The obvious overhanging crack in the groove above.

140. Adrenalin Direct 90ft E2/A3
(1) 25ft 4b. Start in the large corner below the sandy cave, and climb the wall trending slightly left to the cave. A good contender for a black spot!
(2) 65ft A3/6a. Peg with difficulty up the crack above the right side of the cave, then follow a diagonal crack to Adrenalin and finish up this. Stacked 'blades in shakey placements.

At the end of The Pit the rock becomes very sandy, and the rock to the right of this point to the top corner of the quarry is known as **RED WALL**.

141. Knuckleduster 80ft Hard VS   **
Start at the base of the arête just right of the sandy cave
(1) 55ft 5a. Step left into the crack and follow it past the horizontal break and over the overhang to a large ledge.
(2) 25ft 4c. Starting on the arête move up delicately until the groove on the right can be gained and followed to the top.
(2a) 25ft 5b. (Fist Finish) Climb the short crack in the back wall and continue up a vague groove above.

142. Triffid Wall 55ft A2   *
From Knuckleduster pitch 2, swing left round the arête to peg a steep left-slanting crack, finish up the groove on the left as Adrenalin. Still not free!

143. Thin Air/Hot Air 90ft E5   *
(1) 50ft 6a. A bold pitch. Climb the smooth wall just right of the blunt arête to PR. Pass this by a hard move to gain a short groove leading to the break and the belay ledge of Knuckleduster.
(2) 40ft 6b (†). An even bolder pitch. Leave the belay ledge by its right arête, to attain a hold in the bottom of a shallow groove. Enter this groove by a desperate mantel and finish direct.

144. Nothing Fantastic 70ft E3 ★
5c. Fifteen feet right of the blunt arête is a rightwards-curving crack, follow this, with an awkward move rightwards above the PR, then climb direct to the horizontal break and the large ledges of Blackout. Climb the thin crack above the ledge to finish.

145. Blackout 65ft VS ★★
Another classic Wilton route, which is not as difficult as it might seem, though there are many capable leaders who might disagree. At the north end of the quarry, just past the final rise in the quarry floor, is a pedestal which marks the start.
(1) 45ft 4b. Up the pedestal, then the groove behind for a few feet, until a traverse left can be made to a ledge. Left again is another ledge and PB.
(2) 20ft. Climb up behind the belay veering right.

146. Clapped Out 45ft E4 ★
6a. From the top of Blackout's initial groove, surmount the overhang (PR) and struggle up the continuation crack above to the top.

147. Master Spy 65ft E4 ★★★
6b. Follow Clapped Out to the roof then launch out tentatively right along the undercut flake (easier than it looks) for 15 feet to a vertical crack and rest. The crack above holds out right to the end.

148. Counter Intelligence 60ft E4 ★★★
6b. Eight feet right of the start of Blackout, an impressive vertical crack leads to the right-hand end of the Master Spy roof. Climb the crack (PR) and pass the roof, then traverse leftwards to a PR and a nasty mantel to finish.

149. Master Spy Direct 60ft E4 ★★★
6b. The obvious direct connection of the two previous routes; excellent.

150. Wipe Out 60ft E2 ★★
5b. The awesome hanging groove 10 feet right of Blackout never relents, and has a real sting in the tail.

151. Black Mamba 55ft E4 ★★
6b. Start in the centre of the steep wall right of Wipe Out, and climb slots to a sloping ledge and PR. Move up to gain a standing position on this ledge, BR, then make a particularly venomous move up and left to gain the base of an easy groove. Finish up this.

152. Shaggy Mamba 55ft E6 ★★
6b. Break out right from the BR of Black Mamba, and make desperate moves to gain good holds on Shaggy Dog. Finish as for that route.

153. Black Dog Blues 55ft E5 †
6b. Climb Black Mamba to the PR and either lurch/jump or make a lo..o..ong reach up and right for a ledge and continue up the cleaned groove above, PR.

154. Shaggy Dog 45ft E4 ★★
5c. From 15 feet up Kettle Crack, swing left onto a ledge on the face, PR. Move left and climb straight up the wall to a somewhat 'out there' finish.

155. Kettle Crack 40ft E2
5c. The crack left of a huge block supported by an iron bar.

156. Fall Out Chimney 40ft Hard Sev ●
4a. The ugly chimney on the right; don't touch it with a bargepole!

157. Myrmidon 55ft E5 ∗
6b. The thin crack in the arête to the right is climbed (crux) to a long reach right which gains ledges on Overtaker's Buttress. Join and finish up that route.

158. Overtaker's Buttress 60ft E2
5b. Climb the groove in the narrow buttress on the right to a sloping ledge, move left along this to the arête and finish up this, passing a small overhang.

159. Twazack Left-Hand 50ft VS
4c. Farther right is a deep bay. Start in the left corner of this and climb up to a large block which forms an overhang. Move left and up the shallow groove which bounds this block on its left, to a small ledge on an arête on the left. Finish direct.

160. Twazack Right-Hand 50ft VS
4c. As for Twazack Left-Hand to the block, then climb the corner/groove which bounds the block on its right.

The following two routes centre on cracks on either side of the steep arête which marks the right side of Twazack's bay. The stability of the upper section of this arête gives great cause for concern, and these routes are probably best left alone.

161. Rebellion 50ft E1 †
5b. The crack on the right side of the bay, (gained from the grass ledge on the left) moving right at the overhang to the subsidiary corner.

162. Roll Over 50ft E2 †
5b. Just right is a clean-cut S-shaped crack at the top of the crag. From the grassy ledge on the left, swing round the arête and climb the steep crack above. R.I.P.

163. Dinosaur 80ft Hard VS
(1) 40ft 4c. Ten feet right is a corner with a wide crack in it. Climb this to a swing right onto the belay ledge.
(1a) 40ft 4c. Climb the corner for 10 feet to a niche, then move up and right to a good hold which enables a swing right to be made to join Great Slab. Follow this to the belay.
(2) 40ft 4b. The crack which forms a continuation to the corner.

164. Knock Out 30ft VS ∗
4c. From the belay of Great Slab, climb the crack on the right of Dinosaur.

165. Great Slab 85ft VS
Start beneath the centre of the impressive slab at the north end of the quarry.
(1) 30ft 4b. Mantel onto the slab, and climb via a rust flower, to a large grass ledge on the left of the slab.

(2) 55ft 4c. Cross the slab at its sandy weakness, then climb the groove to a small overhang. Traverse right along a small ledge to the arête. Finish up this on its left.

166. Virgin's Dilemma   65ft   Hard VS   ★★
A bold problem; not quite so common nowadays!
5a. Start just left of the large corner groove of 999, move up onto the slab and climb to the rust flower. Step right here and climb the slab above direct, passing PR to enter a shallow chimney.

167. 999   60ft   Hard Sev   ★★★
4c. The open groove on the right gives a good well protected route, with its crux at the top.

168. Left Edge   25ft   Hard VS   ★
4c. From the grassy ledge in the corner, climb the left arête and finish as for Great Slab. Good, bold climbing.

Right of the grassy ledge, the rock arcs round rightwards and becomes **THE GRAVEYARD**; an uninspiring piece of rock on the whole but with one or two exceptionally good lines.

169. Coffin Crack   20ft   VS
4c. From the wide grassy ledge in the top corner of the quarry, climb the crack in the left wall.

170. Green Chimney   20ft   Hard Diff
The aptly-named chimney starting from the angle of the large ledge.

171. Susan   20ft   VS
4c. The crack which slants right from the back of the ledge.

172. Chance Encounters   30ft   E3   ★
5c. A direct line up the small diamond-shaped buttress just right, PR.

173. La Morte   40ft   Hard VS
5b. Start below a sandy cave and climb ragged cracks, passing the cave on the left, and continue to a ledge. Finish up the wall above via a small pod.

174. Undertaker's Crack   35ft   VS
4c. Traverse right from the wide grass ledge to the base of a hand-jam crack. Climb this to a niche below an overhang (PR). Leave the niche to the left and then finish up the short wall above.

175. Join the Army, Get Yourself Killed   60ft   E4   ★★
The impressive wall left of Soixante Neuf.
6b. Gain a ledge in the wall left of Soixante Neuf either direct from the ground, or by a traverse in from the left above the cave. Clip the PR above the ledge (hard and dangerous if you're less than average stature) then step left and finish direct.

176. Soixante Neuf   45ft   E2   ★
5c. Gain a niche and finger crack, then up this to a ledge on the arête. Finish direct or gain the ledge on the arête from the front face via a mantel.

177. Graveyard Direct   30ft   Sev
Climb the obvious chimney in the centre of the wall to a ledge, then up the hanging chimney above.

178. Graveyard Ordinary 45ft Moderate
From the initial chimney go up ledges on the right, and finish up a narrow chimney.

179. Bolton Buttress 35ft Sev
Just right is a short triangular buttress. Climb this, then step across the wall at an obvious ledge and finish up Graveyard Direct.

180. Mary 30ft V Diff
The layback corner on the right, then finish up the short blocky corner.

181. Saturation Point 40ft Hard VS
5a. The narrow face 5 feet right of the corner.

182. Digger's Spade 35ft Sev
Farther right is a V-shaped fault filled with blocks, with a tree and a sandy cave below it. Gain the cave from the left, then climb over a dob to the Spade, and pass behind it to finish on its left.

183. Catalepsy 40ft Hard Sev
Just right is a thin crack. Climb this to a ledge, then continue via a sloping ledge on the wall above to the right side of the Spade. Finish over the blocks above.

184. Neddy's Walk 35ft V Diff
Climb a short groove behind a bush to a ledge, then move up a series of ledges and finish by a mantel over the overhanging wall on the right.

185. Crash and Burn 50ft Hard VS
5a. Follow the curving crack 12 feet right, then finish up the leaning jam crack on the left.

186. Ape 20ft V Diff
The wide crack 15 feet right.

187. The Overhang 20ft VS
4b. On the right is a small buttress with a double overhang. Climb the crack on its left-hand side to the break, then traverse right and finish up the arête.

188. Horror Arête 25ft VS
5b. Go over the nose on the right by a gymnastic move, and finish up the arête above as for The Overhang.

189. Avoidance 25ft Diff
Start 10 feet left and traverse left to finish up the arête of The Overhang.

190. Chocky 20ft Sev
The chock-filled corner on the right of the buttress.

TRAVERSES

191. Grey and White Girdle   335ft   Hard VS   *
A massive circumnavigation of the big walls with sustained climbing on most pitches. Allow 5 hours; it is no longer necessary to bivouac on this route, though food drops are optional.

(1) 55ft 4c. Climb Dandelion Groove for 30 feet to a ledge on the right; foot-traverse this rightwards to a PB, 10 feet left of Remembrance Corner.

(2) 50ft 5a. Gain the corner and climb round the arête to a PR. Descend slightly to the sandy belt and traverse awkwardly right to a small corner. Step down here into a small cave and down again to belay on the iron spike of Patience.

(3) 40ft 5a. Regain the horizontal break and follow it rightwards to join Patience at the foot of its ramp; follow this ramp to a belay on Western Terrace.

(4) 65ft 4b. Reverse Western Terrace to its initial rib and climb down this until it is possible to move right, along a series of unstable flakes, to gain Frightful Fred at the top of its chimney. Follow that route to its PB.

(5) 40ft 4b. Climb Frightful Fred to an obvious ledge on the right, overlooking Bohemian, PB.

(6) 50ft 4c. Descend diagonally right (PR) and enter a loose and sandy cave. Leave this cave (thankfully) by its right-hand end and hand-traverse along the horizontal break to Knuckleduster. Continue this traverse around the blunt arête to gain and climb a short groove (as Thin Air) to the huge ledge on Knuckleduster, PB.

(7) 35ft.   Either continue as for Plenty of Zzzzs (4c), or climb the short thin crack in the wall above the PB and move right to join Blackout's second pitch, up which a finish can be made.

192. Plenty of Zzzzs   135ft   E2   *** †
An extension to the traverse is possible which provides a fitting climax to the previous seven pitches. Can be done as a route in it's own right. Start at pitch 7 of Grey And White.

7a. 50ft 4c. As for Grey and White, but at the top of the short crack, traverse right over ledges to reverse the crux slab of Blackout and a belay under the roof of Clapped Out.

8. 85ft 5b. Do Master Spy's roof and swing right into Wipe Out. Move right across the wall of Black Mamba, and on to a ledge and PR on Shaggy Dog. Go right across Kettle Crack to a final stiff move to reach a BB. Either abseil off from here (preferable) or go right to finish up Fall Out Chimney, (lethal). Whilst the block above the BB seems stable, it is inadvisable to hang on the rusting iron bar which appears to support it!.

193. Tombstoned   130ft   Hard VS
A traverse of The Graveyard is possible, the line is obvious but lacks any sort of appeal.

WILTON TWO (SD 696 134)

THE CLIMBS are described from LEFT to RIGHT.

The section on the left when entering the quarry is known as **SCOUT WALL**. At the extreme left of this is:

1. **Arête Not**   25ft   Hard Sev
4a. Follow the arête as near as possible.

2. **Concrete Crack**   30ft   E3   ★★
6a. Start 2 feet left of Cement Mix. Pull up and move left into the obvious thin crack, then climb this to a finish up Cement Mix.

3. **Cement Mix**   30ft   E1
5b. Climbs the obvious, semi-rubble-filled groove 15 feet left of the corner.

4. **Tosser's Wall**   35ft   E4   ★ †
6b. The steep wall between Cement Mix and Short Corner.

5. **Short Corner**   30ft   E1
5c. Follow the corner on the right easily to a PR near the top. Pass this by a couple of hard moves.

6. **Start**   25ft   Diff
Follow vertical drill-holes 6 feet right of the corner and finish up a short groove.

7. **Boomerang**   25ft   Diff
Fifteen feet right of the corner is a sloping ledge at 10 feet. Gain this and move up the slab above, then swing diagonally right and finish up the niche above.

8. **Puss Soldiers**   30ft   E4   †
6b. A serious line up the wall left of Shallow Groove, TR.

9. **Shallow Groove**   30ft   Hard VS   ★★
5b. The obvious steep groove 20 feet right of the corner.

10. **Shallow Green**   30ft   E2   ★★
5c. Make committing friction type moves up the slabby nose just right to an overlap and PR. Move right to gain a good hold, then pull boldly onto the wall above and climb this.

11. **Shukokia**   30ft   E3   ★
6a. Climb the shallow groove on the right, then continue up the thin crack with a difficult move to finish.

12. **Kung Fu**   30ft   Hard VS   ★
5a. Climb to a sentry box just right, gain entry to this and finish straight up above the break.

13. **Misunderstandings**   30ft   E1
5b. A steep line of scoops just right of Kung Fu.

14. **Roopy Roo**   25ft   Hard VS
5b. Start 10 feet right and climb a series of scoops to a grassy finish.

15. **Median Crack**   30ft   Hard VS
5a. Start 3 feet right and climb the wide crack to a ledge, then finish up the wall above.

16. **The Bod**   30ft   E1   *
5b. Good climbing up the left-facing groove 3 feet right.

A traverse of Scout Wall is possible. **The Traverse of the Beer Drinking Gods** (E4 6a, 6a) starts at Arête Not and traverses the walls in two pitches finishing up The Bod. Obviously, there is 'crater potential' on much of the route!

17. **Ace of Spades**   30ft   E3   *
6a. Climb the steep groove right of The Bod. Short and Sharp.

18. **Tweeker**   40ft   E3   ***
5c. Climb Throsher to the second large ledge, then traverse left to below a hanging groove. Nip up this (PR), to a rest below the roof, from where a quick tweek on the nipple helps pass the roof and gain the top.

19. **Throsher**   25ft   VS   **
4c. The thin crack, just left of the arête which overlooks the pit.

20. **Ledge and Groove**   30ft   E1
5b. Climb to the ledge at 10 feet, and swing right, around an arête, into a groove above the pit; up this boldly to the top.

The next four routes start from the large ledge in the bay to the right. This can be reached from Throsher by a long step right, or by an easier traverse from lower down on the right.

21. **Twin**   25ft   E2
5b. The next groove, which starts from the left side of the large ledge. Variation: **Smut Ball Fungus** (E4 6a) moves right from Twin at 8 feet and climbs the wall above.

22. **Volper**   25ft   Hard VS
5a. The crack and shallow groove in the centre of the left wall.

23. **Scout Cleft**   25ft   V Diff
From the darkest recesses of the cleft, mantel onto a ledge on the left then go back right into the cleft to finish.

24. **The Axe Wound**   25ft   E6   * †
"One small step for the Aardvark, one giant leap for mankind!" 7a. The radically overhanging wall right of Scout Cleft, 2BRs.

25. **The Spoiler**   30ft   VS
4c. Climb the crack on the right arête of the bay, then steep slabs lead to the top.

The next route starts 25 feet right, on a gently overhanging wall just past an unclimbed crackline.

26. **Against All Odds**   30t   E5   ***
6c. Once a 'Last Great Problem' of the quarries, the S-shaped feature

in the steep wall left of Frostbite more often than not lulls one into a false sense of security before violent rejection just below the top. Side runners.

27. **Frostbite** 25ft E2 *
5b. The shallow corner which bounds the leaning wall on its right.

28. **The Curve** 25ft Sev *
The right-slanting crack 3 feet farther right, which bounds the steep slab on its left.

MAIN WALL
To the right is a break containing an easy way down. Farther right is Main Wall, a series of clean buttresses increasing in height to the magnificent Wilton Wall on the right, behind the right-hand edge of the firing range.

29. **The Hornet** 25ft Hard VS
Alias 'Keep off the Grass.'
5a. Start just left of the initial crack of The Bee, at a short groove. Climb this avoiding an illegal ledge on the left, then finish up the short wall above.

30. **The Bee** 30ft E1 *
5b. At the base of the descent route is a short diagonal crack leading to a ledge at 10 feet. Climb this then step down left onto the face and climb boldly to a break and the top.

31. **The Wasp** 30ft E3
6a. Climb the short arête right of The Bee to a ledge, then climb up using the thin crack in the rib above.

32. **Laying the Ghost** 25ft E2 *
6b. From a few feet up Slanting Slab swing left into a thin crack (PR) and follow this to the top.

33. **Slanting Slab** 25ft Sev *
Climb the narrow slab 10 feet past the short rib of The Hornet.

Round the arête is a blank overhanging wall (unclimbed as yet) its right edge forming the bulging corner of Direct.

34. **Savage Stone** 25ft E4 **
6c. Climb Direct for a few feet, then swing left into the hanging groove and climb it desperately past one good hold and one PR.

35. **Direct** 25ft Hard VS
5a. Layback up the corner which bounds the leaning buttress on its right.

36. **Kukri Crack** 20ft V Diff
The clean crack, obvious by its name, in the wall right of Direct.

Descent from routes in this vicinity is by the stepped corners just right; **Three Corner Climb**.

37. **Spline** 35ft Diff
Up a shallow corner on the left arête of Deep Groove to a large ledge,

then the corner on the left .

38. **Deep Groove** 30ft Diff
The large groove to the ledge, then the corner above.

39. **Meandering Molly** 35ft Hard V Diff
From 6 feet up Deep Groove traverse right to the arête, then up this and the centre of the short wall behind.

40. **Cross Tie** 30ft Sev
Climb the arête for 10 feet then move left into the centre of the wall and finish up this.

41. **I'm Cured Bouncy Bouncy** 25ft E1
6a. Start slightly left of The Rapid Rambler and climb the short wall to a ledge, finish easily.

42. **I'm the Rapid Rambler; Fondle Fondle** 30ft VS   †
4c. For the person who's done everything. Takes the overgrown corner groove 4 feet left of The Mud, exiting leftwards.

43. **The Mud** 25ft VS
Aptly named climbing up the crack 3 feet left of Flake Crack.

44. **Flake Crack** 35ft Sev   *
Follow the obvious flake crack; very sandy after wet weather.

45. **Big Dorris** 40ft E2   *
"It's just a pity a donkey's climbed it" John Monks.
5b. From the base of Flake Crack climb diagonally right to a thin crack in the centre of the wall, then follow this with increasing difficulty to the top.

46. **Painted Smile** 45ft E5   * †
6c. Climb Big Dorris for 25 feet, to a no-hands rest and runners. From here, break out right and gain a PR by desperate finger tearing moves. Finish slightly easier. Don't trust the PR!

47. **Falling Crack** 45ft E2   **
5b. The prominent crack in the centre of the wall is followed to a hard move into a niche where the crack narrows, finish more easily over the overhang.

48. **Wilton Wall** 45ft E3   ***
6a. Climb Falling Crack for 10 feet then traverse right on a detached block to a crack. Climb the crack, with a hard move to stand on a flat hold. Enter the upper groove by a further hard move and gain the large ledge. Finish easily. The direct start is 6a.

49. **Pigs on the Wing** 45ft E5   ***
6b. Start just left of The Swine. Climb up left, then straight up on small holds to gain good holds (NR) leading right across the wall to The

Swine. Climb the thin crack just left of The Swine to the ledge. **Pigs Direct** (E6 6b ★★★) is a much bolder alternative, continuing direct up the wall from the good holds and NR.

50. **The Swine** 45ft E3 ★★
6a. Start 10 feet left of Iron Orchid and climb diagonally rightwards (crux) to gain good holds just left of the arête at 20 feet. Continue to a PR and finish straight up.

51. **Iron Orchid** 50ft E4 ★★
6b. Climb the right arête of the Main Wall to a PR at 25 feet, move up then traverse right to another PR in an overhanging scoop. Climb the blunt right arête of the scoop to gain the large ledge.

52. **Dancers at the End of Time** 80ft E4 ★★★
(1) 20ft 5c. Start under Saturday Crack and traverse up and left to the arête. PB.
(2) 60ft 6b. Continue traversing left at the same height, crossing Wilton Wall and Falling Crack to finish up Big Dorris.

53. **Two PVC Girls Go Slap Happy** 35ft E5
6b. The wall just left of Saturday Crack, 2PRs.

54. **Saturday Crack** 30ft Hard VS ★
5a. Right of the Main Wall the wall falls back; climb the prominent V-groove at this point.

55. **Dirty Corner** 25ft V Diff
Start 3 feet right and climb the wide crack to a grassy ledge, then finish up the corner itself.

56. **Flake Traverse** 50ft Hard V Diff
Start 5 feet right of the corner and climb up ledges for 10 feet, then move right to the obvious wide flake and traverse behind this to finish up Smokey.

57. **Flight of the Condom** 30ft E1
5b. Start as for Flake Traverse but ascend the wall above, moving right into Loosen'ard to avoid a loose finish.

58. **Loosen'ard** 30ft Sev
The crack on the left of the Great Flake.

59. **Flying Motorcyclist** 30ft Hard VS
5c. Climb the thin finger crack in the centre of the wall, then finish as for Smokey.

60. **Smokey** 30ft V Diff
The wide crack on the right side of the Great Flake.

61. **Ringing Wall** 30ft E1
5b. Up the centre of the wall on the right, using loose flakes.

62. **Buttocks** 30ft V Diff ★
The short crack in the centre of the next buttress, then move left and finish up a short, chimney groove.

63. **Crack and Chimney** 30ft Moderate
The crack on the right of the buttress is either climbed direct, or via a crack 3 feet left.

WILTON THREE (SD 695 135)

Wilton Three is the first quarry on the right when approaching from the A675 up Scout Road. The quarry is one of the most popular in the whole Lancashire area, and is very well used on warm summer evenings by locals to work up a sweat and a thirst before a session in either the Wilton Arms or the Bob's Smithy.

ORANGE WALL
The first recorded climbs are on the clean buttress at the left side of the quarry and directly behind Wilton Two.

1. **Twin Cracks** 20ft Diff
The corner left of the chimney is gained from the left, then the parallel cracks are climbed direct.

2. **Sneck** 20ft Sev
Gain the large ledge just right, then climb the blunt arête finishing on the right.

A gully on the right is the usual descent for climbs in the vicinity.

3. **Zee** 20ft Sev
Layback the loose crack just left of Great Chimney.

4. **Great Chimney** 25ft Moderate
The wide chimney on the left of the wall, finishing left at the capstone.

5. **Orange Wall** 30ft VS
4b. The wall right of Great Chimney can be climbed by several routes.

6. **Orange Crack** 25ft Hard Sev
4a. The jamming crack on the right side of the wall, which forms the left side of a leaning pedestal. The wall immediately left of the crack is taken by a poor Hard VS: **Cracked Orange**.

7. **Justine** 20ft Sev
The layback crack which forms the right side of the pedestal.

8. **Orange Groove** 30ft V Diff
The right slanting chimney just right, very popular.

9. **Monolith Crack** 25ft VS
4b. Just right is a half ship-shaped monolith. Climb to a good hold and thus the right crack of the monolith. Finish up the steep wall above.

10. **Cedric** 25ft Sev
The stepped groove 12 feet left of the corner.

11. **Orange Squash** 30ft E3 †
6a. Start midway between Cedric and Orange Corner. A hard start gains an obvious undercut at 10 feet, and the ledges of Cedric on the left. Move back right onto the wall and climb it by a steep crack.

12. **Orange Corner** 25ft Hard V Diff
The corner which limits the wall on its right. Often muddy.

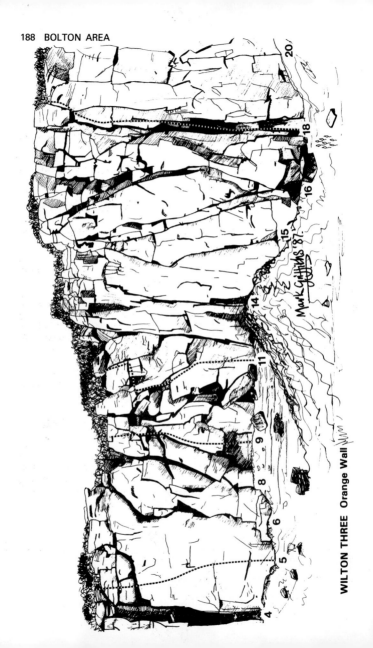

WILTON THREE Orange Wall

Mark Griffiths '87

CONSTABLE'S OVERHANG AREA
The rock now turns a right-angle and becomes a slabby wall split by several prominent cracks.

13. Oak Leaf Wall 30ft Sev
The line of ledges 12 feet right of the corner.

14. Oak Leaf Crack 30ft Diff   *
Right of Oak Leaf Wall is an obvious straight crack, climb this in its entirety.

15. Forked Cracks 30ft VS
4b. Just right two cracks converge to form an inverted Y. Climb the right one. Can be climbed direct; 5c.

16. Parallel Cracks 35ft Sev   *
Gain the hook then take the twin, parallel cracks on the left.

17. The Groove 35ft Hard V Diff   *
From the metal hook move up into a chimney/groove which is hard to enter but soon eases.

18. Slime Chimney 40ft V Diff   *
The deep chimney which cuts the left wall of the recess opposite the quarry entrance. The capstone is negotiated on the right.

19. The Grader 45ft E3   ***
5c. Start from Slime Chimney but swing right around the arête at 15 feet, to the base of a diagonal crack. Enter the crack by a hard move and follow it to join Lightning at its triangular block. Pass this by a further hard move and finish as Lightning. A direct start is possible at 5c.

20. Lightning 45ft E3
5c. Climb the vertical crack in the wall just right of The Grader, then step right to join the ledge at mid-height on the back wall. Hand-traverse back left to a block and finish up a thin crack.

21. Thunder 45ft Hard VS
5a. Climb the left corner of the recess to the ledge, then continue more awkwardly up the corner to the top.

22. Constable's Overhang 45ft E4   ***
6b. A fantastic route with quite a reputation. Climb the peg-scarred crack (or the wall just left; easier) in the back wall of the bay to a ledge. Step right off the ledge and climb a steep crack to a PR (Rock 3 above). Fight up the dogleg crack above to an entertaining exit onto the slab above.

23. Nameless Edge 40ft Hard VS   †
5a. The corner which limits the recess on its right.

24. Slipshod 45ft E1   *
5a. Climb the right wall of the recess until a scary and exposed move right round the arête gains Green Slabs, finish up this.

25. Green Slabs 40ft V Diff
The aptly named slabs are climbed until at a large detached block it is possible to traverse left and finish up the arête.

26. Fallout 35ft VS
4b. From Green Slabs climb straight up the overhanging wall above using a rocking block.

27. Pulley 40ft Sev
Climb the crack just left to a hard move onto a slab in the corner. Then a move over some blocks, followed by a mantel leads to an exit gangway leading left.

28. Block and Tackle 35ft Hard V Diff
The open blocky groove left of the arête left of Central Crack.

29. The Arête 35ft VS
The arête just left of Central Crack.

30. Central Crack 35ft Hard VS ★★★
5a. The striking, perfect crack opposite the quarry entrance is one of the most popular routes here.

31. Crack and Slab 30ft Diff ★★
To the right is a large ledge at half-height, which can be gained by 4 methods:- (a) up the obvious flake right of the arête; (b) up the arête; (c) up the first crack left of the arête; (d) up the second crack left of the arête (b and c are harder than Diff). From the ledge climb onto a large block and finish up the short crack on the right.

32. Ascendveass 20ft Hard VS ●
4b. In the short upper wall, above the flake start of Crack And Slab, is a horrendous looking groove. Don't climb it!

33. Chockstone Crack 20ft Hard V Diff
The short crack at the extreme right, using 2 chockstones.

WATERFALL BUTTRESS
The rock turns a right-angle and becomes Waterfall Buttress. At first this is broken and vegetated but soon becomes a solid buttress which sometimes has a waterfall.

34. Bloomer 40ft Sev
At the left side of the back wall climb the crack which forms a shallow groove at the left.

35. Groper 40ft Hard Sev
4a. Climb the shallow groove 15 feet right, then step left and finish on poor holds.

36. 30-Foot Wall 40ft VS
4c. Climb 40-Foot Corner onto the slab, then go diagonally left to the arête and follow this to the top.

37. 40-Foot Corner 35ft VS
4b. The deep corner left of Waterfall Buttress proper.

38. Canine Crucifixion 40ft E2 ★★
5c. The left edge of Waterfall Buttress proper is an arête. Climb the crack just right of this to its end. Move up and right here then back left to finish easily up a short corner.

39. Brastium 40ft E1
5b. Fifteen feet right, climb the steep crack. This route is sometimes

obscured by a waterfall and in these conditions the grade may alter somewhat.

40. **Betty's Wall** 40ft Hard VS   ★★
A good route which is somewhat marred by a little loose rock.
5a. From the crumbling ledge on Route Four move left and up to the base of a shallow groove (PR), then finish up this.

The two thin cracklines just right are taken by **Cabbage Man Meats the Death Egg** (E3 5c †) and **Hodgepig Boogy** (E3 5c †).

41. **Route Four** 30ft Sev
Further right a white streak runs down the rock; climb the loose crack which this hides.

42. **Route Three** 25ft V Diff
The delicate crack 10 feet right.

43. **Route Two** 25ft Hard VS
5a. From Route One, traverse left beneath the overhanging wall to join and finish up Route Three.

44. **Route One** 20ft Diff
The short, block-filled corner on the right.

An easy series of ledges in the corner gives an easy descent **(Route a Half)**.

RAPPEL WALL AREA
Right of the descent route, the next continuous area of rock is called Rappel Wall Area.

45. **Barbecue** 45ft Sev
Climb direct to the ledge halfway up Rappel Wall, then finish up the poor crack above, just right of Rappel Wall.

46. **Rappel Wall** 55ft V Diff   ★★
Follow the obvious weakness which splits the wall from right to left, to a chockstone at two-thirds height. Then move left and exit via a sandy scoop.

47. **Shivers Arête** 45ft E1   ★★
5b. Climb Canopy for a few feet but continue left to the arête (spike runner), press on up the arête to a PR and pass this by a hard move, to gain the top.

48. **Canopy** 45ft Hard VS   ★
5a. Start in the corner of Kay and climb diagonally left to the bottom of a thin peg-scarred crack; follow this passing a small overlap.

49. **Kay** 45ft VS   ★★
4b. The deep corner on the right; very good (when clean).

50. **Crooked Crack** 40ft VS   ★★
4c. From the deep corner gain the ledge near the bottom and from the right of this climb the crack which splits the overhang to a mantel on the lip, then follow the crack, or escape to a grass ledge on the right and finish to the left.

51. The Gay Dwarves and Mr Plod Go to the Tupperware Party 35ft E2
5b. Climb the dirty wall between Crooked Crack and Mo direct, on disposable holds.

52. Mo 35ft Hard Sev ★
4a. To the right is an orange patch with a crack on either side. Climb the wall below, then use both cracks until it is possible to finish, using the right one.

53. Miney 30ft Hard V Diff
The thin, ragged crack on the right is gained by the wall on the right, and is climbed using holds on the wall.

54. Meeny 25ft V Diff
The wide crack on the right is reached by a subsidiary crack, then climbed on jams, or as a layback.

55. Eeny 20ft Hard Diff
The short crack starting halfway up the wall is reached by climbing the wall below.

56. North Wall 20ft V Diff
Up the centre of the short buttress which stands out on the right.

THE PLAYGROUND
This is the more broken area on the right.

57. North Corner 20ft V Diff
The short corner set back a little, and slightly lower.

58. Curver 20ft V Diff
The crack just to the right.

59. Short Chimney 20ft Diff
To the right, and at the end of the trough in the quarry floor are two chimneys. This is the shorter left-hand one.

60. Belly Wedge Buttress 20ft V Diff
Straight up the narrow buttress between the two chimneys.

61. Belly Wedge Chimney 20ft Hard Diff
The right-hand chimney.

62. Belly Wedge Wall 25ft V Diff
Climbs the wall right of Belly Wedge Chimney.

63. The Slab 20ft Diff
Forty feet right at a slightly higher level is a small slab. Numerous variations are possible – backwards, upside-down, no hands etc.

64. Unnamed Crack 20ft Diff
Farther right again, above the trench in the quarry floor, is a tower. Climb the crack on the left side.

65. Hanging Arête 20ft Hard Diff
Climb the steep arête of the tower.

66. Right-Hand Route 20ft VS
4c. The right wall of the tower is split by a peg-scarred crack. climb these strenuously to a break, go left to finish up Hanging Arête.

67. **Rodin's Requiem** 20ft E4   *
6c. Start just left of The Square, at an overhang. Surmount the overhang with the utmost concentration and then tackle the wall above.

68. **The Square** 20ft VS   *
5c. Thirty feet right of the tower is a cubic block on the hillside. Climb its right-hand side. Alternatively, from the small overlap make a long and awkward reach left to gain a sidepull and gain the top.

69. **The Third Party** 465ft E3
(1) 70ft 4c. Climb Twin Cracks to a small ledge on the right arête, then traverse to Great Chimney. Continue along the upper ledge of Orange Wall and round the arête, then descend a little and cross to Monolith Crack. Some difficult moves past large blocks at the same level lead to the ledge halfway up Cedric.
(2) 70ft 5c. With a situ PR traverse to the corner and descend this to a large ledge. From the right of this ledge continue at the same level, then move up slightly to The Groove. Move up and right, then belay below the capstone on Slime Chimney.
(3) 60ft 5c. Descend the chimney until it is possible to follow a short crack (Grader) to join Lightning, then continue into the left corner of the recess and gain the sloping ledge. Cross this to the right corner of the recess and descend very awkwardly for 8 feet until at a ledge a traverse can be made to join Slipshod. Follow this to Green Slabs and belay on the large block. (It is advisable to place a runner at the top of Slipshod to protect the second).
(4) 35ft 4b. Cross to the ledge at the top of Pulley, then move round the arête and with hands on the obvious break traverse to Central Crack. A hard move to a high foothold enables the ledge on Crack And Slab to be reached.
(5) 150ft. Secure one end of a 150-foot rope to the block and then, using a 'third party', get the rope fixed to one of the fence posts above Rappel Wall. Make a tyrolean traverse to the large ledge below Rappel Wall, climb to Rappel Wall, then descend until it is possible to traverse right on an obvious line to a belay on Shivers Arête.
(6) 80ft 4b. Go along the ledge to Kay and ascend this until with feet just above the PR, it is possible to traverse to a ledge above Crooked Crack. Descend Mo for 10 feet, then continue the traverse until it is possible to finish up Eeny.

An excellent low-level traverse (6a) is possible round practically the whole quarry, and boulder problems litter every spare inch of rock.

WILTON FOUR (SD 696 134)

Over the years this quarry has become needlessly neglected by the majority of climbers, but there is no need for this as it contains routes as good as any of the other quarries. It is the smallest of the four quarries on this site and lies at the top of Scout Road, just before the sharp bend at the top.

SANCTION WALL
The first routes are on the very steep wall on the left side, and the descriptions work rightwards from here.

1. Sally 20ft VS
5c. From the flat area at the base of the steep wall, climb the thin crack 15 feet left, up the banking.

2. Teachers Crack 30ft E4 *
6c. At the base of the hollow are 2 obvious cracks. This is the first of these.

3. Hell's Bells 30ft E5 ** †
6b. The second crack past a powerful undercut move and PR.

4. White Horse 30ft E4
6b. The crack just left of Haig. A bold lead; no gear until the crux has been passed!

5. Haig 25ft E2 *
6b. Start at the left side of the cutaway roof. Climb to the roof and pass it on its left side to finish up a crack with one hard move.

6. Johnnie Walker 20ft VS
5a. The crack on the right side of the square-cut overhang.

7. Long John 20ft VS
5c. The crack 15 feet left of the right arête of this wall.

8. Neat Whisky 15ft VS
6a. An interesting problem up the wall 3 feet left of the obvious arête, via an obvious pocket.

9. Dimple 20ft VS
5b. Start 10 feet right of the arête and traverse diagonally left to the top of the arête.

10. Mort Subite 20ft E5 †
6c. Just left of the arête of Glenfiddich, climb a thin crack, passing the overlap with extreme difficulty. RP protection.

11. Glenfiddich 35ft Hard VS *
5b. Climb the arête with a PR, finish on the right wall.

12. Suspended in Cryonics 30ft E5 †
6c. The wall right of Glenfiddich is boundless in its complexities, has one BR, and a hidden BB on a ledge at the top, abseil off.

13. 100 Pipers 25ft Hard Sev
4a. The deep corner on the right.

14. Cutty Sark 35ft Hard VS
5b. The V-shaped groove 15 feet right of the corner.

FRIDGE-FREEZER ZAWN is the name given to the small buttress situated in the pit on the right, the most striking feature of which is a steep arête.

15. Lady Ice 35ft E4 *
6b. Further right, past an impossible looking wall, is an impressive

arête, rising menacingly out of the rubbish tip. Climb this arête on its left side, PR, BR.

16. **Cold Emotions** 30ft E4
5c. The impressive arête rising menacingly etc, etc. This time on its right side with NO gear; the situ gear on Lady Ice having been placed tantalisingly out of reach!

Farther right are two walls at a slightly higher level: **COCKTAIL WALLS**

17. **Inverted Triangle** 25ft Hard Sev
4a. Start at the foot of a triangular slab and climb this trending right to the top.

18. **Vat 69** 25ft VS
5a. Climb the obvious arête 15 feet right to an awkward finish.

19. **Dewars** 25ft Hard Sev
4a. Start 3 feet right of the corner and take a direct line to the top.

20. **Clan Dew** 30ft Sev
Climb the crack 3 feet right to a large ledge, then finish up the niche above.

21. **Cossack Crack** 35ft E2
5b. Climb a vague crack 2 feet right of the next steep arête.

22. **Smirnoff** 40ft VS
4c. From the gully on the right, gain the large overhang and layback round it on its left. Finish up the flake above.

23. **Martell** 35ft E2
5c. The centre of the wall between the gully and the dirty corner.

24. **Dry Cane** 30ft E2
5c. Start 12 feet right of the dirty corner at the right of the crag, and climb the wall behind.

25. **Gordons** 25ft Sev
The first crack on the right wall of the dirty corner.

26. **EKU 28** 35ft E3   †
4a. Climb the thin crack 6 feet right of Gordons and finish leftwards.

27. **Bacardi** 30ft Sev
The next, thin crack.

28. **Pedestal Crack** 20ft Diff
The aptly-named wide crack.

29. **Daiquiri** 20ft Hard Diff
The crack and wall 4 feet right again.

30. **Mild** 50ft Sev
From 10 feet up Cider follow an obvious traverse line left, eventually finishing up Bacardi.

31. **Cider** 25ft Diff
The shallow groove 15 feet right of the pedestal.

32. **Bitter** 30ft Diff
From the start of Cider follow a right leading line to the top.

An interesting low-level traverse at 6a starts from the triangular slab which faces the quarry entrance, and continues to the final route. Never more than 2 feet off the ground, protection is difficult to arrange for the second man.

MINOR CRAGS

MONTCLIFFE (SD 656 122)
Opposite Pilkington's Quarry, off George's Lane in Horwich. Several large bays though only one with any real possibilities. Many lines have been climbed in the past though not recorded.

1. **Show us yer Topo's**   35ft   E1   *
5b. The overhanging groove leading to a slabby upper section and exiting on the left.

2. **The 10p Giro**   30ft   E2
5b. On the wall right of the slabby arête right of Show us yer Topo's, the peg-marked crack in the middle of the wall.

MOOR GATE QUARRY (SD 665 111)
This quarry which lies by the side of the B6226 at the Blundell's Arms, has been noted as a possibility, but a raft would be essential.

PILKINGTON'S QUARRY (SD 660 120)
Just off George's Lane in Horwich, an impressive working gritstone quarry which has unfortunately been re-opened. In the last edition 13 routes were described, and more existed. The quarry is notable for having one of the finest untouched gritstone walls anywhere which would give some immaculate routes if the quarrying ceased.

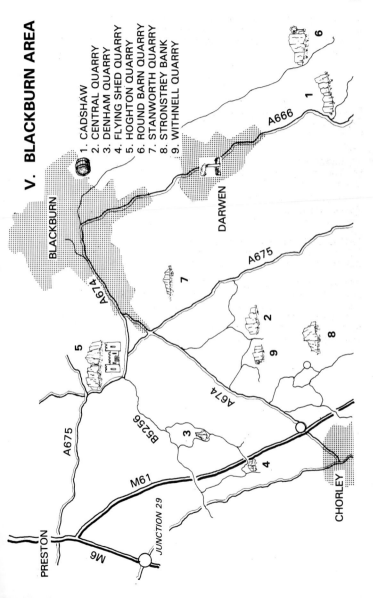

V. BLACKBURN AREA

1. CADSHAW
2. CENTRAL QUARRY
3. DENHAM QUARRY
4. FLYING SHED QUARRY
5. HOGHTON QUARRY
6. ROUND BARN QUARRY
7. STANWORTH QUARRY
8. STRONSTREY BANK
9. WITHNELL QUARRY

V. THE BLACKBURN AREA

Compiled by Dave Cronshaw
With assistance from Goi Ashmore, John Ryden, Rob Scott
and Ian & Roger Vickers

The crags within the Blackburn area have continued to develop since the last guide, as have all the other areas in the guide. Hoghton especially has seen an intense couple of years with even more aid eliminations, and new routes of every type – all in superb positions.

A couple of miles down the road, Stanworth is now a changed crag; many thousands of tons of spoil have been dumped in the centre of the quarry, and although many routes have disappeared as a consequence, some excellent routes remain. Nearby is Central Quarry, a huge circular quarry with more than its fair share of loose rock. Recent activities here have unearthed some good routes though, and much remains to be done.

Denham remains popular as an evening training ground, probably because it stays in the sun when all other crags are in shadow. The other main crag in the area is Cadshaw, where many a budding rockstar has taken his/her first tentative steps; the rocks here see a constant flow of traffic, whilst the quarry opposite (which has been neglected over the past few years, only enjoyed by a few die-hard enthusiasts) should now become more widely used as a result of recent cleaning and placing of permanent bolt belays. Round Barn Quarry is also fast reaching maturity, and Billinge Hill Quarry will provide some 'city centre bouldering' for the Blackburn crowd. Of the smaller crags in the area, Withnell (not quite so small) has seen many developments, while Flying Shed and Stronstrey Bank remain ideal for an evening visit.

BILLINGE HILL QUARRY (SD 658 283)

By Ian & Roger Vickers

SITUATION AND CHARACTER

Situated in Billinge Woods, a country park on the north-west fringe of Blackburn, this quarry provides the closest realized climbing ground to the centre of the town. The rock is good quality gritstone, similar to Hoghton (in texture if not in stature), but is only between 25 and 30 feet high and about 30 yards long.

APPROACH AND ACCESS

The quarry is best approached from the Billinge End Road entrance to the woods, where there is a small car park and toilets. Walk up the main path from here, to an old iron gateway on the left at the end of the flat section of the path. The quarry lies at the rear of the pond which lies beyond the gateway, the pond being best circumnavigated on its left side, to reach the rock.

THE ROUTES are described from LEFT to RIGHT, starting at an obvious rightward-slanting ramp.

1. **Pockets** 4a
Start at the foot of the ramp and climb the wall, using the obvious pockets.

2. **Ledgeway** 4a
Climb the ramp, moving left to follow the ledge system to the top.

3. **The Monkey's Gangway** 4b
Climb the ramp but step up and right to climb the upper slab direct.

4. **Monkey's Direct** 6b   *
Climb the wall direct to join the finish of Monkey's Gangway.

5. **Roote's Arête** 5a
Climb the faint arête and slab direct.

6. **Roote's Groove** 4b
Climb the faint groove just right of Roote's Arête, and finish up the crack above.

7. **Ripper's Ramp** 4b
Follow the ramp right of Roote's Groove and the wall above to an overlap. Finish direct.

8. **Spider's Crack** 3c
Climb the left-slanting crack right of Ripper's Ramp.

9. **Barry's Wall** 5b
Climb the wall right of Spider's Crack, and finish up the slab above.

10. **Mad Monkey's Mantel** 5c   *
Start 4 feet right of Barry's Wall and mantel onto the large hold at 6 feet. Finish direct.

11. **The Monkey's Sand Pit** 3a
Climbs cracks to the left of the obvious arête to a sandy hole. Finish direct from the hole.

12. **Paddy's Arête** Hard Sev
4a. Climb the arête to a crack and finish up this.

13. **The Big Greenie** VS
4c. Climb the big green corner to the overhangs, reach over to good jugs and swing right then finish direct.

14. **Squirrel Nutkin & the Park Warden Went to the Three Bears' Underwear Party** E3
6a. Start 3 feet right of the corner and climb the slab direct. Peg runner at mid-height.

15. **Lady C's Lost Lover** Not led
The slab between Squirrel Nutkin etc. and Randy Gardener's Groove, via a very thin crack and slight arête.

16. The Randy Gardener's Groove Hard Sev
4a. Climb the groove by a series of mantelshelves, passing a niche.

17. Where the Hell is Goldilocks VS
4c. Climbs the big corner at the meeting of the two walls – desperate when wet, yet seldom dry!

OVERHANGING WALL
Several lines have been top-roped on this wall as it is seldom dry and protection is poor. When it eventually does dry out, it should give several desperate leads for an aspiring hard-man.

There are many variations to the lines described, and the crag can be girdled at several points. Little is known of the history to the quarry, so apologies must be made for any obscure route names which are not those of the first ascensionists, whoever they may be!

CADSHAW QUARRIES (SD 708 180)
By Dave Cronshaw

SITUATION AND CHARACTER
Cadshaw lies two miles south of Darwen just off the A666 Darwen – Bolton road. There are several quarries on the site, with heights ranging from 15 feet in the Small Quarry to 75 feet in the Main Quarry. The rock is of variable quality gritstone, but on the whole is much better than appearances might suggest.

APPROACH
Fifty yards north of the B6391 Turton road (Green Arms Lane) is a bus stop, and a track signposted 'Egerton' leads through woods and around the shoulder of the hill into the main quarry in 10 minutes.

HISTORY
Although climbers had visited the quarries in the pre-1950s, the first serious attempts on the Main Quarry was John Wareing and Tim Dowberkin's impressive Green Slabs in the early 60s. In 1964 Les Ainsworth decided to explore the quarry whilst waiting for his partner to arrive. The result of this exploration was Les's first new route, Klud, which was only overcome after a mammoth two-hour struggle with the overhanging summit sods. Les had more success on his solos of the neighbouring routes Ku and Klux and by 1965 he had persuaded others across to the quarry. With Paul Hamer he climbed Baboon and the classic Orang Outang, then went on to add The Ape with Les Houlker and John Mason. In 1968, Les turned his attention to Weasel Quarry where he did Instant Insanity with John Mason. Things now lay dormant until 1973 when Dave Cronshaw found an alternative finish to one of Les's earlier routes to produce Delusion, and also around this time more routes were added to Weasel Quarry, one of which was named Allsopp's Arête which was thought to be a fitting tribute to Allan who had recently died.

1976 saw Dave's free ascent of the old aid route Gorilla with Rick Walsham, and Rhesus Negative with Phil Warner (one of his earlier aid routes). Dave Knighton and Dave Lyon paid a brief visit one day when lectures didn't appeal, and stayed long enough to add Kashmir.

The buttress above the mineshaft in the Main Quarry began to cause concern during 1975 and was eventually blown up professionally following year, destroying two of Les' earlier routes (Klukard and Mandrill) and also affecting the girdle, Little X. Shortly afterwards, Dave climbed the right corner of the recess – Resurrection Shuffle, and also Salamander. Later in the year Cronshaw cleared out the rotting aid wedges and then free climbed the fine Monkey Business. The year finished with States Wall being discovered and with three routes added in a previously neglected area.

Ian Lonsdale paid a brief visit and added Bombay Door, and then Mark Liptrot free climbed Monkey Crack and the desperate Marmoset. Things started to hot up again in 1987 whilst guidebook work was going on. Dave Etherington started to visit the quarry with a new eye for a line and spotted some obvious gaps. The first of these gaps to be filled was Slap Happy which was eventually accomplished with Jeff Hope and is in effect a direct version of Jeff's route Rhesus Positive, added the previous year. Among the other routes to fall that year were Teddy's Boy (Jeff and Dave) and then The O-Zone by Dave Cronshaw and John Ryden and lastly Picnic On Hanging Rock by Cronshaw and the up-and-coming Ian Vickers.

SMALL QUARRY
This is the short quarry, which lies just to the left of the track, about 400 yards from the main road. It has some good problems on clean rock.

YARNSDALE DELF
This is the large quarry, also known as the Main Quarry. THE CLIMBS are described from LEFT to RIGHT starting on the complex wall to the left of the main amphitheatre.

1. **Ku** 45ft Hard V Diff
At the left end of the complex wall are two 'eyeballs' above a 7-foot high pedestal. From the top of this pedestal, step right and go up trending slightly right to a short wall and the top.

2. **Time Out** 45ft E1   †
5c. Start 5 yards right at a small corner/groove. Climb this to flakes on the right then gain the short slab above on the left (PR), finish direct. The flakes can also be gained by a finger traverse from the left.

3. **Yarnsdale** 45ft Hard VS
5b. The next shallow groove to a ledge, step left and through a narrow chimney to easy ground.

4. **Klux** 45ft Sev
Just right is a block overhang at 10 feet; layback around this to a ledge and take the shallow recess above.

CADSHAW QUARRY

5. **Baptism** 50ft VS
4b. Start at the base of the rib at the left side of the amphitheatre. Climb up to a ledge and the flake above, turning the overhang on its right.

6. **The Wog** 55ft V Diff
Climb easily up a series of ledges in the left corner of the amphitheatre until it is possible to traverse left across the cracked wall near the top, to finish up the arête.

7. **Baboon** 60ft Hard Sev
4b. Up the corner 7 yards right to a ledge at 10 feet. From a higher ledge (PR) make an awkward move right and surmount the butterfly overhang above to reach a large ledge. Finish up the crack in the short steep wall above.

8. **The Ape** 65ft Hard VS   ★★
5a. On the right is an overhang at 12 feet, with a hanging groove on its left. Gain the groove and climb it to its top, then step left to a small ledge on Orang-Outang. Or, from halfway up the groove go diagonally left, below a bulge, then pull up right and make an airy mantel onto the same ledge. Continue up the left edge of the slab above.

9. **Orang-Outang** 70ft VS   ★★★
(1) 40ft 4c. Up to the overhang at 12 feet, then hand-traverse right until a gymnastic mantel can be made onto a large ledge. Climb the wall above on its left to a large ledge, NB.
(2) 30ft 4b. Gain the ledge on the left and make an exposed swing onto the ledge on the skyline. Finish up the short wall as for Baboon.

10. **Green Slab** 65ft Hard VS   ★★
(1) 40ft 4b. Start at a V-groove below a bulging arête. Climb the groove to a ledge on the left (on Orang-Outang), then take the thin crack in the shallow corner to the belay ledge of Orang-Outang.
(2) 25ft 5a. Climb the steep slab by its corner.

11. **Slap Happy** 65ft E4   ★ †
6b. Climb the edge just left of the start of Green Slab to the ledge of Orang-Outang. Step right and slap up the bulging arête direct to a ledge then step right and ascend the left side of the slab.

12. **Rhesus Negative** 75ft E1   ★
5b. The leaning crack in the slab to a ledge on the arête. Stand on the flake and move up to a small overlap (PR), move right and pull up at a short crack to gain easier ground above.

13. **O-Zone** 65ft E3   ★ †
5c. Takes a direct line up the centre of the slab. Go up to a thin dog-leg crack in the slab left of Gibbon. Climb this and move up left to gain a tiny ledge on the horizontal break. Carry on direct up the slab (BR on left) to a short crack, finish diagonally left.

14. **Gibbon** 65ft VS
4c. The oft-damp corner which bounds the long slab on its right.

15. **Gorilla** 70ft E1
Takes a line up the centre of the back wall of the amphitheatre, just left of the old mineshaft.
(1) 30ft 5b. Climb the overhanging crack to a ledge and iron spike

belay.
(2) 40ft 4c. Climb the wall behind to a small ledge near the top, traverse off right to finish behind a tree.

16. **Salamander** 75ft VS   *
Start at the left side of a square recess, behind blocks where the mineshaft used to be.
(1) 45ft 4c. Climb the crack in the left wall of the recess to a ledge on the arête. Continue up the corner above to a large ledge on the right, NB.
(2) 30ft 4a. Finish up the steep corner on the right.

17. **Resurrection Shuffle** 75ft E2   *
(1) 45ft 5b. The right corner of the recess, over several roofs to a large ledge, NB.
(2) 30ft. Up the corner behind, as for Salamander.

Farther right, past a rather unstable corner which has been climbed (black spot?), the ground level rises, and the next obvious feature is a waterfall, which sometimes flows down a series of clean rock steps.

18. **Primate** 50ft Sev.
Start just left of the waterfall at a corner/groove; climb this to a ledge at 20 feet then follow ledges in the corner above. Finish left at the top. The ORIGINAL START climbed the waterfall until a traverse left could be made to the ledge at 20 feet; slightly easier.

19. **Waterfall** 45ft V Diff/Impossible
Takes the series of clean rock steps by easy though often wet mantels, to a loose finish. The route is graded for dry conditions, otherwise it will be found to be an ungradable exercise in masochism.

20. **Bandarlog** 35ft Hard Sev
4b. At the top of the mound on the right is a deep hanging V-groove; climb this to a finish on the right.

21. **Klud** 40ft Hard Sev
4a. Ten feet right is another groove, climb this over a bulge then up past an overhang to exit on the left.

The next four routes have a common finish, so in order to avoid the hanging gardens above, a ring bolt abseil point has been planted near the top for those who do not possess green fingers.

22. **Delusion** 50ft VS   *
4c. Up the shallow groove 4 feet right to a ledge on the right, then traverse diagonally right for 10 feet to finish straight up past a break.

At a lower level are three cracks splitting the bulging wall.

23. **Monkey Crack** 45ft E2
5c. Takes the left hand crack.

24. **Monkey Business** 45ft E2 ★★
5b. The impressive crack just right.

25. **Marmoset** 45ft E4 †
6c. The desperate thin crack on the right to its end, cross the blank wall and go left to finish.

26. **Chimpanzee** 30ft Sev
The right hand corner of the wall, stepping off right at the top.

SECOND QUARRY
The following routes are situated in a large bay 100 yards further right.

27. **Picnic at Hanging Rock** 45ft E3 ★★ †
6a. At the left side of the bay is a wall with a niche at half height. Scramble up to a belay beside a large block. Climb up into the niche and take the crack above to the horizontal handrail, traverse left for a few feet then, using a small sloping ledge, go up the wall trending slightly right. **Variation** (E2 5b ★): hand traverse the break rightwards to a dynamic swing-up which enables the arête to be gained. Continue more easily to the top.

28. **Teddy's Boy** 30ft E2 †
5c. The leaning wall to the right, bounded on the left by a grassy rake. The route takes the overhanging wall and crack to a small tree near the top. Start below the top crack, climb up and left of a thin crack, to a horizontal break. Step right and pull into the flake/crack to finish.

STATES WALL
To the right of the last bay is a long, leaning wall parallel with the stream; this is States Wall. The first routes here start in the deep corner on the left. All the routes at present end at a long ledge upon which there is a convenient abseil point.

29. **Utah** 60ft Hard Sev
4b. From the arête left of the deep corner traverse past a pointed block to below a small inverted triangular niche. Up to this, then diagonally right to a large ledge. Gain the flake above and exit onto a sloping ledge, go up to the long ledge and PB on the right, AO.

30. **Colorado** 45ft VS
4c. From the base of the deep corner climb the short wall on the left to the large ledge. Move up to an awkward sloping ledge above and continue up a short V-groove to the long ledge.

31. **Blind Alley** 45ft Hard VS ★ †
5a. Start just right of the corner and climb the wall to a square niche. Step right and pull through the centre of the overhangs above, finishing up a shallow corner to the long ledge.

32. **California** 50ft VS
4c. Climb the wide crack on the right to the overhang, pass this on its right to a ledge above. Traverse left to the PB.

WEASEL QUARRY
This quarry lies hidden in the trees on the other side of the stream, opposite States Wall.

33. Instant Insanity   50ft   Hard VS   ★★
5a. This route is somewhat unique by starting on quarried rock and finishing on natural grit. Start at the left side of the amphitheatre, at the crack nearest the arête. Climb the crack until it is possible to traverse round the arête at half height, to a small ledge overlooking the stream, finish directly above.

34. The Loony Bin   40ft   Hard VS   †
5b. Start as for Instant Insanity but climb direct to the top on wobbly holds.

35. Kashmir   45ft   Hard VS   ★
5a. Start 8 feet right at an obvious wide crack and follow this to the horizontal break, then step left to a short crack and from the top of this swing right into a niche and exit right at the top.

36. Bombay Door   45ft   Hard VS   ★
5a. Follow Kashmir to the horizontal break, then step right to a crack. Climb this and move left to the niche, exit right at the top.

37. Boogie Mamma   40ft   E1
5b. The leaning block-filled crack on the right.

On the remaining routes in the quarry, a preplaced rope hung from the top will be necessary to enable a belay to be made at the top of the routes.

38. Allsopp's Arête   30ft   Hard VS   ★
4c. Start just right of the left arête of the next buttress, by a tree close to the rock. Climb the steep crack to a ledge, continue up just right of the arête.

39. It'll All End in Tears   35ft   E1
5c. Climbs the wall in the centre of the buttress starting from a ledge at 5 feet. Pull into a small niche then climb the thin crack above, step left and finish up a large flake.

40. Quarry Groove   35ft   Severe
4a. The groove just right to ledges on the right. Finish up a small flake.

41. Spilt Milk   35ft   Severe
The weakness 10 feet right of Quarry Groove, to finish up that route.

42. The End   30ft   Hard Sev.
4b. Up the centre of the next buttress, cut through the overhang by a V-groove.

SUNKEN QUARRY
This small hidden quarry may be reached by following the green track for 150 yards, around the hillside to the right (towards Cadshaw Rocks), and provides some interesting problems up to 25 feet high.

CADSHAW CASTLE ROCKS (SD 708 182)

By Allan Allsopp with recent update by Dave Cronshaw

SITUATION AND CHARACTER

Cadshaw Castle Rocks or Fairy Buttery is a small natural outcrop of sound rock situated on the sunny side of a pleasant valley, opposite Cadshaw Quarry. It is an ideal place for beginners.

APPROACH

The rocks are reached by following a path down from the quarry to the stream. Cross this by a footbridge and ascend a short slope to arrive at the foot of the rocks.

HISTORY

In 1937, Allan Allsopp wrote a guide to Cadshaw Rocks which described about thirty routes. These included The Niche, Pagan's Progress, The Mantelshelf, Central Buttress, Central Wall, Split Block Crack and the Girdle. It is likely that most of these routes were the work of Allan himself and he continued his developments through the war years, until by 1951 all but a few of the present routes had been climbed. Around this time a problem known as Altar Direct (now a part of Druid's Direct) was climbed. The execution of this problem had to be very precise, and it is thought Jim Nightingale was the originator; he actually conquered the problem wearing a pair of leather breeches which gave his knees extra purchase on the rock – bad style but effective!

The last remaining gaps at the crag now were the double overhangs (at that time) of the unled Split Block Overhang of which the first lead is unknown, and Druid's Face which was occasionally top roped but was left to Nightingale to lead (amidst stiff competition) in 1961.

THE CLIMBS are described from RIGHT to LEFT.

1. **The Staircase** 25ft Moderate
The short easy-angled slab at the right end of the rocks.

2. **Druid's Corner** 35ft Hard V Diff
Start 7 feet left of the right edge of the crag. Ascend to a square notch on the arête and continue up this on its right.

3. **Niche Indirect** 50ft Sev
From Druid's Corner make a rising traverse past a small flake to the niche in the centre of the wall, traverse right to the arête and finish up this.

4. **Druid's Face** 40ft E2   ★★★
5b. Gain the niche from directly below, and climb over the overhang above via a crack. Move up right to a slight depression in the upper wall. Reach up for a hidden hold and so the top; superb.

5. **Pagan's Progress** 45ft VS   *
4c. A good climb. Left is an overhang at 8 feet (The Altar), start up a vague corner and turn the overhang on its right then step back left onto The Altar. Traverse left to a ledge and climb up into the recess above (The Crow's Nest). Using the block above (The Coffin) as a right foothold, climb the short wall above.

6. **Druid's Direct** 45ft E3   **
6a. Start below the centre of the overhang and make some precarious moves onto The Altar. Climb straight up and over the second overhang, finishing up the rippled wall. A delicate yet strenuous route.

7. **Pagan's Direct** 40ft Hard VS   **
5b. Boulder up the nose which forms the left edge of the buttress, and go up to the coffin. Hand traverse this to a thin crack in the wall above, finish up this.

8. **Pagan Wall** 35ft Sev
The narrow wrinkled wall on the left-hand side of the buttress.

9. **Corner Chimney** 35ft Moderate
The block-filled cleft in the corner.

10. **East Face Climb** 35ft Hard V Diff
Start 8 feet left and follow a more or less direct line up the wall, stepping onto a large flake, to a poor finish.

11. **Column Climb** 40ft Diff   *
Up the corner above the prominent rock column, gain a flat triangular ledge and climb leftwards to the top.

12. **Crack and Wall** 35ft Sev
The sharp edged crack 6 feet left to a good ledge then the short wall above, or climb diagonally right from the ledge at V Diff.

13. **Overhang and Wall** 35ft Hard Sev
4b. The small triangular overhang just left is climbed direct to the good ledge, finishing up the wall just right of the corner crack.

14. **Overhang Crack** 35ft Hard V Diff   *
The thin crack left of the overhang to a good ledge, then the steep corner crack to finish.

15. **The Mantelshelf** 35ft Sev   *
Polished holds up the wall on the left lead to a difficult mantel at 12 feet. Step left and follow the crack which bounds the overhang on its left.

16. **Blue Lights** 35ft VS
4b. Follow The Mantelshelf to its namesake, then go carefully over the overhang above, the stability of which gives great cause for concern.

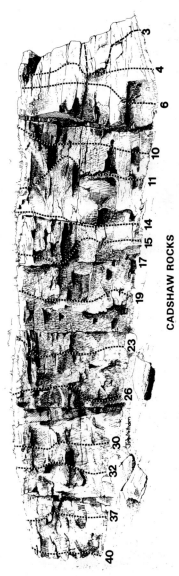

CADSHAW ROCKS

17. Oak Tree Chimney 30ft   V Diff
The wide block-filled crack to the tree.

18. Tyro's Delight 40ft   Moderate
From 12 feet up Oak Tree Chimney, gain the good ledge on the left then leave the left end of this ledge via a ridge.

19. The Slab 30ft   V Diff
The steep slab and wall on the left. Numerous variations are possible, the best being on the left.

20. Central Chimney 30ft   Hard V Diff
The chimney behind the projecting leaf of The Slab.

21. Central Buttress 25ft   VS
5a. The narrow buttress on the left, direct.

22. Central Crack 35ft   V Diff   ⋆
The corner crack, exiting on the right at the constriction.

23. Central Wall 35ft   Hard Sev   ⋆
4b. Just left is a clean slabby wall, climb it by its centre, passing through the Bull's Horns (a gap in the overlap which splits the wall at half-height) and the steep wall above to a recess below the top overhang. Finish left or right through this.

24. The Snout 30ft   Diff
The polished nose on the left is gained with difficulty, then good holds lead more easily to the top.

25. Snout Wall 30ft   V Diff
The thin crack in the wall which forms the left edge of The Snout.

26. Zig Zag 30ft   Hard V Diff
Start in the short V-Groove just left. Pull over rightwards onto a small ledge and continue steeply to the top.

27. West Corner 30ft   V Diff
The corner just left, finishing up the right branch.

28. West Chimney 30ft   V Diff
The block-filled cleft right of West Slab.

29. West Slab 30ft   V Diff
Climb the steep slab on the left diagonally rightwards into Western Chimney. A more direct line up the slab is possible; VS 4b.

Left again is an overhang at 15 feet, bounded on each side by cracks. Care should be taken with the rock in this vicinity.

30. Split Block Crack 30ft   Hard Sev   ⋆
4b. The thin corner crack on the right of the overhang, with surprisingly awkward moves through the bulges.

31. Split Block Overhang 25ft   Hard VS
5a. Climbs direct over the overhang on sloping holds.

32. Split Block Climb 25ft   Sev   ⋆
4a. The shallow hanging groove on the left side of the overhang.

33. West Wall 20ft   Sev
The face climb just left, passing an overlap at half height.

34. Curving Crack 20ft Hard Diff
The prominent hand crack on the left.

35. West Rib 20ft V Diff
The rib on the left has a difficult finish on sloping holds.

36. Easy Chimney 20ft Moderate
The obvious deep cleft.

37. West Mantelshelf 25ft Hard Diff
The short wall to a broad ledge, then up the wall just left of the chimney passing a small ledge (the West Mantelshelf).

38. West Buttress – Ordinary 30ft Diff
Start just right of the left arête of the crag and climb diagonally right to the top.

39. West Buttress – Direct 25ft V Diff
From the start of West Buttress – Ordinary, take a direct line to the top.

40. The Bulges 25ft V Diff
The bulging arête with an undercut start is climbed on the right.

41. West Face 20ft Hard V Diff
The short, steep end wall of the crag.

42. Girdle Traverse 180ft Sev   ★★
There are numerous variations to this traverse, and belays are possible at many points.
Start from the notch on Druids Corner and traverse the wall past the niche, to the top of the nose. Move round into Corner Chimney then make an ascending traverse to the triangular ledge on Column Climb. Go along to Overhang Crack and climb down a couple of moves to gain the ledge of The Mantleshelf on the left. Cross to Tyro's Delight and cross Central Wall at roughly the same level, step down to the ledge on Zig Zag and follow this to West Chimney. Move up then traverse left across to the top of Split Block Overhang. Descend to a narrow ledge and go round the rib into Easy Chimney. Gain the ledge on West Mantelshelf and descend obliquely left until an easy line leads round the arête, crossing West Face to finish.

CENTRAL QUARRY (SD 641 217)

By Goi Ashmore and Rob Scott

SITUATION AND CHARACTER
Basically the quarry consists of a broken wall on the left and a much better series of buttresses on the right which finally drop down to the forbidding Main Wall. There are several marked boulder problems on the buttresses to the left and on the first tier on the right-hand side. The first major climbs lie on the higher tier of the right-hand walls. After a long low stretch is Southworth's Bay – identifiable by the boiler plate on its right-hand side.

APPROACH
Central Quarry lies on the sharp bend of the Abbey Village to Withnell

road when coming from the A675 Bolton – Preston road.

HISTORY

This rather esoteric quarry was first visited in the mid 70's by Robin Barley and Jerry Peel, whilst Barley was actually doing research work in the quarry, and it was this pair who excavated two big routes in the shape of the now defunct Vendetta and Co-Axial. These routes have never had a confirmed second ascent, which is perhaps just as well as the rock was extremely poor and so ashamed of itself that large sections have now fallen down.

The next activity occurred in 1978 when Robin Barley, Les Ainsworth and Dave Cronshaw paid several visits, climbing most of the current routes on Birch Buttress. The most worthwhile of these routes was undoubtedly The Birch which was originally climbed with the capping bulge in situ. The quarry then enjoyed well deserved obscurity until John Morrissey and Dave Carpenter tenuously ascended Gibbering Crack, a route which has since had a facelift. It was this trundling that attracted Goi Ashmore to the quarry, who soloed Little Matchstick Owen's Route, A Thing of Hate and I Put my Trust in You, before loosing his suicidal urge and retiring to Withnell.The last route in the quarry to date was Riding High, memorable for the high ground-falls encountered on its first two ascents. Climbed in mid-December it was too cold to differentiate between holds and icicles. The fact that it was the holds which became detached and not the icicles just about sums up the nature of the quarry. The boulder problems are mostly the work of Morrissey and Dave Carpenter.

SOUTHWORTH'S BAY

1. **Rubber Bullet** 20ft Hard Sev ⋆
4b. Climbs the groove in the centre of the buttress behind the boiler plate; unprotected.

2. **Spy** 25ft VS
5a. Climbs the wall on the left of the middle buttress of the bay, finishing up the obvious block.

Fifty yards farther left is **TREE BUTTRESS**, obvious by the large birch tree at its top.

3. **Camina** 35ft Hard V Diff
Just left of the grass slope at the right end of the buttress, two flakes can be followed easily to the top.

4. **Lode Star** 35ft VS
4c. Start just right of the obvious arête and climb up until it is possible to traverse left onto the large ledge on Pot Pourri. Finish up the arête.

5. **Pot-Pourri** 40ft VS ⋆
5a. Start just left of the square-cut arête with a corner groove at its top. Climb to the overlap (PR), then make a long reach to a good hold and

continue to the ledge. Finish up the groove above.

6. Mad Barney 40ft VS
4b. Start 10 feet left and climb the wall and corner above to an exit over a jammed block.

7. Paul Mitchell Can't Climb 40ft Lethal! †
5b. Just left is an obvious triangular chimney. This horrendous route takes this via several levitating blocks then uses some highly dubious holds to gain the thin crack above, to finish up Bizz Energy, or more likely in a morgue.

8. Bizz Energy 45ft Hard VS
5a. Left again is a slabby wall which is cut away at its base. Pull onto this wall below an obvious PR (the use of stacked boulders at the start is illegal). Pass the PR and follow the right side of the wall above.

9. Verboten 40ft Sev
4a. The large corner on the left.

10. Sabre 50ft E1 ★★
5b. Climb the sandy wall just right of The Birch to an overhang, then go boldly over this to reach a hanging flake crack, which can be followed to a grassy finish.

11. The Birch 55ft Hard VS ★★★
5b. A much better route than first appearances might suggest Start directly below the birch and climb a crack to the overhang. Gain the inverted triangular niche above, then finish up the thin crack above, or via the groove on the left.

Thirty yards left past some broken rock is an obvious cracked grey wall.

12. Riding High 35ft Hard Sev
4a. On the right-hand side of the wall is a disjointed crack system split at half-height by a ledge. The route takes these cracks.

Round the arête is **PALE WALL**, obvious by the half-height terrace and large rock fall at its base. Tree belays well back.

13. Gibberish Crack 40ft Hard Sev
4a. The initial resurrected crack of the wall proves very dusty.

14. Little Matchstick Owen's Route 35ft Hard VS
5c. Six feet left of the initial crack is a very thin crack with a pocket at 10 feet. Use this to gain the terrace then continue up the obvious dual crack system.

15. A Thing of Hate 30ft Hard VS †
5a. Thirty yards left of Pale Wall is an obvious slab, climb this bridging up the scar, then swing slightly right and finish direct. **Direct Finish** (E2 5c †): the obvious unprotected scoop.

MAIN WALL

This is the large gloomy buttress at the far right hand side, generally obscured by a profusion of slime, although there is some potential here if equipped with industrial sand blasting equipment. Two routes were described in the last guide; **Vendetta** (VS 4c) and **Co-Axial** (Hard VS

5b), but they have now fallen into a state of disrepair and can only at present be recorded as unjustifiable. An aided traverse of the wall exists, using either pegs or friends, with huge pendulums to avoid the looser sections.

No routes lie on the left-hand side at present.

DENHAM QUARRY (SD 592 228)

By Dave Cronshaw and John Ryden

SITUATION AND CHARACTER
The quarry lies 5 miles south east of Preston, near the village of Brindle. Climbing here is on variable quality gritstone and being west-facing, is ideal for an evening visit.

APPROACH AND ACCESS
The quarry is under the ownership of Chorley council, having been bequeathed to the borough for 'public enjoyment'.

From the M6 (junction 29) follow the A6 south for about one mile to a small roundabout at Clayton Green. Turn left here onto the B5256 and continue for about half a mile to another roundabout. Follow the left turning from this roundabout and cross the M61 almost immediately, then after a further quarter of a mile turn right into Holt Lane and follow the road round until it is possible to drive into the quarry on the left a few hundred yards farther on.

If approaching from Blackburn or Hoghton, turn onto the B5256 from the sharp bend on the A675, which is midway between the Royal Oak and the Boar's Head, then follow the road through Brindle and turn left after about half a mile into Holt Lane. The Blackburn – Leyland bus route runs along the B5256.

HISTORY
The early history at Denham is still rather vague although it is known that various parties climbed here during the 50's, making first ascents and at least one guidebook was written to the crag. This guide was handwritten and had a very restricted circulation. Les Ainsworth was shown a copy of the booklet but it was in the days before photocopiers and Les was unable to make a duplicate. One route stood out in his mind however, a route called the Green Caterpillar which is probably now the line taken by Narrow Slab, the Caterpillar having unrolled itself in the 1960's.

Les 'discovered' the crag whilst taking a rather circuitous route back to college and soon set about climbing all the obvious lines with Paul Hamer; in many cases re-climbing lines which had been done previously and renaming them with such inspired names as Mohammed the Mad Monk of Moorside Home for Mental Misfits, and also adding some routes of their own such as Gnomely, the Mediaeval Melancholic, The Layback and Main Break, whilst Concave Wall was done by John McGonagle. Hank Pasquill made a fleeting visit and left having made the first free ascent of Dry which was one of the routes done by the previous generation of Denham devotees. The locals now believed that there was little remaining to be done in the quarry, but this illusion was shattered when Dave Knowles claimed Mad Karoo in the summer of 1969. No-one had attempted routes on this wall, and at first there was some scepticism about the route, and then uncertainty as to its proper line. Re-reading the description showed the true line, and two more obvious gaps suddenly came to light. Dave Cronshaw and Les Ainsworth now turned their attention to this wall and Dave clocked up Time, with Les in tow. The pair then switched leads for Les to complete End of Time; a brilliant route which unfortunately had to resort to a little aid to reach the break. Next in line was the obvious traverse of the large horizontal fault which did not succumb without a little tussle with a large block which fell onto Les's shoulder near the top whilst he was placing his first runner. Les confessed to feeling "a little naked in the way of protection" as a fall would have been nasty, and thus the route was named Complete Streaker. Soon after Les climbed Our Man From Cairo and Timepiece. Things were then dormant at Denham for some time until Dave Knighton appeared on the scene in 1977. With Eric Dearden he converted the old aid route Sticky into a free route with just one point of aid (later eliminated by Dave Kenyon); That's All It Takes. Knighton then turned his attention to the right arête of the wall and soon produced the superb Flick Of The Wrist, and the year ended with Nigel Bonnett claiming the short arête above the pool on the 'Last Day But One' of his holidays.

1980 saw Tony Brindle 'Going for the One', followed closely by Eric's Arête by Dearden, and then in 1981 attentions turned to the Overhang Area when Cronshaw forced two interesting routes through the roofs with Chronometer and Chrono-Logical, the aid route Super Indirectissima having been done by Les and Ian Cowell a few years previously.

In 1982 Cronshaw renewed his attentions to the aid route Torreador, and after a couple of failures he completed the route free, with John Ryden, as Bullworker. Then 1983 saw Greg Rimmer knocking off Jimmy Sideways, whilst Malc Haslam retaliated with the neighbouring Lock off Locomotion. This latter route became derailed later, when a huge block fell from the roof, rendering it obsolete. This pair clubbed together with Mick Ryan and visiting kiwi Roland Foster to establish Screaming Meemees whilst Eric Dearden had returned to the main walls of the amphitheatre and put up Cyclops.

Preston ace, Andrew Gridley arrived on the scene in 1987 when he climbed the fiercely technical problem, Fujari, followed closely by more intimate contact on his Private Palpate. Finally, after numerous small fillers-in by various climbers, the latest addition of any note was made early in 1988 when Cronshaw took a dive which nearly ended head-first into the pool when he fell from the top moves on Acapulco.

THE CLIMBS

The quarry is conveniently divided up into three areas; the Pool Area on the right, which provides the best climbing; the Overhang Area marked by the great overhangs on the left side of the crag; and the

Intermediate Area which lies between the other two.

THE CLIMBS are described from RIGHT to LEFT.

POOL AREA
The first three routes are all poorly protected.

1. **Ashimoto** 35ft Hard Diff
From the centre of the end wall follow an obvious line of ledges and a ramp to a finishing groove.

2. **Waldo** 35ft Hard Sev
From the foot of the ramp on Ashimoto, mantel onto the left wall then up to a large ledge (and the first and only runner, in a borehole) finish easily right.

3. **Short Circuit** 40ft E1   * †
5b. Climb the wall between Waldo and Our Man From Cairo direct via a borehole at half height.

4. **Our Man from Cairo** 40ft Hard VS   *
5b. Climb the left-facing groove for 15 feet, high PR, then make an awkward pull out right onto a small sloping ledge. Move across to another small ledge on the right then up left, finishing past 3 prominent nebs.

5. **Gnomely** 40ft Hard VS
5a. From the sloping ledge on Our Man From Cairo move up and left to ledges, then follow the weakness above.

6. **Narrow Slab** 40ft Hard Diff
Climb the centre of the narrow slab to the left, turning the capping overhang on the left.

7. **Splash Arête** 45ft V Diff   ***
Just above and left is a large ledge, gain this and then up to a further two ledges and traverse left to the arête and disproportionate exposure. Finish airily up the arête.

8. **Last Day but One** 35ft E2   *
5b. From the large ledge, climb the obvious right arête of the pool to finish as for Splash Arête.

Around the arête, an aid route climbs the steep wall above the pool. The next 5 routes have a common start in the corner recess at the left edge of the pool.

9. **Wet** 85ft Hard V Diff
From the corner traverse right, moving down slightly to reach the right corner, climb this over large ledges. Waterwings advisable.

10. **Damp** 70ft VS
4c. Follow Wet to the centre of the wall, then reach up to a mantel ledge and climb the shallow groove above to the terrace, finish directly up the wall behind.

11. **Acapulco** 60ft E2   * †
5b. The shallow groove in the wall left of Damp is gained from below on creaky flakes. From the terrace take the problem wall left of Damp via two pockets.

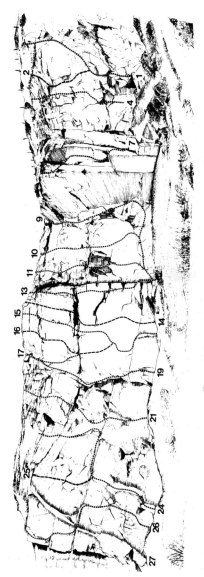

DENHAM QUARRY The Pool Area

12. **Dry** 55ft E1
(1) 30ft 5c. Climb the corner recess without respite, to the terrace.
(2) 25ft 4b. Move up left to a ledge on the arête, then take the stepped ledges on the right to finish.

13. **Flick of the Wrist** 60ft E2 ★★
5c. Climb the corner for a few feet to a swing left around the slabby arête. Climb over the bulge above with difficulty, past an ancient BR, to the horizontal break. Pull over the overhang to a ledge and then finish up the arête.

14. **That's All it Takes** 65ft E4 ★ †
6b. Start 15 feet left of the arête and gain a footledge at 5 feet. Use peg slots and small flakes to reach an overlap. Surmount this on its left to a cave in the break. Leave the cave by a flake in the roof and climb the upper wall on widely spaced but positive holds. Actually takes more than most people have to give!

The following six routes start from the large ledge at the base of the wall. Protection is generally lacking, thus making these routes serious undertakings. Various problems exist on the short wall below the ledge.

15. **End of Time** 70ft E2 ★★
5b. From the large ledge mantel onto a small ledge on the right at 10 feet, then move up right to gain the break with difficulty. From the left side of the cave, climb the overhang on large but awkward holds and finish direct.

16. **Time** 65ft E1 ★
5a. From the mantel at 10 feet on the previous route, continue direct via a pocket to the break. Go diagonally right a few feet, passing another pocket, then climb a shallow scoop and finish to the right above this.

17. **Mad Karoo** 65ft Hard VS ★
4c. Follow Time to the horizontal break, then trend left and climb the wall on flakes, just right of the shallow corner.

18. **Complete Streaker** 95ft VS ★★
A little naked in the way of protection.
4c. Climb Concave Wall to the obvious horizontal break. Traverse this almost to the arête, PR, gain the ledge above the overhang and streak up the blunt arête in a fine position.

19. **Concave Wall** 60ft Sev
Climb easily over ledges in the angle of the wall, then finish up the shallow groove which forms the corner.

20. **Bevel** 80ft V Diff
From the ledge, traverse left across ledges to where D.C. left his mark for posterity. Go up and right to a large ledge then follow the diagonal break leftwards, finishing over poor rock.

21. **Monk Puzzle** 60ft Hard VS
(1) 30ft 5b. Start 20 feet left of the angle of the wall, directly below the chiselled D.C. Climb up past a curious hole to a ledge then up right to a large ledge and poor TB.

(2) 30ft 4c. Follow the flake above to a small overlap then straight up passing some friable rock.

Between the angle of the wall and the first pitch of Monk Puzzle are some interesting boulder problems:
  (a) The obvious scoop just left of the angle of the wall (5b).
  (b) The shallow peg cracks right of Monk Puzzle (5c).

There is also a low level traverse from the corner of Wet, to Green Finger Crack at 5a – 6a depending which bits are missed out.

22. **Brittle Nerve** 55ft E3
6a. The obvious right slanting weakness 15 feet left is climbed (PR) to the large ledge, continue up the easier wall above.

23. **Timepiece** 90ft Hard VS ✱
5a. From a circular rock feature just left, climb the steep wall on slots to the left end of a large ledge. Hand traverse out left along the break, passing an obvious groove. Traverse left round the arête to finish up a short crack.

24. **Mohammed the Morbid Mogul** 85ft Sev
Left again is a shallow corner, climb this to the large ledge then traverse easily right to D.C.'s epitaph. Step up and left then direct to finish up a crack in the short wall above.

25. **Private Palpate** 55ft E4
6b. From where Timepiece traverses off left, climb the thin crack in the wall above past 2 PRs.

26. **Going for the One** 70ft E2
5b. Start midway between the two Mohammed climbs, move up to a small overlap and step right to climb the left side of the thin flake above. Traverse off left to Mad Monk and stride across its groove to gain a thin crack. Climb this until it is possible to swing left to finish.

27. **Mohammed the Mad Monk of Moorside Home for Mental Misfits** 50ft VS ✱✱✱
4c. The appealing right-leaning groove at the left side of the Pool Area. At the top finish slightly right, or follow the old peg crack.

28. **Mohammed Arête** 50FT E1
5b. From the start of Mad Monk, climb the wall just right of the arête passing a thin crack.

29. **Mohammed the Mediaeval Melancholic** 45ft VS
4c. Climb the left side of the arête to finish up a short crack.

30. **Green Finger Crack** 35ft VS
4b. The obvious loose-looking flake crack 20 feet left is gained by delicate moves to start.

31. **Cyclops** 30ft Hard VS
5b. Start 10 yards left below a small overhang. Climb over the overhang, passing a large hole on the right.

RIGHT INTERMEDIATE AREA

32.   Eric's Arête   30ft   E1
5b. The slightly friable right arête of the area.

To the left are three grooves:

33.   Den Diedre   20ft   V Diff
The first groove.

34.   Tower View   20ft   V Diff
The middle groove.

35.   Tower Groove   25ft   Diff
The deep V-groove on the left.

36.   Ledgeway   20ft   Moderate
The broken series of ledges in the corner on the left.

37.   The Clangers   20ft   Hard Sev
4a. The ancient peg crack just left.

38.   Notions of Disposability   25ft   E1   †
5c. From the left edge of the wall make awkward moves up the right side of the arête.

39.   Albert's Arête   20ft   Hard Diff
The arête on the right of the large bay, gained easily from the left.

40.   Nuts   35ft   Hard Sev
The grassy corner in the centre of the bay. Carry a machete.

41.   Pop   35ft   Hard VS
5a. Start 10 feet left of the corner, below a niche. Gain this direct via a small hole at 10 feet, and continue to the top.

42.   Rivet   35ft   VS
4c. To the left are twin cracks. Up these to a ledge on the right, then exit awkwardly up and left.

43.   Fujari   35ft   E5   †
6c. The line of cleaned holds in the wall on the left provides a desperate sequence of moves on undercuts, to gain a short finishing crack (2PRs).

44.   Aviemore Arête   30ft   Sev
The arête on the left with a loose finish.

There is a low-level traverse around the area with one 5c move.

LEFT INTERMEDIATE AREA
The area of rock stretching left contains generally easy climbs, but they are in danger of disappearing under a cloak of vegetation.

45.   Hough   30ft   Hard V Diff
Start as for Curving Crack but climb the short, thin groove and square niche above to a heathery finish.

46.   Curving Crack   35ft   Diff
The wide curving crack, finish to the right by scrambling over heather.

47.   Slanting Groove   30ft   Diff
The shallow groove snaking right, then the groove above.

48. Thin Finger Crack 35ft VS
4c. The peg-scarred crack just left.

49. Groove and Wall 40ft Hard Sev
4a. Climb the groove on the right of Low Rib, to the top of the rib, then finish direct. Care needed with rock on the top wall.

50. Low Rib 40ft Hard V Diff ★
Start at the rib which projects from the lowest ground level and climb this for a few feet until forced left. Continue to the top of the rib, then climb up and left to a large ledge on the arête, follow this to the top.

51. Finito 35ft Hard VS
5a. Start 8 feet left at a corner with a hole on its left wall, and climb this on its left until it is possible to move right to finish.

Just left of the main buttress is an isolated slab, **Slabracadabra** (5b) takes the centre of this, after an awkward start using shallow cracks.

FAR INTERMEDIATE AREA
The short buttress 20 yards left.

52. Sprain 20ft VS
4c. Start just left of the right arête of the buttress. After a difficult start climb over the overhang by a V-shaped groove.

53. Midget 20ft V Diff
Start in the angle of the buttress, then step right onto a nose and surmount the overhang above.

54. Nosey 20ft VS
5b. Ascend the overhanging nose on sidepulls then climb straight over the overhang above.

55. The Ceaseless Tide 20ft VS
5c. Just left of Nosey is a blunt rib; climb this and the wall above.

56. Fingerbore 20ft VS
4c. Start 3 feet left and climb direct to the overhang via boreholes, then finish up the groove on the left.

57. Abrasions and Lacerations 40ft VS
5a. A right to left traverse of the area just below the overhanging band.

OVERHANG AREA
The next climbs are on the final section of unbroken rock, which presents itself as 3 buttresses, before it drops down to the lower level and the Great Overhang.

58. The Edge 30ft V Diff
Keep to the right side of the buttress.

59. Trigular 30ft Moderate
Up the centre of the next buttress, past a triangle chipped in the rock, to a ledge, then right to finish.

60. Extra 40ft Diff
The right corner of the next shallow bay, finish to the left.

61. Intra 40ft Hard V Diff

Climb the centre of the bay, passing between the overhangs.

62. Lintel   30ft   Sev
Climb the overhang which Intra avoids, swing round the overhang on its left, then finish easily.

63. Central Buttress   40ft   Diff
Climb the left side of the bay to the overhang at 12 feet then traverse left and follow a line of boreholes to the top.

64. Central Buttress Direct   45ft   V Diff
Climb the Central Buttress directly, starting behind a small bush.

65. Cuckoo's Nest   30ft   Hard VS
5b. To the left and at a higher level is a steep slab. Climb this just right of the corner, via a pocket.

66. The Layback   30ft   VS
4c. The corner crack.

67. Dislocation   30ft   V Diff
From the base of Layback move up left and climb the corner, borehole runner.

68. Wings   30ft   E1
5c. Below and left of the previous route is a butterfly overhang. Starting up a short rib climb the overhang by a short hanging groove, then the arête above.

69. Butterfly   30ft   Sev
Start just left. Climb a flakey wall and the 2 corners above.

70. Step in the Clouds   30ft   Sev
From behind some large blocks on the ground climb up to a ledge (or gain the ledge by the ramp on the left, better). Gain the top of the block behind then traverse right to a small ledge and an easy finish.

71. The Funny Farm   30ft   Hard Sev
4b. Climb the corner groove where the ground level drops, at the overhang pull out right, then finish straight up the steep ramp.

72. Quasimodo   35ft   E1
5b. Climb the arête on the left to a sloping ledge, then finish up the groove above. An alternative start is possible by climbing the corner on the left of the arête: **Quasimodo Left-Foot**.

73. Super Indirectissima   45ft   A2
The obvious line of ancient bolts across the Great Overhang, finishing with an awkward free move.

74. Screaming Meemees   40ft   E3
6a. Climb the roof crack (Friends) and a short corner above the narrowing of the roof, just left of the previous route.

75. Bullworker   35ft   E3   ★★
Free climbs the old aid route Torreador.
6a. Start 20 feet further left and climb a slabby rib to the overlap. Enter the steep peg crack above and follow it to the top.

76. Main Break   50ft   Hard Sev   ★
4a. Left again is a steep rib leading to a break in the overhang. Start

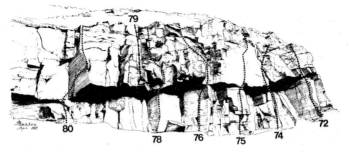

DENHAM QUARRY Overhangs Area

left of the rib and climb up through the break, then step left and climb a slab.

77. Ganglion 110ft VS
4a. Climb through the overhang as for Main Break, but traverse left above the roof for 20 feet. Either step up and swing left across a bottomless groove, or move down to cross the groove (or maybe jump across it?). Continue along, crossing a V-groove then climb a short arête and broken rock to finish. Poor protection.

78. Chronometer 40ft Hard VS
5a. Further left the overhang is broken by a hanging groove. Climb a rib to the overhang, then from a good hold above, make a long reach right to enter the groove. Climb it then exit left to a ledge, finish easily above.

79. Crono-Logical 45ft E2 ★
5c. Follow Chronometer to the good hold but make a committing swing leftwards onto a jutting block. Make an impressive mantel onto this and finish easily. Excellent protection is available but needs a little thought.

The blocks lying on the ground to the left are the remains of a rib which used to form the start of **Lock off Locomotion** (E2 6a). This route hand-traversed the lip of the roof leftwards to finish up the next route. It has not been ascended since the demise of the rib.

80. Jimmy Sideways 45FT HARD VS
5a. Where the large overhang ends is an undercut slab with a sycamore beneath its left side. Step off a boulder into the corner then gain the rib on the right and so to the top.

81. Rockdancer 45ft Hard VS
5a. From the boulder at the start of Jimmy Sideways climb a crack in the centre of the slab until it is possible to traverse right into the corner. Finish on the right.

82. Rocking Horse Droppings 35ft Sev
Twelve feet left of the sycamore is a short wall. Start at the left side of this and step up, then move right across the wall to a finish up the right side.

FLYING SHED QUARRY (SD 583 217)

By Les Ainsworth, Dave Cronshaw and John Ryden.

SITUATION AND CHARACTER
The quarry lies across the M61 from Denham, and a visit to both crags can easily be combined. The disused end of the quarry consists of several buttresses on the right hand side, the most striking of which is about 60 feet high. Beyond this the rock rapidly deteriorates and quarrying is still continuing.

APPROACH
From the small roundabout on the B5256 by the bridge over the M61 about 200 yards on the Leyland side of the Denham turning, turn away from Denham, and continue for about 100 yards to the Lord Nelson. Turn left here and continue to the Duke of York, then take a small turning on the left about 150 yards farther on. Car parking is possible here below the miraculous 'flying shed', provided that care is taken not to block access.

HISTORY
Flying Shed was rapidly developed in 1981 by Les Ainsworth, Dave Cronshaw, John Ryden, Roger Vickers and John Grundy. Of note are Les's Lancastrian and Dave's Barrier Reef, whilst Roger and his son Ian opened up, and climbed the first routes on Optrex Slab; Epheseus and Giza.

THE CLIMBS are described from LEFT to RIGHT.

BARRIER BUTTRESS
The main feature of this buttress is a prominent overhang which guards access to the upper wall.

1. **Spiral Galaxy in Virgo** 55ft Hard VS
5a. Above the left side of the barrier overhang is a deep triangular niche at three quarters height. Start below this and climb to a small niche below the barrier overhang, then surmount the overhang with difficulty using a springy block under the roof and the flake crack above. Continue to the deep niche and exit from this over the right side of the roof to finish up the blocky groove above.

2. **Handless Corpse** 55ft Hard VS
5a. Break through the overhang as Lancastrian, then move left and up a short ramp. At the end of this ascend the right leading shallow chimney/depression trending right slightly at the top.

3. **Lancastrian** 65ft Hard VS ★★★
5b. The route breaks through the barrier overhang above the left side of the altar, at a cone formed by a borehole which runs diagonally right, and a left leading scoop which meets it at its top. Gain the altar from its left side (borehole runner on altar), then step up onto a foothold below the overhang. Reach over the roof towards the base of the

borehole, and using this and a hidden pocket, pull up to the top of the cone (PR). Step right onto a small ledge, then climb up for 12 feet to overhanging blocks and move right to a prominent ledge on the arête. Climb more easily up a series of ledges and finish on the left.

4. **Cornishman** 55ft E3 *

5c. Gain the altar as for Lancastrian. Above and right of the drill hole is a small triangular hole in the roof. Using this reach over the roof and make a difficult hand traverse right on poor holds for 5 feet. Then make a very difficult mantel over the roof. Climb the slanting crack above by strenuous layaways to an easier finish.

5. **Jaws** 50ft Hard VS

5a. Below the right side of the barrier overhang is an obvious rock fin. Climb to the top of the fin from its left, then continue easily for 20 feet to a small overhang. Use dubious blocky holds on the right to reach the crack above the overhang, then make a difficult layback to reach better holds and ledges on the left. Finish more easily straight to the top.

WONDERS WALL

The wall to the right of the barrier overhang is known as Wonders Wall.

6. **Colossus of Rhodes** 50ft Sev *

Take the obvious line which slants up from the right side of the rock fin. It is possible to finish up the crack on the left side of the top block at Hard Sev, but this is not as pleasant as the direct line.

7. **Barrier Reef** 75ft Hard VS **

5a. A girdle of Barrier Buttress, starting at a sentry box 10 feet right of the rock fin. From the top of the sentry box swing left, then traverse to the top of the fin. Move up for 10 feet, then traverse left above the barrier overhang to reach Lancastrian. From the top of the cone step down left to a sloping foothold, then move up slightly to the top of the overhang of Spiral Galaxy, then move round the arête, and finish up over blocks.

8. **Knossos** 45ft VS *

4c. Start 3 feet right of a square-cut sentry box and climb up to a ledge on the left. Finish up the steep crack system which forms a direct continuation of the start.

9. **Mycenae** 40ft Hard Sev *

4a. Climb to the niche on Petra, then exit left to gain the top.

10. **Petra** 40ft Sev

Six feet right is a deep crack which forms the drainage channel when the crag is wet. Climb this to a niche, then exit on the right and finish up Epheseus.

OPTREX SLAB

The next routes lie on the steep, wavy slab on the right.

11. **Epheseus** 45ft Sev

Starting 4 feet right of the deep crack, take a direct line using two drill holes at mid-height.

12. **Giza** 40ft Hard Sev
4a. Start below the next drill hole, 3 feet right, and climb direct to the next drill hole, then step left and finish.

13. **Coliseum** 40ft VS
4c. Start from the left side of a rock toe which is 3 feet right of Giza, and climb up to a shallow depression, then continue direct to the top.

14. **Angkor** 35ft Sev
Start up the break which bounds the wavy slab on its right, then continue direct to the top.

WONDERS BUTTRESS
To the right the rock becomes broken, but then after 15 yards it presents itself as a short, compact buttress, known as Wonders Buttress.

15. **Terra Cotta Soldier** 30ft Hard V Diff.
Climb the arête on the front of the buttress, then finish to the right at the top.

16. **Acropolis** 30ft Severe
Ten feet right is a right-slanting weakness. Climb the left side of this.

17. **Flying Shed** 25ft Severe
The right side of the weakness, 3 feet farther right.

18. **Chichen Itza** 25ft Hard V Diff.
Start 10 feet right, and climb into a small, deep V-shaped depression, then step left onto an arête and finish up this.

SMALL WONDERS BUTTRESS
This is the small buttress 50 yards farther right.

19. **Canyonlands** 35ft Sev
Start in the vegetated corner at the left of the buttress and gain the highest of two horizontal cracks, then follow this round the arête until a finish can be made at the right side of the front face.

20. **Yellowstone** 25ft Hard VS
5a. Straight up the centre of the buttress, starting at an overhang and finishing up a thin crack.

21. **Tetons** 25ft V Diff
The right arête of the buttress, finishing just right of Canyonlands.

To the right is an easy bay with no routes as yet, and then:

22. **Oblique** 25ft V Diff
Start below a square chimney recess at the top of the crag and then climb to this and an exit on the left.

HOGHTON QUARRY (SD 626 265)

By Dave Cronshaw

SITUATION AND CHARACTER

This magnificent quarry lies below Hoghton Tower, just off the Blackburn – Preston road (A675). In the past it was a mecca for the 'bash-and-dangle brigade', though now its boasts is that of an excellent free-climbing arena which provides varied climbing in interesting positions; ranging from steep slabs and walls to an abundance of overhangs. Because of the northerly aspect of the main walls, they may need a short spell of dry weather before they come into condition. Liqueur Wall, though, faces south and provides good climbing in a sunny situation.

APPROACH AND ACCESS

The land on which the quarry lies is part of the de Hoghton Estate and it is used as a breeding ground for game birds. It is their desire that these birds are not disturbed and after extensive B.M.C. negotiations it has been agreed that climbing should only take place between February 1st and June 30th each year; the quarry is regularly patrolled by gamekeepers, who have an uncanny knack of recognizing climbers' cars, and a visit outside these agreed times will result in instant eviction.

To reach the quarry from the A675, Blackburn – Preston road, take the lane (Chapel Lane) which leads down by the side of the Boar's Head pub. After about ½ a mile and just after crossing a railway bridge, take a short track which breaks off rightwards and follow it down to fields. Cross over the railway at a gate and enter the tree-infested grounds of the estate. Turn left and follow a cleared path for 100 yards to a muddy cutting. Continue up this small gorge, which leads into the quarry. Parking is available at the small hamlet, at the side of the small chapel, though special exhortations are made about consideration for the community.

HISTORY

As far as is known, the quarry was first used for cliff assault practice by the armed forces during the second world war.

In the 1950s more conventional methods were used to scale the crag: quarries were popular as training grounds on which aid techniques could be practiced in preparation for the bigger walls in the Alps. During 1955 John 'Fritz' Sumner pegged Ten Minute Traverse, using custom-made 1-inch pegs specially made for the ascent by Keith King. Sumner also went on and aided the imposing Rhododendron Buttress which gained some notoriety amongst the local climbers when Tony Crook (attempting the third ascent) fell from the lip of the overhang when a peg foothold came out. His belayer, John Britt, only just succeeded in preventing an impressive 80-foot crater all the more impressive as no belay plates were in existence at that time! The following year Alan Atkinson left the commonly used bivouac spot (the Waiting Room) by a different route and attacked the roof-crack above using wooden wedges. On the lip of the roof, Al had the disconcerting experience of watching the wedges in the back of the roof slowly work loose and drop out as the crack widened slightly. He named the route Scimitar Crack for obvious reasons, though it is now known as Dangler.

Towards the late 50's Hoghton had become established as a centre for artificial climbing, attracting Joe Brown and Ron Moseley, together with other members of the Rock and Ice crew, and this set made several aided ascents though details are sketchy. In the early 60s a number of free routes had been done, such as Cave Route, Zig Zag, Partnership, Bowker's Crack and a free version of Route One. Mostly these were climbed by various combinations of John Hamer, John Wareing, John (Aussie) Parkinson and Bill Bowker. Meanwhile, aid routes continued to be put up until the late 60s, including Terry Wareing and Ian (Spider) McQuirk's bolting extravaganzas, Terry's Torment and Drupe.

In 1965 Les Ainsworth and Paul Hamer free-climbed Overhanging Crack; not by design but simply because Les did not trust the rotting wooden aid wedges. At this time though, the big problem was an unfinished aid route which was set to breach some impressive territory up the huge roofs left of Hoghton Walls. Up to 1966 many teams had pegged the first pitch up to The Pasture and then John Hamer and Aussie Parkinson climbed this free, also adding a variation start called Patella. Within a couple of months Stan Bradshaw (who had recently partnered Les Brown on Praying Mantis on Goat Crag) had finished the route on pegs. Later, John Hamer set out on a free ascent (as a peg route) but managed to keep going without using aid, and thus completed Mandarin – one of the best routes in the whole of the area. Hamer followed this success with an attempt at Hope Not which ended prematurely with both John and Aussie dangling below the Pasture. After a short rest they completed the route however. Around the same time Stan Bradshaw put up an impressive display by soloing the first ascent of Wilkinson's Sword Edge.

Liqueur Wall had been spared the attentions of the new-router up until 1967, when Les began to explore the area, immediately making solo first ascents of Kummel and Kirsch. Later in the year The Wasp was added: Les and Paul Hamer had both made protracted attempts at the route and had actually reached a point about 15 feet below the top. They left it there and returned two weeks later to complete the route, only to be told that Brian Molyneux and Geoff Hamridding had aided it the week before. Les and Paul free-climbed the route soon after, though this was something of an anticlimax, again having joined the ranks of an aid route that had been free-climbed, rather than being the first major deliberate free-climb at Hoghton that Les and Paul had dreamed of. Ascents of The Wasp and Mandarin opened up another new area of rock and Boadicea was soon aided by Phil Paget and Roger Grimshaw. This lucrative period ended in 1968 with Tony Makin and Terry Devaney adding yet another route to Hoghton Walls which turned out much easier than the rest of the routes in the area and so was a free climb which they called Thespis.

Just as the guide was going to press Geoff Fishlock and Paget completed the mammoth task of traversing the main areas of the crag, from what was then Shake Not (now Lamentably Gentlemanly), to Ergonome's Enigma. The resulting traverse (Tobacco Road) was a route of epic proportions and included many artificial sections.

During the early 1970's the main preoccupation was the clearing of vegetation from the area beyond Rhododendron Buttress and when this task was completed, some good routes were discovered by Les Ainsworth, Dave Cronshaw, Bob McMillan and Rob Meakin. The most notable of these were Chattox (with 1 PA), Creme de Menthe, Goldwassre and Molotov Cocktail which succumbed to Dave and Les, Rob and Bob's Book of Fate, Malkin Tower (Bob) and Demdike (Les and party) which was probably best of all. In 1972 Dave and Les returned their attentions to the Main Amphitheatre to tackle the mighty Goliath's Groove and to make the first free ascent of Slime Corner which seemed an appropriate name under the prevailing conditions! The following year Strong's Flake received its first lead from Dave Pyecroft, having been top-roped many years earlier by Frank Strong.

A lull followed, and things remained quiet until Dave Knighton appeared on the scene in 1976. This long, hot summer saw Knighton cleaning and free-climbing Rhododendron Buttress, which immediately heralded the start of a new wave of development at the crag. Knighton soon added to the crag's repertoire with Fallout (with a point of aid John Tout) which was a different proposition then because of loose blocks (cleaned off and freed by Ian Lonsdale the following year). From Fallout, Knighton spotted what was later to become Highway Star and then Knighton teamed up with Lonsdale for the latter to steal War of Attrition. In 1977 Knighton and friends went to work on Boadicea and transformed it into a brilliant free climb though retaining 1 point of aid; an indiscretion which was later eliminated by Ron Fawcett, together with the tension move on War of Attrition. Ian went on to free-climb Goulash (with Paul McKenzie) and to rid Ten Minute Traverse of its aid, with Nadim Siddiqui.

Knighton's onslaught continued unabated; Lady, Visions of Jan, Sheer Heart Attack and the particularly bold line of Keep It Coolin' were soon in the bag, and Knighton then turned his attention to free-climbing the girdle traverse, which he renamed When The Levée Breaks. Flight of the Rat was added in 1978 though unfortunately necessitated a peg and long sling to bypass a particularly stubborn block in the overhang. Knighton then climbed Every Face Tells A Story with Jenny Hyslop. In June the following year Cronshaw joined forces with Knighton for his free ascent of Rhododendron Arête, though this was not without incident as Knighton took a spectacular flier before succeeding.

A month later some new blood arrived on the scene in the shape of Dave Kenyon and Malc Haslam. This pair began to slowly work through all the crag's remaining gaps and aid routes and soon Maraschino had been rid of its aid and the last stubborn aid points on Dangler were eliminated (the aid having been reduced to two points by Cronshaw a little earlier). Kenyon and Haslam began to make a series of technical testpieces such as Speech Impediment and New Wave. In April 1981 Ian Lonsdale joined Kenyon to add a top pitch to Ian's earlier route

Black Pudding Team Special, and the next year Kenyon free-climbed Dave Knighton's old aid route Candlemass to produce a very hard and very classy route – The Excitable Boy.

During the summer of 1983 Gary Gibson pulled in to open All Roads Lead To Rome, a classic pitch which was soon smouldering under the smell of burning rubber and hot on Gary's heels came Malc Haslam and Greg Rimmer with For God's Sake Burn it Down. Cronshaw retaliated further, and with Mick Ryan, found Golden Delicious more to his taste. Kiwi Roland Foster was also operating in the area at the time and was particularly impressed by Hoghton. Foster took an immediate shine to the steep wall to the right of The Wasp, up which Mark Leach and Ian Conway had forced a free version of the old route Shake Not (Spider Rider) the previous year. Foster decided that Spider Rider needed straightening out, thereby avoiding the escape rightwards onto the arête, and succeeded in climbing Lamentably Gentlemanly with John Noblett; a 'Friend bending pitch'. Looking at the chalk marks snaking up the wall later, Foster noticed the expanse between it and The Wasp, and over several days he filled the space with Getting Rid of the Albatross, Hoghton's first E6.

Kenyon, along with Foster, transformed Dave Peace's dream of a 'Burning Desire' when they free-climbed Gath, another super-route, and then Foster turned his attention to the Keep It Coolin' Wall, playing serious Mind Games and La Lune Dans La Carniveau. Malc Haslam returned with Ronnie Marsden to produce and direct Greg Rimmer: The Motion Picture, a very serious line under the Pasture.

The monsoons played a very large part in 1985, and no new routes were climbed that year. 1986 was a far better year however, starting in April when Cronshaw and John Ryden climbed yet another new route on Hoghton Walls, naming it Burning the Phoenix – which requires a certain amount of faith in 'Friends'. The lanky figure of Paul Pritchard started to get a look in now, and pulled over the roof in the top pitch of Knickertwister to produce On the Brink (the first pitch had been free-climbed by Fawcett in the 70s) and within days his belayer, Phil Kelly, with Ann Smith, had climbed the blatantly obvious crack below the Mandarin traverse: Let's Go Play at the Adams' – a wicked trip. Pritchard then moved up in the world, to the Pasture to be precise, where he added Void and over two days managed the serious and stratospheric traverse of the lip of the Keep It Coolin' wall: Do the Aqua Melba. Kelly, who followed both these routes, fell off the very first move of the latter and swung out right past the arête of Mandarin, over the top of the trees and finally came to rest hanging in free space in no mans land.

By July, Andrew Gridley had completed The French Lieutenant's Marrow, a superb slab climb just left of Slime Corner's main pitch utilizing bolt runners, and a contender for one of the best pitches at Hoghton, and at the same time Cronshaw became attracted to a partially-cleaned line over the roofs below War of Attrition. Dave succeeded though this ascent was a little tainted when he was forced into using a rest point whilst trying to gain the upper wall. Kenyon was duly informed of yet another incursion into his domain and he repeated the route, without the rest point, to give Biodegradable Man. One evening in August Cronshaw dashed over the border and kidnaped Ian Lonsdale away from Wilton just long enough to create The Luddite, a free version of an ancient aid route just right of The Excitable Boy, then Dave co-opted Kelly into his team and the pair climbed a line between The Luddite and The Excitable Boy, aptly named Hoghton Weaver. Then these two found themselves Steppin' in the Slide Zone, trying to gain access to a sloping ledge just left of Easy Route.

In April 1987 Cronshaw turned to the much-neglected Flight of The Rat and after a quick abseil to remove a sandy block, both he and Kenyon led the first pitch, then Cronshaw returned the next weekend with John Ryden to add a direct finish. Finally, as a climax to his new-routing in the quarry, Dave Kenyon recently succeeded in free-climbing Silverside, a fitting finale to the history of a quarry that is fast reaching maturity.

THE CLIMBS are all described from RIGHT to LEFT.

HOGHTON WALL is the large open face which rises from the end of the muddy cutting, and which is bounded on its left by the Main Amphitheatre.

1. **Lamentably Gentlemanly**   70ft   E5   **
6b. Start 20 feet right of The Wasp. Climb the short wall, with care, to the sandy break. Climb the crack above, 3 PRs, to the stepped overhang. Pull over this leftwards into a short corner to finish.

2. **Getting Rid of the Albatross**   80ft   E6   *** †
6c. Start between Lamentably Gentlemanly and Wasp, below a small niche above the break. Climb the short wall to gain the niche and continue up flakes and slots on the right to the left end of the stepped overhang, step left and fight up a thin crack (crux) to finish.

3. **The Wasp**   80ft   Hard VS   **
5a. The impressive corner at the quarry entrance is climbed in its entirety to a large ledge on the right.

4. **The Sting**   25ft   Hard VS
5a. The short continuation corner above The Wasp.

5. **Goulash**   90ft   E1
5b. Climb the thin crack 8 feet left of The Wasp, then traverse right along the horizontal break and finish up the final few feet of Wasp.

6. **All Roads Lead to Rome**   130ft   E5   ***
6b. Start 5 feet right of Boadicea and climb the thin crack and wall (BR) with increasing difficulty to a grassy ledge, traverse left and finish up Boadicea.

7. **Boadicea**   120ft   E2   ***
5c. An excellent route which takes the obvious crack 20 feet left of The Wasp, past two breaks to finish up a bulging crack, passing a tree near the top.

8. **For God's Sake Burn it Down!**   125ft   E4   *
6b. Climb the crack left of Boadicea, past a small overlap to a break. Step left and go up to a PR, then make some thin moves to gain a second break. Move right to a crack, finishing up the last few moves

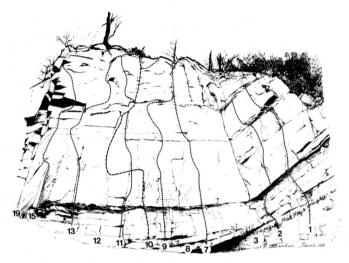

HOGHTON QUARRY Hoghton Wall

of Boadicea.

9. Every Face Tells a Story 120ft Hard VS ★★
5b. Start at a crack just right of Thespis. Climb the crack past a bulge then continue to the first horizontal break. Climb the wall above to the PR on Burn it Down. Either go left to a finish up Lady, or use the peg for aid to gain a second horizontal break and follow this right to finish up Boadicea. The aid peg can be omitted at E3 6b.

10. Thespis 120ft Hard VS ★
Start in the centre of Hoghton Wall at a right-facing flake/groove.
(1) 45ft 4c. Climb the groove then traverse left along the obvious ledge to a peg belay.
(2) 75ft 4c. Climb the wall and short corner above to a break. Step right to a peg (possible belay), then up the shallow groove to a tree at the top.

11. Burning the Phoenix 120ft E4 ★★
The crack and wall 5 feet left of Thespis.
(1) 75ft 5b. Climb the crack to a ledge at 35 feet, continue in the same line to the grassy break. Step right to a PB.
(2) 45ft 6a. Traverse left for 10 feet and climb the wall (PRs) to an overlap, (Friend runner). Over this on the left and up a short awkward wall to a ledge. Belay on the right at the tree.

12. Lady 125ft Hard VS ★
(1) 35ft 4c. The break 4 feet left of Burning the Phoenix to belay as for Thespis.

(2) 90ft 5a. Traverse right to the end of a narrow ledge, then climb straight up the wall above to the first horizontal break. Follow cracks above to the second horizontal break (PR), then foot traverse this right for 10 feet to the final peg-scarred crack of Boadicea and finish up this.

13. Route One 115ft VS ★★
(1) 45ft 4b. Start a few feet right of the arête which forms the right boundary of the Main Amphitheatre. Climb up the obvious crack, then up the wall diagonally left to a large ledge and bolt belay.
(2) 40ft. Up the corner to a mantel, then follow a line of ledges right to a PB below an obvious block overhang.
(3) 30ft 4c. Climb the overhang on its left.

14. Golden Delicious 130ft E3 ★★★
(1) 40ft 5c. Climb the thin crack (PR), just right of the arête, to the large ledge, BB. **Variation** (6a †) The slanting crack on the left joins the parent route at the peg runner.
(2) 90ft 5c. From the left of the ledge climb to the roof. Pass this on the left and gain the traverse ledge of Mandarin (situ peg) go up to the overhang and move left onto the exposed arête. Climb up to a small triangular overhang and step left (crux) to finish up a crack. Trend right to the tree belay on Mandarin.

15. The Knickertwister 120ft E5 ★★★
(1) 50ft 6a. Start as for the alternative start to Golden Delicious, but climb the corner, then bear left to a vertical crack which leads to the large ledge and BB.
(2) 70ft 6b. **(On the Brink)** Climb the crack above the belay, to the roof and move right under this. Make a long reach to a slanting hold on the lip (BR) and make a dynamic move onto the wall above. Go up this and trend leftwards to finish up the easier top section of Mandarin.

The next five routes have a common start at the easy-angled corner on the left.

16. Blind Eye 55ft E5 ★ †
6c. Takes the diagonal overlap on the right, starting up Let's Go Play At the Adams' and finishing up Knickertwister (BR). Serious towards the top.

17. Let's Go Play at the Adams' 55ft E5 ★
6a. From 2 feet up the corner, gain the thin crack in the yellow wall on the right. Up this to a poor PR and up to another PR. Finger-traverse right along the break to the large ledge and BB, abseil off.

18. Ten Minute Traverse 120ft E3 ★★
(1) 60ft 5b. Climb the corner to some iron spikes then up and move right to gain a large flake; foot-traverse the horizontal break right until it is possible to step round onto the belay ledge of Let's Go Play At the Adams'. It is also possible to hand-traverse the break (harder but better protected).
(2) 60ft 5c. Climb the corner at the right end of the ledge to the roof, then straight up the crack above (PRs).

19. Mandarin 120ft E2 ★★★
A superb climb which can be climbed in a single pitch if desired.

(1)   65ft 5b.   Up Ten Minute Traverse to the large flake and follow this to an overhang. Or; from the spikes continue straight up a short chimney and over another overhang to reach the same point, **Patella** 5c. Go over the overhang then up the short wall to the roof. Traverse left onto the large grassy ledge (The Pasture) and BB.
(2)   55ft 5b.   Traverse back under the roof to gain an obvious traverse ledge. From the end of this bridge up to the overhang and pass this on the right then continue to a niche. Exit left round an arête to an exposed finish up easy rock to a tree belay.

WAITING ROOM AREA
The Waiting Room is the name given to a conspicuous ledge at the right side of the Main Amphitheatre, at about 25 feet, just left of some large blocks on the quarry floor. The first four routes to be described lead to the ledge itself from which it is possible to descend easily by an abseil from an excellent belay.

20.   **Twin Spikes**   30ft   Hard V Diff
Climb the ledges on the left side of an easy-angled corner to a ledge on the left, then climb up past two large iron spikes and traverse left to the Waiting Room.

21.   **Groove and Ledge**   25ft   Sev
The groove on the left.

22.   **Blunt Arête**   25ft   Hard VS
5a. The blunt arête between Groove And Ledge and Slanting Crack, with a long reach to finish.

23.   **Slanting Crack**   25ft   Hard VS
5b. The crack which goes diagonally left across the orange wall on the left. At the overlap step right and make an awkward mantel into the Waiting Room.

24.   **Greg Rimmer – The Motion Picture**   60ft   E4   ★★
6a. Start as for Slanting Crack and follow the continuation flake to the break, traverse left to a hanging groove. Up this to a ledge, move left and up to The Pasture.

25.   **Dangler**   50ft   E4   ★★★
6b. From The Waiting Room climb the short corner which starts below a roof with an obvious circular crack, surmount this (crux) and up to a large roof, which is avoided by a traverse to the left. Finish up a short wall to reach The Pasture.

26.   **Sheer Heart Attack**   40ft   E2   ★
5c. From the left side of The Waiting Room, make a move round the arête to a good hold, PR, then climb the arête to a small ledge. Continue up the flake crack above. then make a difficult mantelshelf onto the horizontal break, then step right and up another crack to The Pasture.

THE PASTURE
The large ledge at mid-height on the right of the amphitheatre is known as The Pasture. It can be reached by abseil, or by various routes. Also it can be left by any of 10 routes, or even by B.A.S.E. jumping (not recommended).

The first five routes to be described climb rock which is sometimes friable and due to difficulties in arranging good protection these routes are serious undertakings.

27. Do the Aqua Melba 70ft E6 ★★ †
Serious climbing in a sensationally exposed position. Start from the right end of The Pasture, BB.
6b. Dance right, along the lip of the roof to the good hold below the small overhang on Golden Delicious, then follow this to finish.

28. Void 55ft E5 ★★
6b. From the start of The Aqua Melba, climb up past a small sloping ledge on the right at 10 feet, to a PR. Step left to a large hold and finish straight up.

29. La Lune Dans La Carniveau 55ft E5 ★
6b. From the BB, climb direct to a PR, move right and finish straight up.

30. Keep it Coolin' 55ft E3 ★★
5b. Start at the large block behind the tree. Climb straight up for 10 feet to a small ledge, then make a rising traverse right into the centre of the wall, and up to a PR. Continue direct to the top.

31. Mind Games 45ft E5
6a. Start as for Keep it Coolin' but climb direct up the wall.

32. Disowned 45ft VS
5a. A poor route. Start just right of Partnership and take a direct line up the corner.

33. Partnership 55ft VS
4c. A line of mantelshelves in the corner above The Pasture, starting and finishing on the left.

34. Claymore 40ft Sev
From the start of Partnership, continue straight up to a large ledge, and then finish up the left-slanting ramp.

35. Hope Not 50ft Hard VS ★
5a. The steep crack 12 feet left. Strenuous at 40 feet. Exit to easier ground past a sloping ledge on the right.

36. Spazzm E1
5c. A direct finish to Hope Not.

37. Silverside 50ft E6 ★★ †
Free-climbs the bolt route in the wall left of Hope Not.
6c. Climb up past old bolt holes to gain a short peg-scarred crack which slants leftwards to a large ledge.

MAIN AMPHITHEATRE
This is the name give to the distinctive main area, which contains much excellent climbing.

38. Burning a Nun 60ftE5 †
6b. The counter line to Greg Rimmer. Start in the shallow corner 30 feet left of Slanting Crack. From a ledge at 6 feet, traverse diagonally right, past a thin curving crack, to gain a hanging groove. Up this to a ledge then cross to join Sheer Heart Attack. Follow this to the horizontal break, step left and over the overlap to finish.

HOGHTON QUARRY
Rhododendron Buttress Area

39. Sirloin 50ft VS
4b. Climb the shallow corner past a flake to a ledge, then move easily right until it is possible to climb up through an obvious gap in the overhang to The Pasture

40. Slime Corner 130ft Hard VS   *
(1) 50ft 5a. The broken wall in the centre of the amphitheatre, just left of Sirloin, to a large ledge just left of The Pasture.
(2) 30ft 5a. Up the corner to a ledge and small tree on the right.
(3) 50ft 4b. Up the ledges to a large ledge from which it is possible to walk off to the right. Move left along this, then up the wall using old chiselled holds, and finish up the short wall above.
(3a) 30ft **Original Finish**. Continue up the groove over ledges to the top (easier and not in keeping with the rest of the route).

41. Five Minute Traverse 30ft Sev.
From Slime Corner pitch two, traverse up and right onto The Pasture.

42. Spleen Road 135ft VS   *
A high-level girdle of the left side of the Main Amphitheatre.
(1) 85ft 4b. Start from the 'walk-off' ledge near the top of Slime Corner. Stride across the corner then step down to gain an obvious line of ledges which lead to a blunt arête on Highway Star. Continue along the break to join Goliath's Groove below the final flake, NB.
(2) 50ft 4c. Traverse the ledge to the arête, then step onto the front face and continue left along the bad belt (PR in Rhododendron Buttress) to a ledge on the left side of the buttress. Finish easily to a tree belay at the top.

43. Baron of Beef 105ft A2/E4   †
Start midway between Slime Corner and Fallout, below a short hanging groove.
1) 45ft A2. Using skyhooks in bolt holes, then up the wall above on pegs to belay on Slime Corner.
(2) 35ft 6b (†). **(Canibalistic Inclinations** *) Up the shallow corner on the right and over the overhang to a ledge and tree belay.
(3) 25ft. The short wall by a crack in its centre.

44. New Wave 45ft E4
6b. Starting up the thin crack just left, gain the hanging groove on the right, PR. Then continue up the flake above to the large ledge.

45. Fallout – Direct Start 45ft E2
5c. Start up initial crack of New Wave and swing left into a flake/groove. Go up this to the roof, move right and up to the large ledge.

46. Fallout 140ft E2   *
(1) 55ft 5b. Climb the corner below the right side of the Main Overhang to a ledge, then traverse right to the good ledge on New Wave; up this to The Pasture.
(2) 85ft 5b. From the left side of the ledge climb up to an indefinite groove and follow this to a large ledge at its top. Up the short corner then finish up the break on the left.

47. The French Lieutenant's Marrow 80ft E6   ***
(1) 50ft 6b. A strenuously thin climb. Start at Slime Corner pitch two and climb the steep slab between that route and Fallout to a grassy

ledge, BB. Either walk off home or continue up:
(2)   30ft 4b.   The old chiselled holds of Slime Corner to finish.

48.   **Highway Star**   100ft   Hard VS   *
(1)   30ft 5b.   Start as Fallout pitch two, make a rising traverse beneath
the groove of Fallout, to a BB above the Main Overhang.
(2)   70ft 5a.   The obvious crack in the blunt arête above the belay to
a break. Step right and continue to the top.

49.   **Main Overhang**   55ft   A1
The obvious line of bolts over the large overhang, finishing on the
belay ledge of Highway Star.

50.   **Flight of the Rat**   135ft   E4   **
(1)   55ft 5c.   Start at the obvious easy chimney beneath the left side
of the Main Overhang. Up this to a ledge on the right and climb a steep
friable rib until it is possible to move right onto the left side of an
undercut slab. Go up and right (Friend) over the overhang to the belay
of Main Overhang.
(2)   80ft 6a.   Step back left to regain the crackline and follow this with
increasing difficulty to the top.

51.   **Burning Desire**   90ft   E5   ***
This very strenuous route takes the crack 6 feet left.
6b. From a ledge, gain the crack and follow this until level with the lip
of the overhangs. Finger-traverse right and move up to a borehole.
Move left to regain the crackline and follow this to finish.

52.   **Deaf School**   100ft   E2   *
5b. Follow Goliath's Groove for 30 feet to a sloping ledge on the left of
an overhanging scoop. Layback right past a PR on the lip, to a break.
Traverse right for a few feet, and then up the top of Burning Desire to
a break, which can be hand-traversed right to a rhododendron. Finish
direct.

53.   **Goliath's Groove**   90ft   Hard VS   *
5a. The deep corner groove at the left of the amphitheatre. At the top
layback the flake on the left.

RHODODENDRON BUTTRESS
Rhododendron Buttress is the impressive buttress which is situated at
the left side of the Main Amphitheatre. To the left of the buttress itself
the rock becomes more broken, and the area is bounded on its left by
an impressive leaning wall.

54.   **Rhododendron Arête**   95ft   E3   ***
6a. The left arête of the amphitheatre, starting up a crack slightly right
of the arête, to a ledge, then continue past a small overlap to a very
small ledge below impending rock. From here go up and right to
another ledge, then step left and finish up the arête.

55.   **Cave Route**   140ft   Hard Sev   **
(1)   50ft.   Climb the short steep slab at the left of the amphitheatre,
then up a corner groove to a small overhang. Move left to the cave,
then climb direct to a large ledge (PB).
(2)   50ft.   Traverse left over poor rock, then continue the traverse at
a slightly higher ledge until it is possible to step around an arête to

Wobbling Groove. Up for a move, then left and up easily to a large ledge on pitch three of Zig Zag.
(3) 40ft. Up the corner as Easy Route to a muddy ledge on the right, then either up the crack in the steep slab which overhangs the corner, or the crack on its right.

56. Rhododendron Buttress 60ft E2 ★★★
5c. A classic route which takes a dramatic line directly up the front face of the buttress. From the right end of the first belay ledge on Cave Route, cross the wall up left to a good ledge below the overhang. Surmount this by a crack and continue to the sandy break, step left then follow the thin crack (crux) to the top.

57. War of Attrition 65ft E2 ★★
5c. A fine climb. From the good foothold over the roof on Rhod. Buttress, traverse left with difficulty to below a right slanting overlap. Surmount the overlap via a thin crack, then climb the groove and short wall above to finish up a finger crack on the left of Rhododendron Buttress.

58. Biodegradable Man 65ft E5 ★★
6b. From the second pitch of Cave Route climb up to the roof (old BRs), then swing right (PR) and make some exhilarating moves over the roof to gain the slanting overlap of War of Attrition. Continue up this to finish.

59. Terry's Torment 55ft A2
This aptly named route climbs over the left of the roof on manky bolts from the Cave Route belay ledge.

60. Strong's Flake 45ft E2 ★
5b. From the belay ledge of Cave Route, climb the massive flake on the left, which rises from the left side of the buttress. Friable rock to start.

61. Finger Traverse 45ft VS
5b. Climb the short layback crack just left of the start of Cave Route, then finger-traverse left with increasing difficulty until the ledge widens. Climb the corner on the left, then either step round to Bowker's Crack, or finish on the right.

62. Pandora's Box 50ft E1
6a. A rather artificial route, but interesting and varied. Start below the left end of the Finger Traverse ledge, and gain the ledge by a technical mantel up a scoop on the arête, or more easily by using a chipped hold on the right. Move right, and climb the thin crack until it is possible to swing right and up into the cave of Cave Route. Hand-traverse left to the top of Finger Traverse, and then step back right and climb to the large ledge on Cave Route.

63. Bowker's Crack 25ft VS ★
4c. Just left is a short wall. Climb the right corner of this.

64. Speech Impediment 25ft E2
6b. Takes the crack between Bowker's Crack and Cyclops, finishing up a blank-looking wall.

65. Cyclops 25ft VS
4c. The crack at the left side of the wall.

66. **Visions of Jan** 105ft E2 ⭐
(1) 30ft. Up the corner 2 feet left of Cyclops to a ledge, then up to the ledge above (tree). Finish at a larger ledge on the right (NB).
(2) 45ft 5b. Scramble right easily and then up to the base of the shallow overhanging corner. Up this past a PR on the left wall to a ledge at the top. Tree and NB's on left.
(3) 30ft 4c. Follow the left-slanting groove to a ledge, then surmount the overhang which is split by a wide crack, and scramble through rhododendrons to finish.

67. **Wobbling Groove** 80ft Hard VS
5b. Start at Visions of Jan pitch two. Climb up and left to a ledge on the right of a blunt arête (junction with Cave Route), then follow a thin crack into a shallow scoop. Pull out of this onto a ledge at the start of the traverse on Choice Exit, (PR on right), then move left and up into a groove and follow this past 2 PRs. Finish up a groove on the right.

68. **Choice Exit** 75ft VS ⭐
5a. Start behind the birch tree left of Visions of Jan pitch two. Climb a corner crack to a ledge, then up to a sandy break and move right to a small ledge, PR. Continue along right to a tree belay on the right.

69. **Easy Route** 120ft Hard Diff ⭐
(1) 50ft. Start 20 feet left, at a short, easy-angled slab. Gain a ledge on the left, step right, then reach the large ledge above, either direct, or (easier) by traversing right and then mantleshelving back left.
(2) 70ft. Proceed up a series of ledges in the centre of the bay. At the top of the corner make a muddy landing on the right, then step back left across the corner and finish through undergrowth.

70. **Easier Route** 120ft Hard Diff
(1) 30ft The obvious weakness 15 feet left of Easy Route.
(2) 90ft As for Easy Route. to the muddy ledge, then walk right along this finish up an obvious short break.

71. **Zig Zag** 120ft Hard VS ⭐
Start below the corner which marks the junction between Rhododendron Buttress and Overhanging Crack Areas.
(1) 35ft 4b. From a small ledge at 8 feet, traverse right on small ledges until an awkward move round the arête makes it easy to gain the ledge above. Belay as Easy Route pitch two.
(2) 30ft 4c. On the right of the ledge is a corner, (hook belay). Climb the corner then easily up up to a large ledge on the left. BB.
(3) 20ft 5a. The hanging groove on the right to a tree.
(4) 35ft. The stepped wall behind.

72. **Steppin' in the Slide Zone** 45ft E2 ⭐
5c. Start at Easy Route's first belay. On the left is a borehole in a blunt arête; climb this (TR) and make an interesting move onto the sloping ledge above. Climb ledges then continue up the thin crack in the wall above to a large pocket. Leap for the top.

OVERHANGING CRACK AREA
Past the Main Amphitheatre the rock becomes a little more broken until the impressive leaning wall of Overhanging Crack is reached. This area extends from the right side of the leaning wall to a deep corner round

the arête.

73. Che 80ft Hard VS ⋆
(1) 30ft 4c. Climb the corner made with the large leaning wall on the left, to a large ledge. NB.
(2) 50ft 5b. Step left onto the leaning wall, then gain the hanging groove on the right, and climb this to a ledge, go up to the obvious inverted triangular niche, finish straight up.

74. Overhanging Crack 70ft Hard VS ⋆
(1) 35ft 5b. The deep crack up the left side of the leaning wall to a large ledge and tree belay on the left. Awkward to start.
(2) 35ft 5a. Scramble up and left to a higher ledge then climb the T-shaped crack making an exit to the left.

75. Black Pudding Team Special 75ft E2 ⋆⋆
(1) 45ft 5c.The peg-scarred arête on the left. Climb the arête, exiting on the right to a large ledge and tree. Scramble up and left to BB.
(2) 30ft 5c. Make a delicate traverse left to the arête and up this past PRs.

76. Drupe 70ft E1/A1
5c. Round the left arête of the leaning wall is a crack, climb this to the break then continue up the wall and over the overhang on bolts.

77. Ergonome's Enigma 70ft A2 ⋆⋆
Up the thin crack 9 feet left into a niche above the overlap. Leave the niche by a crack on the left and follow this to the roof. Traverse right under the roof for 5 feet, to a thin crack splitting it, over this then the overhang above to finish up the scooped wall.

78. Suicidal Tendency 55ft E1
5b. The route follows the 'rising damp' break which cuts across the face below the initial overlap of Drupe. Start at the left and finish at Overhanging Crack.

79. Device Diedre 45ft VS
4c. The corner which limits the wall on its left. Finish right.

LOOKOUT AREA
The area from Device Diedre to the break at the far end of the quarry is known as the Lookout Area. Until the early 70's much of the rock hereabouts was cloaked with vegetation, but its removal has revealed a wide variety of climbs, including several in the easier grades. Although many of the climbs in this area are excellent when they are free of vegetation, the very nature of the rock means that these climbs will always be in danger of being lost under a veil of rhododendrons. To maintain the routes in good condition requires only a modest effort on every ascent, but if this is neglected only a major gardening effort will save them. Visiting climbers are therefore asked to assist with maintaining this area.

80. The Luddite 60ft E3 ⋆⋆
5c. Start in the centre of the wall on the left. Climb to an overlap, BR. Move right and up a short crack to a horizontal break. Up the wall above to BR, step left and finish direct.

81. Hoghton Weaver 75ft E2 ★

6a. Start as for The Luddite but at the BR gain the short break up and left, then go up to a second break. Move right to a very thin diagonal crack and follow this to an overlap and PR –junction with The Excitable Boy. Traverse left to a crack and finish up this.

82. The Excitable Boy 55ft E4 ★★

6b. Start in the corner on the left. Climb this (bold) to a ledge. Step right to gain the main crack and follow this to an overlap and PR. Make some baffling moves onto a small ledge then make a long reach to the top.

HOGHTON QUARRY
Excitable Boy Area

83. Assheton Arête 60ft Sev
Climb the arête just left of The Excitable Boy for a few moves then pull round into an easy angled groove. Climb this to a ledge and move up to a block. Pass this on its left to gain a ledge and finish up the short break behind.

83a. Direct Finish VS
4c. From the groove on the parent route, climb the obvious crack above, as Hoghton Weaver.

84. Royal Declaration 65ft Hard Sev
4a. Start at a lower level, 10 feet right of an overhung corner. Climb a short crack and the groove above, until it is possible to ascend the shallow corner to a ledge on the right. Finish easily.

85. Book of Fate 70ft Hard VS *
5a. From the first ledge on The Motorway gain a higher ledge on the right, then a triangular niche. Move up, then diagonally right to a shallow corner and up to a large ledge on the right. Traverse back across the face to some obvious large holds and an easier finish. Poorly protected.

86. Hermit of Tower Wood 60ft V Diff
From the triangular niche on Book of Fate continue up the shallow corner to the top.

87. The Motorway 120ft Moderate
Probably the best easy way down for most of the routes, because of this the route is marked with red paint. Start 20 feet left of the overhung corner and follow a sloping ledge left to a large ledge (HARD SHOULDER). Scramble up for a few feet to another ledge complex (CENTRAL RESERVATION), continue left across this to reach the top.

88. Sliproad 65ft V Diff
Starting 5 feet left, gain the ledge above and move to the HARD SHOULDER. From the right of this follow small holds to the ledge above, then continue past two ledges to a vertical crack. From the base of this go diagonally right for 15 feet until the top can be reached easily.

89. Lookout Ridge 90ft Hard Diff
The left wall of the bay ends at a long arête, which starts at a much lower level. Follow this to the top (HARD SHOULDER), then go up for a few feet and finish easily up the final blunt arête to reach LOOKOUT POINT.

90. Lookout Gully 95ft Diff
The gully bounding Lookout Ridge on its left. Finish as that route.

91. Trunk Road 60ft V Diff
The series of short corners on the left of Lookout Gully to the HARD SHOULDER.

92. Malkin Tower 70ft Sev
(1) 55ft. Where Lookout Gully and Trunk Road split there is a vertical

crack. Follow this to a large ledge, then continue up the groove behind, which is best entered from the left. PR not in place. Belay on Central Reservation.
(2) 15ft. The wall behind, to reach LOOKOUT POINT.

93. **The Trial** 60ft Hard VS
5b. Start 10 feet left of Malkin Tower at a lower level. Climb the crack (awkward to start) to a large sloping ledge. Then go up the short wall behind to easier ground, finishing up the groove above to the Central Reservation.

94. **Chattox** 80ft Hard VS *
Takes the break through the large overhang which stretches across the top of the quarry at the Blackburn end.
5b. From the corner on the left, climb a weakness 7 feet right until it is possible to move back to the corner at a drill hole (spike). Move up this a few feet then move right and up to the obvious break which splits the overhang. Surmount the overhang (PR) to gain the hanging corner above. Step left to a good pocket and continue to a small niche. Finish straight up.

95. **Demdike** 100ft Hard VS **
Despite appearances a very good route.
(1) 45ft 5a. Climb the cracks just left of the corner to a PR at 30ft, step left to gain a line of flakes leading diagonally right to a large niche, NB. It is possible to start this pitch by starting up Scoop and Wall, to gain the flakes on the right.
(2) 55ft 4c. Climb to the overhang, then traverse left to an arête. Step up to a ledge then from this move up on small holds to a wide crack on the right. From here either finish straight up, or, keeping low, move across to a small niche and make a rising traverse right to finish at the top of the hanging corner of Chattox.

96. **Scoop and Wall** 70ft Hard Sev
Start at the far end of the quarry, 10 yards right of an obvious easy way up the short end wall.
(1) 25ft 4a. Climb the crack to a small ledge. From the left of this gain the massive ledge and tree belay.
(2) 45ft 4b. Climb the crack in the corner until it is possible to traverse right to the arête on a sloping ledge. Move up to a ledge, then finish up a short slab.

97. **Scoop and Wall Direct** 35ft VS
4c. Start at Scoop and Wall pitch two and follow it to the sloping ledge, then continue straight up over a large block, step left and finish direct.

98. **Suspended Animation** 60ft Sev *
(1) 20ft. The crack 10 feet left.
(2) 40ft. The flake crack behind the tree to a ledge on the left. Gain the next ledge, then finish easily up the arête.

99. **Wilkinson's Sword Edge** 30ft E1 *
5b. Start from the large belay ledge of Suspended Animation and climb the vertical razor-edged arête just left.

100. **The Minihang** 25ft Hard Diff
Set back from Wilkinson's Sword Edge is a large overhang. Climb the

V-groove to the overhang, then step right and climb the wide crack which splits it.

LIQUEUR WALL

To the left the quarry curves round and back towards the main area past a stretch of rock known as Liqueur Wall. At the extreme right end it is very short and the following two routes start here:-

101. **Ouzo** 40ft Diff
Start 8 feet left of the easy way down the short end wall, and follow an easy line of ledges left to finish up Strega.

102. **Strega** 30ft Hard V Diff
Start in the corner on the left which contains two overhangs, and climb the wall just right of this corner.

The following four routes have a common start at the deep corner which bounds the main sweep of Liqueur Wall on its right.

103. **Advocaat** 60ft Sev
Up the corner to a massive ledge at 30 feet, then move right for 6 feet and climb to the top via a series of three strenuous mantels.

104. **Chartreuse** 60ft Sev
From the massive ledge, step left and continue to a higher ledge on the right, then finish more easily.

105. **Grand Marnier** 65ft Hard Sev
4a. From the massive ledge, traverse left to the arête and climb this.

106. **Wilt the Stilt** 50ft E2
5c. Climb the arête between Grand Marnier and Creme De Menthe, direct.

107. **Creme de Menthe** 50ft VS   ★
4b. The next corner, which contains 4 overhangs.

108. **Curacao** 55ft Hard VS   ★
5b. Climb the groove 8 feet left, to a PR below the capping overhang. Move up and right to a small ledge, and from the right of this continue with difficulty, until at 30 feet a good flake handhold ends the difficulties. Finish more easily, passing the final overhang on the left.

109. **The Effect of Alcohol** 60ft E2   ★
5c. To the left is a deep corner, with a fallen pedestal below it. Climb the corner to the roof, then improvise rightwards round this, layback up and continue to the top.

110. **Winston Groovy** 55ft E4
6a. Climb the wall on the left on sloping holds and the thin crack above (PR) to a ledge. Move right finishing up the centre of the wall above the roof.

111. **Kummel** 65ft Sev
4a. In the centre of Liqueur Wall is a deep corner, climb this to a large ledge at its top. From the right of this ledge climb up a prominent flake and then finish easily.

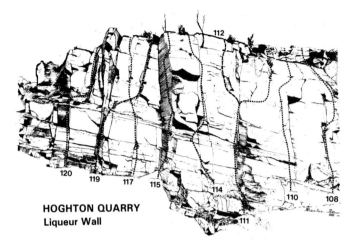

HOGHTON QUARRY
Liqueur Wall

112. Trappistine Finish 55ft Hard Sev *
The continuation corner above Kummel.
4b. From the second ledge on Kummel, step up left to another ledge,
then climb the corner above.

113. Kirsch 65ft Sev
4a. From the second ledge on Trappistine Finish, climb the left-hand
corner.

114. Benedictine 55ft E1 *
5c. Start 10 feet left and climb cracks to a ledge, then step right and
climb the crack which bounds the overhang on its right, until a step left
can be made onto the wall above the overhang. Finish direct.

115. Maraschino 50ft E3 **
6a. The thin crack which splits the wall on the right of Tia Maria. At
three-quarters height move right, then finish up the arête.

116. Tia Maria 50ft VS
4c. The deep corner on the left of Liqueur Wall.

117. In the Pink 50ft E1 *
5c. Takes the crack between Tia Maria and Cirrhosis. Start up the crack
10 feet left of Tia Maria to a large ledge and climb the crack in the
leaning wall above.

118. Cirrhosis 50ft E1
5b. Further left is a short arête leading to a large ledge. Climb the crack
on the right of this to the ledge, then continue up the groove above to
the top. Situ PR.

119. Goldwasser 60ft VS *
4b. Climb the thin groove on the left of the arête to the ledge, then
follow a right leaning ramp to the top.

120. **Sloe Gin** 50ft VS
4c. Start at the extreme left, below a large square-cut recess. Gain the recess and exit on the right to a large ledge. Traverse right then climb the obvious corner. Variation: **Pastis** (Hard VS 5a) From the recess, exit left to the ledge. Up a groove and diagonally rightwards to the top section of Sloe Gin.

On the wall directly facing Liqueur Wall some climbs have been done, but these have now become overgrown.

GIRDLE TRAVERSES:

121. **When the Levée Breaks** 495ft E2   **★★**
A girdle of the main part of the crag.
(1) 130ft 5a. Climb The Wasp for 60 feet, to the horizontal break, then hand-traverse left past a small bush until beneath the short corner on Thespis. Move up to stand on the break and continue along to the belay ledge of Route One.
(2) 35ft 5b. From the left-hand edge of the ledge foot-traverse the sandy break across to the flake on Mandarin. Climb down and across left to the Waiting Room (part of Ten Minute Traverse in reverse).
(3) 70ft 5b. From the left-hand side of the Waiting Room, pull up and round the arête to a good hold (PR) and traverse across to reach Sirloin. Climb the crack on the left to gain the large ledge on Slime Corner, PB.
(4) 120ft 5b. Traverse left as for Highway Star to the hanging ledge above the Main Overhang. Step left into a crackline and follow this to the horizontal break and traverse left into Goliath's Groove below its final flake, NB.
(5) 60ft 4c. Cross the ledge on the left to the arête, then step onto the front face and cross at the bad belt (PR in Rhododendron Buttress) to a ledge on the left side of the buttress. Traverse left across the top of the corner on Visions of Jan to gain another small corner, tree and NB.
(6) 40ft 5a. Reverse mantel down to a break, then make an awkward move left to where the ledge widens (2 PR's) and traverse left to a BB below the groove on Zig Zag.
(7) 40ft 4a. Climb the corner on the left to a muddy ledge and then take the crack in the steep slab above, as for Cave Route, to finish.

122. **Preston Guild** 130ft VS/A2
A rather uninspiring peg girdle of the Overhanging Wall Area.
(1) 70ft. Starting from the left side of the first belay ledge on Zig Zag, step onto the leaning wall, as for Che, and continue across, until pegs have to be resorted to in a feint crack. Belay as for Overhanging Crack.
(2) 60ft. Easily up a large flake to the ledge behind, then go under the overhang of Drupe and follow a line past Ergonome's Enigma to an obvious exit through the overhangs.

123. **Molotov Cocktail** 170ft VS
A girdle of Liqueur Wall.
(1) 90ft 4b. Up Strega for a few feet, then traverse left under the second overhang, and continue at this level to Creme de Menthe. Surmount the overhang above, then go diagonally left to a small ledge just left of the top of The Effect of Alcohol. Traverse along this until it

is possible to drop down to a large ledge on Kummel. Step left onto another ledge and belay on the left side of this.

(2)   80ft 4c.   Tension left to the arête, then go round this to the deep corner. Up the corner to a horizontal crack which leads to the base of the ramp of Goldwasser, then finish up this.

ROUND BARN QUARRY (SD 728 191)

By John Ryden

SITUATION AND CHARACTER

For the most part the quarry is composed of two tiers and all the climbing (as yet) is on the more stable upper tier. The rock on this tier is generally solid, though it would be advisable to clean any intended new route before leading. The shaley lower tier does deter some climbers, but as there are no climbs on it, this is unnecessary as some of the climbs here are very worthwhile.

Standing at the first concrete block, at the top of the quarry track, North Walls are immediately ahead (Fo and Manque De Ville lining up with the neighbouring, taller concrete block), to the left and adjacent to the demolished brick shed is Scarey Buttress. To the right above the lower quarry and to the right of a grassy descent route, are Terrace Walls, which provide access to No Future Walls as the terrace eventually drops into the void. Lancashire Wall lies at the right (southern) end of the quarry, above the top of the second quarry track.

Following the manic surge of development in the late 70s (was that really ten years ago?!) the moor and mother nature have done their best to reclaim the rock for the flora and fauna; some impressive rock falls and trundles have taken place over the intervening years, and some await the unwary.

APPROACH AND ACCESS

Five miles south of Blackburn on the Edgworth road is the Crown and Thistle pub. Past the next group of houses on the left, a well-marked footpath leads directly into the quarry in 200 yards. Limited parking is possible about 50 yards before the houses.

HISTORY

Numerous parties had undoubtedly visited and dismissed Round Barn Quarry, including John Spencer and the rest of the Wilton 'crew' whose main explorations centred on a vast 300-foot route around the walls, roofs and doorways of one of the buildings in the quarry floor. They named this route the Big Wet, but, as happens to most routes here, it was demolished/fell down.

The first real wave of development began in the early seventies when Dave Cronshaw, Bob MacMillan and Les Ainsworth made a bid for glory with the prospect of including the routes they climbed in the forthcoming Lancashire supplement of 1979. When the cleaning was over, ascents were made of Sough, Last Straw, Red Rose Rib and an initial batch of routes on Lancashire Wall. The old 'Crags' magazine chronicled these developments, unwittingly spurring John Ryden to visit the crag, and the result was 'simultaneous' ascents of many routes. Certainly Black Pudding was the work of Les, but the two Johns (Ryden and Grundy) spiced it up and took the true line to produce Mustard. Later, Dave Cronshaw began his protracted campaign on the Lancashire Wall, while Nigel Bonnet and Steve Marsden stole a real gem in the shape of The Pross, which subsequently saw off a good few attempts at a repeat.

John Ryden dug out many of the dodgier 'Eiger Sanction' areas, and in more recent years, a series of shorter and cleaner buttresses have been the focus of Cronshaw's attention with ascents of Forbidden Fruit, Hold In The Wall and Gay Deceiver in 1984 and Burgess, Third Man and MacLean in 1987.

Round Barn Quarry remains less than popular, and the moor above is attempting to regain its hold on the rock. This is a pity, because it is a fine place to climb; full of character!

THE ROUTES are decribed from LEFT to RIGHT. Beyond the remains of the ruined building on the left of the quarry entrance, is a series of small buttresses (left of Scarey Buttress). The last of these is of compact rock, capped by an overhang, with an obvious corner/groove on its right. There is a belay stake in place at the top.

1. **Burgess** 25ft Hard VS
5a. Fifteen feet left of the corner/groove, follow a series of widely spaced holds which lead to a break in the overhang.

2. **Third Man** 25ft E2   †
6a. The disjointed crack system 10 feet right.

3. **MacLean** 25. VS
4c. The corner/groove itself, with a long reach to finish.

The next buttress on the right gives:

4. **Gay Deceiver** 30ft Hard Sev   *
4b. The blunt arête on the left side of the buttress, marked by a small inverted niche near its base.

5. **Hold in the Wall** 30ft Hard VS   *
5b. Climb up the centre of the wall via 'The Hold', PR.

6. **Forbidden Fruit** 25ft E1
5c. The twin cracks just right.

SCAREY BUTTRESS
This unstable buttress is undercut by a cave, and as the fallen pillar is actually the remains of two previous routes, there is good reason to suspect the rock's stability.

7. **Thundercrap** 25ft Sev
The obvious jamming crack 6 feet left of the recently formed corner groove. The rock at the top requires attention.

8. **Blackfoot Sue**   30ft   VS
4b. Starting to the right of the cave, follow the crackline on the left of the Scarey Monster's Eyes to a cleaned stance at the top.

NORTH WALLS
This is the name given to the series of walls opposite the quarry entrance. A good path descends the angle between Scary Buttress and North Walls. The first buttress at the base of this path contains two routes.

9. **Lost Arrow**   25ft   Hard VS
5a. Surmount the overhang and continue up the crack left of the arête.

10. **Limbo**   25ft   Sev
Takes the crack up the centre of the inside wall, traversing left along the horizontal break to finish.

11. **Downward Bound**   25ft   V Diff
The arête of the small buttress immediately right.

12. **Star Sailer**   45ft   VS
4c. Climb the corner left of The Pross to the overhang then hand traverse right to finish up that route.

13. **The Pross**   45ft   E1   **
5c. Almost directly opposite the entrance is a clean buttress marked by a curious hole beneath a neb. Ascend a crack on the right of the arête, then traverse round and up to the hole. Move right below the roof and then finish up the crack directly above the arête.

14. **Ghost Dancer**   40ft   E1   †
5c. Start a few feet right. Climb the wall direct via a flake and a small sandy pocket.

15. **Ho**   40ft   VS   **
4b. The crack 8 feet right. The rock is broken for 25 feet until the inside face of the third buttress is reached.

16. **Gogo**   25ft   VS
4c. Starting by large fallen blocks, climb the left side of the arête until it is possible to pull over to gain a sandy ledge and the top.

17. **Polo**   20ft   Sev   *
The deep groove 8 feet right.

18. **Sough Direct**   25ft   Sev
Climb the wall immediately right via mantelshelves.

19. **Sough**   35ft   V Diff   *
Start on the front of the third buttress on the North Walls. Make a high mantel, then trend left and up to finish.

To the right is a wall with a square cleft in the middle at half height.

20. **Fo**   30ft   Sev
Climb the crackline on the left edge of the left wall. The right wall has a ledge at its base with a quarry spike protruding from it.

21. **Manque de Ville**   25ft   VS   *
4c. Start just left of the quarry spike, move up, trending right to the

arête via a sandy pocket. Then move back left and through the overhang (good incut over the top).

22. **Lonesome Traveller** 30ft VS ★★
4c. The arête bounding Gogo on the right. It is taken direct, using the thin crack.

23. **Spanish Stroll** 30ft V Diff
To the right is a V-groove, climb this directly, finishing on the left.

24. **Barn Owl** 30ft Diff
From the base of the groove trend right up the wall to finish up the arête.

25. **Barnstormer** 30ft Sev
The groove on the right, climb directly to the top.

26. **Last Straw** 35ft Hard VS ★★
5a. On the right are two grooves capped by triangular overhangs at 9 feet, and separated by a thin rib. Climb the wall 3 feet left of the left groove on awkwardly spaced holds to a small overlap, over this to the top.

27. **Wop** 30ft Sev
From the recess below the left triangular overhang, climb the crack on the left of the overhang and then finish direct over doubtful blocks.

28. **Pencil** 30ft V Diff
Climb the rib between the two grooves, then step left and continue to the top.

29. **Trevor's Answer** 30ft VS ★
4b. Climb the arête on the right side of the right triangular overhang. Awkwardly spaced initial holds lead to a sandy pocket. Continue direct up the arête.

Immediately right of the arête is a wall at the base of the descent route.

30. **Ron's Dilemma** 25ft VS
4b. Start at the foot of the descent route, and climb via awkwardly spaced finger holds to a resting position at half height. Continue directly to the top.

To the right of the descent route is a steep slab with a conspicuous crack splitting it.

TERRACE WALLS

31. **Flake Out** 20ft V Diff
Start 6 feet left of the crack at a sandy pocket, and climb to the top via a second sandy pocket.

32. **Crackling** 25ft V Diff
Climb the first conspicuous crack directly to the top.

33. **Barnacle** 30ft Sev ★
Start at the lowest point of the slab, 6 feet right of Flake Out. Make a difficult move to the horizontal break and continue direct to a sandy pocket, then trend right to finish.

34. Clog & Billycock 20ft Diff
The cracks 6 feet right.

35. Barnraker 20ft Diff
Climb flakes to finish at a curious sandy 'cave'.

36. Red Rose Rib 30ft Sev ★★
The arête right of the slab. Start on the left, then mantel onto the arête and finish on the left.

37. Red Rose Wall 20ft Hard Sev
4b. The crack just round the arête.

38. Shear Brow 20ft Hard Sev
4a. Past a descent route is a prominent square-cut roof. Climb the groove to this, then exit left.

39. Killing Floor 25ft Hard Sev
4a. Climb the rib on the right of the groove, stepping right at the roof to finish.

40. Stubby Pinnacle 20ft Hard Diff ★
Right again is a pinnacle. Step right from the top of this and follow a crack to the top.

41. Railroad Groove 25ft Sev ★
Just right is a right-slanting groove with an overhang at the bottom. Climb this, finishing left at the top.

42. Right Track 25ft VS
4c. The hanging crack just right, provides an awkward start, more so as the undercut block has shed another 2 feet.

43. Flake and Groove 30ft VS ★
4b. Gain the flake crack on the right of the corner. Up this, then back into the corner groove to finish.

To the right is an obvious undercut slab: Black Pudding Slab.

44. Mustard 35ft VS ★★
4c. Directly up the centre of the slab, starting by a thin finger-crack on the right edge of the overhang.

45. Black Pudding 35ft Hard Sev ★
4b. Takes a diagonal line from the extreme bottom right of the slab to the top left.

46. Offal Corner 35ft Sev
The obvious dirty corner on the right.

Right of Black Pudding Slab the rock steepens and the terrace extends another 30 feet before falling away to the shale beds below. This section is known as **NO FUTURE WALL**.

47. Gardeners' Question-Time 25ft V Diff
The half-height buttress immediately right of Black Pudding Slab is split by a square-cut recess. Mount this!! and finish up the left edge of the slab above.

48. Ah-Med-It 25ft Sev
The hanging crackline 8 feet right, starting from a fallen block.

49. **Blackburn Buttress** 45ft VS
4c. Immediately right is a large block overhang. Climb the short wall on the left of this, then make a sensational mantel right onto a ledge above the overhang and follow ledges to the top. It should be mentioned that doubts have been expressed about the stability of the block overhang in the past, but it continues to defy gravity.

50. **The First Third** 40ft Hard VS   *
5a. Start beneath the right end of the block overhang.Climb directly up the arête and then up the corner crack through 2 overhangs to a final groove. Finish direct on heathery moves. It is also possible to step to a quarried stance to avoid the heather.

To the right the access ledge terminates above shaley walls.The upper wall has been dedicatedly trundled, gardened, dismantled, reassembled and a top ledge excavated. From this ledge a couple of terminal moves up consolidated moor lead to a belay stake.

51. **Rising Dread** 40ft Hard Sev
4b. At the end of the access ledge twin cracks/grooves lead up to a ledge at 25 feet. Sandy moves right lead to the top ledge and a grovel finish.

52. **Helter Skelter** 40ft V Diff
From the end of the access ledge step right to an obvious niche. Up this till forced out on the right wall, then up to the top via two ledges.

Above the centre of The Void is a recess and ledge with PB (The Cuckoo's Nest). This is the start for the routes between Sometimes a Great Notion and Complete Control, inclusive, and can be reached by the following route:-

53. **Cuckoo Waltz** 20ft Sev
From the end of the access ledge traverse right and up slightly across a friable-looking break, to reach The Nest, or ascend the first 12 feet of Helter Skelter and then descend diagonally right.

54. **Sometimes a Great Notion** 30ft Hard V Diff
Step left up sandy ledges from the Nest, and then follow the left slanting ramp.

55. **One Flew Out** 30ft Hard Sev   *
4a. The corner/groove immediately above The Nest, finishing up parallel cracks above the overhang.

56. **Armagideon Times** 30ft Hard VS   **
5b. Climb the wall immediately right of the arête on thin, awkwardly spaced holds. PR low down on right.

57. **Complete Control** 40ft VS   *
4c. Traverse right from The Nest past a PR and step down to a corner niche. Climb directly up to a ledge on the right, then step back left above an overhang to finish up a thin crack.

ISOLATION WARD
This is the large sloping ledge at the right side of The Void which can be reached by an awkward descent via the broken heathery corner to

the south, or by abseil. The next two routes start from at the base of the slope.

58. Equaliser 30ft Sev
Climb diagonally left from the foot of the descent rake to join a crackline above the niche on Complete Control.

59. Suspect Device 40ft Hard Sev
4a. From the bottom of the rake climb directly up to an obvious corner/groove finish.

The remaining routes lie 200 yards farther south, on **LANCASHIRE WALL**, the steepest and cleanest area of rock in the quarry.

60. July Wakes 35ft Hard V Diff
Start in the centre of the first wall and climb this, veering right and finishing up the arête which bounds the left side of the Lancashire Wall recess.

61. Dawn Chorus 35ft E2   *
5c. The arête right of July Wakes on its left-hand side, 2 PRs.

62. Mudlark 20ft Sev
The short corner on the left side of Lancashire Wall. Move left at half height and then regain the corner above.

63. Vixen 30ft Sev
Right of the deep corner some cracks split the wall. Climb the left of these.

64. Foxhead 30ft Hard Sev
4b. The right crack to the horizontal break, just left of the 'Fox's Head', then finish up the wall above as for Vixen.

65. Gulag Archipelago 35ft E1   **
5b. At the point where the ledge below Lancs Wall deteriorates into shale, there is a conspicuous hanging groove. Gain this with interest, and continue to the top.

The final routes start from the large grassy ledge at the right of Lancashire Wall. This can be gained from the left via the shaley ledge, or by an airy step down from the right.

66. East Lancs 35ft VS   **
4c. From the left of the grassy ledge climb up a groove to a small overhang at 15 feet, then traverse left below this to a hanging groove on the left of a pedestal. Finish up this (crux).

67. Legendary Lancashire Heroes 90ft Hard VS   **
5a. A traverse of the suspended section of Lancs Wall, from right to left. Start up East Lancs and continue along the obvious horizontal crackline from the overhang at 15 feet to a resting position on Gulag Archipelago. Awkward moves left then lead to better holds and the finishing crack of Vixen.

68. Lancashire Lad 30ft Hard Sev   *
4b. The obvious groove which starts just to the right.

69. Yorkshire Queer 25ft Hard VS
5a. The leaning crack 6 feet right of the next corner.

70. Psychlops 25ft E3   ★★
5c. Takes the curving crack immediately left of the large 'eye'. Gain the crack and continue strenuously on awkward holds.

71. Lancashire Lass 25ft Sev
The corner on the left of the airy step.

STANWORTH QUARRY (SD 638 241)

By Dave Cronshaw

SITUATION AND CHARACTER

Stanworth quarry lies 1 mile north of Abbey Village, and to the east of the A675 Bolton – Preston road. The quarry provides varied climbing on generally good gritstone in small sheltered bays. The bay seen from the stile as one approaches the crag is all that remains of Apollo Buttress but despite its diminished height it still contains worthwhile bouldering. On the crest of the infilled quarry are two telegraph poles; the one to the left lies above South Pole Buttress while the right-hand one lies atop North Pole Buttress. The wall at the far end of the quarry is known as The Equator.

APPROACH

From the roundabout where the A674 and A675 cross, the quarry can be reached by travelling towards Bolton and taking the first track on the left (signposted to Stanworth Farm) after the transport cafe. After a couple of hundred bumpy yards the track arrives at a stile and parking on the right, at the northern end of the quarry.

HISTORY

It was not until the mid sixties that climbing began at Stanworth; Ray Evans and Ken Powell climbed around 20 routes here during 1965 but unfortunately made no records. A year later, in 1966, Les Ainsworth and Paul Hamer rediscovered the quarry and climbed eight routes which were later to be lost under a pile of rubble. Both Les and Paul were so enamored with the place that they immediately forgot all about it, and it was not climbed on for the next ten years, when Les remembered the crag while researching into the forthcoming supplement. He managed to coax a small team out for a look on a snowy December day. This visit turned out to be extremely productive and within a fortnight, members of the team had ascended around forty routes, including such climbs as Amundsen (in icy conditions) and Meridian by Dave Cronshaw, African Queen and Eskimo Nell by Al Evans, Ganges and Euphrates by Phil Warner and 'big' Ian Horrocks, and Peary and Amazon by Les Ainsworth. In 1982 Dave Kenyon and Malc Haslam contributed Floodgate and Stranded Passenger and free ascents of both Brasilia and Rally.

1985 saw a year of dramatic change when it was proposed to fill in the quarry with spoil from the adjacent slate quarry. However, these plans were modified by careful BMC negotiations to ensure that the minimum of climbing was lost.

When the dust had settled a series of routes were claimed but some doubt arose as to whether or not they had been led. It turns out though that one of the routes (Sub Zero) had actually been climbed in 1983 by Dave Kenyon and Greg Rimmer but was left unrecorded. Kenyon set about re-establishing his crown, by repeating all these routes; many succumbed fairly quickly but the most stubborn of them (Mount Vinson) needed many visits to complete.

Despite the widespread tipping in the quarry, North Pole Buttress has retained its original height and the small undercut buttress to its right contains the first route to be described. The remaining routes working RIGHT to LEFT from here.

1. **Dynamo** 15ft 5c
Takes the overhanging wall via a hole.

2. **Toit Groove** 20ft Hard VS
5a. Climb the overhanging groove on the left side of the wall.

NORTH POLE BUTTRESS is distinguished by having a telegraph pole above it.

3. **North West Passage** 25ft Sev
Start at the right side of North Pole Buttress, behind a bush, and climb the deep groove stepping right near the top to a ledge and exit.

4. **Rust Never Sleeps** 40ft VS   *
4b. Start 20 feet left of North West Passage, below a sentry box at 10 feet. Gain this and climb the groove above until it is possible to step left onto the slab above the overhang, then finish direct.

5. **Vega** 35ft Hard Sev
4b. Start in the deep corner just left and finish up the V-groove which cuts through the overhangs.

6. **Arctic Circle** 15ft 5c
The blunt arête 10 feet left, to the break.

7. **Shale Surprise** 20ft E2
6a. The wall just left again to the break.

8. **Eskimo Nell** 40ft Sev   **
The wide crack to the roof. Move left through the roof to finish.

9. **Spitting Image** 40ft E6   *
6b. The wall on the left moving left into the centre at the crux. Continue over the exciting overhang above, PR on the right in break.

10. **Sub Zero** 40ft E6   *
6b. Climb the wall on the left, direct to a hole below the break, and finish directly over the roof above.

11. **Peary** 40ft VS   *
4c. Start immediately below the telegraph wires and either ascend the groove, or the flake crack to the overhang (PR). Climb the overhang direct by exciting moves.

12. **Energy Vampire** 40ft E2
5c. Climbs the thin crack in the wall 6 feet left (PR).

13. **Nansen** 35ft VS
4b. From a ledge at 3 feet climb the wall on the right, eventually gaining the blunt arête on the left just below the large ledge, then continue to a drill belay. Ascend the overlap 4 feet right of the corner crack (PR) on good holds.

14. **Hudson** 25ft Hard V Diff
On the left is a glacis; gain this from the left and continue to the drill belay. Descend by abseiling from the drill.

15. **Bering Strait** 30ft Sev
Climb the chimney crack to the top of the 'Icicle', then climb the wide corner crack above to finish.

16. **Abruzzi** 20ft VS ★
4c. Climb the rib on the left.

17. **Baffin** 35ft Hard VS ★
5a. Ascend the very shallow depression on the left to the large ledge, then finish up the crack above.

18. **Ross** 20ft VS
5a. The wide crack on the left.

19. **Barents** 25ft VS
4c. Starting 3 feet left, climb up the centre of the wall and continue to the top.

20. **Blacky Woo Woo Bon Bon Pipkins** 25ft Hard VS
5c. Climbs the centre of the steep wall on the left which contains some bore holes.

21. **Pack Ice** 25ft V Diff
The flake crack just left.

22. **Melt** 25ft Sev
The wall on the left. Gain a sloping ledge at 8 feet then finish up a short corner.

23. **Spitsbergen** 30ft VS
4c. Start down to the left and take the shallow groove and corner.

To the left is a grassy banking giving an easy way down. On the other side of this is a left facing corner.

24. **Edge Game** 25ft Hard VS
6b. The problem right arête of the corner.

25. **Mason Master** 25ft Hard Sev
4b. The corner and short wall above.

26. **Jack the Lad** 25ft Diff
The wide crack with a pedestal at its base, to a step left near the top.

27. **Haymarket** 25ft 6a
The problem wall between the previous route and Thorn Hill, without recourse to the edges.

28. **Thorn Hill** 25ft Hard Diff
The ragged crack on the left.

29. **Beano** 25ft VS
5b. The steep slab starting at two finger slots. Move up and left then straight up to finish.

30. **Cancer** 20ft Sev
The thin crack via a mantel at half height.

31. **Goll's Wall** 20ft VS
4b. The slab between Cancer and Tropical Corner.

THE EQUATOR
At the end of the quarry the rock increases in height, and this end wall is known as The Equator.

32. **Tropical Corner** 20ft Hard Diff
The chimney at the right corner of The Equator.

33. **Monsoon** 20ft VS
5a. Start a couple of feet left of Tropical Corner, leap for an obvious high jug and gain a flake on the left to finish.

34. **Too Hard for Greg Rimmer** 20ft 6a
The wall and flake/groove 10 feet left of Tropical Corner, starting at a small finger slot.

35. **Edge of Extinction** 25ft E3
6b. Left is a right-leading flake/crack, take this and the short groove to finish. PR.

36. **Floodgate** 25ft E1
The crack 3 feet left.

37. **Blue Nile** 30ft E2
5c. Left again is a ledge at 6 feet. From this climb the converging cracks to an awkward finish.

38. **Luxor** 30ft Hard VS
5a. On the left is a protruding column of rock at half height, pierced by a borehole. Gain the niche on the right of this then move right and finish up a short hanging groove.

39. **White Nile** 30ft Hard VS   *
5a. Start in the corner on the left and after a painful start, follow the thin crack to the top (borehole runner on the right at half-height).

40. **Stranded Passenger** 35ft E4   *
6c. Just left is a letterbox at 10 feet. Gain this, then move right and follow a thin crack and wall above to the top.

41. **African Queen** 50ft Hard Sev   **
4b. Seven feet right of the obvious arête is a crack which forms an inverted Y. Climb this to a ledge and cave, then step right onto grass. To finish either, walk off, or ascend the corner which lies above and to the left.

42. **Tigris** 30ft Hard VS
5b. Gain a slanting flake from African Queen, or direct, and finish up the arête.

43. **Euphrates** 45ft E2   ★★
5b. Climbs the arête direct.

44. **Ganges** 50ft VS   ★★
4c. Six feet left of the arête a line of small ledges leads to a large neb.
Follow these (PR) then step right onto the arête and continue more
easily to the top.

45. **5.14** 40ft E6   †
6b. The wall between Ganges and Amazon. Start slightly right (obvious
handhold?), move up and go left to a foothold then finish direct through
the break. Would have been better named 5.12b.

46. **Amazon** 50ft Sev   ★
Follow the wide crack which leads left from the Ganges Delta. At the
top step right, then exit left. Belay stakes well above.

47. **Brasilia** 55ft E3   ★
6a. Start 5 feet left of the dangerous loose corner. Climb up to a thin
crack, climb this to reach a small groove which can be followed to a
sandy cave. Scramble off to the left.

48. **Machu Picchu** 35ft VS
4b. Twenty feet left is a broken groove, climb this to gain a left-trending
corner to finish.

SOUTH POLE BUTTRESS
This is the buttress opposite North Pole Buttress and also has a
telegraph pole above it.

49. **Fuchs up the Pole** 15ft 5b ★
Start directly below the pole and gain the slanting ledge on the left.
Finish up the shallow groove.

50. **Mount Vinson** 35ft E7   ★★ †
6c. Left of Fuchs up the Pole is a chimney. Start 15 feet left of this at a
line of hanging flakes. Power up the flakes passing several overlaps.

51. **Meridian** 35ft Hard VS   ★
5a. The conspicuous crack 10 feet left to a difficult finish.

52. **Amundsen** 20ft Hard VS   ★★
5b. Further left at a higher level; the classic jamming crack.

53. **Rally** 20ft E4   ★★
6b. About 20 yards left is an overhanging buttress. Rally takes the brutal
thin crack which splits the leaning wall.

STRONSTREY BANK QUARRY (SD 619 186)

By Goi Ashmore

SITUATION AND CHARACTER
Situated high on the west edge of Anglezarke Moor, above the hamlet
of White Coppice, this small quarry is composed of sandy gritstone up
to 30 feet high, and it offers some pleasant climbing despite its dark
enclosed atmosphere. Care must be taken as some of the tops still

contain loose rock as do many of the climbs.

APPROACH
The best approach is from White Coppice cricket ground. From Anglezarke, continue up the hill for two miles and follow the White Coppice signs into the village. Cars can be parked at the cricket ground except on match days, when it is best to park on the rough track by the reservoirs. Cross the bridge and strike up the obvious track leading off right. This track leads to just below the quarry, The Bank itself can be reached by scrambling up the depressingly-steep gully 200 yards before the quarry. Black Brook Buttress is found by following the track direct from the bridge, up the valley for ¼ mile.

HISTORY
The quarry was mainly developed by Colin Dickenson with John Cottingham, Frank Menzies and Bob Scoltock, between 1972 and 1974, with subsequent additions from Karl Lunt (Screaming Abdabs) and Kev Glass, who also added routes to the previously neglected outlying buttresses. Stronstrey has seen little activity since then except for Gong and Boredom (details unknown) and Reunion Wilderness which was inadvertently soloed by Goi Ashmore during guidework.

The numbers included in brackets after some route descriptions refer to the numbers painted on the rock. Heights are not given. The first climbs lie in a bay on the right as one enters the quarry, and are described from RIGHT to LEFT.

1. **Gong** Sev
The initial crack system.

2. **Small Wall** Diff
The isolated block on the left.

3. **First Night** V Diff (2)
Climb a right-slanting crack above a small cave.

4. **Butch** Hard Sev (3)
4a. Up parallel cracks just left of First Night. At the square recess move left.

5. **Deck of Cards** Diff (4)
The broken corner 15 feet left.

6. **Stacked Hand** Hard VS (5)
5c. Climb the centre of the steep slab on the left.

7. **Notch**
5b. A boulder problem up the arête with an obvious notch 30 feet left.

Twenty feet left are two sets of slabs. The next two routes take the cracks in the lower slab.

8. **Lay Off** Sev (7)
The cracks on the right of the slab.

9. **Coppice Crumble** Diff (8)
The corner crack.

10. **Feeble Finger** Hard Sev (9)
4a. The right crack on the next slab.

11. **Pinchblock** Sev (10)
The crack 10 feet left.

12. **Grapevine** Hard Diff (11)
The slab just right of the corner.

13. **The Mole** Diff (12)
Climb onto a small pedestal just left of the corner and finish up this.

14. **The Max Factor** VS (13)
4c. Cracks in the blunt arête just left.

15. **Muddy** VS (14)
4b. The next 'muddy' crack.

16. **Flake Crack** V Diff (15)
The crack just left, which forms the right side of a large flake.

17. **Boredom** Sev
Traverses the horizontal break from the corner left of Flake Crack to The Mole.

18. **Cannine Crawl** Hard VS (16)
5a. A strenuous route up the overhanging jamming cracks just left of the corner.

The next climbs lie on the opposite face of the quarry, on a large broken overhanging wall.

19. **Screaming Abdabs** VS (17)
4b. Start on the right below a piece of angle-iron embedded in a crack, and climb the right slanting crack, taking care not to dislodge the whole rockface.

20. **Stron** Hard VS (18)
5b. Start 15 feet left and climb into a shallow cave, then exit via the right crack.

21. **Coppice Cave** Hard VS (19)
5b. As for Stron, but take the left-hand exit.

22. **Stopgap Swinger** VS (20)
4c. Start 15 feet left and climb the short chimney beneath a wide V-groove, passing a large chockstone.

23. **Finger Five** VS (21)
4b. Twenty feet left are two cracks forming the left corner of a blank wall; climb these. The blank wall appears to be the quarry's last great problem.

24. **Greyhound Track** Sev (22)
The left-slanting groove 5 feet left.

25. **Rampant Digit** Sev (23)
The V-shaped groove just left.

26. **Dog Lead** Diff (24)
Climb up blocks and a crack to a ledge on the right, then finish direct.

27. Chevalier Diff (25)
Twenty-five feet left, past a broken gully is a flat-topped triangular block. Climb onto this then the indefinite arête above.

28. Pathos V Diff (26)
This route takes the left side of a wide block-filled crack-cum-groove.

29. Sportos VS (27)
4c. The fine, curved crack 10 feet left.

30. Decadent Diff (28)
Start 10 feet left and climb up to a grassy ledge, then finish over large blocks.

31. Swinging Brick V Diff (29)
Start on the front of a small protruding buttress. Climb over the capstone and finish just left of Decadent.

32. Thinger V Diff
Mantel onto the top of the slab and then continue up small ledges to finish just left of a small tower.

33. Thwinger Sev
Climb the wall on the left, keeping to the right of a small overhang and a red groove.

34. Radio Gnome Invisible VS
4c. The crack and small corner 6 feet left.

35. Mam Diff
Climb into a pod just right of the right arête.

36. Reunion Wilderness Hard VS   †
5a. The arête right of Wam on its left-hand side.

37. Wam Sev
Takes a line up the highest part of the front face on good holds to a solid chockstone, then finish up the jamming crack.

38. Sam Sev
From a large ledge 20 feet further left, follow holds diagonally left onto a sloping slab, then up small holds to the top.

STRONSTREY BANK (SD 620 187)
The Bank itself is on the route to the quarry, but is nearer to the village. It consists of an isolated buttress at the N end of the bank.

39. Beyond the Realms of Death Sev
From a small ledge at the foot of the left edge, follow a crack left onto the arête, then move up and back right round the arête and finish straight up.

40. Anthem Hard Diff
Fifteen feet right, gain a triangular ledge, then bear left over ledges to gain the top few feet of Beyond the Realms of Death.

41. The S-Bend Diff
The chimney on the right.

42. Bleak Outlook 5b
The arête at the far end of the arc, on it's left-hand side.

BLACK BROOK BUTTRESS (SD 623 189)
This is the small crag on the left bank of Black Brook, above the cricket ground at White Coppice. It is identifiable by an old mine level. The routes are on the solid buttress farther right.

43. **Bastille Day**   Hard Sev
4a. The obvious shallow chimney near the left edge.

44. **Bomber**   Sev
Mantel onto a sloping ledge 5 feet farther right, then follow the corner crack to the top.

WITHNELL QUARRY (SD 633 217)

By Goi Ashmore and Rob Scott

APPROACH
From the A675 at Abbey Village follow the Brinscall road for nearly a mile, passing Central Quarry, to a surfaced track (Butterworth Brow) which forks left. Follow the track to the massive quarry on the left. Parking is possible in the various lay-bys, but care must be taken not to block the quarry gates.

CHARACTER
The quarry is a rough semi-circle of shattered walls guarded by dangerous scree runs. Much potential exists here for trundling, but normal climbers should not be deterred as most of the climbing lies away from these walls. The first area of any note is the small square buttress situated under the prominent hillock on the far left of the quarry. Rock here is sound and a belay stake is in place.

HISTORY
This huge quarry, which only closed down in 1974, saw its first activity in 1977 when two unknown climbers put up a now deceased route in the Subsidiary Workings. The first really major wave of development however, occurred in 1978 when Dave Cronshaw and Les Ainsworth discovered Brick Buttress and ascended five routes before encountering access difficulties caused by the local water bailiff.

The crag lay dormant until the late Kev Glass solved most of the other obvious gaps on the buttress during guidebook work in 1981. The best of these was undoubtedly the undergraded Marie, Marie.

The first climbs away from Brick Buttress came in 1986 when Cronshaw remembered the hidden New Walls and returned with John Ryden to create Split Screen and the crag's hardest route, Emotional Paralysis which had previously been attempted on sight without much success by Goi Ashmore, who now turned his attention to the remaining lines on Brick Buttress, producing some good pitches such as The Factory Syndicate and the direct finish to Blinkers.

1987 was a busy year which saw a huge trundling effort to unearth

WITHNELL QUARRY Brick Buttress

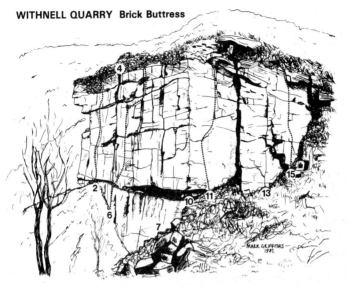

MARK GRIFFITHS
1987.

routes in the previously neglected Main Quarry. First to fall was Honest Onions And Rotten Garlick by Goi, followed by a solo ascent of the previously aided Moscow Wall which took six hours to clean and as many minutes to climb. A few others have also started to make a mark; Rob Scott added Council Orifices and Pete Swales was responsible for Crakatak, but the quarry's plum lines remain untouched due to a short term access ban imposed on the crag in late 1987. This ban should not prove permanent and developments will soon begin again at this interesting quarry.

BRICK BUTTRESS

1. **Hookworm** 25ft Hard Sev
At the left side of the buttress is a crack with an old drill embedded in its base. The route takes this crack.

2. **Strangle** 25ft Hard Sev
4b. The series of irregular cracks 5 feet right.

3. **Tangle** 25ft Hard VS
5a. Just left of Wangle is a short wall capped by a small overhang. Mantel over this then continue to the top break, finishing up the crack just left.

4. **Wangle** 30ft Hard Sev
4c. The obvious crack at the top of the banking.

5. **Mangle** 35ft Hard VS   *
5a. Takes a series of indefinite cracks 10 feet right.

6. **Dangle** 40ft Hard VS
5b. Climb the thin crack system which gains Mangle from the left.

7. **Gaffer** 40ft VS
4c. The wide crack 10 feet left of the right arête of the buttress.

8. **Marie, Marie** 35ft E1 ⋆⋆
5b. Fine climbing up the thin crack just left of the arête (PR).

9. **Criminal Neglect** 70ft Hard VS †
5a. Climb Wangle for 12 feet, then follow the obvious thin traverse line which leads to Arête-Toi. Finish up this.

10. **Arête-Toi** 30ft Sev ⋆
The arête direct (PR).

11. **Weezy Wonk** 30ft Hard V Diff
Start just right of Arête-Toi, and follow stepped ledges to the top.

12. **Scrabble** 30ft V Diff
The next arête.

13. **Blinkers** 25ft Hard VS ⋆
5a. The centre of the wall just right, finishing over the bulge on hidden holds.

14. **Old Granny Glass** 25ft Sev
The crack that limits the wall on it's left.

15. **The Evil Fencepost** 20ft VS
4c. The wall just right.

There is a short break in the rock followed by a short steep wall.

16. **The Factory Syndicate** 20ft E1 ⋆ †
5c. Climbs the wall direct from the top of the banking via a small orange flake and small layaway. Unprotected with a bad landing.

17. **Exercise One** 20ft VS
5b. Climb The Factory Syndicate until hands can be placed on the higher of the mid-height breaks and feet on the lower. Traverse right to left in this manner.

There is also a low-level traverse from The Factory Syndicate back to the first route with some 5b climbing, and a poor 4c problem over the overhangs right of The Syndicate.

A prominent track runs through the qy at this point. On the other side of this is **THE PROMONTORY**; a tongue of rock separating the subsidiary quarry from the main workings. The climbs here are sound though protection is sparse. Nut belays throughout.

18. **The Funnel** 20ft Hard Diff
The groove on the left arête of the end face of The Promontory.

The following routes are reached by following the path which leads down rightwards from the base of The Funnel.

19. **Out of the Locker** 20ft 5b
Thirty yards right of The Funnel is an obvious crack in an overhanging

wall and eight feet left of this is a scoop; follow this to finish via the obvious pocket.

20. Moscow Wall 50ft Hard Sev   *
4c. Just left of the right arête of the end face of The Promontory is a layback crack. Follow this, then make awkward moves up and left to a large ledge. Trend up and right from this for 10 feet then finish direct up the flakey scoop.

21. Honest Onions and Rotten Garlick 50ft Hard VS
5a. The obvious slab 50 yards right of the right arête of the end of The Promontory is climbed by the scoop on its right until an awkward move can be made onto the large ledge. Finish up the obvious V-shaped groove. A direct start is possible via the mantel ledge on the left of the slab at 5b.

THE SUBSIDIARY WORKINGS
This is the small low section left of The Promontory. Most of it is broken and only the better routes are described.

22. Murder 20ft 5b
Twenty yards left of The Funnel is an obvious arête which is somewhat harder than it looks. Climb it on its right side.

23. 'Enery 20ft VS
5a. The first overhanging block is surmounted slightly left of the pocket at the top of it's initial slab.

24. Crakatak 20ft Sev
Thirty yards left is the last clean cut face of this side of the area. The route takes the cracks up its left side.

25. Incandescent Geography 20ft VS
5a. The dirty leaning wall at the left-hand end of the back wall. Fortunately it has no belay.

26. Council Orifices 30ft Hard Sev
4a. A hundred yards right of the junction of The Promontory and the Main Walls is an obvious council road spike. Use this to gain access to the scree platform below. The route takes the obvious left-slanting crack.

NEW WALLS
This is the hidden wall almost directly opposite Brick Buttress. The wall leans about 5°, with a discontinuous ledge running it's length. Extreme caution must be exercised with the shale tier at the top although all the current routes avoid this.

27. Slab Dab 40ft Sev
At the top of the left-hand banking is a wide excavated chimney, climb this until it is possible to step right to finish up the obvious slab.

28. Emotional Paralysis 55ft E3   **
5c. At the far left-hand side of the wall is a thin crack, follow this to the break, PR. Swing right then climb the exposed wall above on slots.

29. Split Screen 50ft Hard VS   *
5a. Just right are twin cracks, take these stepping left or lowering off to avoid the loose finish.

MINOR CRAGS

HOGHTON BOTTOMS (SD 628 263)
A short and somewhat dusty natural grit crag, below the viaduct on the Blackburn – Preston railway line, just past Hoghton Quarry.

KEMP DELF (SD 723 277)
A small quarry about 100 yards south of the B6234 at Stanhill. From the bend on the Blackburn side of the village a track below some transmission lines leads directly into the quarry. Some climbing has been done including some good bouldering, and there are possibilities for about a dozen climbs of up to 30 feet. As it is so conveniently located it certainly appears worth further development.

KNOWL HEIGHTS QY (SD 684 222)
A small quarry ½ mile mile west of Darwen centre contains some problems including an obvious off-width crack: **Flash** (5c).

From Manor Road, alongside Bold Venture Park turn right into Westland Avenue and park here. From the top of the avenue follow a track which leads off right and take the right-hand fork just past some cottages. The quarry is on the left before some trees.

STAR DELF (SD 717 317)
A small quarry consisting of three clean slabs just off the Rishton – New Inns road. Climbing has obviously taken place here in the past as an ('un-natural') line of polished holds climbs the central slab. Further across the fields lies Rabbit Delf which has potential for a 25-foot roof climb.

VI. THE PENDLE AREA

Compiled by Phil Kelly
with assistance from Andrew Gridley, Rob Smitton and Jon Sparks,
with acknowledgements to Malc Haslam

The area which surrounds Pendle Hill is one of great beauty, within which are four crags, each with it own distinct character. The limestone of Witches Quarry, near Downham, offers excellent climbing at all grades, on good sound rock in pleasant situations. Climbing is banned here at present though it is hoped that this access problem will soon be resolved (consult the BMC for the latest news). Another limestone crag is the Trough of Bowland Quarry which though not very extensive, has a number of good climbs.

On the gritstone side of things, Craig Y Longridge has brought a new dimension to climbing in the area, and is probably now the bouldering mecca of the north! Craig Y Longridge is very useful for a short visit because that is all most people can manage, the crag overhanging for its whole length and the climbing tending ever so slightly towards the strenuous!

Farther north and in complete contrast is the recently re-discovered Thorn Crag; a gem of natural gritstone set high on the wild, wild moor on the Forest of Bowland. Thorn Crag is well worth the walk needed to reach this unspoilt place and to enjoy the superb climbing there.

CRAIG Y LONGRIDGE (SD 619 384)

By Rob Smitton

APPROACH AND ACCESS
The crag is best approached from Longridge by heading northeast from the town centre along the road signposted 'Jeffrey Hill'. Where the road forks, bear right following the sign to the golf course and continue for another 500 yards, passing a large caravan site on the right. Shortly after this a gravel pull-in and iron gate will be seen on the right. Park here, go over the stile and left over the fence into the field where the crag will be seen. No access problems have arisen but please respect the farmer's fences and livestock.

SITUATION AND CHARACTER
Craig Y Longridge has matured rapidly since its unveiling in the 1986 supplement – it is a unique crag now providing arguably the biggest and best concentration of high-standard bouldering in the region. Looking like one side of some drunken railway cutting, it consists of a 100-yard long straight wall tilting continuously 30 degrees beyond the pumpy side of vertical. Because of this, climbing here can at first be demoralising: an open-minded attitude to failure can be useful on early

visits, but persistence should quickly confer the strength needed to unlock some of the finest problems in the Northwest.

The rock is generally good gritstone although care needs to be taken with the top three feet on account of the looseness: topping-out is strictly for those bored with life, the normal practice being to reach the top of the good rock and then either downclimb or jump off. Unfortunately the crag faces southeast and is therefore quite slow to dry after rain and suffers badly from seepage.

HISTORY

The history of Craig Y Longridge is very short and to-the-point. Andy Gridley (Grid) and other members of the Longridge Crazy Gang first discovered the crag in 1983 and climbed five routes; John Marsden climbed Thug, Steve Sharples added the open corner of New Stone Age, and Grid ascended Neolithic Technology and two others. They kept quiet about the actual location of the crag because they realised just what big potential it had, but accidentally Grid let it slip in the pub one night and the race was on...

Paul Pritchard immediately became a devotee of the crag as it seemed to suit his style well, and he began adding new routes such as Central Icefall Direct (covered in verglas at the time!) Slug The Thug, Dyno...Bucket, and The Howling and Wobblebottom. Phil Kelly climbed the poor Semen Scream and repeated many of the earlier routes including Grids' Company Of Wolves, after others had failed. Pride of place though went jointly to Pritchard who traversed the obvious horizontal break in duvet and gloves to create Ascent Of Man, and also to Grid who fell slapping for the top on what was to become 30 Feet Of Pain, during a solo attempt. This problem was later solved by Pritchard though using the safety of a rope and situ 'peg runner!

Grid continued his developments during 1985 with Spah's Daehniks and Descent Of Man, whilst Tim Gridley climbed Thin Tim's Footsteps and Timothy's Route as well as belaying big brother on Red Animals which was named after the Heysel stadium disaster.

As news of the crag spread Rob Smitton began visiting and soon usurped Grids' crown. Rob began by adding Black Jake and Babylon Blitz late in 1985, just as the supplement was going to press. Mark Leach got a short look-in and put up The Gauntlet, Imitation Arapiles and Like A Slug But Sucks (think about it) which were all named by Pritchard. Kelly returned to climb Muscles In Their Imagination, but not before Will Steel had completed Waiting In The Wings just to its left whilst waiting for Phil to complete his line. Muscles... was later improved by Rob when he lined the back of some of the deeper pockets with waterproof cement to stop seepage!

In 1986 Rob continued to beaver away and climbed a series of excellent traverses including Bend of the Rainbow and Tarot Plane (Kelly had done the latter a couple of months previously and called it Horizontal Heavyweight), which it is hoped will one day be linked by a traverse of the whole crag; what a prospect! Rob's other efforts from 1986 include Grow Wings and Still Raining, Still Dreaming and a magnificent effort in neatly painting new lines at the base of the routes to help with identification. Mick Lovatt climbed Big Marine the same year and claimed it to be the hardest problem on the crag, though 1987 saw Malc Haslam add the excellent Eat 'em and Smile which is probably harder, together with Smitton's Mr. Skin, Grids' Unnatural Selection and an earlier Mark Leach problem; Fertile Delta which possibly gets to be top of the 'tick-list' at a meaty 6c.

THE ROUTES are described from LEFT to RIGHT and can be located by numbers painted on the rock.

1. Session's End 5a
Traverse right as far as The Race.

2. Easy 3a

3. Peasy 3b

4. Pudding 4a

5. Pie 4b

6. Gauzebush 4a

7. Absolute Beginners 4a

8. Bramble Ramble 4a

9. The Race 4c

10. Escalator 4b

11. Snail Trail 4c

12. Paul Pritchard's Jacket 5a

13. Stoning a Leper 5b
Exit leftward out of the cave.

14. Pay the Witch 5c   *
Exit rightwards from the cave and pull quite boldly up the headwall.

15. Late Pickings 5a
Climb the left arête of Rifted Victim, starting from directly below.

16. Rifted Victim 5b
Surmount the protruding blocks and pull leftwards into the groove. One of the few routes on which it is possible to top out.

17. Naked Lunch 4c
Another route destined for greatness.

18. Black Jake 5b   *
An exciting finish up the headwall on small, rather shy holds.

19. Timothy's Route 5c   **
Unusual in that it is possible to top out in relative safety. Only 5a to touch the top.

20. Wobblebottom 5c   ***
Snatch up to the break, step right and surmount the short juggy arête above. Mind the cars.

21. Seven-A 6a   *
Gain the top by undercutting an unfriendly horizontal slot; feels dangerous on first acquaintance.

22. Bomb Squad 6a   *
A ridiculous lock-out involving another unhelpful orifice.

23. Tarot Plane 6a ***
The first of the excellent traverses: go left from Central Icefall Direct to link up with Session's End and so reach the end of the crag. A hard, low variation when crossing Snail Trail and P.P's Jacket makes it particularly good value.

24. Central Icefall Direct 5a *
Can be used as a 'Bachar Ladder' by dispensing with the footholds.

25. Hitting the Wall 6a
A low traverse from Central Icefall Direct to Pump 'til you Jump; greasier than a mechanic's rag!

26. Babylon Blitz 5b *
Climb the wall using footholds in Central Icefall Direct and top out using the short, leaning arête and hanging garden to the left.

27. 30 Feet of Pain E3 ***
6b. An excellent route on which it is advisable to take a rope. The peg protection for the crux headwall can be backed up by a Friend.

28. Haardvark 6a
Big and exciting but sandier than the Sahara.

29. Cruel Country 6b **
A high level counter traverse above Hitting the Wall, from Pump 'til you Jump to Central Icefall Direct.

30. Pump 'til you Jump 5c *

31. Twelve Dreams 6b
A very low-level traverse from Pump 'til you Jump to Mad Aardvark's Tea Party.

32. Still Raining, Still Dreaming E3 **
6b. Climb the wall immediately right of Pump 'til you Jump (Friend protection high up).

33. Grow Wings 6b ***
Although it has been soloed, in situ peg protection can be used near the top. The lower half is the crux, but the finish requires unwavering optimism.

34. Imitation Arapiles 6a **
Good, committing climbing into and beyond the cave at 20 feet.

35. Going Deaf for a Living 6a **
A higher-level counter traverse above Twelve Dreams from Mad Aardvark's Tea Party to Pump 'til... Embarrassingly difficult for the short-legged.

36. Mad Aardvark's Tea Party 6a
Almost ungradeable: either lock out Rambo-style or leap for the obvious jug at 12 feet.

37. Gruts 6a **
Traverse tenaciously from Mad Aardvark's Tea Party to Muddy Wobble Block; a bit like doing pull-ups sideways.

38. Like a Slug but Sucks 6b *
A very hard start is followed by a bold and rather dirty finish.

39. **Slug the Thug**   5c

40. **Dissenting**   5c
A variation to Slug the Thug, stepping left slightly and climbing the wall above the niche.

41. **Piledriver**   5c
A short-lived route whose most crucial hold fell off on the second ascent. Possibly impossible.

42. **Added Incentive**   5c

43. **Muddy Wobble Block**   5a
As bad as it sounds.

44. **Mr. Skin**   6c
Traverse from Muddy Wobble Block to Semen Scream with the crux passing Blatantly Slimy Slug. Jump off where the good holds end or continue as far as Bend of the Rainbow for 1st prize.

45. **Waiting in the Wings**   5c

46. **Muscles in their Imagination**   6a

47. **Weir Aardvark**   5c

48. **Blatantly Slimy Slug**   5b   *
Short but interesting.

49. **Company of Wolves**   5b

50. **The Howling**   5c

51. **Dyno...Bucket**   5b

52. **Semen Scream/Harry Hodge Pig**   5c   *
Some confusion exists over the rightful claims of these two route names to the same piece of rock. Declared a draw.

53. **Smeg City**   5c   **
A satisfying problem on excellent rock. Jumping for the first good jug reduces the grade.

54. **The Gauntlet**   6b
A nasty little number with a spine chilling landing.

55. **Big Marine**   6b   *
A thrilling lurch off tinies for the top.

56. **Renal Failure**   6c   **
A rarely repeated problem; similar to but harder than Big Marine.

57. **Push to Prolapse**   6b   **
Hard slapping for the top off that Longridge rarity – a good (?) undercut.

58.   **Bend of the Rainbow**   6c   ★★★
Longridge's best traverse and possibly best route of any kind. Traverse thoughtfully from a lonely jug to the right of Push to Prolapse, until bridged smugly across New Stone Age.

59.   **Eat 'em and Smile**   6c   ★ †
So far unrepeated. An indifference towards torn flesh seems to be essential.

60.   **Rug Thug**   6b   ★★
A hard and unrelenting problem on small fingerholds up the vague crackline.

61.   **In Excess**   6a   ★★★
Hard and surprising climbing all the way to the top. Parachute descent.

62.   **Porridge Gun**   6a   ★★
Yet another excellent route on superb rock.

62a.   **Fertile Delta**   6c   ★★
Longridge's most gymnastic problem, a direct start to the jugs on Porridge Gun via a small L-shaped fingerhold.

63.   **Anal Cave-In**   6b   ★
Not the major challenge of this wall but good nevertheless and with one very awkward move.

64.   **Scorched August**   6a   ★
An under-rated route that doesn't get the attention it deserves.

65.   **New Stone Age**   5c   ★
Longridge's 'Good Book'. Awkward moves up the big groove line.

66.   **Unknown Arête**   5b   ★
Climb the arête, mainly on the outside.

67.   **Unnatural Selection**   6c   †
Traverse crab-like from New Stone Age to Jacob's Ladder. Deformed limbs might be helpful.

68.   **Missing Link**   6c   ★
A very rarely repeated problem; the height factor seems to be crucial.

69.   **Moschops**   6a   ★★
Committing and exciting. The landing, if wet, needs to be treated with respect.

70.   **Ascent of Man**   5c   ★★★
Traverse the high break from Jacob's Ladder to New Stone Age; brilliant. Never desperate but a test of strength, stamina and nimble-footedness — like ballet sideways.

71.   **Jacob's Ladder**   5b

72. Spah's Daehniks   6a
The boldest route here, with an uninviting landing. Traverse the high break from Jacob's Ladder to Runaway.

73. Orifice of Faeces   6a   *
Fine attractive climbing on good rock; shame about the name.

74. Neolithic Technology   6a   *
Very similar to Orifice of Faeces.

75. From Ape to Aardvark   6a

76. Descent of Man   5c   **
Traverse low from Runaway to Jacob's Ladder. An on-sight link-up with Ascent of Man would be impressive.

77. Runaway   4a

78. And She Was   5a

The crag now degenerates into an arena for real climbing with vertical faces rising up to considerable heights. Unfortunately the routes in this section of the crag have only received a handful of ascents and natural protection is scarce, and so the routes must be approached with some caution.

79. Some Friend   5a
Located bashfully behind the tree. Probably better to climb the tree instead!

80. Thug   5a

81. Headline   5a

82. Unnamed   5a
Climb the wall direct to an in-situ sling.

83. Bwink Bwink Bonk   5c

84. Shaps Master Flasher   6a

85. Thin Tim's Footsteps   E1 5a

86. Red Animals   E2
5c. Go straight up to BR and continue past two shallow caves.

THORN CRAG (SD 596 571)

By Andrew Gridley

SITUATION AND CHARACTER
This pleasant little esoteric beauty is situated in some of Lancashire's most inspiring yet bleak landscape. The crag offers everything for the gritstone afficianado, from first class bouldering to full blooded routes of all grades – and all on excellent rock!

The main crag is split into two tiers, and THE CLIMBS are described from LEFT to RIGHT beginning with the upper. Apart from the main crag there are many outlying boulders, the most significant of which has been named and described.

APPROACH

Thorn Crag lies at the crest of the fell which can be seen from and to the right of the Trough of Bowland road. To reach it by car when travelling from Dunsop Bridge, follow the road which passes the Trough of Bowland Quarry and continue along it for a further 3 miles until, on a sharp left hand bend it is possible to turn right into a cul-de-sac leading to the sleepy hamlet of Tarnbrook. Follow this road to the hamlet, parking on it's fringes with consideration for the small community. The crag can be seen on the left skyline. On foot now, walk through the hamlet to a gate and follow the path for about ½ a mile, until it is possible to branch up left across the fell to the crag without being too conspicuous. An alternative approach is to follow the track leading directly up the hillside behind the hamlet, to the shooting huts. Then branch off rightwards to the crag. PLEASE NOTE: no dogs allowed under the Lancashire County Council Access Agreement.

HISTORY

The first climber to visit the crag was probably Alan Atkinson and his friends from Blackpool in the 1950's, who would tramp the surrounding moors on most weekends, often walking up the Trough of Bowland with huge rucksacks full to the brim with beer, to doss in the shooting hut below the crag. It was Thorn Crag that introduced Alan and his friends to climbing and they would happily swarm all over the crag in blissful ignorance of climbing in other areas, and in fact when they did widen their horizons, it soon became apparent that they had been climbing routes that were a good match in terms of difficulty, to routes in other areas. The friends still continued to trek the moors together though they soon began to realism that it was easier on both body and soul on a Sunday morning to go climbing on the crag than to trudge the moors all day with a thick head.

The modern wave of developments began in 1985 when Andy Gridley and Paul Pritchard (both fully paid-up members of the Longridge Crazy Gang) discovered a small boulder field on the side of the moor. On closer examination, it turned out to be two tiers of perfect natural gritstone attaining a maximum height which initial appearances from the road could not suggest. Both climbers were surprised to discover an ancient and rusting peg in the route now known as Prior Visit, and they realised they were not the first to discover the crag.

Honours between Pritchard and Gridley were even, though most routes were bound to have been done before. Two of Paul's routes (Epée Edge and Kissing the Pink) were undoubtedly first ascents, as was Grid's ascent of the off-width roof crack Air Aardvark.

As news of the crag spread, Owain Jones and Steve Edmondson paid a visit, and stayed the weekend, sleeping under the crag. Owain made the second ascent of Kissing the Pink and went on to claim a route that Paul and Grid had managed to evade; the awesome looking off-width crack on the right-hand side of the upper tier – Grimly Fiendish was billed a 'like Goliath but with runners' and looks excellent, as does the crack to its left, New Rose which Owain climbed and Steve repeated immediately after.

Dave Cronshaw and John Ryden made the effort one winter's day and trudged up to the crag to see what all the fuss was about. They were pleasantly surprised at what they found, but even more surprised when Grid appeared through the mist and rain to 'keep an eye on' the raiders. The two sides joined together for Cronshaw to lead The Fireman's Slippery Pole before a swift retreat to the pub.

UPPER TIER

1. **Pelvic Thrust**   35ft   Severe
4a. Start 10 feet left of the central crack of the first buttress, climb up trending leftwards then finish direct.

2. **The Fireman's Slippery Pole**   40ft   VS   †
4c. Climbs the central crack direct.

3. **Kissing the Pink**   30ft   E4   *
5c. The right arête; bold with a big fall potential.

4. **Toro Toro Aardvark**   30ft   Hard VS   **
5a. Twenty feet right of Kissing The Pink is a small buttress split by two cracks; climb the right-hand crack direct.

Right again an impressive buttress thrusts it's presence forwards. The first route on this buttress is the wide crack 15 feet right of the bulging arête.

5. **Grimly Fiendish**   35ft   E2   *** †
5c. The aforementioned offwidth, an ascent of which proves an unforgettable experience. Good wires.

6. **New Rose**   35ft   E1   *
5c. Climb the crack right of Grimly Fiendish to the capping roof, then surmount this to gain the top.

Farther right is a mass of boulders within which are some good problems. Walking into the boulders by the obvious path finds Pinch 'n' Pull and Button Moon on the left, and Flying Pleb on the right.

7. **Pinch 'n' Pull**   5a

8. **Button Moon**   5c.

9. **Flying Pleb**   5a
Takes the obvious small overhang on the right.

LOWER TIER
The lower tier is more broken but sports many good routes.

10. **The Fallen Madonna with the Big Boobies**   30ft   E1   *
5b. At the far left of the tier is a broken area, this climb takes the left arête of the first solid buttress.

11. **Prior Visit**   30ft   VS
4b. Six feet right of The Fallen Madonna etc is a crackline containing a fossilized peg, take this direct.

12. **Long Shore Drift**   30ft   E2   *
5c. Climbs the short wall right of Prior Visit and joins Termination to

top out.

13. Termination 30ft Sev
4c. Climbs the crack direct.

14. Banana Land 20ft Diff
A large isolated buttress stands in front of the next wall; this climb takes the easy left arête.

15. Look no Hands 20ft Sev
4c. Take the centre of the boulder below Termination.

16. Epée Edge]25ft E4   ★★
5c. Back on the lower tier, this route climbs the left arête of the slim buttress on the right.

17. Aardvarks Don't Dyno 25ft E1   ★
5b. Right of Epée Edge is another arête; climb this direct.

18. Air Aardvark 15ft E1
6a. Forty feet right of Aardvarks Don't Dyno, the tier begins to regain it's height, climb the roof by the obvious offwidth.

19. Ride a Wild Aardvark 25ft Hard VS   ★
5a. Takes the arête at the far right of the crag.

HALF-WAY BOULDERS
Three hundred yards below the edge is a fine little collection of boulders containing problems of all grades and offering light relief on the arduous trek to the crag.

TROUGH OF BOWLAND QUARRY (SD 628 519)

By Jon Sparks

APPROACH AND ACCESS
The quarry lies above the road through the Trough of Bowland from Dunsop Bridge, half a mile north of Sykes Farm. There is good parking by the small waterworks directly below the crag, though the crag is actually hidden from view here. The simplest approach is to walk a short way up the road to where it crosses the stream. A gate gives access to an obvious track which leads directly to the crag in only a few minutes.

SITUATION AND CHARACTER
The quarry faces roughly southwest and gets plenty of sun, so most of the rock dries quickly apart from one or two seepage lines and after prolonged rain there is some drainage from the hillside above. The right side of the crag has a large number of trees and the routes here are generally dirtier and slower to dry. The crag is limestone of quite a compact nature, but with a number of detached blocks. Good protection is often hard to find. The climbing is generally of a balancey nature, with a predominance of sloping holds; the routes are often steeper than they appear from below which can be quite disconcerting at first.

HISTORY

Though easily accessible, the quarry is only briefly seen from the road which may explain its relatively slow development. The initial lines, including Bowland Wall, Owl Wall and the girdle were climbed by J. Ingham Riley and friends. Whilst checking the routes for the first Lancashire guide, Ian Cowell missed the line of Bowland Wall and found himself on what is now Guillotine, the name resulting from a potentially nasty rockfall which sliced his rope in two. The route was completed later by Les Ainsworth. That was the state of play until 1977 when Roger and Glenn Brookes added Owl Stretching Time and Deceptive Bends (then described in two pitches with a belay on Owl Ledge).

In 1987, during guidebook work, the present writer devised the variation to the girdle though this involves only negligible amount of new climbing.

THE CLIMBS are described from LEFT to RIGHT.

1. **Left Edge** 35ft V Diff
Several lines are possible, all of which lead to a finish entirely composed of loose blocks. If undeterred, the best start is probably by the left-facing slab starting below the large tree.

Just past this is a small but very steep diamond-shaped wall which gives an interesting but somewhat fragile problem.

2. **Owl Stretching Time** 60ft VS ★
4c. Follow the rib right of the steep wall to a large ledge on the left (belay possible, but rather pointless). Move up awkwardly just left of a large projecting block and then straight up the wall above on good jugs to twin trees. Pleasant but over all too soon.

3. **Bowland Wall** 80ft Hard Sev ★
Start just right again. Climb up and slightly left, then move left to the large grass ledge. The large ramp on the right is both awkward and bold to start; follow it to broken ledges and finish diagonally up the fine wall to the leftmost of the large trees.

4. **The Guillotine** 70ft VS ★
4b. Start as for Bowland Wall but move awkwardly right just before the large ledge, past blocks to gain the lower parallel ramp. Follow this boldly to its end then move up to the broken ledges on Bowland Wall. Continue straight up the wall using a right-slanting crack.

5. **Captain Beaky** 65ft E1 ★
5a. A very direct line up the highest part of the crag. Start just right of Bowland Wall at a short left-facing corner; climb this and continue up the steep black wall (bold) to finish as for Guillotine.

6. **Owl Wall** 75ft Hard Sev
Climb the short corner as for Captain Beaky then follow the narrow

slab/ramp to a ledge with several trees (Owl's Nest Ledge). Climb the wall behind and move slightly right to another tree. Or, (easier and often drier) move right and climb an obvious break to the tree, as for Owl's Nest Direct. Finish leftwards to the large trees, the last few feet being quite loose.

7. **Deceptive Bends** 70ft Hard VS   ★★
5a. Start a few feet right below a white crystalline wall. Move up on to this and climb diagonally right to cross Owl Wall, just left of Owl's Nest Ledge. Climb the wall above trending slightly left then straight up to the trees; the best route on the crag.

8. **Owlet** 30ft Hard Sev
4b. Climb directly up to Owl's Nest Ledge.

9. **Owl's Nest Direct** 65ft Hard Sev
4b. A wide and rather dirty crack runs up to the right end of Owl's Nest Ledge. Follow this then step right and up an obvious break to the higher tree, and finish as for Owl Wall.

10. **Primrose Route** 60ft V Diff
Very dirty and not recommended. The original first 'pitch' took the large easy-angled slab (or hanging garden!) to the large tree, but a more direct approach is probably better. From the tree climb up to a ledge and swing left to a deep groove, go up this and finish up the left edge of a broken slab.

11. **Original Route** 30ft Moderate
High up the slope on the right, climb the right side of a block left of the last area of rock, then up the centre of the wall above, passing a small tree.

12. **Girdle Traverse** 155ft Sev
(1) 70ft. Climb Original Route to the top of the block, then descend the left side of the block to a tree. Up easily as for Primrose Route for a few feet until a traverse can be made to Owl's Nest Ledge.
(2) 85ft. Descend Owl Wall until just above the foot of the ramp, a traverse can be made to join Bowland Wall; follow this to the large grass ledge then continue leftwards to finish up Left Edge (after reading the warning in that route's description).
(2a) 55ft. VS 4c ★. **Variation**: From Owl's Nest Ledge step up then diagonally left to gain the ledges on Bowland Wall. Reverse this until just above the large protruding block. Step left onto the block and finish as for Owl Stretching Time. There is hardly any independent climbing and the girdle is less complete, but it is higher, better and safer.

WITCHES QUARRY (SD 810 444)

SITUATION AND CHARACTER
The quarry is limestone which on the whole is of good quality. In some parts the rock is covered by an easily-removed lichen which hides excellent rock. Belays at the top are sometimes a long way back, and it is advisable to carry extra rope to reach them. The quarry is probably

the one referred to in 'The Lancashire Witches' by Harrison Ainsworth, hence its name.

APPROACH AND ACCESS

This quarry lies east of Downham and just north of Pendle Hill. To reach the quarry from Downham, (when coming from Chatburn), take the road which bears left immediately after the Asheton Arms, and follow this for about two miles. At the top of a steep hill the quarry can be seen on the right a few yards from the road. Climbing is at present NOT ALLOWED on this crag, though when it is, it is essential that all climbers visiting the crag obtain permission to climb from the farm just up the road. DO NOT plan a visit to this crag without first consulting the British Mountaineering Council at their offices in Manchester to check up on the access problem. If they say that access is out of the question, then DO NOT try a visit. Access is banned at the time of writing.

HISTORY

The climbing history of Withches Quarry probably began around the early 1960s, but the early history is very vague. Certainly, Beelzebub, Broomstick, Thrutch and several other of the easier routes had been climbed by the mid-sixties as had Peel Off, though this route used an aid peg which was eliminated in 1969/70 by Mike Haslam. Mike also climbed Witch Bane, though he called it Central Wall originally.

Next on the scene were Les Ainsworth and friends who added Black Mass, Abbot Paslew and The Shrew, together with Warlock Wall and a protracted campaign against Sorcerer's Apprentice, the final result being definitely worth the effort though.

The Lancashire guide of 1975 contained all the routes known at the time, and helped focus attention on the crag, which it otherwise would not have seen. Ron Fawcett paid a visit and free-climbed The Reeve and Prayer To Absent Friends then Al Evans discovered the popular free version to Witchcraft. Al also repeated Fawcett's climbs thinking them to be first ascents. In 1975/76 Gordon Fishlock, Pete Black and Ronnie Marsden climbed Witch Way and Black's Magic, as well as Witch Arête and Witchcraft Crack with John Wilmott and Ron Valovin respectively.

Nothing further was done until 1978 when Dave Kenyon took over the explorations, starting with Tarrot Wall and working through the obvious lines and not so obvious eliminates, to add almost thirty routes including Witchfire at Lammas, Waxen Doll, Brimstone, The Dark One, Ducking Chair and Black Orchid. The only other people to get any sort of a look in over this period were Dave Cronshaw who added Satan's Slave, Gordon Lancaster climbed First Impressions, Martin Atkinson with a direct finish to The Dark One, and Jerry Peel with The Nameless One.

As the 1983 guidebook came out, however, the landowner began to object to climbers using the quarry, citing litter and nuisance as his main objections, and so no climbing has taken place in the intervening years. Things look bleak as to whether or not this gem of a crag will be restored to climbers, but we remain hopeful.

THE CLIMBS are described from LEFT to RIGHT.

TWISTON WALLS

This is the stretch of rock from the extreme left of the crag to the right side of the obvious long, horizontal overhang. The most prominent feature of the wall is the deep overhung corner crack of Beelzebub.

1. Hrothgar 25ft VS
4c . From the foot of the next route, climb up to and follow an obvious line of holds leading left for 6 feet, then finish direct.

2. Avenging Angel of Death 25ft Hard VS
5b. The arête of the small, detached buttress at the far left of the crag.

3. Belladonna 30ft V Diff
Climb a crack 5 feet right of the short corner at the left of the crag, to a ledge. Finish up the right of the two cracks above.

4. Farrak 30ft Hard VS
5a. Climb the wall just right, using an obvious crack at 12 feet to gain a ledge. Climb the wall above via a thin crack, moving right to a tree at the top.

5. Broomstick 30ft Hard Sev   ★★★
4b. Fifteen feet right of the short corner is an obvious wide crack. Follow this to its top.

6. The Omen 35ft Hard VS
5a. Start at the foot of Alice and pull over a bulge, then continue up to an obvious tree stump. Pass this on its right to a small ledge, step left then climb direct to the top, just right of Broomstick. Runner in that route.

7. Alice 30ft Sev.
The wide crack right of Broomstick, behind a protecting leaf of rock.

8. Elizabeth 35ft V Diff
Just right is another flake; climb this, then finish as for Alice.

9. Seven Years After 35ft Hard VS
5b. Climb the bulge between Elizabeth and Jennet, then continue direct up the wall above.

10. Jennet 40ft Sev
From Elizabeth, move right under a bulge to short flake crack. Up this, then finish direct.

11. Coven Crack 40ft Hard Sev
4b. Seven feet right is a shallow cave at ground level. Climb the flake crack above this, then step left and finish as for Jennet.

12. Hemlock 50ft Sev
A direct line from the right side of the cave. Surmount the large overhang on its left, then finish diagonally right.

13. Cauldron Cracks 45ft Sev
Follow an obvious weakness 4 feet right, passing the large overhang on it's right.

14. The Shrew 45ft VS   ★★
4b. Climb the blunt arête 10 feet left of Beelzebub to a ledge on the right, then climb the overhang by the flake crack which splits it, and

finish direct.

15. **Warlock Wall**   45ft   Hard VS   *
5b. Climb the thin overhanging crack 5 feet right, to a ledge on The Shrew. Move onto blocks on the right of the overhang and finish direct.

16. **Mist Over Witches**   45ft   E2
5c. Immediately left of Beelzebub use undercuts to reach round the bulge to a short crack, which can be used to reach a second crack. Step left above the bulge and move up (bolt runner) then step right and reach round the overhang to better holds. Surmount the overhang and finish as for Warlock Wall.

17. **Beelzebub**   45ft   VS   *
5a. The obvious overhung corner crack about 50 feet right of Avenging Angel of Death: it is best climbed facing left.

18. **Witchfire at Lammas**   45ft   Hard VS   **
5b. Start just right and surmount the square-cut overhang to gain a small ledge below a second roof. Climb this via a good flake hold, and continue up the short wall above to a junction with Beelzebub.

19. **Abbot Paslew**   45ft   VS
4c. Starting 3 feet right, climb to a small ledge at 15 feet, beneath a small overhang. Over this overhang and the one above to an easier finish.

20. **Halloween Outing**   45ft   Sev
On the right is a cracked wall, climb the left crack.

21. **Witches' Brew**   45ft   Hard Sev
4b. Climb the cracks 3 feet right, until it is possible to step right above an overhang and finish up the wall above.

22. **Witches' Favourite**   45ft   Hard VS
5a. Climb the cracks as for Witches' Brew, but continue in a direct line through the bulge at the top.

23. **The Flying Magician**   45ft   Hard VS
5b. Climb the corner just right, to below an overhang. Surmount this to gain a ledge on Witches' Brew. Finish up that route.

24. **Cracklap**   45ft   Hard Sev   *
4b. Right again is a system of wide cracks trending left. Climb these.

25. **Darkness**   50ft   E2
5b. Immediately right a thin crack leads up to a bulge. Follow this with difficult moves round the bulge to reach a small ledge (PR). Traverse up and left to a tree belay.

26. **Familiar's Fall**   50ft   Hard VS   *
5a. The next obvious feature is a shallow corner leading to the left side of a large overhang. Climb this corner, then layback the overhang to an easier finish.

27. **Satan's Slave**   50ft   Hard VS
5a. Starting 10 feet right, climb a short crack to a long ledge. Gain good holds below an overhang (PR not in situ) and climb it and the wall above (PR) to a ledge and short finishing groove.

28. Thrutch 50ft VS
4b. Start below the right side of the long ledge and climb up to it. Then continue up a groove, to finish up an obvious clean, wide crack at the top.

CENTRAL WALL
This is the steep continuation wall where the crag is at its highest, which is further identified by the large, pointed boulder (The Magician's Hat) at its foot. It provides some of the best middle-grade climbing on the crag.

29. The Spell 55ft Hard VS ★★
5a. Climb the steep wall between Thrutch and Witch Bane to a ledge on the left. Move up, then step right in an exposed position, to gain a horizontal break (PR on right). Finish direct.

30. Witch Bane 65ft Hard VS ★★
5a. Start from the large pointed boulder (Magician's Hat) and follow a right sloping ledge to below an obvious groove. Climb the groove to a ledge on the right (Malkin Ledge), then step left and finish up a flake crack.

31. Waxen Doll 65ft E3 ★★
5c. Follow Witch Bane until just left of the groove and directly below a PR. Ascend to the PR, then move left to a second PR and up to a horizontal break (PR). Make a move left along the break, then finish direct.

32. Resurgent Spirit 55ft E4
6a. From the first PR on Waxen Doll take a direct line to the top.

33. Devil Worshipper 55ft E4
6a. Starting 6 feet right of the Magician's Hat, climb easy, cleaned-rock to a short groove immediately right of that on Witch Bane. Climb this groove and the overhang above to a gangway, then follow this easily left to Malkin Ledge. Climb the steep wall at the back of this ledge by some intricate moves to a tree at the top.

34. Black Mass 65ft Hard VS
5b. Fifteen right of the Magician's Hat is a thin, undercut crack. Gain the crack from the left and climb it and the wall above to a ledge (The Gallery), then follow an easy gangway left to Malkin Ledge, and finish up the short, overhanging groove on the right.

35. Brimstone 60ft Hard VS ★
5a. The first section of this climb ascends the fine crack on the right. Climb a short wall to gain the crack, then follow it to The Gallery (PR). Step left and climb the intimidating wall above, surmounting a small overhang on good holds to finish up a left slanting crack.

36. Dark Secrets 60ft Hard VS
5a. From a point 10 feet up Peel Off, step left into a groove, and follow this to The Gallery (PR). Continue up the blunt rib, just right of the peg, to below an obvious small roof. Pull over this and then up the wall to finish. From the small roof an easier finish is possible by moving left and then finishing up Brimstone.

37. **Peel Off** 60ft VS   ★★★
4c. Start 3 feet left of the gully which limits Central Wall on the right.
Gain a ledge at 15 feet (The Boiling Pot), then step up and hand-traverse
left to The Gallery (PR). Finish up the flake crack above.

38. **Crucible** 60ft Hard VS   ★
5b. Follow Peel Off to The Boiling Pot, then continue in a direct line to
a ledge below a shallow groove (it is possible to step left here to
arrange runners on Peel Off). Climb the groove, using holds on the
right wall, to a large ledge and an easy finish.

39. **Cloven Hoof** 60ft E1
5b. From The Boiling Pot, step right and follow an obvious line of
pockets and cracks up the wall, to gain a slab and easier climbing to
the top.

SWEET DREAMS BUTTRESS
The section of rock which stretches right from the Central Gully, and
ends in a dome-shaped, overhanging wall.

40. **Witch Arête** 55ft VS
4c. Just right of Central Gully is a short wall, capped by a bulge, at the
left side of which is a thin crack. Climb this crack to gain the arête, and
after a short detour into the gully, follow this to the top of the crag.

41. **The Necromancer** 55ft Hard VS
5c. Six feet right is a shallow scoop at 15 feet. Gain this direct and climb
it to a ledge above. Surmount the bulge via a thin crack and a long
reach to a good hold, and either finish direct, or (better) move left onto
the arête and follow this to the top.

42. **Witch Way** 65ft VS   ★
4c. Separating the short wall and the overhanging face on the right is
a slabby wall. Climb this to the right side of a slab, then traverse this
left in a good position to join Witch Arête, and finish up this.

43. **Satanic Rite** 30ft VS
5a. At the left side of the dome-shaped buttress is an undercut groove
capped by an overhang. Climb this groove, stepping left to surmount
the overhang at the top.

44. **Sweet Dreams Left-Hand** 35ft Hard VS
5c. Starting at the centre of the dome-shaped buttress, climb directly
to the top and a difficult finish.

45. **Sweet Dreams** 35ft Hard VS   ★
5b. This route takes the groove at the right side of the wall. Follow the
groove and continue direct up bulging rock to a good hold. Move right
to finish.

46. **The Nameless One** 25ft VS
5b. Ascends the steep wall between Sweet Dreams and the edge of the
buttress.

WITCHCRAFT BUTTRESS
A fine steep buttress, offering some fine climbing in the higher grades.
It is identified by the large overhang which spans the top of the wall.
The climbs are reached by short, easy scrambles.

47.   **Witchraft Crack**   55ft   Hard Sev
A poor climb which takes the obvious shattered crack at the left side of Witchcraft Buttress, escaping left when the going gets tough.

48.   **Witchraft Left-Hand**   45ft   E1
5b. In the steep wall on the right is a thin crack. Gain the base of this crack from the left, then climb it and move up right to gain a good flake. Continue up the wall on good holds to finish.

49.   **Witchcraft**   50ft   E2   **
5b. Start 10 feet right and climb a short, bulging wall to a ledge on the right. Continue up the groove above, until it is possible to move up and right over a slight bulge. Step left to arrange some NRs, then traverse back right on small holds to gain an arête, which is followed to the top.

50.   **The Dark One**   50ft   E3   **
5c. The big groove which runs up to the left side of the large overhang. Climb the groove to a good hold at 15 feet (PR on left), then step right and follow a thin crack up to the overhang. Using undercuts, make a long reach and a bold move round to better holds and the top.

51.   **Prayer to Absent Friends**   50ft   E1
5b. Bridge up the wide-angled corner right of The Dark One to the roof. Pull up left into a short bottomless corner below a second roof and make a long reach right to a hidden jug, which enables a swing to be made onto the front face. Finish up a line of flake holds which are not always above suspicion.

52.   **The Ducking Chair**   50ft   E3   **
6a. The wall on the right has a niche at 15 feet containing a peg. Gain this direct (crux), and climb through its apex to a crack in the roof above. From the crack, reach up and left to small holds, and use these to get established on the headwall and an easier finish.

53.   **Black Orchid**   55ft   E2   **
5b. Using thin left-slanting cracks, gain the niche on The Ducking Chair from the right (PR), then follow another crack back right to a ledge on the arête. Finish by moving up and left to gain a ledge just below the top. Serious in its latter stages.

54.   **Return of the Incubus**   50ft   Hard VS
5a. Climb the narrow wall right of the arête on the right edge of Witchcraft Buttress, to a good ledge on the arête. Step right and continue to the top.

DOWNHAM WALLS
The remainder of the quarry, after a grassy break.

55.   **Baalbreth**   35ft   Hard Sev
4a. A series of short walls, starting from a clump of trees at the left side of the wall.

56.   **The Reeve**   30ft   VS   *
4c. The system of narrow cracks splitting the face to the right.

57.   **Satan**   30ft   VS
5a. Just right is a groove. Climb a short wall to gain the groove, then follow it to the top.

58. Walpurgis Eve 30ft Sev
Four feet right is a short crack, follow this to a mantel, then continue direct.

59. Serenity 35ft Sev ★★
From the mantel on Walpurgis Eve, step right and move up to the higher of two ledges. Turn the arête on the right, and finish up the left edge of the slab.

60. Tibb 30ft Sev
Just right two grooves meet at half-height to form a Y. Climb the scrappy left-hand groove.

61. Pendle Groove 35ft Hard Sev
4a. The right-hand groove.

62. Downham Racer 35ft E2
5c. Climb the the steep wall just right, to a sloping shelf, and continue up a short groove to a tree and a good ledge. The slabby wall at the back of the ledge provides a good finish, taken more or less, up its centre.

63. Tarot Wall 35ft VS
5a. From a ledge at 6 feet on Mouldheels, move up and left to a triangular niche, then up and left again and follow an obvious crackline up the left side of the wall.

64. Mouldheels 40ft V Diff
The right-slanting groove on the right.

65. Black's Magic 50ft Hard VS
5a. Just right is a low bulge flanked on its right by slabs. Climb the centre of the bulge onto the slab, then step right and climb a shallow scoop with difficulty to a ledge on the right. Finish up a short wall on the left.

66. Nance 40ft V Diff
Up the slabs on the right of the low bulge to a deep groove which starts at mid-height. Follow this to the top.

67. Witch Trial 30ft Hard VS
5c. The thin, peg-marked crack ("HVS A1" scratched at bottom) with one PR. Finish up a fin of rock.

68. Diabolos Vobiscum 30ft V Diff
Climb the wall between Witch Trial and the arête on the right, past a small tree to a ledge. Finish up the rib above

69. Wicca 30ft V Diff
Just round the arête are two cracks. Climb the left crack, then step right to finish up the slab.

70. First Impressions 30ft Hard Sev
4b. The right crack, finishing up the slab.

GIRDLE TRAVERSES:
71. Sorcerer's Apprentice 245ft Hard VS ★★
A traverse of the Twiston and Central Walls.
(1) 60ft 4a. Climb Broomstick until it is possible to traverse at

mid-height to Alice. Continue in the same line to Cauldron Cracks, move down and belay on the ledge below the overhang on Shrew.
(2) 90ft 5a. Traverse awkwardly above the corner of Beelzebub, step down and follow the horizontal break across Cracklap and Familiar's Fall, to a belay at the right of the long ledge, (in Thrutch).
(3) 65ft 5a. From the ledge move up and right to the horizontal break. Hand-traverse right (PR) on good holds to Malkin Ledge and reverse the easy gangway of Black Mass to a PB on The Gallery.
(4) 30ft 4c. Step right and finish up Peel Off.

72. Hubble, Bubble, Toil and Trouble 100ft E1 ⋆
5b. A right to left traverse across Witchcraft Buttress. Start as for Return of the Incubus, and climb up to a ledge on the arête. Reverse the thin crack of Black Orchid into the niche (poor PR), and continue into the corner of Prayer to Absent Friends. Climb the corner to a roof, then traverse left under it to gain an arête by an awkward move. Step up and continue left along the obvious line to finish.

MINOR CRAGS

COLD STONE (SD 709 608)
This remote 'boulder' would be an immaculate crag any closer to the road. The most worthwhile of a series of outcrops east of Thorn Crag (Wolfhole Grag, Bull Stones and Reeves Edge all give to rock).

Best approach from the Slaidburn to Higher Bentham road. Parking after crossing the River Hodder.

NEWCHURCH-IN-PENDLE QUARRY (SD 820 392)
A small quarry just off the Sabden Hall road about ½ a mile from the centre of Newchurch, would appear to warrant further attention. Some climbs have been done on the short right wall, but none have yet been recorded on the main 50-foot slab.

NOGARTH (SD 845 394)
Several interesting slabs up to 60 feet long, just over a mile north-west of the centre of Nelson. Just a pity it is not a few degrees steeper.

WISWELL QUARRY (SD 753 370)
This small quarry consists of an overhanging face 40 feet high with a couple of old bolt routes and a traverse **The Maze** (A2). On the easier-angled wall on its left is a Hard Sev: **Sideline**.

Park in the lane 50 yards before Wiswell Moor Farm, then from a gate opposite follow a winding track to the crag which is situated below the radio mast.

VII. CARNFORTH AREA

Compiled by Jon Sparks
with assistance from David Craig, Phil Stone, Brian Davison
and Jason Kaushal

The crags described within this section, apart from Farleton, all lie within the Silverdale – Arnside Area of Outstanding Natural Beauty: a compact and intricate – even confusing at first acquaintance – region of winding lanes and a seemingly haphazard topography, rich in wildlife, with many fine woodland and coastal walks. The charm of the surroundings adds much to the pleasure of climbing on the fine white limestone which surfaces irrepressibly all over the place; it is said that the name 'Silverdale' derives from the colour of the rock.

The area also enjoys a relatively benign micro-climate; low-lying, mild and relatively low in rainfall, often dry when it is raining in the Lakes (Ambleside is only 20-odd miles away). Virtually all the crags face west or south and dry quickly. Some, such as Woodwell, deep in the trees, are slower to get wet at the onset of rain, but also slower to dry afterwards. This is particularly noticeable when the trees are in leaf, less so in winter. Two crags in particular stand out as drying almost instantaneously – Warton Upper Crag and most of Trowbarrow Quarry – and on these two, all year-round climbing is certainly possible. All this makes the Carnforth area an ideal one to escape to when the weather is bad elsewhere.

The crags fall naturally into two main groups, with the two large quarries giving much more serious climbing than the remaining, mostly natural, outcrops. Here the accent is generally on fun, with the climbs being soloed by the bold and top-roped by the timid more often than they are led – at least at Woodwell and the three Warton crags. Subtle variations in rock and situation give each crag its own distinct character, the most individual (and the largest) being Jack Scout Cove, the part-time sea-cliff, and Farleton with its more upland setting.

As well as the crags detailed there is a myriad of small outcrops which would – and do – yield a few boulder problems and short routes to dedicated explorers. North from Jack Scout Cove, for instance, the cliffs are continuous, virtually all the way to Arnside, though they are mostly low and/or shattered. They do however offer a good bay-side walk with the possibility of picking off a few routes, scrambles and problems, together with some intriguing traverses.

Of the two big quarries, Trowbarrow feels relatively friendly with its open, westerly aspect and easier-angled areas. The extraordinary range of rock-type (like a condensed field-course on the many varieties

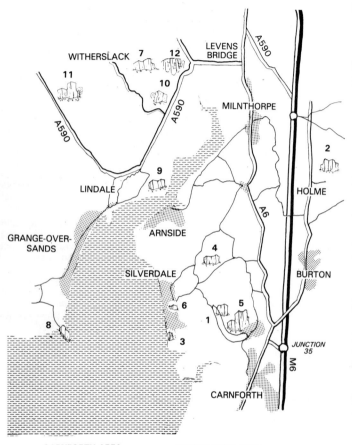

CARNFORTH AREA
1. CRAG FOOT
2. FARLETON
3. JACK SCOUT COVE
4. TROWBARROW QUARRY
5. WARTON
6. WOODWELL

WHITBARROW AREA
7. CHAPEL HEAD SCAR
8. HUMPHREY HEAD POINT
9. MEATHOP QUARRY
10. MILL SIDE SCAR
11. WHITESTONE CRAG
12. WHITE SCAR

of limestone) offers something for almost every taste, from some of the best easy routes on limestone anywhere, to some very hard and serious challenges. Main Wall is a uniquely theatrical piece of rock, complete with seating for hundreds amongst the tumbled boulders which lie at its base.

Warton Main Quarry is something else again: stark, sombre and uncompromising. At the best of times it is impressive, and on gloomy days the atmosphere can be quite daunting and overpowering. Though facing south much of the quarry is enclosed and there is always a tremendous feeling of release in climbing out of shadow into sunlight, from the oppressive pit to flowery terraces with a great sweeping panorama. Though not the easiest crag to come to terms with, those who do make the effort usually feel well rewarded and many believe its better routes to be amongst the finest in the county.

GRADED LIST FOR CARNFORTH AND WHITBARROW AREAS

E7
Maboulisme Merveilleux

E6
Agent Provocateur
Super Duper Dupont
Stretchy Peroneum
Phantom Zone
Torture Garden
Exequy

E5
Videodrome
Super Dupont
Perverted Start
Sylvester Strange
Cosmic Dancer
Electric Warrior
Introducing the Hardline
Flight Path
Wargames
A Vision of Things Gone Wild
Countach
Twisted Sister
Stan Pulsar
Mighty Fly
Comes a Time (direct)
Blow Job
Driller Killer
Dry Grin
Wodwo

Cain (direct)
True Path
Brainstrain
Humphrey Hymen
Doubting Thomas
Perverse Pépère
War of the Worlds

E4
La Mangoustine Scatoflange
The Route of all Evil
Poetry in Commotion
Scary Monsters
Ivy League
Beers for Fears
Witherslack Flange Finish
Flash Imp
The Firing Squad
Spectral Wizard
Cadillac
Cain
Bleep and Booster
Killer Queen
Oddballs
Dune
Telegraph Road
Android

E3
Interstellar Overdrive
Shot by Both Sides

The Book of Invasions
Android Original Finish
Terminal Trajectory
Crimes of Passion
Chain Reaction
Prometheus Crisis
Cryptic Cripple Club
Moon-Loon Connection
A Fistful of Steroids
Moonchild
Lunatic
Up the Neck

E2
Birdbrain Meets Clothears
Sniffin' the Saddle
Galactic Timebreaker
Izzy the Push
Triggerfinger
Sleeping Sickness
Cracked Actor
Cyborg

E1
Touch of Class
Atomic Bong
New World
Cosmic Debris
Plastic Iceberg
Virility
Javelin
Just Like a Woman

Hard Vs
Hollow Earth
Born Free
Vespers for the Dead
Limestone Rain
Sungod
January
Fall of the House of Usher
The Third World
Icicle
Assagai
Missing Words

CRAG FOOT (SD 479 735)

APPROACH AND ACCESS
The crag lies just south of Crag Foot hamlet, where the two roads from Warton to Silverdale re-unite, on the lower road. It is possible to park on the grass verge directly below the crag but a much better space lies less than 100 yards north.

SITUATION AND CHARACTER
At first sight the crag seems tiny — some find it comical — but appearances are deceptive and it is in fact taller than most of the local crags. It is extremely sheltered from most winds and stays dry even when raining (the girdle traverse, under umbrella overhangs, is a particularly good bet). Most of the routes are quite steep with good overhangs, some of which are surprisingly easy: definitely worth the walk.

HISTORY
Crag Foot was literally unearthed, and most of the routes climbed, by Al Evans and John Girdley, in time for the 1975 guidebook. Subsequent additions have been eliminate in nature and there isn't much room left!

THE CLIMBS are described from LEFT to RIGHT and descents are possible at either end of the crag by slightly awkward scrambling, or by abseil.

1. **Achilles' Heel** 45ft VS
4c. Start at a shallow groove below the obvious roof crack. Climb up and left to a pedestal/ledge then step left and over the bulge, go up the left edge of the slab to finish up a ragged flake crack.

2. **Left Foot Eliminate** 50ft Hard VS   **
5b. The striking roof crack above the start of Achilles' Heel is as good as it looks, but unfortunately often dirty. Climb the groove to the overlap and bridge uncomfortably over it then move right to below the crack and power up it.

3. **Footsie** 50ft VS   *
4c. A surprisingly tricky route; the guarded may want a runner or two in the tree! Climb the steep wall behind the obvious large tree and very awkwardly gain a niche below the crack of Left Foot Eliminate. Move right for a few feet, as for the girdle and finish up and obvious short crack.

The large overhang between Footsie and Stilleto can be climbed direct at 5c.

4. **Stilleto** 50ft Hard VS   *
5a. Start about 10 feet right of the tree. Climb the wall to the overhang, step right and climb a short groove onto the hanging slab (this section is hard, but can be avoided on the right). The hanging crack above is 'easy when you know how.'

5. **Right Foot Eliminate** 50ft Hard Sev   *
4b. Start a few feet farther right and find the line of least resistance up the wall, moving right to a projecting tree. Climb the right side of the large flake then make some exciting moves right, around the overhang, to easy ground.

6. **Toe and Heel** 45ft Hard VS   *
5b. A direct line below the finish of Right Foot Eliminate, using a short groove on the lower wall and hidden holds on the bulbous overhang above. Good climbing throughout.

7. **Nonopod** 45ft Hard VS
5b. The rock and the protection are rather dubious. Climb the bulging wall just right of Toe and Heel to the girdle break, then climb the shattered right side of the bulbous overhangs via a sort of groove.

8. **Athlete's Foot** 40ft Hard V Diff
The obvious set-back break 10 feet right of Nonopod. The trees are generally better than the rock.

9. **Pseudopod** 45ft VS   *
4b. A surprising route where the rock improves again at the right end of the crag. There is a large overhang, almost a shallow cave; this can be climbed direct (about 5b) or, more easily, by its left edge. Climb the slab to an amenable overlap and continue to the large overhang, split by an obvious crack, which sooner or later reveals its secret.

10. **The Plimsoll Line** 130ft VS   ***
A great little girdle, even when it isn't raining; full of character.
(1) 80ft 4c. The first of the hanging slabs is gained as for Achilles' Heel. Traverse delicately right then awkwardly round to below the crack

of Left Foot Eliminate. Move round resolutely onto the second hanging slab, behind the large tree and cross pleasantly right to belay on the large flake of Right Foot Eliminate. Thoughtful ropework pays dividends on this pitch.

(2) 50ft 4b. Step down to the tree and traverse below the overhang. Continue at much the same level and grapple briefly with the tree on Athlete's Foot to gain the slab below the large overhang of Pseudopod. Purists and masochists will continue rightwards to finish up a vile cleft, but the final crack of Pseudopod is altogether a better alternative.

FARLETON CRAG (SD 539 796)

By David Craig

SITUATION AND CHARACTER

The climbing edge is a ¾ mile long belt of limestone which girdles the main scarp of the fell that used to be called 'the Gibraltar of Westmorland'.

The rock is sound on the whole, although some large and useful reference features have fallen down recently. The crag dries relatively quickly, though it is screened by trees in summer.

APPROACH AND ACCESS

The crag is near to the M6, five miles north of Carnforth. Leave the A6070 just south of Farleton Village at Holme Park Farm (zinc-topped silo) and follow 'Public Bridleway: Clawthorp Fell'. 150 yards past a wooden gate, at a rising double bend, walk north (uphill) until a path climbs through trees to meet the stratum on the right, where it rises into a continuous 30-foot high edge.

HISTORY

Unlike many of the crags in the area, Farleton is well hidden from any real distance, so it is quite reasonable to speak of it as being truly 'discovered', at least in a climbing sense. This honour fell to a group of climbers including Ian Dobson and Roger Gott in the late 1960s. They climbed Farleton Crack, Appleton Crack, the Earwig routes, Idleness and Doodlebug. Augmented by Stew Wilson, this group added a further batch of routes, probably most notable of these being The Shriek of Baghdad which still stands as the classic of the crag (as its polished state testifies!) The introduction of Bill Lounds in the late seventies brought some harder additions, including Agrippa and Enyoka. Bill and Stew, meanwhile, visited the quarry and ascended Uhuru.

Allan Austin sneaked past the frontier guards from Yorkshire, to add the technical gems of Roughneck and The Gent, and Ian (Sherpa) Roper led The Family Way. Sporadic development has continued over the years but more recently Dave Bates, Tony Mitchell and Tom Walkington gave the crag a fresh examination, coming up with some desperate routes and problems.

THE ROUTES are described from RIGHT to LEFT.

1. **Lumumba** 30ft Hard Sev
4a. A few feet left of an easy way down, climb the right-hand part of the wall using fingery edges, and finish up a split above the horizontal break.

2. **Enyoka** 30ft Hard VS
5b. Near the left edge of the wall climb cracks and a short steep corner to the break. A delicate mantel, an incut and a long reach lead to jugs on the lip.

3. **Eggyoka** 30ft V Diff
The open corner just left of Enyoka.

4. **Monkey Wrench** 30ft V Diff
The bulging buttress 5 feet left of Eggyoka, leading to wide cracks above the break.

5. **Rock Ivy Line** 30ft V Diff
The well-garnished crack 5 feet left of Monkey Wrench.

6. **Anaconda** 35ft Hard Sev
4b. The smooth finger-crack 4 feet left of Rock Ivy Line.

7. **Primrose Path** 140ft Sev   *
Nice horizontal gymnastics, starting up Lumumba then girdling steadily northwards, through a flourish of yew antlers, striding across to a buttress and finishing at the south end of a steep, pock-marked wall.

8. **The Coil** 6c
A desperate problem up the slender crack in the centre of the wall.

9. **The Pill** 45ft Hard VS   *
5b. The left-hand side of the wall is split by a polished layback crack; climb this to the break, hand-traverse right and finish over the bulge.

10. **The Family Way** 30ft VS
4c. Climb the layback edge and the easier cracks above.

Fifteen yards north of The Family Way, past some broken buttresses, the wall steepens again.

11. **Green Machine** 30ft Hard VS
5b. Ten feet left of a tall hawthorn; climb fingery edges to the break and continue up the thin diagonal crack in the wall above.

12. **Pudding Club** 30ft Sev   *
The open, blocky groove just left of Green Machine.

13. **Dimple, Dimple** 20ft Hard VS
5b. The wall 5 feet left again.

14. **Clayfire** 20ft VS
4c. The thin finger-crack in the wall left of Dimple, Dimple.

15. **Flaykier** 20ft VS
4c. The steep rough edges, 6 feet left of the tree-choked grooves.

16. **Cracker** 20ft Hard VS
4c. The crack on the left, with an undercut start, passing little overhangs.

17. Prowler 20ft VS
5a. Just left is a wedge-shaped prow; climb it by its nose.

18. Caliban 20ft Hard Sev
4b. Climb the centre of the strangely wrinkled wall just left of Prowler.

19. G Squared 35ft Hard VS
5a. Fifteen feet left is an ash tree close to the crag; climb the thin crack behind it to the break, traverse left and follow a second crack to the top.

Five yards left is a rib which bounds a deep recess.

20. Pork Chop 30ft Hard VS ★★
5a. Pull over the first overhang on the rib and climb directly over the overlap.

21. Doodlebug 40ft Hard Sev ★★
4b. The square-cut chimney at the right of the recess.

22. Instant Whip 35ft VS
4b. Climb directly up the groove in the centre of the recess, and finish over a bulge.

23. Idleness 30ft VS ★
4c. Climb the flake crack at the left of the recess and step left to a good foothold just below the overhangs. Jam the crack which splits the overhangs to finish.

24. Feet of Clay 35ft Hard Sev
4b. Climb the square-cut groove beneath a hefty ash, then finish via jugs and branches or (harder) by the dimpled scoop on the right.

25. Fat Good Crack 30ft VS
5a. Five feet left of Feet of Clay, climb the fine layback flake and dimpled bulges above.

26. Doggo 30ft Hard Sev
4b. Eight feet left of Fat Good Crack, climb a stepped crack to a ledge, then finish up the scoop.

27. Earwig Two 35ft VS
4c. Left of a shattered white area, climb shakey rock to a jagged beak, then semi-hand-traverse right to a chimney; climb its outside, the inside line reduces the route to severe.

28. Earwig One 30ft Hard VS
5a. Climb to the beak (as for Earwig Two) then gain an awkward groove which leads to the top.

29. Agrippa 30ft E1 ★
5b. Fifteen feet left of Earwig One, a crack runs through the centre of a small roof. Climb up under it and overcome the roof by painful jamming.

30. Herod 35ft VS
4c. A few feet left of Agrippa, climb the thin groove to the left end of the overhangs and continue via a crack with a tree stump.

31. **The Shriek of Baghdad** 40ft VS ★★
4c. Six feet left of Herod, layback up a smooth flake/crack, hand-traverse left at the top to gain a niche and exit from this by a crack. A **Direct Finish** is possible at 5c.

32. **Watching the Motorway Flow** 35ft VS ★
5a. Eight feet left of The Shriek and round an arête, climb the crack in the right wall which contains an ash near its top.

33. **Slime Gut** 30ft VS
4c. The corner left of Watching the Motorway Flow.

34. **Girdle Traverse** 85ft VS ★★
A strenuous route stretching from Idleness to Slime Gut.
(1) 25ft 4c. Climb Idleness to the good foothold and hand-traverse left using the break, to belay on a ledge with a tree.
(2) 60ft 4c. Continue at the same level to the wall of Agrippa. Trend down slightly to the first crack on Agrippa and climb this to the roof. Hand-traverse left to The Shriek, step round the arête on the left, and finish up Slime Gut.

35. **Appleton Crack** 35ft Hard Sev ★
4b. Climb the smooth V-shaped groove a few feet left of Slime Gut, step right under the overhang and follow the wall left of Slime Gut to the top.

36. **Hazy Daze** 25ft Hard Sev
4b. The twisting crack 6 feet left.

37. **The Easy Way** 25ft Diff
The cracked corner left of Hazy Daze.

38. **Farleton Crack** 30ft V Diff
The wide, steep crack with a tree growing near its foot.

39. **Deb's Wall** 6b
The wall of a steep narrow cleft a few feet left of Farleton Crack.

40. **Deb's Crack** 30ft VS ★
4c. The steep narrow cleft. Layback up it then jam over the bulge at mid-height.

41. **Super Dick** 30ft Hard VS ★
5a. Climb the prow on the left, starting on its left and using the edge of the next route for the left-hand. Move up and out onto the prow at half-height.

42. **Pleb's Chimney** 30ft V Diff ★
The polished chimney on the left.

43. **Heatwave** 30ft VS
5a. The smooth wall on the left; move diagonally right on tiny holds to a stump. Without using this, make a hard move to stand in the break beside it, and finish on good holds.

44. **Shower Crack** 30ft V Diff ★
Up the crack immediately left of Heatwave.

45. Avalanche 25ft V Diff
Follow the line of the corner on the left, climbing the front of the wall which forms the containing wall of an easy way down.

46. Pleasant Wall 30ft Sev
Twenty-five yards left of the easy way down, a large block or 'dummy wall' leans against the main crag. Immediately right, climb onto a block and then go up a rough wall to the top.

47. Scraper 30ft Sev
The crack just left of the 'dummy wall'.

48. The Gent 25ft Hard VS
5b. The wall to the left has a wide crack near its right end. Climb the wall just to its left, using tiny flakes (much harder variations are possible a few inches right).

49. Roughneck 25ft Hard VS
5b. Climb the left-hand section of the wall to a 12-inch vertical crack and use it to gain the rounded break, then finish more easily.

50. Rough Crack 25ft Sev
Layback up the crack on the left.

51. The Spoon 20ft V Diff
The smooth scoop on the left, which is entered by a traverse from the right or direct (harder), is followed direct.

The edge now loses height but continues to offer excellent bouldering possibilities, as does the stratum above, with superb vistas across to the Lakeland mountains.

UPPER CRAG
Ten minutes walk to the north, near the summit of the fell, is a fine high prow, visible from both the A6070 and M6. The prow itself gives fine, sound climbing and there are routes (dodgier) to both its right and left.

1. Buckshot 45ft Hard Sev
Twenty yards right of the prow a triangular grey overhang juts out. Climb up to it, traverse left and continue to the top via steep, ivy infested cracks.

2. Avoidance 65ft Hard Sev   *
4a. Climb the right of two chimney/grooves to the headwall below the roof of the prow. Traverse right, then finish up a short corner and crack.

3. Rose Amongst Thorns 55ft VS   **
4b. Climb Avoidance and move left, using the split in the headwall and its left-hand corner, to climb up under the roof. Swing left onto the arête and an airy finish.

4. California Dreaming 60ft Hard VS
5b. Fifteen feet left of Rose Amongst Thorns, climb the loose wall to a

small overhang and a shallow groove above (PR). Follow the groove to the break and move right to climb the crack which splits the overhang.

5. Blood on the Tracks 60ft Not Led
5b. The groove and crack 8 feet left of California Dreaming.

6. Silent Jim 50ft Hard Sev
4b. Fifteen feet left of Blood On The Tracks, climb to a jutting flake then trend right to a tree. Continue right on suspect rock and exit up a groove just left of the overhang.

FARLETON QUARRY (SD 536 809) lies behind the village of Farleton, and consists of a single wall of rock, with a crumbling earthy top. A good case for a minor crag! THE CLIMBS are described from LEFT to RIGHT.

1. Yoruba 30ft Sev
The good crack at the left side of the wall; the tree at half-height proving useful.

2. Hark to Bounty 30ft VS
4c. Direct up the centre of the wall between Yoruba and Ebo.

3. Ebo 35ft Hard Sev
The steep loose crack in the centre of the wall.

4. Uhuru 45ft E1
5b. Farther right is a block at the foot of the wall. Climb the steep wall above this, then a thin crack to a bulge. Continue on small holds to the final bulging wall which is climbed strenuously to the top.

5. The Pit 20ft V Diff
The short corner on the right.

6. Mister Universe 120ft Hard VS ★
5a. Traverses the wall from right to left, the first moves being the hardest. From the large ledge in the corner, move onto the wall using a good flake. Hard moves then lead to a niche from where a break can be followed to a finish up Yoruba. A variation is **The Pit and the Pendulum** (VS 4c 1 point of aid): the wall can be girdled from left to right, with a rope move from the peg on Uhuru to cross the difficult rock.

JACK SCOUT COVE (SD 459 736)

APPROACH AND ACCESS
The crag is just north of Jenny Brown's Point near Silverdale. It can be approached by walking back along the shore from the point. An alternative approach is from the gate and National Trust sign halfway down Lindeth Lane – this is easier provided a good parking space can be found near the gate. From the gate trend half-right to find a sloping rake leading to the cove.

SITUATION AND CHARACTER
Jack Scout Cove is the nearest thing in the Lancashire guide to a sea-cliff, though the routes (especially at the left side) are only sea-washed at high spring tides. Even then most of them are accessible by abseil or by a potentially exciting traverse from either end. More often the outlook is over extensive sand and mud flats, laced with glittering channels and with a huge bird population. The crag gets all available sun from just after mid-day until the very last moment, which makes it a delightful spot.

The rock is variable, but rarely poses major problems, while the routes are longer than on most of the neighbouring crags, with some very good lines: the strongest of which is the gently rising break of The Onedin Line. Generally the holds are good and the angle just off vertical, giving some good Severes and even more VS's. The crag has been rather neglected, except in the beach-party season, but it deserves and needs a revival. More traffic would check the encroachment of vegetation; however please note that this is National Trust land and there should be no 'gardening' as such — wardens do patrol the area, if conscience alone is not enough!

At the right-hand side there are few belays at the top and it is necessary to scramble up (easy) grass to belay on rather rickety fenceposts. For peace of mind it is a good idea to link several of these, and so sufficient slings need to be carried. Few of the routes lend themselves conveniently to top-roping.

HISTORY
The first known routes here were done in 1969, including the line now known as Cave Route which was originally led by Carl Dawson and named Contraband. Also climbed at this period, and also under a different name, was the classic The Onedin Line; led by 'a charming young lady called Sheila' (sorry if that sounds like the first line of a limerick). Other visitors included Bill Lounds, Chris Eilbeck, Dave Thompson and various Kendal climbers, but systematic development and recording had to wait until 1978 when John Girdley and various members of Lancaster University M.C. took the crag to the cleaners. Most of the route names date from this period, even if the routes themselves had been done before. Practically the only subsequent addition of any note was The Bermuda Triangle, climbed by Owain Jones and his father early in 1983.

Around the same time, regrettably, the coincidence of high tides and westerly gales resulted in some damage to the routes, with In the Wake of Poseidon being the most seriously affected. Even more sadly the bad weather, combined with the shifting of the channels, led to the disappearance of the fine carpet of turf which used to occupy most of the cove. Jumping off the low-level girdle is now a much less inviting prospect, and the whole appearance of the crag and its environs has been marred, though this might encourage people to climb more and laze about less when they visit the crag! Whether the turf will ever regenerate is in the lap of the gods; the main Kent Channel apparently shifts every 75 years or so, so it could be a long wait.

The most prominent features are the girdle break and a tall, narrow cave in the centre of the crag. Most of the better routes are in this area and it is an obvious focal point; THE ROUTES will be described first working RIGHTWARDS from this cave, and then the left-hand section is described later. Descent is possible at either end, usually more pleasant at the seaward end.

1. **Cave Route** 30ft Hard VS   *
5a. Bridge up out of the cave and move right to a yew and prickly stance. It is possible to escape by scrambling, though easier to abseil.

2. **Sexless Wedge** 30ft Hard VS
5b. The overhanging rib on the right demands forceful climbing.

3. **Brant's Little Brother** 30ft VS   *
4c. The obvious V-shaped groove has several chockstones, which rattle cheerfully but seem to be going nowhere. Great fun.

4. **Masochism Tango** 30ft Hard VS
5b. The blunt rib right of Brant's Little Brother is climbed direct.

5. **Jackal** 50ft Hard Sev   *
4b. Just right again is a fine steep crack. Climb this to the girdle break, move right and then up to a small tree. Move rightwards again to a small but prominent right-angled groove in the headwall to finish.

6. **Victim of Life** 50ft Hard Sev   *
4b. A few feet right are two thin cracks: climb these to the girdle break, then follow Jackal to finish.

7. **Spring Tide** 50ft Sev   *
Just right, an obvious series of crazy jugs (which may be occupied) lead to a breach in the overhang. Above this step right then climb up to finish up the same groove as the previous two routes.

8. **Crying Crocodile** 50ft VS   *
4c. About 8 feet right there is an obvious deep crack. Climb this to the overhang and take this directly (there is sometimes a PR). Finish by the slab and that groove again.

9. **Laughing Hyena** 50ft E1   *
5b. Climb the flaky groove on the right to the overhang and over this on good holds. Climb straight up the slab to an overhang just right of the finishing grooves of the previous routes. This is quite bold but there is something to go for. Finish direct.

10. **Vietnam Defoliation Squad** 70ft VS
4c. Just left of the start of the girdle break there is a short groove: climb this, crossing the girdle to gain the slab. Follow the traverse line at the top of this, crossing Laughing Hyena just below its crux, to finish up a short square groove – yes, that one again!

11. **Morecambe Bay Eliminate** 60ft VS   *
4c. Start in the same place, but continue up the hanging groove to a tree, and finish up the clean groove above.

12. **Sad Eyed Lady** 60ft VS
4c. A few feet farther right is a large white groove: climb this and escape left, with some relief, to the tree on Morecambe Bay Eliminate. Finish up that route.

The crag now deteriorates, but presently things improve again, just before an obvious, jutting, cracked rib.

13. Bird of Prey 45ft VS *
4b. Six feet left of the arête, an obvious clean V-shaped groove leads to a bulge at about 30 feet. Traverse left for a few feet and finish up a shallow groove past a sapling.

14. Cornish Raider 40ft VS
4c. The thin crack a few feet left leads to the same finish.

15. Scout Rock 45ft VS *
4b. The crack in the arête looks loose but feels sound − so far!

16. The Kitchen Sink 35ft V Diff
Ten feet right is a ledge with a short square corner above it: climb this to an obvious flake with a wide crack behind it, move left (treating the flake with respect) then back right to finish by a short crack and slab. Both The Kitchen Sink and the next route are open to innumerable variations, though rarely hard.

17. The Great Gonzo 30ft Diff
About 30 feet right there is a blank slab above a small recess. Climb this on good holds to a ledge then continue to a further ledge and finish rightwards via a grassy ramp.

The following routes are described LEFTWARDS from the cave.

18. In the Wake of Poseidon 50ft E3 †
A large rock-fall, of which the scars can still be seen, has completely changed the upper part of this route; the upper wall is still friable. 5c. Climb a shallow flake/groove and the wall above, a few feet left of the cave. At the girdle break traverse right to belay, or finish up the groove above and slightly left.

19. Elusive Valentine 50ft VS *
4c. Climb the thin crack in the wall on the left with difficulty, and continue straight up the wall. Above the girdle break is a jutting rib; pull over on large holds and finish up the rib.

20. Curlew Calling 50ft Sev *
Five feet left is a groove, climb this and the wall above, crossing Elusive Valentine, to finish up a groove.

21. Celebration Day 50ft VS *
4c. Just below the girdle break are two opposing flakes; climb up to these and move left to finish up a groove (as for Nomad).

22. Nomad 50ft VS *
4c. Start about 6 feet left, just right of a rockfall scar; pass the small overhang with difficulty, continue direct to the girdle and step right into a finishing a groove.

23. Unreal City 50ft VS
4c. Directly above the rock-fall scar is a deep crack. Climb up to this and follow it to the girdle break. Pass the overhang with a long reach for a good jug.

24. **Question Mark** 55ft V Diff
Start from a fallen block on the left, step into a crack and climb it to a ledge at 15 feet. Traverse right (loose) to the crack of Unreal City, go up to the girdle break and back left to the yew tree stance. Finish behind this (advisable to stay roped).

"he area on the left is rather broken and very vegetated in its upper reaches; it would hardly be worth exhuming even if it was allowed! The next route starts about 10 yards left.

25. **Courtesan's Chimney** 50ft V Diff
The obvious deep chimney half-way up the crag – reach it direct and escape to the left at its top. Recent rock-fall has made this climb cleaner though care should still be exercised. About 15 yards left, past another unimpressive section, is an arête.

26. **Atlantic Affair** 60ft Hard VS
5b. The wall left of the arête is split by a prominent crack near the top. Start on the left side of the wall, crossing to the right at half-height.

27. **Sailing By** 50ft Diff
The unappealing chimney in the angle left of Atlantic Affair.

There follows another unattractive wall, but this improves after about 20 yards.

28. **Armada** 60ft Sev
Climb the white wall to a hanging flakes; these are pleasant but the vegetated scramble above is less so.

29. **Bermuda Triangle** 45ft Hard VS   *
5b. Climb the hanging crack and grooved arête a few feet left.

30. **Holly Throttled Groove** 50ft Diff
A particularly repulsive route in the back wall of the bay behind a huge erect boulder and obvious by its name.

31. **Lemming's Ville** 50ft Hard Sev
4c. Just left, climb the crack, or the enjoyable slab on its right, into a bottomless groove. The upper reaches are yew-shadowed but surprisingly clean and pleasant.

32. **Superstar** 40ft VS
4b. A few yards left is an understandably unclimbed corner. Climb the wall on its left, taking great care with the rock at a shattered bulge, eventually moving right to finish.

A stone wall lies a few yards farther left, an easy descent comes down just beyond it. There are two girdle traverses:

33. **Sea-Level Girdle** 350ft 5c   *
Doesn't always live up to its name! Though not sustained it has some good sections. Right of Spring Tide it is relatively easy, a fact which is sometimes very useful to know.

34. Onedin Line   150ft   VS   ★★★
The pièce de resistance! A superb outing, especially at high tide. Start
at the right end of the break on a choice of ledges (not so much choice
at high tide!)
(1)   60ft 4b.   Gain the break and follow it left to a stance in the trees
above Brant's Little Brother.
(2)   90ft 4c.   Move awkwardly left across the groove and the top of
the cave then continue along the break to another prickly stance. It is
advisable to stay roped together for the 'scramble' off above.

TROWBARROW QUARRY (SD 481 758)

By Jon Sparks and Dave Bates

APPROACH AND ACCESS
Just south of Silverdale station (accessible by bus as well as by rail),
a road branches east, over the railway. About half a mile on, it runs
through dense woodland on both sides. There are several parking
spaces (sometimes muddy) towards the eastern end of this stretch. A
number of paths lead roughly north through the wood, converging at
the southern entrance to the quarry, five minutes from the road. The
approach to the quarry is not obvious but the entrance is marked by a
'keep out' sign.

Before planning to climb here, read the 'Crag Environment' section at
the beginning of this guide: at some stage you are likely to be asked
to leave, therefore bear this in mind before going to discover this
quarry's particular charms.

SITUATION AND CHARACTER
Most of the quarry walls face west, catch plenty of sun and dry quickly,
but there the generalizations end. Few crags or quarries can offer such
a diversity; the rock varies enormously in character and its reliability
runs the gamut from very good to diabolical. Some of the climbs are
also dreadful but a good number are outstanding, with something of
real quality at almost every grade from V Diff upwards.

Main Wall is so eye-catching that on a first visit the other attractions
can easily be overlooked, but Assagai Wall is a very classy piece of
rock, while Asylum Wall and Red Wall offer contrasting styles of
desperation. The areas of rock in between, whilst being less obviously
attractive also have some very worthwhile routes.

The easiest descents involve considerable treks to the ends of the
quarry, and possible shortcuts are mentioned at appropriate points in
the text.

HISTORY
The early history to the quarry is obscure but undoubtedly the
easier-angled lines such as Original Route and Jomo were ascended

by persons unknown well before the real explorations began. In 1968 and 69 a number of harder lines were climbed, mostly by Bill Lounds with a variety of partners. Amongst these routes were Rumal and two which are now some of the most popular climbs in the quarry, Assagai and Coral Sea. Those who know the latter route today may be surprised to know that it only succumbed after a heavy cleaning session

Lounds soon added Izzy the Push, the first venture onto Red Wall, with a couple of aid points, while Essence of Giraffe by Stuart Butler, Miles Martin and Stew Wilson was more heavily aided.

It may seem strange that the stunningly obvious lines on Main Wall were not attempted first, but in the early days they were not as obvious as they are today. In fact they did not exist at all until about 1970, when the quarry owners blasted an area indicated now by a huge cone of Debris. Whatever the intentions of this act – and its legality has also been highly questioned – it served to open up (literally) the wall to climbers. At the time no-one thought Main Wall would remain standing for long, and some people still find it hard to believe. Al Evans top roped the left-hand crack in the wall (later to become Aladdinsane, though it was horrifically loose at this time) and then cleaned and led the classic Jean Jeanie, which has lost all its loose holds in the intervening years and is now substantially easier; the cracks have widened over the years and intense debate goes on as to whether this is due to mechanical shifts or merely to the removal of the cracks' loose linings (surely a bit of both). Shortly after these first forays a young up-and-coming waif by the name of Ron Fawcett led the aptly-named Aladdinsane, while Ben Campbell-Kelly added Touch of Class, which has recently become harder with the loss of holds from its pod.

The 1975 guide brought the quarry under scrutiny from many more climbers: Major Tom (Andy Hyslop) and Harijan (Bill Lounds) soon succumbed and Al Evans claimed a major coup with the first free ascent of the now-classic Cracked Actor. In 1976, Yorkshireman Pete Livesey climbed the 'blank' wall of Javelin, possibly without encroaching onto Assagai as much as everyone now does. The fine Sleeping Sickness fell to Dave Hilton and Phil Garner and this is another route which has increased in difficulty since the first ascent. The following year Lounds achieved completely free leads of Nova Express, Green Tony and Izzy the Push, but several of the Red Wall routes were still described as 'not led' in the 1979 guidebook supplement, even some in the '83 guide. In 1979 Lounds and Ken Bliss cleaned Yellow Wall (a job which is never quite finished) and climbed Earth Eater and Street Boy Blues. Lounds later caught Al Evans cleaning a line on the Main Wall, obliging him to lead the pitch, which he did with initial reluctance, though ultimately with success creating Hollow Earth, and thereby clinching his hat-trick of what are probably the three finest routes on the wall.

Around this time Dave Knighton added two characteristically fine, hard and bold routes; Makin' Magic, between Cracked Actor and Aladdinsane, was for some reason omitted from the '83 guide which led to a very confusing situation recently when Mark Liptrot claimed the same line (calling it Pacific Ocean) and then Dave Bates climbed the wall left of Cracked Actor and quite coincidentally called it Making Magic. The situation was resolved by Bates altering his route's name to Magic Making. The second of Knighton's contributions was A Sense of Doubt, a rarely repeated route up the blankest part of Assagai Wall.

Knighton was sometimes a controversial figure, frequently criticised for top-rope practice and pre-placing protection, but when A Sense of Doubt finally received companions in 1984 similar tactics were employed. The first neighbour moved in in 1984 when Owain Jones and Steve Edmondson added Scary Monsters, followed at the end of the year by the brilliant Doubting Thomas by Dave Bates. These two routes marked the end of a seven year lull in new routing at Trowbarrow, in which intermittent access difficulties must have played a part. 1985 though was slightly busier than the previous year with several first free leads on Red Wall, including Willy the Fink by Ron Fawcett and Wrongo Sal by Owain Jones who also added (after a good deal of practice) the very hard and serious Exequy though not without a couple of falls. Tom Walkington and Dave Bates signed the year off by girdling the wall, something which is often seen as a sign of maturity (for the wall, not necessarily for the climbers!)

Across the quarry, the wall below Original Route, with its countless micro-holds had long held a single route, its name throwing down a gauntlet: 'The Great Unled'. Several teams had designs on the pitch, and it came in for a good deal of top-rope practice. There was nearly a nasty accident when a block being used as an anchor pulled out; luckily it missed the three climbers but it succeeded in destroying most of their gear! The Great Unled even suffered the placing of two bolts, but before the route could be attempted, Paul Carling declared before witnesses that he could do it without. Forced to put his money where his mouth was, he duly chopped the bolts and led the line with marginal skyhook and micro-wire protection. Dave Bates and Tom Walkington added a neighbour, The Nut House, a similarly serious adventure, though subsequent routes have not followed the fine ethical example, and the slab has acquired three more routes, two of which utilize bolts. Perhaps in the light of earlier experiences, top-roping is considered too dangerous.

Back on Red Wall Mark Liptrot disposed of the penultimate 'not led' when he led Burrough's Blues. Various gap-fillers and variations have been added, most of them by the indefatigable Dave Bates; Blow Job is a substantial offering from a very capable climber. Perhaps the most significant addition of 1987 was Tony Mitchell's solo ascent of Twisted Sister, shortly after having made the first solo ascent of Exequy.

One can't say there are too many lines left to go, but it would certainly be premature to suggest the crag was 'worked out'. On the other hand it is very much to be hoped that – as a quarry – it is worked out, once and for all,

THE ROUTES are described from RIGHT to LEFT, starting just past the bank which crosses the quarry floor (one of the 'long hike' descent routes comes down here).

1. **Baby Walker** 35ft Sev
Direct up the centre of the stepped buttress: loose and non-descript.

2. **Lonely Wall** 45ft E1 *
5a. A surprisingly good route, but a serious lead since the loss of its peg runner; it takes the diamond-shaped wall 40 yards left of Baby Walker. Start behind the three small trees growing very close to the wall and climb up to a ledge, then up and left to the horizontal break (Friend runner strongly advised) about 3 feet right of the drill-mark. Go straight up to the bulge and cross it diagonally rightwards. Tree belays. The upper wall is very loose and it is probably preferable to descend the grassy ramp.

3. **Boulderdash** 50ft Hard VS
5b. Twenty yards left is another buttress. Climb the centre of the lower wall with difficulty (an easier alternative exists on the left); finish by the easier blocky crack on the left.

On the left and set back is a steep, broken wall. A couple of routes have been made here but are entirely unpopular, for reasons which should be obvious.

Left again and farther forward is a more compact white wall. A poor route (**Blue Daz** 40ft Sev) takes a line up its right-hand edge. The two routes on the front are altogether more superior.

4. **Square Deal Surf** 40ft VS
4c. A worthwhile route and better than it looks. Start at the lowest point of the wall. Gain the right end of the ledge, move up the small corner and diagonally right to a short deep groove. Go up and then back left on a sloping ledge to finish up pleasant twin cracks.

5. **Biological Agent K9** 35ft Hard VS *
5b. The thin crack in the upper wall, 10 feet left of the finish of Square Deal Surf, is fine and well protected, but the lower wall to reach it requires care.

To the left and slightly forward is an insecurely-laminated grey wall. At its left is a deep flake crack above shot mark '156' (**First Cut** 30ft Diff).

Left again, above the debris cone, is the steeper and more appealing **YELLOW WALL**. This gives good climbing when clean, but unfortunately the cracks tend to ooze mud if conditions are at all damp.

6. **Willy the Disk** 50ft Hard VS
5a. Start 10 feet right of shot mark '155.05' and climb direct up cracks to the top.

7. **Earth Eater** 50ft VS
4c. Start at the shot mark and climb as directly as possible, moving right near the top.

8. **Street Boy Blues** 60ft E2 *
5c. Start left of the shot mark and move up to two, parallel thin cracks. Climb to the bulge and pass this using the obvious diagonal crack. The final wall is easier.

9. Sleeping Balls 50ft VS
4c. A semi-girdle. Follow Street Boy Blues to the horizontal crack at 10 feet, then follow this and finish on the right.

MAIN WALL
This imperious wall dominates the quarry. Its solidity is often called into question, but it has remained substantially unaltered for some time now. Fossil holds on the face require careful handling but the cracks are generally sound and clean. The top few feet of some routes can be loose and earthy.

10. Helden 90ft E1 * †
5b. Climb the groove on the very edge of Main Wall to an overhang on the right. Break out left along a horizontal crack to the corner on Warspite. Move up to the roof and pull round this on its left, finishing up the short headwall.

11. Warspite 85ft Hard VS *
5a. An adventurous route starting up the big corner at the right side of the wall. About 10 feet below the roof a horizontal break leads left to the arête. Move up, then left along the first horizontal crack until a wide crack can be taken to finish.

12. Warspite Direct 85ft E1 **
5b. The next corner runs up to a roof at half-height. Gain the corner from the right and climb to the roof. Move right and climb the crack splitting the roof – strenuous and spectacular. The widening crack above is a bit of an anticlimax.

13. Hollow Earth 90ft Hard VS **
5a. Start as for Warspite Direct, but move out left just below the roof to gain the superb, sustained diagonal crack, joining Harijan near the top.

14. Rock & Roll Suicide 35ft E2
5b. A bold alternative finish to the previous route. About 8 feet short of the junction with Harijan the crack widens to hand-jam size. Step up and then right on small holds, and continue up with some anxiety until better holds arrive.

15. Harijan 95ft VS ***
4c. Start up the corner for a few feet, until a horizontal crack leads awkwardly left onto the face. Follow it left and then up the obvious jamming crack to the top. Care needed to avoid rope drag.

16. Touch of Class 95ft E1 **
5b. A few feet left an obvious pod/crack splits the overhang. Move left beneath this and climb it with difficulty (well-protected with Friends). The fine jamming crack above leads to a junction with Harijan. Finish as for that route. A poor but much easier variation starts just right of Jean Jeanie and climbs the wall until a horizontal crack leads rightwards to the base of the jamming crack; Hard VS 5a.

17. Major Tom 105ft E1 *
An unsatisfactory line redeemed by some fine climbing.
5b. Start as for Touch of Class but after the crux take a gently rising thin crack leftwards to join Jean Jeanie: follow this until it dog-legs

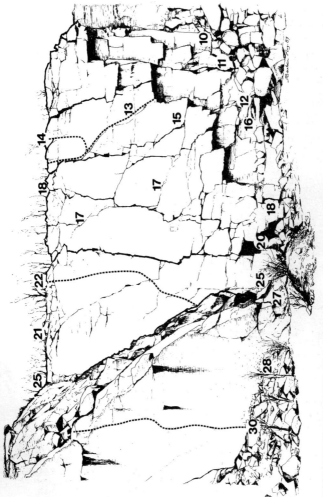

TROWBARROW QUARRY Main Wall Area

right, then move out left to finish up a fine diagonal crack.

18. Jean Jeanie 100ft VS ★★★
4c. The central crackline is a classic of its grade; sustained and quite strenuous but with good protection and resting places. Climb the blocky wall to gain the crack proper and follow it to the top.

19. Blow Job 100ft E5 ★ †
6a. Follow Jean Jeanie until it dog-legs right at about 40 feet. Step left to a thin crack and climb this to a small niche (PR – hard to clip). Continue direct, with much trepidation to a second PR, then up to meet a good crack (Major Tom) and so to the top.

20. Aladdinsane 95ft E1 ★★
5a. The wide crack above the cave has a bold and awkward middle section.

21. Cracked Actor 100ft E2 ★★★
5b. Follow Aladdinsane to the base of the straight section of the crack then move out left to the thin diagonal crack. Follow this crack, the first 20 feet are very sustained but can be well protected. Finish via the horizontal breaks on the left.

22. Makin' Magic 95ft E3 ★
5c. Climb Oniscus for 10 feet then follow the thin crack in the Main Wall to a move right to gain Cracked Actor. Follow this for a few feet then move right onto the face and climb this direct via a peg runner.

23. Magic Making 95ft E1
5b. Follow Makin' Magic until it moves right to join Cracked Actor. At this point move left and follow a thin crack until an awkward move gains the horizontal breaks and the finish of Cracked Actor.

24. Space Oddity 180ft E1
5a. A devious and unsatisfactory attempt at a girdle; it finishes in a fine position but apart from this there is every reason to think a right to left girdle would be better. Follow Oniscus for 30 feet to a horizontal crack which leads to the junction of Aladdinsane and Cracked Actor, then move down slightly and go right along a horizontal break to join Jean Jeannie. Up this until it is possible to step right to hollow earth, and traverse right to the base of the wide crack of Warspite Direct. Move right along the second horizontal crack to Heroes, then step up and continue the traverse above the large roof until it is possible to finish past large blocks on the arête.

25. Oniscus 105ft Sev
The corner between Main Wall and Red Slab gives a poor, loose and vegetated route. It might improve with traffic – if it ever got any!

26. Red Slab 120ft VS
The expanse of slabs left of Main Wall can be climbed almost anywhere. The easiest line starts roughly in the centre, with a rightwards detour at the steeper section. A couple of narrow crystalline slabs on the left give the best finish. The thin right-facing corner just right of Original Route also leads quite nicely to this finish: 4c.

27. Original Route 120ft V Diff ★
The slabby rib on the left is technically easy but quite serious; what

protection there is being behind perched flakes. Move right after 60 feet then finish up the back of the bay behind. A better but harder finish (Severe) is to move right from the ledges to the narrow crystalline slabs, and finish over the nose.

Below the rib is the steep 'crozzly' slab of **ASYLUM WALL**

28. **Memoirs of a Lunatic** 30ft E5
6b. Follow the obvious streak at the right side of the wall, with one bolt runner.

29. **The Idiot** 35ft E5
6a. A bold line up the lesser streak just left.

30. **The Asylum** 40ft E5
6a. Takes a line just left again. Climb 10 feet to a PR and then up to a good nut placement. Step right and climb direct to the top.

31. **The Nut-House** 45ft E5
6a. A direct line up the wall just left again, with one PR of its own; the peg on The Asylum is also clipped.

32. **Diaries of a Madman** 40ft E5
6b. Follow Rampant to a small elder tree, climb up to a BR then step left to a vague crack and climb up to the apex of the slab.

33. **Ramp Ant** 110ft Sev   ★
The red ramp bounding Asylum Wall on its left leads very pleasantly to broken ledges and a choice of finishes. There now follows a very broken section with no climbs and no appeal. A few yards farther left the quarry wall stands forward again.

34. **Crematorium** 110ft Hard VS
5a. Climb the steep, shattered and often wet, groove in the angle. At a bulge move left onto a slab then continue to a belay at 50 feet. Move back right and climb right of a crack, past an overhanging block, then left and up a crack to a groove and wall finish.

35. **Jomo** 120ft V Diff   ★★★
A fine varied outing, marred only by the terrace at half-height. The start feels both hard and bold but the angle soon eases. Start below the rounded light-coloured rib behind some saplings. Climb this to easy slabs and bear left to a diagonal crack. Climb this to the terrace and block belays. Follow the steep gangway behind to the small roof, which is passed (easier than it looks). Step right onto the fluted wall to finish.

36. **Pigfall** 100ft Sev   ★
Start as for Jomo, but when the easy slabs are reached move up to the foot of a fine arête. This is exposed and poorly protected but never very hard.

37. **Pig in a Poke** 60ft Hard VS
4c. A variation on Pigfall. At the foot of the arête step right (block and sapling – possible belay) below a steep clean slab and climb it with scant protection.

38. **One of these Days** 70ft E3
6a. The fine narrow wall between the upper part of Jomo and Pigfall.

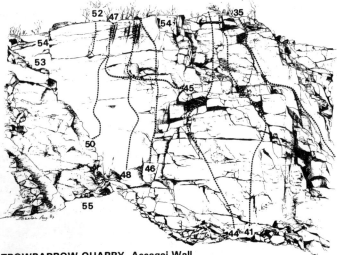

TROWBARROW QUARRY Assagai Wall

39. Very Ordinary Route 120ft Moderate
Climb the cracked groove left of Jomo (often used as a cheating start to that route) to large ledges and block belays. From the upper left end of the terraces finish up cracks and blocks. A poor climb, but a handy descent route – with care!

40. Crinoid 110ft V Diff
Round to the left is an obvious deep chimney. Reach this by any of several possible lines and climb it to the terraces. Finish by the groove at the left side of the upper wall (left of Night Flight).

41. Sluice 100ft Hard VS   *
A bold wall and surprising finish make this climb much better than it looks.
(1) 55ft 5a. Climb the wall left of the chimney at a brown streak, to horizontal cracks and welcome runners. Climb the diagonal jamming crack to the terraces.
(2) 45ft 5a. Climb the centre of the upper wall via a thin right-facing corner, to the crack in the overhangs for a pleasing finale. A blinkers-type route (**Shady Blade** E2 5c) climbs the narrow wall right of this pitch and left of Jomo.

42. The Pate 50ft E2
5c. Start as for Sluice but continue direct up the bald, bold arête right of that route's jamming crack.

43. Incantations 50ft Hard VS
4c. Climb directly up the centre of the wall to the terrace.

44. Night Flight 105ft VS
(1) 60ft 4c. Start in the centre of the wall and climb diagonally leftwards by a series of small ramps/ledges (poorly protected) then up into a recess below cracked roofs. Climb horizontally rightwards to escape the roofs and up to belay on the terrace.
(2) 45ft 4c. Climb the wall left of Sluice, to a short final crack. A scrappy route has been claimed up the system of grooves to the recess below the roofs on pitch one, making a risky direct exit.

ASSAGAI WALL
This elegant wall is set back slightly and gives some of the finest climbing in the quarry. The upper part, with its striking fluted grooves, is naturally weathered.

45. Assagai 70ft Hard VS   ***
An optional first pitch exists (V Diff) up the blocky groove on the right of the lower wall, but the route proper starts from the left end of the lower terrace.
5a. Traverse left along the obvious line (white rock) then step up and left again to a small ledge. Climb up to the horizontal break, step right and finish up the amazing fluted groove: a splendid pitch.

46. Sleeping Sickness 70ft E2   **
5c. Start up the blocky groove to gain a very thin crack. Follow this and the wall on its right to the traverse of Assagai (this section also makes an excellent bold start to Assagai; 5a). A Friend runner is helpful below the overhang, which is taken by the small groove; difficult and blind. Follow the crackline to meet Assagai near the top or continue straight up the tapering pillar.

47. Javelin 90ft E1   **
A contrived line but offering continuously enjoyable climbing.
5b. Follow Sleeping Sickness to the traverse of Assagai, follow this but continue left to a hidden ledge in the centre of the wall. Move up with difficulty to the break and finish up the central fluted groove.

48. Scary Monsters 60ft E5   *
6a. Start at the lowest point of the wall and climb up to a faint seam at 20 feet (2 PRs). Move up (crux) and right, then back leftwards to a shallow corner which meets the end of the Assagai traverse. Finish up that route.

49. Doubting Thomas 75ft E5   ***
6b. More sustained and possibly more serious than Scary Monsters. Start at the foot of the ramp on the left, at the scar left by a trundled pedestal. Climb direct to two incut holds, make an awkward move to gain a niche and pass the bulge above by a wild leap. Finish up the wall right of Javelin. Peg runners protect.

50. A Sense of Doubt 65ft E4   *
6a. Easier than the two preceding routes but still serious. Start on the ramp above the remains of the pedestal. Step right onto the wall and go up for 10 feet to a break. Move left to a good hold and up to a horizontal crease. Continue to the traverse line of Rumal, and finish up the flutings of Javelin. Three poor peg runners.

51. **Day of the Beanpoles** 55ft E3
Technically the hardest route on the wall, but well protected.
6b. Start 10 feet left of A Sense of Doubt, directly below Sour Milk
Groove. Climb direct up the wall (PR) then finish up the wall left of Sour
Milk Groove.

52. **Sour Milk Groove** 60ft Hard VS   *
5a. Start at the top of the ramp. Step right onto the wall and follow the
horizontal break (Rumal) to an awkward move into the left-hand of the
three fluted grooves; follow this to the top.

Assagai Wall boasts two contrasting traverses, which can easily be
done as a 'round trip'.

53. **Rumal** 75ft Hard VS   **
5a. The lower, very pleasant, horizontal break gives a sustained pitch,
possible in both directions.

54. **Truffle** 75ft Hard Sev   **
4c. An amusing route and very exposed for its standard; best done
from right to left as the crux is then right at the start. From a small
ledge about 10 feet below the top of the crag and just left of Very
Ordinary Route, step awkwardly onto the front of the wall. Continue
with plentiful holds and runners and at the end, step round to belay in
the corner.

55. **Twentieth Century Schizoid Man** 90ft Diff
The slabby ramp up the left side of Assagai Wall is easy but not well
protected. Finish up the short wall at the back of the bay on good holds.

56. **Perseverance** 95ft V Diff
Take a variable line up the slab left of Schizoid Man (poorly protected)
to the sapling ledge. Finish up the short wall at the back of the bay.

The next few routes tackle the chaotic area to the left. Loose blocks are
common!

57. **Quisquillae** 100ft Hard Sev
4a. Left of shot mark "111.82" is a short left-slanting slab/groove. Climb
this then swing right below a broken white wall. Continue up and right
past a short corner to the left edge of a red groove. Follow this to the
saplings and finish up the back of the bay.

58. **Aborigine Wall** 100ft VS
(1) 55ft. Take the paired slabs left of Quisquillae and scramble up to
a ledge below a steep and relatively clean wall.
(2) 45ft 4c. Climb the centre of the wall to a bulge, surmount this
and finish direct (better and more solid than the original finish which
moved right below the bulge).

59. **Boomerang** 110ft V Diff
A devious excursion.
(1) 55ft. Take the larger, left-slanting slab, with a crack on its right,
to a large ledge and block belays.
(2) 30ft. From the right end of the ledge step onto the wall and move
awkwardly round below a large block, then up to the sapling ledges.
Amphetamine Variation (VS 4b). From the block, a bold alternative is

to traverse delicately right across the black slab and up the rib.
(3) 25ft. Finish up the back wall of the bay.

60. Ask Lez 70ft Sev
Take an interesting short corner left of Boomerang, then the distressing corner left of Aborigine Wall pitch two. Definitely not recommended!

Set forward and starting slightly lower is a fine tapering wall.

61. Barrier Reef 65ft Sev
Pleasant climbing up the groove in the right rib of the wall with one or two loose blocks.

62. Coral Sea 65ft VS *s a I know* ⋆⋆
Very popular, a testpiece at its grade.
4c. Pull onto the rib from the left and follow it for a few feet, then step left onto the face and traverse into its centre, then ascend on improving holds, to the top.

63. Coral Sea Direct E1
5c. A desperately 'eliminate' line taking thin cracks just left of the rib then going left at the first opportunity to climb cracks just left of the parent route. **Coral Sea Superdirect** (6b) follows the wirebrush marks.

The broken area to the left is a tempting descent but is also very loose. Round to its left is a cracked wall.

64. Barnacle 50ft Sev
Climb the pleasant wall on good holds, trending slightly left. Several variations are possible.

The deep corner left of this wall, below a large tree, is a more amenable descent route (or root). Very awkward at the bottom, especially if damp. The quarry now turns to face south; this section is lower and very broken. Various lines are possible and some have been ascended, but they are all dirty, loose and unpleasant. Where the wall turns again (now facing east) there is an easy way down for those who have not got lost in the woods behind the northern end. Left of this is a long wall, its upper section very shattered.

65. Hara Kiri 40ft E1 ●
4c (Variable). Not so much a rock climb, more a test of sanity! Climb the lower solid section at its highest point, roughly in the middle of the wall, to gain a ledge. Reverse before it's too late or climb the upper wall by a vague groove, moving left to finish just right of a small tree. Other routes in a similar vein are possible: please report any claims direct to the nearest asylum. Left again, opposite Main Wall is:

RED WALL
This unique wall owes its red colour to haematite contamination, which also accounts for its chronically greasy feel, not helped by the fact that chalk never washes off. In fact the wall is so steep and sheltered that it probably never gets wet directly from rain, but there is some seepage and the cracks can get muddy. The climbing, needless to say, is very strenuous and is popular with local climbers for training. Few pegs are in place and top-roping is the norm — except on the girdle!

66. Drop Acid 45ft Hard VS †
5a. Right of the next route are two hanging grooves below a cornice of tree roots. Start slightly rightwards and climb to the overhang below the grooves. Gain the right-hand groove and climb it, using the left-hand groove as necessary, to the 'cornice' and the top. Looser than it looks (and it looks loose!)

67. Acid Drop 50ft Hard VS †
4c. The shattered groove right of Sepia Typhoid Witness – loose in places.

68. Sepia Typhoid Witness 50ft Not led
6a. The steep, blunt rib just left of the shattered groove which marks the right edge of the wall.

69. Izzy the Push 50ft E2 ★★
5c. Start just left and climb to a large depression, PR above. From the left of the depression, climb straight to the top.

70. Heavy Metal Kid 50ft E3 ★
5c. Start at a block left of Izzy The Push and follow the obvious line of holds more or less direct to the top. Two PRs.

71. Twisted Sister 60ft E5 ★ †
6b. Climb the wall 6 feet right of Exequy using an obvious pocket to gain good finger holds. Continue direct until a move right gains Heavy Metal Kid and follow this until a traverse left gains the finish of Exequy.

72. Exequy 60ft E6 ★★
6b. Takes a line up the wall just right of Nova Express. The crux is between 15 and 20 feet up and is rather serious. After the crux, move right to a good hold in the wall (a Friend runner here will protect against a certain crater higher up) and race up the wall, (PR on left) to the top.

73. Nova Express 50ft E3
6a. Takes the line of depressions 15 feet left of Heavy Metal Kid with two PR's.

74. Willy the Fink 50ft E5
6b. Start as for Nova Express, but climb directly up on the left of the depressions.

75. Fluoroscopic Kid 50ft E4 ★
6a. Start just left and climb direct up the wall to a fine finish.

76. Essence of Giraffe 60ft E3
6a. Start 10 feet right of a pit, towards the left side of the wall. Climb a line of large holds up right to a bird-limed hole then step left to a short blind crack and follow the wall above to finish just left of the yew. Two PRs.

77. Essence Direct 50ft E3
6a. Start just left, at a thin slanting crack. Climb straight up to join Essence of Giraffe at the short blind crack, then move right and climb the wall direct to the top. Two PRs.

78. Limestone John 50ft E2
5c. Start on the left of the pit. Climb diagonally right then make an awkward move which allows a traverse left to be made for a few feet. The wall above is climbed direct.

Right: Dave Cronshaw on 'Non-Stop Screamer' - Lester Mill Quarry.
Photo: Cronshaw collection

78a. Direct Finish E3   *
6a. Instead of traversing left climb the bulging wall above.

79. Mugwump 50ft E3
6a. Start just left and climb the wall bearing slightly left to a hard move at 15 feet, then climb the wall above. Two PRs.

80. Wrongo Sal 50ft E5   *
6a. Start just left again. Bold, sustained climbing leads directly up the wall via a deep hole and spike runner.

81. Burrough's Blues 40ft E3
6a. Up the left edge of the wall starting by the obvious birch tree at the foot of the crag.

82. Red Wall Girdle 180ft E3   ***
One of the best climbs in the area: sustained and well protected climbing with peg belays (in situ at the time of writing).
(1) 70ft 5c. Follow Izzy the Push to the large depression then traverse left at this level to the large upper depression of Nova Express and PB.
(2) 60ft 5b. Move left and down to a traverse line which leads past the bird-limed hole on Essence of Giraffe to a PB.
(3) 50ft 6a. Move up slightly then follow a line of holds to the left, to an awkward move which leads to buckets and the end of the crag.

One last wall, with some easy routes, is hidden from the rest of the quarry. It is most easily found from near the start of the track running westwards out of the quarry. Cross the wasteland and the wall lies below some tall pines. It has been christened **BEETLE WALL**, the reason for this being obvious and is nothing to do with Coleoptera. Several routes have been climbed from about V Diff to Hard Severe. The rock is of passable quality and the climbing is pleasant enough, but undistinguished and lacking positive lines.

The large boulder in the middle of the quarry floor has some good problems, the slabby south face contrasting with the overhangs on the other sides.

WARTON MAIN QUARRY (SD 492 144)

By Dave Bates

APPROACH
The Main Quarry at Warton is the one which dominates the view of the hillside from the M6. The quarry entrance is about half a mile past the Black Bull Inn at Warton, on the upper road to Silverdale.

CHARACTER
Over the past few years, since the last guide, many new routes have been climbed, a number of which deserve to be recognized as amongst the best in Lancashire. Having said this there are also some of the worst, with many being very loose. These routes will be pointed out in order that they can be avoided (or appreciated by those who enjoy a little adventure!)

*Left: Paul Ingham finishing the crux of 'La Mangoustine Scatouflange'.
-Chapel Head Scar. Photo: Paul Cornforth*

THE ROUTES are described from RIGHT to LEFT from the quarry entrance.

HISTORY

Apart from one or two aided forays, now lost in the mists of time and legend (the name of Chris Bonington has been mentioned in connection with early developments here though no details are known), the first attack on the quarry came in 1970 with the ascent on the unmissable line of Plastic Iceberg. The first pitch – hardly immaculate even now – was so loose that, in John Sheard's words "what we needed was a disposable non-climber with a disregard for instability and no need of conventional protection" in other words Pete Livesey, then better known in other sports, who made the first ascent with Sheard.

Dave Knighton was next on the scene in 1976 and with John Wilding he made an epic ascent of the appropriately named White Fright whilst being shot at by a young lad who was to become, in turn, the quarry's main activist in the future. Routes really started to fall in 1977; Dave Cronshaw adding Vespers For The Dead on which his second, Les Ainsworth, was rained off. Les consoled himself with Limestone Rain and Real World, the latter finding the easiest way up the impressive left-hand side of the central wall. 'Big' Jim Cooper added the adventurous Rock Folly, and Dream World with A. Atkinson, but the best lines were snatched by Knighton; despite being decried for his top-rope practices, he created the superb Deceptive Bends and Third World, but regrettably had to resort to aid on Killer Queen, a soaring line up the steep wall right of Plastic Iceberg, though only after taking a 25-foot fall when two holds snapped whilst attempting a lead. Dave then led it by a slightly different line, with two pegs for aid. The aid was finally eliminated in 1982 when a Lakes team led by Ed Cleasby managed a clean ascent to produce a very fine, airy wall climb.

The following year, Dave forged a line up the arête left of Plastic Iceberg giving Fall of the House of Usher, and Andy Hyslop led Dave and Marcus Tierney up Just Like a Woman. The fine line of Cosmic Debris fell (literally?) to alternate leads by Phil Martin and Ian Welsh. As well as being involved in several first ascents, Martin was later to leave his mark in quite a different way: it was his preference for a lie-in that is commemorated by the route name 'Ich Bleib Im Bett'. Later, Neil Foster added Saruman with Andy Wiggans, whilst Steve Parr made a bold solo ascent of Year of the Cat, an alternative start to his own Modern Times.

1980 saw Knighton completing the hardest of his Warton routes with ascents of Terminal Trajectory and Up the Neck, and then things lay quiet for some time until the ugly spectre of 'questionable tactics' arose again. This time though it was Iain Greenwood and Mark Danson who first top-roped and then led Comes a Time using preplaced runners. There was no question though of the superb quality of the route and it has recently been straightened out and improved upon even further by the addition of a direct finish by Dave Bates, followed by Mark Liptrot and Jim Cooper.

The next few years saw nothing of any real note, only a series of indifferent routes by Dave Bates and Jonty Wilson, the best of which were Galactic Timebreaker and The New World. Then in 1984, Tom Walkington and Barry Rodgers breached the large white wall left of Wartberg to give the sustained Oddballs. Shortly after Dave Bates climbed a more direct line (The Mighty Fly) up the wall thinking it to be a second ascent due to the old bolt and peg runners. Dave added a number of major new lines that winter, including the bold Brainstrain and the easier Flash Imp, which manages to wend a surprisingly easy way through the huge overhangs left of Third World. With Walkington, Dave made a frozen, two-day epic traverse of the left-hand side of the quarry, creating Birdbrain Meets Clothears and following this Andy Lee accompanied Bates up Ich Bleib Im Bett.

Through the years, Jim Cooper has soloed a few routes on the Upper Tier, most of which are on rather loose rock. Two recent routes though (Walking on Sunshine and Riding on Air) are of much better quality than their predecessors. Back on the main cliff the pace slowed, with little being done during 1985. 1986 however saw Celestial Cyclone by Bates, a Malham style route on the Year Of The Cat slab, using bolts to lower from the top of the slab. Then 1987 saw the introduction of the E6 grade in the quarry and possibly the area's hardest route with Dave's Torture Garden, a very forceful, very direct line up the Mighty Fly wall: the name possibly refers to the excruciating bridging position Tom Walkington managed to get into whilst seconding the route.

1. **Moon Ribber**   50ft   V Diff
Ten feet left of the first black mark, take the left edge of a left-slanting ramp to the top.

2. **Pipedream**   55ft   Hard Sev
4a. The wall above the second black mark can be climbed with several variations possible.

3. **Papermoon**   80ft   Hard Sev
4a. The shallow groove above the '100' mark. PR at 25 feet. Steep and serious.

Two routes of indifferent quality have been climbed on the wall just right of the large cave:

4. **Home James**   80ft   VS
4b. The wall and slanting cracks just right of Don't Spare the Horses.

5. **Don't Spare the Horses**   85ft   VS
4c. The wall and roofs 20 feet right of Gouffle Connection.

6. **The Gouffle Connection**   120ft   VS   *
This climb has completely changed since the last guide due to a large rockfall (which was clearly heard in Warton Village!)
4b. Start below the large cave. Climb the slabs on the left side until a horizontal break is reached, traverse left along this for 20 feet until an exit upwards (careful) can be made.

7. **Vespers for the Dead**   95ft   Hard VS   **
A good route which climbs the wall left of the cave.
5a. Climb the steep wall 10 feet left of the cave to the top of a small

dome-shaped buttress. Continue direct up the wall above (bold) to gain a thin leftward-curving crack. Follow this until a thought-provoking mantel can be made to join the traverse of Gouffle Connection, finish up this.

8. **Wart Berg** 100ft VS
(1) 40ft 4b. Start 20 feet left of the large cave and climb the obvious crack to the right side of the good belay ledge.
(2) 60ft. Continue up the flake, then finish up an easy corner.

9. **Dog Years** 120ft E2 *
A scrappy start leads to fine open climbing on the upper part of the wall left of Wart Berg. Start 20 feet left of Wart Berg.
5c. Climb the shallow corner to the left hand side of the large ledge on Wart Berg. Continue up Wart Berg for a few feet then follow a thin left-leading break (No. 1 rocks) to a pull on sloping jugs (!) leads to a resting position, PR. Easier climbing leads rightwards to finish.

10. **Mighty Fly** 100ft E5 **
An exciting climb, start as for Dog Years.
6b. Follow Dog Years for 20 feet, then break out left on large holds to a BR. Balance up and right (crux) past 2 PRs to an overlap. A delicate move rightwards gains the break of Dog Years, continue straight up to large holds and easier ground leading to the top.

11. **The Torture Garden** 90ft E6 *** †
A magnificent, sustained route, taking a direct line up the white wall left of Wart Berg.
6b. Start 10 feet left of Dog Years and go up to a PR in a thin groove. Continue up to an old PR, using an undercut jam to gain the BR on Mighty Fly: follow this to the overlap. A puzzling move may gain the next overlap, crux. Bold climbing gains the sloping jugs on Dog Years. Step left to a thin crack and follow this to the break (PR) then direct up to a bolt belay. Abseil off.

12. **Oddballs** 100ft E4 **
A very sustained but well protected route.
5c. Start 15 feet left of The Torture Garden. Climb a thin crack/groove to an awkward step right to a large overlap, PR. Sustained climbing past small wires leads to another PR. A delicate move left (PR) leads to an easier finish. It is advisable to hang a rope down the top loose band of rock to belay on.

13. **Tight Sally** 160ft Hard VS
A loose first pitch leads to good climbing on the upper slabs.
(1) 70ft 4a. Start 10 feet right of the corner of Slack Alice, and climb up to a roof. Pass this on the right, then up slabs to a small ledge and peg belay.
(2) 90ft 5a. Move up and right past a horizontal break onto a slab (PR on right). Step left and follow the slab to the top, nut belay.

14. **Slack Alice** 160ft Hard VS
A frightening route; the first loose pitch leads to an even looser second. Start at the large corner 100 feet left of Oddballs.
(1) 70ft 4c. Climb the corner to nut belays in the cave.
(2) 90ft 4b. Continue up the corner (care with the perched block!) to NBs.

15. **Modern Times** 220ft E1
This route has got looser over the years, the second pitch is rather a perilous journey.
(1) 110ft 4c. Start 15 feet left of the corner and climb straight up the slab past a BR on the left at 40 feet. Move diagonally left with difficulty to the right side of a long narrow ledge. Small stance on the left, Peg and nut belays.
(2) 60ft 5a. Climb right across the wall above to a small niche. Enter the groove above from the left, then climb to an exit on the right; iron spike and peg belay. Breathe again!
(3) 50ft 4a. Climb the wall and groove above to a loose finish on the left; tree belay.

16. **The Year of the Cat** 110ft E2
Another route that has become looser. The protection isn't up to much either! Start 70 feet left of Modern Times in a shallow bay to the right of a large shattered block.
5a. Traverse up and right on an obvious band of good rock: go up the slab above to PR and BR below an overlap; traverse right and climb up to belay as for Modern Times.

17. **Celestial Cyclone** 60ft E3
A 'Modern Times à la Malham' type route lowering off bolt and peg belays at the top of the slab.
5c. Start 20 feet right of Year Of The Cat at a shallow groove. Climb the groove, BR, to gain the slab, BR. Step left then up to a bolt and peg belay, AO.

18. **Galactic Timebreaker** 170ft E2 ★
(1) 70ft 4c. Climb the flake crack 50 feet left to a ledge. From the left end of this go up for 15 feet then traverse left across a slab to a ledge. Nut belays well back.
(2) 100ft 5c. Move back right and up a slab, then over an overlap to a resting place under the roof. Surmount this (PR on lip) and gain a slab which is followed to an overlap (PR). Climb up under the roof then traverse right for 20 feet and finish up a short groove. **Left-Hand Finish** (4c): pass the large roof on the left then up via blocks to the top.

19. **Rock Folly** 310ft VS
Start 60 yards left, at a depression (opposite the weigh house) which gives the only easy way through the main back wall. At the right side of this it is possible to scramble between a boulder and the rock.
(1) 60ft 4a. Climb the groove (some loose rock) or scramble up from the right, then step left onto an easy-angled slab, and move up to a belay.
(2) 80ft 4b. Climb dobs to the pink and grey wall, then move up and right to broken ledges, and continue to the large ledge, peg belay.
(3) 70ft 4a. Walk 20 feet left, then cross a steep slab (PR) and move up to a small niche. Swing left round a block, then ascend the corner above to a belay on the left.
(4) 40ft. Traverse left using dobs, then go up a short corner to a large ledge and peg belay.
(5) 60ft. Walk along the ledge to a broken corner near the left end, and climb this over poor rock, finishing on the left. After the first pitch

of the route there are several variations which would be possible, but all need extensive cleaning.

20. **Crunchy** 80ft Hard VS
4c. Takes the clean slab capped with small overhangs between Rock Folly and White Fright. No start has yet been climbed so the approach is by an abseil from the terrace to a ledge at half-height. Climb the slab above this to overhangs, then move left and climb direct to the top.

21. **White Fright** 150ft Hard VS
Very loose and not recommended. Halfway along the main wall is a large cone of debris with a large ledge on the left. Take the groove on the left of this.
(1) 130ft 5a. Follow the right slanting ramp over dobs to below a small overhang, then step right and swing right onto a ledge (no belay). Move left onto the wall (PR) and go up for 10 feet, then move left and up onto a steep slab (PR). From the PR step up and traverse right into the groove-line and follow this with increasing difficulty (2 PRs) to a sloping ledge. Ring peg belay.
(2) 20ft 4a. Bridge up the corner at the back of the ledge to the terrace, peg belay.

22. **Devils Nightmare** 150ft E1
5b. Climb Limestone Rain but continue the traverse for 30 feet to below a ramp (possible belay). Climb this to a roof (PR), which is turned on the right. Continue up to a large loose flake and round this to enter a scoop. Climb up and right (PR) into a slim groove (crux) which leads to the top. Belays well back.

23. **Limestone Rain** 210ft Hard VS   **
A good route though ascents often take on an epic quality.
(1) 80ft 5a. Up the groove at the foot of Plastic Iceberg until it is possible to step up and right onto a slab. Cross this to a short corner (PR), then climb the steep wall on the right (care should be taken to protect the second for these moves), and go across to the right side of an easy ledge system, PB.
(2) 130ft 5b. Up the shallow groove on the right to the roof, then traverse left to the end of the overhang and go straight up (PR) to another roof. Surmount this on the right using some doubtful blocks, then continue up an obvious layback crack towards the next overhang. At a small ledge on the left either, continue up to the roof then surmount it on its left, or climb straight up from the ledge. Above the overhang follow the obvious groove to the top, then walk well back to a belay.

24. **Dance on a Volcano** 85ft E2
A frightening climb on less than perfect rock.
5b. From the belay on Plastic Iceberg, traverse 15 feet right then follow the right trending crack/ramp line, PR, to a pleasant finish.

25. **Killer Queen** 95ft E4   **
An excellent and airy route.
6a. Start from the belay on Plastic Iceberg. Traverse right to the arête: climb the left-hand side of this until just below the overlap; step left and up to a PR. Pass this to a second overlap and another PR. Step right and climb up to a horizontal break, then go straight up the slab

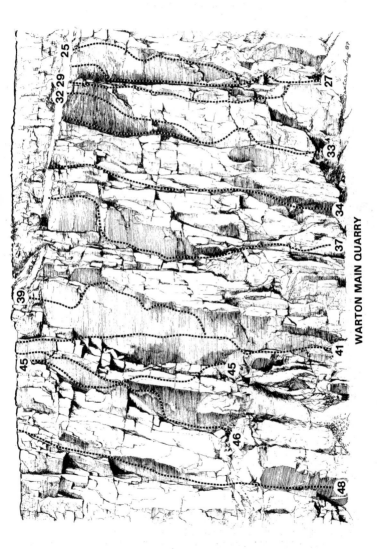

WARTON MAIN QUARRY

above, just left of the arête, to finish. **Variation** (E3 6a): After clipping the first PR, step down and right to the arête. Climb the shallow groove just right of the arête, stretching left to clip the second PR, then finish as for the parent route.

26. **Brainstrain** 105ft E5   ★★
An exhilarating route with a bold finish.
6a. Follow Killer Queen to the first PR, step down and traverse left for 12 feet then make awkward moves (crux) up past a PR to the horizontal break. Step right then make a 'mind-bending' runout past a pod-shaped hole to the top.

27. **Plastic Iceberg** 160ft E1   ★★★
The classic route of the quarry, taking the obvious large deep groove in the main wall. Care is needed with a few holds on the first pitch.
(1) 75ft 4c. Up the slabby groove to a small roof which is passed on the left. A few moves up a ramp on the right lead to a step left into a short groove which is followed to a small stance, peg belay.
(2) 85ft 5b. Sustained climbing up the groove leads to a thin bridging move to gain a PR. Continue to another PR from where an exit can be made to the right. It is possible to climb the wall on the right soon after the first PR: precarious.

28. **Arête Variations** 90ft E1
5b. Follow the second pitch of Plastic Iceberg to an overlap (PR on left) then move down to a small footledge on the left. Traverse left along this to the arête and climb up to a jammed block on House Of Usher. Climb the steep crack on the right and pull onto a small ledge, then finish on the left as for House of Usher.

29. **Fall of the House of Usher** 95ft Hard VS   ★★
An airy pitch with a worrying pull onto a 'way out there' block.
5a. From the belay of Plastic Iceberg swing round the rib on the left onto a short slab. Cross this to the foot of a ramp/groove, (possible belay): follow this past 2 PRs to below the block which guards entry into the upper groove. Make a mind-blowing heave onto the block and continue up the groove with a swing left to finish.

30. **The Demise of Lady Madeline** 75ft Hard VS
The combination of this route and House of Usher make a worthwhile trip.
5a. Follow Plastic Iceberg pitch one for 10 feet, then move left to gain a steep crack: climb this through overhangs, moving left to another crack. Move right and climb over suspect rock (care) to a ledge.

31. **Future Now** 50ft Hard VS
5a. Follow the second pitch of House of Usher to the arête then climb left and break through the overhang on the left. Climb the wall above to the top.

32. **Comes a Time** 115ft E5   ★★
Another excellent route: when combined with the direct finish it makes a superb, three star outing. It takes a direct line up the slab left of Fall of the House of Usher.
6a. From the belay of Demise of Lady Madeline, follow Cosmic Debris for 15 feet (large Hex) then traverse right and up to a thin crack in the

slab. Sustained but well-protected climbing leads to a horizontal break. Move right for a few feet then finish as for Future Now. **Direct Finish** (5c †): Climb direct to the top from the horizontal break, bold.

33. **Cosmic Debris** 170ft E1 *
This occasionally loose but otherwise good route takes the corner line left of Plastic Iceberg to give 3 interesting pitches.
(1) 50ft 5a. From the foot of the corner climb a shattered groove past a PR and then an easy curving flake to a small stance. Good nut belay. Alternative stance 15 feet up the corner on a ledge on the right.
(2) 60ft 5b. Climb the corner above with increasing difficulty to gain the groove above and a nut belay.
(3) 60ft 5b. Continue up the corner to a small roof; layback this and climb to the top.

34. **Saruman** 170ft E2 *
Takes the right-slanting ramp system to the left.
(1) 50ft 5a. Climb the right-trending slab/ramp (which forms a short chimney at the bottom) to a sitting block belay.
(2) 70ft 5b. Climb the wall behind for a few feet, then move left into the slender right-trending ramp. Follow this to ledges at its top.
(3) 50ft 5a. Climb the prominent corner behind (on the left) by a layback, then continue over an overhang to easier ground.

35. **Ich Bleib Im Bett** 170ft E2
A good but rather bold route. Start 20 feet left of Saruman.
(1) 90ft 5b. Follow broken but easy ground up to a large flake at the base of a slim groove. Climb the groove stepping right at the top to a peg belay below a small roof.
(2) 80ft 5b. Step right and up to boldly gain a shallow groove on the left. Follow this to the roof and traverse left under this on good jams to exit onto easier ground to the top.

36. **Up the Neck** 80ft E3 **
5c. From pitch one of Real World move up for a few feet below the overlap then pull over onto the slab (PR). After another step up traverse right (crux) to a foot ledge on the arête. Climb straight up past a second PR to a sloping ledge then continue more easily to the long traversing ledge on Real World. Climb the wall above via a vague crackline to its highest point.

37. **The Real World** 170ft VS **
The easiest way up the left-hand side of the main wall. A rather broken first pitch leads to good groove/slab climbing on the second. It takes the next big corner left of Cosmic Debris.

(1) 70ft. Start below and left of the corner at a short wall of more stable rock. Climb the wall then scramble up and right to arrive at a small ledge, nut belays.
(2) 100ft 4b. Climb the corner, making a delicate move right at 40 feet (crux). Then either traverse the break to the arête and follow this to the top, or continue up the corner for 20 feet then traverse/walk to the arête and so to the top.

38. **The Warton Blues** 80ft E1
5a. From the Real World belay, traverse 10 feet left into a steep

groove/crack. Follow this on less than perfect rock to the top.

39. Deceptive Bends 160ft E1 ***
A classic and very popular climb. Start as for Third World.
5a. Follow the crackline (PR) for 30 feet until a line of holds leads out
to the arête on the right. Balance up this with much trepidation to a
welcome PR (don't look too closely!). Continue to some superb quartzy
pockets and TR. Move thinly up and left, then back right to a good
resting place above the gorse bush. Go up and over the bulge to a PR;
step left to a crack then back right to finish. 30 feet of earthy scrambling
leads to the top. A rope may need to be pulled through to belay. **Direct
Start** (4c): Climb the arête direct to join the original route.

40. Terminal Trajectory 160ft E3 **
Although this route has some fine climbing, it is now more serious
since a PR has disappeared.
5c. Follow Third World for 40 feet, move right onto the slab and wander
up this to the bulge of Deceptive Bends. Pull over this then traverse
right for 10 feet to the arête and finish up a groove.

41. The Third World 150ft Hard VS ***
Another deservedly popular climb, taking the crackline up the centre
of the huge pink slab at the left end of the quarry. Scramble easily up
to the base of the crackline to start.
5a. Follow the crack and make an awkward move over the overlap (PR).
Pleasant climbing leads to a large groove in the overhangs (possible
belay). After a couple of bridging moves a juicy jamming crack on the
left wall is followed to the top. If 45-metre ropes are used it is necessary
to pull one through in order to belay.

42. Flash Imp 160ft E4 **
An intimidating route requiring a cool head. It takes a direct line up the
slab left of Third World, then wends its way through the massive roofs.
Scramble up to the large sloping ledge below the slab to start.
(1) 90ft 5c. Delicate climbing leads to a crux at 30 feet (nut runner
used 15 feet up Third World). Mellow out and run it out to take a belay
at the start of Third World's groove.
(2) 70ft 5a. Move 10 feet left until it is possible to gain a short groove
in the overhangs. Up this then break out left to join Just Like a Woman;
finish up this.

43. Truly Scrumptious 170ft E1
5a. Take the broken groove on the left side of Third World slab until it
is possible to traverse left across the white wall to join Just Like a
Woman at the crux.

44. Dream World 160ft Hard VS
Takes the groove on the left side of the slab.
5a. Follow the groove to the roof. Traverse right to the groove of Third
World, possible belay. Continue traversing up and right to finish up
Deceptive Bends.

45. The New World 150ft E1 *
5c. Climb the white wall left of Dream World's groove, to a PR level
with the overlap on Just Like a Woman. Move left to the rib then climb
a short crack, moving left slightly to climb the wall above to a PR. Pass

this (crux) to an easier finish up a groove. A good if slightly contrived line.

46. Just Like a Woman 130ft E1 *
A worthwhile route best approached by abseil or alternatively by a hairy scramble in from the left.
5a. Climb the corner crack for 15 feet before trending right to a small ledge and PR. The next moves form the crux; palm the arête and if you don't barndoor off you'll reach the overlap. Go over this and up a short groove (possible belay on the left). Make an exposed traverse right to the arête then up and over a small overhang to finish up a friable wall.

47. Shake, Rattle & Roll 130ft E1
5b. Start as for Just Like a Woman but continue up the groove to a hard swing left, PR (crux). Continue up a groove to a broken ledge, possible belay. Step left to gain a thin groove which is followed to the top; care needed with suspect rock.

48. Too Old to Rock 'n' Roll, Too Young to Die 130ft E2
A truly horrendous route, taking a line up the next obvious groove/slab left of Just Like a Woman.
5a. Start at a shallow groove/crack 30 feet left of Just Like a Woman; heart-stopping moves on disintegrating rock gain a delightful slab which is followed with much horripilation (manic laughter an advantage) to finish up a delectable groove.

49. Birdbrain Meets Clothears 360ft E2 ***
A magnificent expedition, girdling the left-hand side of the quarry from left to right.
(1) 120ft 5a. Follow Just Like a Woman to the overlap: traverse right (PR) down across the white wall into the groove of Dream World. Then go delicately across the Third World slab to a peg belay above the gorse bush on Deceptive Bends.
(2) 60ft 5b. After a fight with the gorse bush, traverse right at the same height as the bush to gain Real World, nut belay.
(3) 80ft 5a. Walk across the slab then round the corner to make an awkward move across the Saruman groove. Continue at the same level until a wild swing leads into the final steep corner of Cosmic Debris. Nut belay.
(4) 40ft 5c. Make some thin moves across the horizontal break, crossing Comes A Time and swing round the rib to belay on Fall of the House of Usher.
(5) 60ft 5c. Step down to make an exasperating move (crux) into the groove of Plastic Iceberg (PR). Continue along the horizontal break to finish up the groove just right of Killer Queen.

50. Washington 80ft Hard Sev
4a. A scrappy and poor route. The route lies at the left end of the wall opposite the main back wall, at a point about 75 yards from the quarry entrance. Here are two leaning walls; the route takes the right leading ramp which goes below one of these walls and above the other. Protection is poor.

TERRACE WALL: The remaining climbs in the quarry start from the large terrace which splits the Main Wall above Plastic Iceberg. Access to this ledge is from the left by a short, stepped corner. Two worthwhile routes have been climbed on the right end of the Terrace, the rest are of indifferent quality.

51. Walking on Sunshine 80ft VS ★★
4c. Takes the clean and solid (!) wall right of Polo direct via a thin crack at the top.

52. Riding on Air 80ft VS ★★
4c. Gain the block on Polo and make a rising traverse right to the top of Walking on Sunshine.

53. Three Steps to Heaven 90ft Sev
From the right end of the Terrace, climb the wall to a ledge at 20 feet. From the right of this ledge climb straight up to the top, climbing the left side of a rib 30 feet from the top. Very loose finish.

54. Polo 70ft Hard Sev
4a. Further left is a block stuck to the rock with a shot hole in its centre. Ascend left of the block and step onto its top, then climb thin cracks to a mantel on a large earthy ledge. Continue to the top of the crag.

55. Star Wars 80ft Hard Sev
4a. Start 10 yards right of Sneck. Climb diagonally right for 20 feet, then horizontally right for a further 20 feet to beneath broken rocks at the top. Continue horizontally right for a further 15 feet, and then climb straight to the top.

56. Sneck 50ft Hard V Diff
Towards the left side of the Terrace is a block-shaped nose. Climb the corner on the right of this, passing an overhang at 15 feet. At the top move left and finish over doubtful rock.

57. Rubber Band 45ft Sev
The corner left of the nose, moving right at 20 feet, and then moving left to finish as Sneck.

58. Plastic Band 40ft V Diff
The corner just to the right of the top of Plastic Iceberg

WARTON – THE PINNACLE AND UPPER CRAGS

As these two crags are so close together, and so often visited on the same outing, it seems sensible to describe them together, and to give the best route from one to the other. For ease of navigation and to maximise the benefits of any sunshine there may be, it is recommended to visit the Upper Crag first.

APPROACH AND ACCESS (UPPER CRAG)
The normal starting point is the parking area in the Small Quarry. If this is full there are more spaces a short way up Crag Road, just above a footpath (signposted). The two routes meet by the gap in the wall at the upper end of the Small Quarry. On emerging from the trees a few yards beyond this, go left onto the open ground of the scarp. About 300 yards up this there is a small, right-angled rocky bay with a flat

pavement-like floor. Just above this a narrow path dives into the trees; this leads, after a short climb and more trees, to a level bracken-covered area, with the crag now in sight. The path enters more trees and swings round leftwards almost parallel to the crag, which is eventually reached via a prominent white tongue of scree and a steep grass slope.

UPPER CRAG TO PINNACLE CRAG

A good path leads leftwards from the top, or left-hand end of the crag to the summit trig point. Forty yards on is a small outcrop where the view opens out. Two hundred yards south-west is a small but prominent boulder with a cleft top. Make for this (path virtually invisible in summer) and the top of Pinnacle Crag's descent route is not far beyond this, slightly to the right.

PINNACLE CRAG (DIRECT)

Start as for the approach to Upper Crag, but continue past the rock bay, along the scarp. The Main Quarry appears on the left (though the climbing areas can't be seen) and after crossing a stile the path bears off rightwards, climbing more steeply. On the highest thorny shelf, where small outcrops can be seen ahead, strike off leftward on an oft-muddy, cattle-churned path. Keep to this and soon after it starts to descend slightly, the crag can be half-seen through the trees. This approach normally leads to the Plum Buttress area, instantly recognizable by its large overhangs at head-height. Then again, sometimes it doesn't! Who says there's no adventure left in climbing?

NB: Although Pinnacle Crag is very close to the top of the Main Quarry, attempts at a direct connection are almost certain to end in tears.

WARTON PINNACLE CRAG (SD 491 727)

SITUATION AND CHARACTER

Excellent rock makes this small crag worth seeking out. The usual point of arrival, and the best part of the crag, is the Plum Buttress area. The 'Pinnacle' itself lies quite a long way farther left, and doesn't entirely live up to its name when you do find it, but has a few good routes on its long side (what a giveaway).

The trees can hold moisture for a while in summer, but when bare they do let plenty of sun through whilst giving some shelter from cold winds.

HISTORY

Most of the routes were first done by Stew Wilson and Rod Smallwood, though Dave Powell-Thompson did the very enjoyable Flake and Wall, and Robin Witham shook up The Morning After (so called because it was!). Bill Lounds, Chris Eilbeck and Pete Lucas added the surprisingly substantial Plum Buttress Girdle and Lounds also added the notorious

Plumbline with two points of aid; it is not clear who made the first free ascent. Much more recently Dave Bates solved a long-standing problem with The Crank, while Phil Stone gardened the pleasant Bish's Tipple, as well as claiming several lesser – and less certainly new – routes.

The well-marked descent route is a little to the left of the Plum Buttress Area. THE ROUTES are described first RIGHTWARDS from this, and then back LEFT.

1. The Mushroom   30ft   Diff
Climb the buttress right of the descent gully to the perched block. A good alternative descent as it's nowhere near as polished. The wide cleft on the right is not recommended – as if you needed telling!

2. Fine White Line   20ft   5a
The thin flake cracks at the left side of the next wall are excellent, but lead to nasty vegetation. Carry a machete, or reverse the route.

3. The Morning After   20ft   4c
Climb the centre of the wall via an obvious undercut and crack above: similar comments then apply as for the previous route, or escape rightwards.

4. Clare's Crack   25ft   V Diff
Quite an enjoyable crack, just right again.

5. Flake and Wall   30ft   Sev   *
A satisfying little route. Climb the recess to a bulge, which is passed 'with either difficulty or ease'. Finish direct.

The rock now projects and becomes deeply undercut; this is **PLUM BUTTRESS**.

6. Deadwood Crack   30ft   VS
4c. The obvious line past the dead tree: hard at the start and at the stump (which should not be used).

7. Lone Tree Groove   30ft   V Diff   *
4a. The scoop, where the face curves round, is entered by a hard move from a block. Continue steeply on adequate holds to the tree and an easier finish behind it. Harder for the short. **Lone Tree Variation** (V Diff *): After the hard starting move, venture out right onto the wall, to find some surprising holds leading upwards.

8. The Big Plum   30ft   VS   *
4c after the first move. Round to the right is a 'weakness' in the overhang with a steep corner above. Difficulties at the start are proportionate to height. Common strategies include cairn-building, combined tactics and giving up. **Peach Finish** (VS 4c **): Even more worth getting off the ground for. From the tree at half-height, move out onto the wall and climb it on good, spaced holds.

9. Plumbline   30ft   E3   **
Up-graded by popular demand – this route was formerly Hard VS 5a!

6a. Twelve feet right is another 'weakness'. Climb it and gain the horizontal break (runners on left). Continue by thin, sustained bridging.

10. **Yosemite Rib**   30ft   VS
4c. Pull into the corner groove and step left onto the rib. Follow it direct.

11. **Dihedral**   25ft   Sev
The next corner groove.

12. **The Vine Line**   30ft   Sev   *
6a. The fine undercut slab on the right is gained by a desperate mantel onto the obvious polished little shelf. Or, more often, from the right starting behind the tree (sometimes using it). The holds above are almost too good to be true!

13. **Plum Buttress Girdle**   70ft   Hard VS   *
(1)   30ft 4b.   Start as for Lone Tree Variation, but continue rightwards to belay on the tree of The Big Plum.
(2)   40ft 5a.   Follow the rounded horizontal break rightwards, getting a runner in while you still can. As the break runs out completely, make a long reach up and right to a good hold on Yosemite Rib (crux). Finish up that route.

14. **Bish's Tipple**   25ft   Sev   *
To the right of The Vine Line is a mass of ivy and a deep corner. Climb the right wall of the corner and the left edge of the narrow upper wall.

15. **The Parson's Nose**   25ft   V Diff
Start just right of the nose itself, at an obvious flake which allows a strenuous pull onto easier-angled rock. Finish up the fist-sized crack above.

Poor routes have been done on the undistinguished area of rock to the right, but the next route described is about 15 yards right, on a steeper buttress.

16. **Inspired**   20ft   Sev
4b. Climb the left edge of the lower slab then the obvious crack above. The steep thin crack between this route and the next is harder than it looks!

17. **Supination**   20ft   VS
4c. Above the stump and the carcase of a tall, slender tree (who felled it and why?) is a steep, clean crack, about hand-jam size. Climb it with some difficulty.

18. **Mounting Block**   20ft   Hard V Diff
Just right is a large embedded boulder below a sizeable overhang. From the top of the boulder tall climbers can reach excellent holds; the moves thereafter are strenuous but utterly straightforward. Shorter climbers may have to jump, or use a point of aid!

The next routes will be found round on the front face of the buttress

LEFT of the descent gully, and these routes are described LEFTWARDS.

19. The Gremp 20ft Sev
Climb the right side of the slab; can be varied by using the arête or avoiding it.

20. Skutch 20ft V Diff
Climb the centre of the slab to finish by the obvious flakes.

21. Dollard 20ft Diff
The wide crack on the left can be a struggle; it can also be a cruise.

22. Triplanetary 25ft Hard Sev
4b. Take a direct line up the isolated buttress about 10 yards left.

There now follows a long expanse of broken and often overgrown rocks, though some good problems can be found. Patient jungle-bashing eventually leads to the Pinnacle itself. The more impatient may prefer to go along the top of the crag to find it.

The next route starts at the right-hand corner on the front face of the Pinnacle, where the ground drops away.

23. Weakling's Wall 30ft Hard Sev
4b. Swing in from the right to gain a good hold on the overhanging wall. Move up strenuously to a ledge and finish more easily.

24. The Crank 30ft 6a   ★
A good steep problem up the wall right of The Graunch.

25. The Graunch 30ft VS   ★
4c. This is the clean steep crack, with a surprisingly awkward start. The upper part can be climbed quite elegantly, or as befits the name, it's up to you!

26. Muscles Crack 20ft Hard Sev
4b. The sharp, bulging crack just left. The top block is an optional extra!

27. Bumble Bee 20ft Sev
A decidedly strange route just round the corner. Climb the wide left-slanting crack and make an awkward bridging move out onto the face. Finish more normally.

Explorer-types will find further rock scattered in the wilderness: follow the general line of the crag, slightly downhill. There are many minor buttresses, increasingly overgrown, and one interesting steep wall. Please take a map and compass and/or leave word where you have gone so that search parties will have some idea of where to start!

WARTON UPPER CRAG (SD 494 728)

APPROACH AND ACCESS
See approach section to Warton Pinnacle Crag.

SITUATION AND CHARACTER
The jaunty whiteness of the Upper Crag, fringing the hill-top, catches the eye from a considerable distance, and it comes as no surprise that

it enjoys a wide vista, nor that it has only negligible drainage and gets the sun from first thing until late in the afternoon. Few crags dry faster. The rock too, is excellent; sometimes a bit broken at the starts, but solid, massive and often juggy above. The routes are steep and the abrupt declivity below makes them feel bigger than they actually are. For such a small crag there is also a healthy number of strong natural lines. If only it was a few feet higher...

HISTORY
The crag probably saw an initial wave of exploration by the occupants of the nearby iron-age hill fort, but unfortunately – not yet having invented writing – no records were kept. The recorded history of the crag begins with Robin Witham, Stew Wilson and friends, who worked over the crag for the first Lancashire guide of 1969. There are still some apparent gaps but virtually everything has been climbed, even if no-one can be bothered to write them up and name them.

The normal point of arrival is at the foot of the descent gully, an obvious and polished route in the centre of the crag. This is not, however, unreservedly recommended as a solo descent for absolute novices the easiest way down in this case, is at the far left-hand side. THE CLIMBS are described first RIGHTWARDS from this point, and then LEFTWARDS.

1. **Inverted Stairway** 25ft Hard Sev
4b. The series of overhangs immediately right of the gully; good finishing holds.

2. **Finger of Fun** 25ft Hard V Diff
4a. The obvious flakes on the left wall of a deep V-shaped groove. Awkward to start and to finish.

3. **Judith** 25ft VS   *
4b. Straight up the groove and out over the surprising roof.

4. **Benghazi Groove** 25ft Sev
Start up the groove, but avoid the roof by a tricky move out right.

5. **Sabre Tooth** 25ft Sev
Climb the shallow groove/crack which bounds the right wall of the groove.

6. **Ivy Way** 25ft V Diff
An obvious line on the left wall of the next groove.

7. **Ivy League** 25ft Sev
Climb the back of the groove and exit rightwards.

8. **Space Walk** 25ft 5b   **
The name is not quite as ludicrous as it first seems! The very prominent jutting arête is climbed on its left side; there is really only one hard move, but it's an exquisite one.

9. **Brainwasher** 25ft VS
5a. The wall round to the right, via a thin crack just left of the main one.

10. **Brainchild** 25ft Sev ★
An awkward bulge guards the enjoyable crack.

10a. **Variation Finish** VS ★
4c. From the crack, step right onto a vague rib and finish over the fine juggy overhang.

11. **Seventh Heaven** 25ft Sev
Climb the next deep groove, with an awkward move right into a steep crack at the overhang: easier for the short.

12. **Soft Man's Saunter** 20ft Diff
The obvious blocky corner.

13. **Whippet Wall** 20ft VS
5a. The clean, square wall just right, has a couple of good moves on small pockets which lead to a flake crack.

14. **Lictor** 25ft 4b-5a ★
Just beyond the rib are two siamese-twin cracks; 5a for the left-hand crack alone; 4c, the right-hand crack; 4b when combined!

15. **Fasces** 20ft 4c ★
The wall right of the cracks has more holds than are immediately apparent.

16. **Description** 25ft Sev
4c. The next wall, set back slightly, is steep and tricky until the thin vertical crack is gained.

The corner on the right is about Diff in standard (another possible descent). Beyond the low rib, the wall regains its height.

17. **The Abomination** 20ft Hard Sev
4c. Climb the system of grooves and flakes just left of the 'beak' and of the bulging rib.

18. **The Original Abomination** 25ft 6a
The name originally belonged to this route, but years of usage have transferred it to the easier line on the left. Mount the 'beak' awkwardly, and make a hard move up the bulging rib to better holds.

19. **The Layback** 25ft Hard Sev
4b. The obvious flaky-looking crack on the right.

20. **Flakes** 20ft V Diff
A variable line up the short wall at the very right-hand end of the crag. The thin crack at the left side, avoiding the ledge, is 4b.

Returning to the descent gully, the next route lies on its left wall:

21. **The Plumb** 25ft Sev
4c. Climb the short hanging crack to the left-hand end of the ledge. Finish more easily, direct.

22. **Yellow Edge** 25ft Hard Sev ★
4c. Start below the large nose on the front of the buttress. Climb rightwards to a good but not obvious hold at the base of a small scoop. Move up and slightly right to finish.

23. **Yellow Wall** 25ft V Diff ★★
Climb the right wall of the deep V-shaped groove until it is possible to move out rightwards between the overhangs, onto the nose. Finish straight up.

24. **Sedgewick Wall** 25ft V Diff
Climb the groove, moving left when suitable holds appear. It is also possible to climb the groove direct at the same standard, or to exit rightwards through the bulges, with only slight increase in difficulty.

25. **Freebird** 25ft 5c
The left wall of the groove contains a micro-groove; start slightly to its left and gain the groove using small pockets, and continue with difficulty to the jugs on Sedgewick Wall, the temptation to cheat being ever-present.

26. **Grooves Eliminate** 25ft VS
4c. The steep front face of the buttress, with an awkward bulge guarding the flaky upper groove.

27. **The Gash** 25ft V Diff
Climb the deep V-shaped groove on the left.

28. **Bop Route** 20ft Sev
4b. Start just right of the rib, beneath a spreading yew. Climb up to a short groove then move left across the clean white wall to finish up the rib.

29. **Twin Cracks** 20ft VS ★
5a. Start below the rib. Move up and left around the bulge to pull into the cracks with difficulty. Finish up the all-too-brief arête. A direct pull over the bulge is harder. The short wall on the left is also hard.

30. **Red Mist** 25ft V Diff
4a. Climb the short corner then swing left below the bush and finish up the wide crack or the rib on its left.

31. **Calcarb Arête** 25ft VS
4c. The obvious arête just left, as directly as possible.

32. **Dogfish** 20ft Sev
4a. The pleasant steep wall a few feet left, on good holds.

Beyond the rock 'island' there remains another buttress with two deep horizontal breaks.

33. **Cracked Overhang** 20ft V Diff
4a. Start on the left (easier) or the right (better) and pull round, on to the left side of the rib, and continue without further ado.

The crag now fades into the hillside, with a few shorter buttresses before an easy descent.

WARTON SMALL QUARRY (SD 498 724)

APPROACH AND ACCESS
Warton Small Quarry lies a few yards up Crag Road, immediately north

of the Black Bull. There is parking in part of the quarry itself but if these are full there are more spaces farther up the lane, from where a footpath leads through the trees to the top of the quarry.

A notice at the entrance spells out the official position on access and, of course, description of the routes here does not constitute permission to ignore it.

SITUATION AND CHARACTER
It is hard to imagine a more convenient crag: you can step from the car straight on to the rock, and the pub and a splendid chippy are only yards away. The rock and the routes are quite variable. Some routes are extremely polished, but others have become overgrown which seems to indicate a consensus on their quality. The star attraction of the quarry is the fine low-level traverse; an excellent way to round off a day's climbing on this or the other nearby crags.

The crag is very popular with organized groups and so it is not unusual to find all the easier routes occupied. It also manages to be both sheltered and sunny, but when it does get wet not all parts dry quickly.

HISTORY
The quarry has undoubtedly been climbed on for many years and its easier lines were probably ascended by local youngsters before the 'proper' climbers discovered the crag. The majority of the routes here were first recorded by Bill Lounds, Chris Eilbeck, Stew Wilson, Pete Lucas and Stuart Butler.

THE CLIMBS are described from RIGHT to LEFT. At the extreme right, where it abuts a stone wall, the quarry is very low, and this area is often used as a descent, otherwise abseil or walk round the top end. The low cave here has some good problem exits. A few feet left is a large overhang about 10 feet up.

1. **Sporting Eagle** 20ft 4b
Climb up to the right side of the overhang and move leftwards above it.

2. **Black Bull** 20ft 5c
Climb the overhang, just left of centre; avoid this route when cars are parked beneath!.

3. **The Overhang** 20ft 4b
Start under the roof and move out left to loose jugs at its left side. Pull up to higher and possibly sounder jugs to finish.

The wall on the left (formerly **Gelignite**, 4b) is now overgrown.

4. **Blaster's Groove** 20ft V Diff
The shallow groove with drill marks, below a cluster of trees: very popular and polished.

5. **Blaster's Wall** 20ft 4a
The wall a few feet left gives subtle climbing.

6. Bonnie's Wall 20ft 4c
Climb the wall and the right side of the small overhang.

7. Fool's Gold 20ft 5a
Climb up to and over the overhang just right of the rib.

8. Genius Silver 25ft V Diff
The blunt rib at the end of the car park.

9. Panhandle 30ft Sev
4a. The wall on the left, containing a rusted spike, is in danger of being reclaimed by vegetation but is still a worthwhile route.

10. Manhandle 30ft V Diff
Start 18 feet left below a tree at 8 feet. Climb the wall either left or right of the tree.

11. Gumboot Groove 30ft Sev
Climb the steep corner (just right of the slightly overhanging little wall) and the narrow clean strip above.

12. Delectable Traverse 45ft Sev ★
Start just past the rib bounding the overhanging wall. Climb the rib, or the wall on the left, to an easing of the angle. Traverse left and slightly down, above the line of overhangs, to the arête which leads straightforwardly to tree belays.

13. Townie 30ft VS
4c. Climb the V-shaped groove in the angle, left of the start of Delectable Traverse, over the overhang and finish direct.

14. Out of Townie 30ft VS
4c. Climb the overhanging left rib of the groove of Townie, continue over the overhang, then finish as for Townie.

15. Movie Maker 30ft Hard Sev ★
4b. The rib and roof directly below the finish of Delectable Traverse.

16. Country Boy 30ft Hard Sev
4a. Start below a thin curving gangway on the left. Pull strenuously onto a pedestal and then more easily into an awkward corner. Exit very awkwardly rightwards and continue direct to the top.

17. Connie's Groove 25ft Hard Sev
4a. The overhanging groove on the left.

18. Cracked Corner 20ft V Diff
There is now an obvious recess, reached by a 10-foot scramble. This route climbs the corner above the right side of the recess.

19. Groove and Slab 25ft V Diff ★
From the left side of the recess move awkwardly up a steep groove. Step out left onto a slab then back right to finish up the steep wall.

The overhanging nose on the left was **Burlesque** (Hard VS 5b); lamentably it is now overgrown.

20. Ivy Way 30ft Diff
Start below the highest part of the quarry wall and move up with some difficulty to gain the rightward-leading diagonal break; follow this to the top.

21. The Leaning Tower 35ft VS ✶✶
4c. Start up Ivy Way then move left into a shallow groove. Move up slightly, then left again onto the face, where good holds lead to the top. One of the best routes in the quarry.

22. Quasimodo 35ft 5c ✶✶
Usually top-roped; protection is virtually impossible to arrange before the crux, and the landing is unfriendly. Start about 10 feet left of Ivy Way below an overhang. Climb the rib to the left side of the overhang then pull rightwards onto the front face. Make a tricky move up then continue more easily, joining Leaning Tower to finish.

23. Igor 25ft 5b
Climb the groove just left, with some obvious big flat holds, and finish up the left side of the tower.

24. Original Route 35ft V Diff
Ten feet left is a steep groove containing a moveable block. Climb the groove quite strenuously and move up rightwards towards a tree. Finish by a short crack and leftwards up the final wall. **Variation** (Sev): from the top of the groove, climb straight up the wall.

25. Wailing Wall 30ft Hard VS
5a. Climb the steep, loose wall to the right of Autumn Leaves.

26. Autumn Leaves 30ft VS
4b. Climb the projecting rib to a ledge then, using a good undercut, make a delicate move up to reach better holds on the left (loose) and finish trending leftwards.

27. The Red Groove 30ft Hard VS
5b. The shattered groove on the left.

28. Great Flake 35ft VS ✶
4c. Above and left is a long slanting overhang with a crack beneath. Climb the right end of the overhang and move left using the crack, to a weakness, from where an awkward move leads into a groove, which provides an easier finish. **Direct Finish** (5b): Climb the overhang above the centre of the traverse.

29. Bogie's Groove 25ft VS ✶
4c. Just left of the finish of Great Flake is a shallow groove. Climb this, using the rib on the right, to join Great Flake to finish.

30. Biceps Wall 30ft VS ✶
4c. Climb the steep, smooth-looking wall on the left, with a tricky mantelshelf to reach easier ground.

31. Triceps Wall 30ft VS
4c. Climb the wall on the left which is initially steep.

32. Pete's Route 35ft V Diff ✶
A ledge on the left is the usual start/finish of the girdle. Move up from

this, passing an obvious projecting block, step up and right then continue up the wall to the top, on good holds.

Several routes farther left are now hopelessly overgrown, apart from one short wall which is **Finale Wall** (Sev).

33. Low-Level Girdle 220ft 5b ★★★

A classic of the genre, with well-defined breaks indicating the line for most of the way. The feet should never be more than 5 feet off the ground. The steep wall left of Gumboot Groove is the crux (a hold has recently disappeared, making it harder and the projecting block is becoming a little rickety). Rounding the rib at the start of Autumn Leaves is also very tricky on first acquaintances, but virtually all of the leftward half of the traverse is good. If the car-park section is too easy try it one handed; seriously!

WOODWELL (SD 465 743)

APPROACH AND ACCESS

The crag is very close to Silverdale Village and is a popular local beauty spot. Climbers should therefore take great care not to upset the local people with unnecessary noise and inconsiderate parking, and NO LITTER.

Coming from Warton, turn left after the level crossing and first left again (signposts for the hospital, amongst other things). About ¼ mile past the hospital is a small lay-by on the right, with a signpost to Woodwell. Park here and the first buttress is 30 yards down the path. If the parking spaces are full, continue along the road, turning right at Wolf House Gallery. Shortly after the 30mph signs there is a lane on the right, signposted Hollins Lane and Stankelt. Park on the main road and the lane leads directly to the path itself.

Climbers are asked not to stray beyond the areas described, as other crags in the area all lie on private land.

SITUATION AND CHARACTER

Local beauty spot it may be, but the crag does not have quite the same charm as many of the others in this area. However, for sheer concentration of technical moves it is one of the best around. It is generally used as a training ground and partly for this reason, in the majority of cases, only technical grades are given here. This should not imply that the routes are without any seriousness altogether; leading, say, 4c's here can be far more serious than routes of the same grade at Trowbarrow.

Many of the routes at the right-hand end of the crag are unpleasantly polished, and if conditions are at all damp the whole crag is abominable. The relatively neglected areas north of the well certainly deserve more attention.

Apart from the routes described, many variations and lesser routes exist, as well as several traverses. All those routes described are between 20 and 30 feet high.

THE ROUTES are described from RIGHT to LEFT, as they are encountered using the first approach described above. The first routes can be found by a large tree growing very close to the rock.

1. Clap 5a
Climb the strenuous crack above a fallen block, a few feet right of the tree.

2. Tree Root V Diff
Chimney up between the crag and the tree, then use the tree to reach the top. The grading is traditional!

3. Griddle Groove 5a
The groove just left of the tree; hard to start.

4. The Cad 5c
The wall between Griddle Groove and Creative Urge.

5. Creative Urge 5b
The straight, strenuous crackline, starting from blocks.

6. Cannon Crack 5b
The short overhanging crack on the left, finishing up a steep wall.

7. Long Crack Sev
The next crack is taken direct.

8. Long Crack Groove Sev
The groove on the left.

9. Pussyfoot 5c
On the left is a big flake in the overhang; the main problem is reaching it.

10. Paws for Thought 6a
The bulbous arête on the left.

11. Deryn Groove 5b
The obvious left-facing corner is gained direct, and gives a slippery struggle.

12. Flake Crack V Diff
The obvious crack just right of the yew tree.

13. Battenburg 4b
The thin crack in the centre of the slab, right of the tree.

14. Tree Arête 4c
The arête behind the tree (without using it) to a potentially nasty and rounded finish.

15. Rosie 5c
The thin crack splitting the wall on the left.

16. Pussycat 4b
The next crack.

17. **Tree Corner** 4a
The thin corner on the left.

18. **Cold Comfort** 4b
The wall left of the corner.

There now follows a more broken and generally lower section, where some good problems can be found. The next route is on the front face of an undercut buttress standing well forward from the main line of the crag.

19. **The Claw** 6b   *
Start just right of the arête, by a hard pull, and continue with difficulty. Nearer the well there is another isolated buttress.

20. **The Nose** 4c
Pull into the hanging corner crack and climb it to the bulge. Step right to a good foothold and swing back left immediately to a spectacular finish on suspect flakes.

WELL BUTTRESS
This long wall runs down to the well itself.

21. **All's Well** 4c
A line of flakes starting a few feet left of the twin trees.

22. **End's Well** 4c
Climb awkwardly up the thin groove 8 feet left, and finish up the loose break on the right.

23. **Well What?** 5a
Start just left of the groove and climb the wall.

24. **Shake Well** 5c   *
Climbs the corner on the left, direct.

25. **Get Well Groove** 4b
The groove above the right-hand side of the trough needs a drought to bring it into condition.

26. **Wet Wall** 4b
An accurately-named route up the wall above the trough. Twenty yards left is a wall with a left-slanting ramp.

27. **Rampant** 4c
Follow the ramp and finish either up the crack on the left, or direct.

28. **Bromide** 4a
The dirty crack/groove on the left.

PYLON BUTTRESS
The next section of worthwhile rock lies some way left, through occasionally troublesome vegetation; it can be identified conclusively by the wooden pole a few yards away, at the fringes of the field.

29. **Pylon Crack** 4a
The thin crack at the right extremity of the wall.

30. **Dek's Crack** Sev
The wider and less attractive crack a few feet left.

31. **The Teaser** 5a
The right-hand crack through the overhangs, and the wall above.

32. **Mango** 5b
The central crack, with two stumps; follow it direct and finish up the wall in the same line.

33. **Okra** 5b
The left-hand crack, above the overhang.

34. **Leechee** 4c
The more prominent crack on the left.

35. **Highlight** 4b   *
The flakey wall on the left: the best of the easier routes at Woodwell.

36. **Limelight** 4c
The slanting crack on the left.

37. **Argent** 5c
The arête just right of the gully containing a tree. A thin crack on the left makes the initial moves more amenable.

38. **Bed of Nails** 5b
Climb immediately left of the gully, using holds very close to the gully bed at one point, to gain a spike and an easier finish.

39. **Bed of Knives** 6a
The smooth-looking wall on the left.

40. **Bed of Thorns** 5a   *
Connects the two small niches in the wall by a series of agile moves. The easiest descent from these routes is to follow the sloping and vegetated ledge above the overhangs. With care this soon leads to an easy descent route, though the rock is not above suspicion.

Exploring through the jungle to the left, a long, low wall soon appears, its lines of overhangs giving many enjoyable problems; some surprisingly easy – and some not!

41. **Tom's Traverse** 6c
Start in the middle of the wall, where the overhang is at its highest, and take the lowest traverse line firstly using a thin horizontal crack then by a testing series of crucifix moves on better holds, to finish at a small elder tree. A masterpiece in excavation!

42. **Nothing to Say** 6a
Start just right of Tom's Traverse and climb out of the overhang and up the wall above.

43. **Any Questions** 4c
The wall immediately left of the overhangs is taken direct.

A little farther left is an obvious small pinnacle, with several possible routes of ascent (but first, work out how to get off it!). Just before reaching the pinnacle there is a steep clean wall.

44. **The Enigma** 5c
The short wall immediately right of The Answer.

45. The Answer   6a
The smooth shallow groove leads to a bulge, and finishes via a crack.

46. The Question   6a
The wall between The Answer and Slanting Crack.

47. Slanting Crack   5b
The slanting crackline left of The Answer. Regrettably lachrymose.

48. The Paradox   6b
The wall just left again.

The next buttress is well named **UNDERCUT BUTTRESS**.

49. Cracker   V Diff
The wall and crack at the right-hand side of the wall.

50. Bramble Jelly   5b
The wide break above the small tree is easy; reaching it is not!

51. Ambrosia   5b
The crack at the left side of the wall and paired higher up, is hard if taken direct.

52. Nectar   5a
The crack/corner just round to the left.

MINOR CRAGS

BAINES CRAG (SD 543 617)
Very close to the car-parking space at the top of the Quernmore – Littledale road. This crag is really only a collection of boulders but has some pleasant problems on excellent gritstone; rough, sound and very clean. Called Quernmore Crag in previous editions.

FAIRY STEPS (SD 486 789)
Some confusion may well have arisen from previous guides to this crag as there are in fact two crags here. The Fairy Steps themselves lie in the unmistakable cleft in the upper band of crags, known as Whin Scar. It is said that you are granted a wish if an ascent is made without touching the sides; easy for children, but anything up to 6a for adults, even impossible in some cases. There are short climbs and problems here, on good clean rock, and it is used by organised groups, who are probably responsible for the fixed belay points.

This crag can be reached by a well sign-posted path from the hamlet of Slack Head (leaving the road just below the top of the hill on the Beetham side). From the foot of the steps a path runs directly downhill to the top of the lower (larger) crag. This can also be reached by a slightly shorter but more enclosed route from Hazelslack Tower Farm (SD 477 787).

The lower crag (which is the one referred to as Fairy Steps in previous guides) does, indeed, have a flight of steps, but these are not of supernatural origin, and even Cyril Smith could probably get up without touching the sides (wonder what his wish would be?). To either side of the steps crags stretch away into the jungle, sometimes almost disappearing under luxuriant vegetation, but at intervals emerging again in buttresses of good rock, often surprisingly clean. The 1975 guidebook described 29 routes but there is at least as much rock here as at Woodwell, and of quite similar stature and character. Whereas Woodwell is generally picked clean however, its routes polished, chalked and itemised in the guide, Fairy Steps retains the atmosphere of a crag undiscovered; a place for the explorer and connoisseur alike to pick out problems for themselves at leisure.

HEYSHAM HEAD (SD 407 617)
The cliffs behind Half Moon Bay (sadly no longer a nudist beach) and on the headland to the north, have quite a collection of problems on sandstones of very variable quality. The best rock is on the sea-ward face of the headland, just above high water level, while the higher buttresses just below the old chapel are also quite good, with one or two finishing holds of grave interest (groan).

HUTTON ROOF CRAGS (SD 554 779) AND (SD 566 783)
The tangled landscape of this broken plateau is a delight to explore, but very confusing and a potential nightmare in mist. There are outcrops all over the place but the most continuous are Uberash Breast, just west of the three cairns – a long line of west-facing crags with variable rock and good landings – and The Rakes. Here the rock is generally excellent but seekers of difficulty may feel there are too many good holds. The potential for harder problems lies more in traverses; a red-dot traverse (discreetly marked) exists at the right side. The two tiers behind the main one also yield short problems.

MILLHEAD QUARRY (SD 498 715)
A bit of a slum compared to the other crags in the area; any popularity it may once have enjoyed has now dissipated. Six routes were described in the 1983 guide of which the best (everything is relative!) was **The Main Attraction** (Hard VS 5a) up the centre of the main smooth slab but even this is very serious, with poor protection and suspect rock.

WINDY CLOUGH (SD 536 606)
Reached from the car park on Rigg Lane (SD 526 604): where the track forks go right and follow the obvious path until the crag appears after about 15 minutes. There are outcrops all over the land north-west of the ridge of Clougha Pike but the main concentration is on the western rim of the Clough, giving problems and short routes on gritstone which is a joy to handle. The setting and the views compare with any crag in the area.

Further problems can be found 'over the top', west from the main edge; most notably an undercut wall providing several fiendish mantel-shelves. There is more rock at Little Windy Clough, and close to the summit of Cloughta, but they are only worth the walk if you enjoy it for its own sake. There is also a small quarry of some interest, just beyond the aqueduct, found by taking the left-hand fork of the track.

VIII. THE WHITBARROW AREA

Compiled by Al Phizacklea
with assistance from Paul Cornforth and Paul Ingham

The Whitbarrow Area is wholly within the county of Cumbria, and its boundaries can loosely be defined as the A6 to the east, the A591 to the north and the River Leven to the west. The majority of crags in this section lie within the boundaries of the Lake District National Park, and most of them are limestone.

Since the last guidebook, development in the area has surged forward in leaps and bounds, and excellent bolt protected routes on most crags have become par for the course. Chapel Head has seen major developments with many modern horrors to entice the hard climber, together with the vast array of easier routes it has to offer. Humphrey Head Point has now been equipped with bolt belays at the top of most routes, and so the horrendously loose slope on top of the crag can now be easily avoided. Scout Scar (A.K.A. Underbarrow Scar) has seen billions of bolts placed and numerous routes claimed, creating a very good crag in the Malham mould. White Scar on the other hand has still not realised its true potential, and visits are still only made by a small cognescenti who are crazy enough to revel in the delights of such an atmospheric crag. White Scar has so much scope that it will undoubtedly become a 'crag of the future'.

In the past a rather tentative access agreement to Chapel Head restricted climbing times quite considerably, but not only has the crag seen developments on the new route front; it also has a new access agreement. The ban has been slackened slightly to only five months between the dates March 1st and July 31st. This is thanks to the marvellous work of the British Mountaineering Council, coupled with the environmentally-alert local climbers; everyone visiting the crag is asked to heed their example and continue to respect this unique area.

Thanks to all the good work on new routes and access negotiations, by so many interested people, the Whitbarrow area is now not simply a backwater taking second place to the Lake District crags; it is a major forcing ground in its own right and easily equals the best in the country.

CHAPEL HEAD SCAR (SD 443 862)

By Al Phizacklea and Paul Cornforth

SITUATION AND CHARACTER

Imagine a limestone crag where the sun shines for twelve hours a day, where the rock is peppered with water-worn pockets and drainpipe-like tufa pillars. A crag resplendent in its surroundings amongst rare plants and fruits, interspersed with wildlife and naked bathers. Well, I'm sorry, but the place you're thinking of is probably 1,000 miles away in the south of France. Chapel Head Scar, though, is a good substitute, except that naked bathers are very few and far between!

The crag lies on the Witherslack Escarpment, it faces south-west and is often in condition when the Lakeland crags are under a deluge. It is split into three main buttresses; the Moonchild Buttress is the first to be encountered and lies at the top of the path which leads to the crag; the wall to the right is known as Cyborg Buttress and this is bounded on the right by the impressive, undercut Great Buttress. On the more modern routes protection is from pegs, threads and/or bolts, and descents can be made by abseil from fixed belays. On the routes that 'top out', care should be taken on the loose band of rock that abounds on the summit; descent from these routes is by a way-marked path leading down the right-hand side of the crag.

APPROACH AND ACCESS
Chapel Head Scar is situated directly above Witherslack Hall, 4 miles east of Newby Bridge. From the A590 (Levens – Barrow road) turn off at the Witherslack signs and follow signs to the village. Continue past the village for 1 mile to reach Witherslack Hall. Park here with consideration for the locals, and follow the short dirt track on the right, down to fields. A track then bears left across the fields and into woods; continue through the woods for 200 yards to a clearing where the crag can be seen. A thin path climbs up left from here, passing a notice board at the base of a scree slope. A posted path now runs diagonally right up the scree and swings left to arrive steeply at the base of Moonchild Buttress.

Climbing is banned completely in the area left of Central Gully, it is also banned on the rest of the crag between March 1st and July 31st, though this period may be revised and up-to-date information should be sought from the British Mountaineering Council offices in Manchester. This is not only because of the nesting birds, but also in consideration of the many other types of wildlife which inhabit this important nature reserve. Between these dates, it is essential that the crag is completely devoid from disturbance and in addition to this, a few other stipulations also apply:-
(1)   Use of the marked paths to and from the crag is imperative.
(2)   No gardening is to take place on the crag. Also the trees and foliage surrounding the crag should be respected.
(3)   No litter must be left.

These few rules are a small price to pay if climbing is to continue on this superb crag; the future rests with you.

HISTORY
Surprisingly, it was not the main part of the crag which first attracted climbers, most of the early routes were put up on the Lower Crag which has now been relinquished, from a climbing point of view, under the

new access agreement. A number of routes were ascended in fleeting visits by various climbers, one of them being Unknown Groove which may have been climbed by Chris Bonnington. Al Evans climbed Passion Play and Dandelion Wine, and other routes were done by various combinations of Al, Dave Parker, Les Ainsworth and Dave Cronshaw, many of which were very good climbs though unfortunately not now accessible.

In 1974, Les Ainsworth and Dave Cronshaw climbed The Veil, Starshine and Sungod. The crag received immediate acclaim in the national climbing press and one of the major forces in its development became Al Evans, then news editor for Crags magazine. Although Al did not make many first ascents himself on the Main Crag, he introduced many climbers to the delights of climbing here. One such person was Ron Fawcett who succeeded in climbing Moonchild with Al and Dave Parker. Word of this ascent travelled fast and Pete Livesey turned up with John Sheard and went away with the first ascent of Lunatic, a fine sister route to Moonchild.

Cyborg was the work of Ed Cleasby and Mike Lynch and then Cleasby top-roped Half Life before claiming it. Dave Knighton made what he thought to be the second ascent (in fact it was the first lead) and thought it necessary to place a peg. Cleasby, more legitimately, made the first ascent of Atomic Bong with Andy Parkin in 1977.

Ron Fawcett re-appeared at the crag in 1978 and succeeded in climbing the wandering though excellent War of the Worlds. Development continued with devotees Cronshaw and Knighton (one of the stronger teams operating on rock at the time) traversing the Great Buttress from right to left to produce Cygnus X-1. Cleasby, meanwhile, started work on the line above the swaying tree in the centre of the buttress, which was soon to become Android though it was to employ a little aid. Around the same time Knighton cleaned and geared up a prospective traverse, only to have Cleasby nick it whilst he was away. Knighton and Cronshaw made the second ascent of this traverse (Fast Breeder) and made the obvious connection with Crab Nebulae to give the aptly-named Chain Reaction, showing the rate of developments at the crag at that time.

Cronshaw took the lead to attempt the hanging groove in the upper wall right of Sun God but had to resort to using a rest point to succeed: Interstellar Overdrive. Knighton retaliated by making the first free ascent of Android. 1980 saw Pillar Front being climbed by Iain Greenwood and Steve Hubbard and Apollo's Exit by Mark Danson and Williamson, both routes being real compost heaps.

Development ceased for three years, until 1983 when big George Smith hit the headlines with Al Phizacklea, when they made the first ascent of The Route of all Evil, an excellent climb on superb rock. This route immediately received classic status with the help of the climbing press, and it inspired a young Martin 'Basher' Atkinson to attempt a repeat ascent even though George had told him he would be too short to make the necessary reaches. Suitably peeved, Basher did the right thing and flashed the route, downgrading it in the process. As a final poke in the eye for Smith, Basher also added a direct finish and called it The True

Path.

Al Phizacklea returned in 1984 to start a saga which was to last 15 months, his objective was a line up the severely overhanging rock left of the Android tree. In the meantime Gary Gibson made a flying visit and added Up-Town. Winter of '85 saw Tom Walkington and friends climbing some of the smaller routes right of Central Gully: Winter Pincher, Gully Wall Direct Start, Oddbods, Comedy Show and Veil Direct Start kept them happy for a couple of days. After the summer ban, Phizacklea finally succeeded on his long-standing problem near Android, initially with one rest, and then shortly afterwards (after sandbagging would-be second ascensionists) dispensing with it. This route became Wargames and because of its type of protection (drilled threads) became a turning point in the crags history. Perverse Pépère followed in the same mode by Paul Cornforth and Pat McVey, but instead of drilled threads, it utilized a bolt to protect the crux jump. Steve Hubbard and Tony Mitchell Bleep and Boosted their way up the slim groove left of Moonchild, and then Tony climbed the impressive headwall above Great Gully (passing two appalling bolt runners) to give Darth Vadar.

The floodgates opened and the sounds of the green woodpecker was drowned out by the sound of hammer on bolt driver. Paul Ingham put up the taxing Driller Killer with Paul Cornforth then Corny completed the stunning Super Dupont, right of Android. Steve Hubbard had been attempting a line above Android for quite some time but without success. One day during a warm spell of weather just before the annual ban, he offered Cornforth 'a go', and a few minutes later La Mangoustine Scatouflange was born much to Hubbard's consternation! On the last day before the summer ban, a gripped-up Cornforth made the long-awaited second ascent of Fawcett's War of the Worlds which had lain unrepeated for nearly a decade, and forty minutes later it saw a gripped-up Paul Ingham making the third ascent.

When the crag re-opened in August 1986 competition was hot for new routes. Cornforth succeeded in climbing the curving overlap right of Super Dupont, starting up that route to give Super Duper Dupont. Ingham replied with Phantom Zone, directly up the front of Moonchild Buttress and Mark Greenbank added a diminutive classic in the shape of Warm Push. Steve Hubbard broke out right from the start of Phantom Zone and thus created Stan Pulsar, a real throbber! Two other throbbers were done by Phizacklea when he created The Heinous Penis and L'Flange En Decomposition. Attention returned to Great Buttress where Tony 'Rubber Man' Mitchell swarmed up the flutings left of Wargames to give the shocking Electric Warrior.

Ingham, pressurized by a strong Lancashire team visiting the crag, finally succeeded in redpointing his much-tried line left of Phantom Zone to give Zantom Phone, though not before numerous falls and arriving at the crag that day to find two climbers attempting the route! Yorkshire brat-pack leader John Dunne in the meantime, made the third ascent of Super Duper Dupont (Ingham had already made the second) and the same afternoon, Preston's own Perfect Man, Mick Lovatt, made an impressive flashed ascent. Later, Mitchell, Ingham and

Right: John Mason on 'Truffle' - Trowbarrow Quarry.
Photo: Mason Collection

Cornforth girdled Great Buttress from Electric Warrior to Super Dupont which became the classic Cosmic Dancer.

After a few weeks rest Ingham was back to climb a direct start to Perverse Pépère; a powerful series of moves left of Android and Mitchell put up a route by mistake. While attempting The True Path, he wandered off route and climbed the headwall just right of that route and later called it Flight Path as Martin Berzins unwittingly made the same mistake. Unfortunately for him though he pulled off an undercut which previously accommodated a micro-thread, and in the process plummeted sixty feet, from whence he had come.

Cornforth spent quite a lot of time, firstly equipping and secondly fighting to complete the first ascent of the ridiculously overhanging, fluted area of rock rising out of Great Gully. He finally reached the top in October after a redpoint ascent, on the last dry day, just before the rains took over. Maboulisme Merveilleux was the name, a route to boost your metabolic rate a notch or two!

1987 arrived and Paul Ingham broke out right from Driller Killer to produce Videodrome just before the summer ban, but unlike previous years the ban only lasted a shorter period under the new agreement. Making best use of this situation, Cornforth put up Stretchy Peroneum, a dynamic start to Android. Surprisingly the only other new routes done during 1987 were Mitchell's Agent Provocateur (an extended version of his own Electric Warrior) and Witherslack Flange, which is Corny's continuation finish to La Mangoustine Scatouflange.

THE CLIMBS are described from LEFT to RIGHT, starting from the dirty gully 80 yards left from the point where the path meets the crag. This is the left-hand limit of current climbing here.

1. **Central Gully** 90ft VS
What a pity this one wasn't included in the ban! A disgusting route up loose rock, loose vegetation and solid thorns.

2. **L'flange En Decomposition** 70ft E2
Starts up a shallow groove 10 feet right of the gully. Mediocre climbing which deteriorates at the top.
5c. Up the groove, moving slightly left at it's top, straight up past a square cut flake then through choss to a yew tree.

3. **Gully Wall** 70ft E1
Some pleasant climbing – start as for L'Flange.
5b. Up the groove for 20 feet, move right to a shallower groove, then straight up finishing carefully at a tree. **Variation start**: the tricky groove 5 feet right of the normal start (20ft E2 5c).

4. **Winter Pincher** 50ft E3
6b. Climb the shallow, hanging groove (PR) 15 feet right of L'Flange to a tree, AO. Short and fierce.

5. **Oddbods** 50ft E3
Another short, difficult problem.
6a. The little groove, PR, 5 feet right of Winter Pincher.

6. **Strongbow** 50ft E2
Better protected but awkward climbing for it's grade.

Left: Unknown climber on 'Cyborg' - Chapel Head Scar.
Photo: Cronshaw Collection

5c. The hanging groove 5 feet right of Oddbods to a yew, AO.

7. Comedy Show 50ft E2
The fourth little groove 5 feet right again.
5c. Up, up and away to the tree. AO.

There is a horrendous hanging gully guarded by a short wall and yew tree at the end of the wall. The next route starts 10 feet right of here, behind a small tree.

8. The Veil 70ft VS
Good climbing tho' care is needed with a few temporary holds.
4b. Up left along a ramp to a ledge, traverse right to a blocky ledge and tree. Move up to a bush, traverse right to the rib and finish at a yew above. AO, or climb the flake above to finish at the top. **Variation: Direct Start** (20ft Hard VS 5a) The rather pointless thin crack that leads to the blocky ledge.

9. The Heinous Penis 70ft E2
An unsatisfactory route, which fails to climb the smooth pillar to the right of The Veil.
6a. Climb the centre of the wall to PR, then pull up right to TR. Climb the rib above – just left of Starshine, traverse left to the blocky ledge on The veil, finish up this; supersedes Pillar Front.

10. Starshine 80ft E1
Starts up a shallow groove 20 feet left of Sun God.
5b. Up the groove to the ledge, then the disposable groove above leads to a yew, AO.

11. Interstellar Overdrive 90ft E3 *
Some exciting climbing, start midway between Starshine and Sun God.
6a. Up a vague groove (TR) to the dead, rickety tree on the ledge. Use this to gain TRs below the roof then make some wild moves out right to the hanging groove (PR) which leads to the top, AO.

12. Sun God 70ft Hard VS *
Good climbing up the prominent flake line which is 10 feet left of the point where the path meets the crag.
5b. Up the strenuous flake to a dead tree, then continue up the bulging flake behind to the yew, AO.

The crag now steepens into an impressive rounded buttress of good rock: the **MOONCHILD BUTTRESS**.

13. Zantom Phone 90ft E5 ** †
A searing climb just right of the flake of Sun God.
7a. Up Sun God for 10 feet, then pull out right onto the steep wall to BR. Step right then back left to an obvious sidepull, BR. Then climb directly up to the hollow flake on War of the Worlds, passing BR. Move up to the roof, pull right into the smooth, hanging groove, BB up right.

14. Phantom Zone 90ft E6 **
A superb, sustained, fingery climb. Start where the path meets the lowest point of the crag.

6b. An awkward start gains the BR, move up and left to a PR, then grit your teeth and go like hell up the wall (BR) to where it eases, PR. Move up and left to a hollow flake; junction with Zantom Phone – finish as for this.

15. Stan Pulsar 90ft E5 ★★
A fine route with a puzzling start.
6b. An awkward move to the BR (as Phantom Zone), swing right to BR and stand on the ledge above (if you can!). Climb the groove above to a rest and PR on War of the Worlds. Pull right into the hanging groove above (NR) and finish up the superb crack to BB on Zantom Phone.

16. War of the Worlds 130ft E5 ★
A wandering line but gives quality climbing.
6a. Start up Moonchild to the PR, then traverse left for 15 feet to a groove, up to a resting place and PR, Traverse left for 15 feet to a hollow flake, then up to the roof, pulling right into the smooth groove to finish – or fall off. BB up right.

17. Bleep and Booster 90ft E4 ★
The shallow grooveline left of Moonchild; bold climbing. Care is needed with a few disposable holds near the top.
6a. Up Moonchild to the PR, swing left for 5 feet to a shallow groove. Up this awkwardly to a black bulge. Move left and pull up to gain another groove and PR; up this until it is possible to step left onto a slab. Finish up a short flake to a tree. Either belay here or on BB 10 feet left.

18. Moonchild 80ft E3 ★★
The classic route on the crag. Start up a steep polished groove 10 feet right of the point where the path meets the crag.
5c. Up awkwardly to a PR (bold) then rock over right to a scoop. Pull out left on superb holds to a second PR, then up right to a small tree. Climb the flake above to a bunch of saplings – finish left at a yew, AO.

19. The Moon/Loon Connection 120ft E3 ★★
A brilliant combination.
5c. Climb Moonchild to the saplings, then traverse right to a tree belay – junction with Lunatic. Finish up that route

20. Lunatic 90ft E3 ★
The upper groove is a fine contrast to the lower wall. Start below a flake some 20 feet up Great Gully.
(1) 50ft 5c. Climb to a sapling, then up the flake above to gain a ledge. Climb up to a big ledge and tree belay.
(2) 40ft 5c. Gain the superb open groove on the right which leads to the top.

21. Darth Vadar 50ft E5 ★
May the force be with you!
6a. Climb either Moonchild or Lunatic to the tree belay. Move right into the groove on Lunatic, and to the hollow flake on the right, (poor BR). Up to a small flake, step right across the obvious niche. Climb the wall

above to the break (PR), finish out right up a loose groove. A harder variation is to gain the niche from below.

22. Maboulisme Merveilleux 70ft E7 ★★★
For men only! Start 30 feet up Great Gully at a BB. Unfortunately a slow drying route.
6b. Follow the line of bolts and a thread through the huge impressive leaning wall-cum-roof, using a variety of weird contortions, to finish direct above the last bolt.

23. Dune 200ft E4 ★
A traverse of the Moonchild Buttress that gives a scary pitch for both leader and second. Start up Starshine.
(1) 40ft 5b. Climb the groove to the ledge, move right to the dead tree, Belay.
(2) 100ft 5c. Move down and dash right across the wall to good holds, BR, PR, then up and right to a rest and PR on War of the Worlds. Traverse delicately right to below the black bulge on Bleep and Booster. Step down and swing right to a good jug on Moonchild, PR. Move up right to a tree, climb the flake above to saplings. Belay on the yew out left to give some sort of protection for your poor second.
(3) 20ft 4b. Move out right to the tree belay on Lunatic.
(4) 40ft 5c. Climb the open groove on Lunatic.

24. Great Gully 60ft V Diff ●
The tapering vegetated gully that leads to a yew in a cave. AO. The best line is on the left.

25. Captain's Crack 60ft Hard Severely Grotty ●
The broken crack up the right-hand side of the gully that leads to the cave. Excitement is limited to the fight with the brambles.

26. Apollo's Exit 25ft E2
5c. The short, awkward crack through the cave roof (PR on lip). Belay well back.

27. The Route of all Evil 100ft E4 ★★★
Excellent climbing up the smooth white wall right of Great Gully. Start at a short right facing flake 20 feet left of the fallen tree that blocks the path.
6b. Up the flake then climb to the top of the shallow groove in the middle of the wall. Move left and up to a good horizontal break (TR), step right and up flakes to a second break (TR). Traverse left to a good rest, PR, and pull up right on good holds to a flake (PR, finish out right to the top, (easier to go left − CHEAT!).

28. The True Path 85ft E5 ★★★
Brilliantly brutal! A direct finish to the previous route.
6b. Up The Route of all Evil to the second break, TR. Move up and leftwards to a good NR then make wild moves on a one-finger undercut to finish up the headwall.

29. Flight Path 85ft E5 ★★★
The smeary right-hand finish to The Route of all Evil.
6c. From the TR in the second break on The Route of all Evil, move slightly rightwards, then climb straight up the headwall passing a BR.

30. **Cyborg** 100ft E2 ★
Some very good climbing in the lower half. Start as for The Route of all Evil.
(1) 70ft 5c. Up the corner to the flake, then traverse right for 20 feet to a stumpy tree in the middle of the wall. Go straight up to a small ledge and sapling then move out right, PR, across disposable holds and up to a yew tree.
(2) 30ft 5a. The rib and crack out left; brittle rock.

31. **The Omega Factor** 100ft E3
Start directly behind the fallen tree.
(1) 60ft 6a. Up awkwardly to the niche, get poked in the eye by the holly and escape left, TR, to gain a good flake then up to the tree on Cyborg. Move right, climb to an overlap and up the groove out right, finishing at a yew as Cyborg.
(2) 40ft 5c. Move right to beneath a shallow depression in the steep wall and climb this to the top.

32. **Garden of Eden** 100ft VS ●
Junglebashing: Start 30 feet right of the fallen tree, below a forested wall.
4b. Climb past a tree to a ledge at 20 feet, move across left to a crack. Bushwhack up this and struggle through bushes to a tree. Finish up fairly clean rock.

33. **The Rocinante** 90ft Hard sev
The steep right facing corner at the left-hand end of Great Buttress. Start at a short clean flake 40 feet right of the fallen tree. Now reclaimed by vegetation.
4b. Up the flake to a large yew. Move left into the corner; up this through a holly to a dead tree, then finish up the groove behind.

GREAT BUTTRESS is the next, steep buttress of clean rock, with a very undercut base.

34. **Half Life** 90ft E3
Some brittle rock and poor protection. Start as for The Rocinante.
6a. Up to the yew, climb this to gain the horizontal break. Step left and move into a wide scoop. Climb this until it steepens then traverse right to gain an open groove which leads to the top – carefully!

35. **Up Town** 80ft E3 ★
A more direct line on Half Life, with better climbing.
6a. Up Half Life to the break, step right and gain a stalagtite (TRs). Up this to a higher TR then step left and up, joining Half Life. Traverse right to the open groove and finish up this.

36. **Atomic Bong** 150ft E1 ★
A climb that improves to a fine delicate finish. Start as The Rocinante.
(1) 80ft 5a. As for Half Life to the break, traverse 25 feet right to a tree-strewn ledge, then straight up to belay in a round niche above.
(2) 40ft 5b. Traverse right for 15 feet to a flake. Up this, then tiptoe back left to a loose flake which leads to the top.

37. **Chain Reaction** 190ft E3 ★★
A superb, delicate traverse of the Great buttress which has a strenuous

finish.
(1) 70ft 5a. Up Atomic Bong to belay on the tree strewn ledge.
(2) 120ft 5c. A sustained pitch. Traverse right along the break to a flake on Wargames, step down and move across right to a runner on Android. Move delicately right and up to gain a rest and runners on the hanging flake above. Traverse strenuously past several TRs under the roof to a hanging belay at the far right end. AO.

The original route on the buttress – **Fast Breeder** – climbed the previous route to the hanging flake and then finished direct.

38. **Electric Warrior** 40ft E5 *
A short, hard route up the lower wall 30 feet right of The Rocinante.
6b. Climb the rice crispie flutings past 2BRs then step right to BB under the shattered roof.

38a. **Agent Provocateur** 30ft E6 **
6c. The continuation line of Electric Warrior, climbing directly through the bulge via a painful one-finger pocket.

39. **Cosmic Dancer** 125ft E5 **
An entertaining low traverse of Great Buttress.
(1) 80ft 6b. Start up Electric Warrior to the belay, then traverse right past TR on Wargames and reverse part of Android to a BB on La Mangoustine Scatouflange.
(2) 45ft 6a. Climb to the second BR on La Mangoustine Scatouflange and slide across right to Super Dupont. Up this to its BB then go right along the roof to TB at it's right-hand end.

40. **Wargames** 80ft E5 ***
Super climbing with a strenuous start. Start below a tiny yew 25 feet left of Android.
6b. Up to the yew and crank up past PR to TR, then move right into the hanging groove to gain a rest above (TR). Climb just right of the very shallow groove above to a good hold and NR, move out left to a corner that leads up to the roof. Just over this is a line of jugs (PR), swing right along these to a niche. Pull up to a hanging belay. AO.

41. **Stretchy Peroneum** 35ft E6 **
A dynamic direct start to Android, starting left of the tree.
6b. Climb boldly to the first bolt. Move leftwards on undercuts to gain a 'squashy' position beneath the roof, BR. Pull over this, slapping wildly, and climb the wall above to a junction with Android.

42. **Android** 95ft E4 ***
Excellent climbing once you reach the rock! Start up the ash tree at the centre of the foot of Great Buttress. Low in the grade.
5c. Climb the tree to an ancient PR. Move left along a branch to a tiny TR, then start climbing! Pull into the scoop on the left, up to a PR then step down and across left to PR. Climb the steep thin flake above until it eases – junction with Chain Reaction. Move delicately right and up to gain a rest below the hanging flake; climb this to it's top, and traverse off right to a hanging belay (this avoids the loose top wall). AO.

43. **Android Original Finish** 150ft E3 *
A poorer finish but still worthwhile.

(1)   105ft 5c.   Up Android to the junction with Chain Reaction then traverse left along the break to belay on a tree strewn ledge – part of Chain Reaction in reverse.
(2)   45ft 5b.   Move back right along the break for 15 feet, pull directly over the bulge past 2 tree stumps, up to a flake – junction with Atomic Bong, move left to another flake to finish.

44.   Perverse Pépère   85ft   E5   ★★
The direct on Android gives the best jump in the guide!
6b. Follow Android to the first PR, move up to a BR then crank up and dyno for a jug, TR. Climb delicately up to the top flake on Android, up this to belay on the right. **The Perverted Start** (80ft E5 6c ★) is a useful route if you can't stand that bloody tree! Climb the fluting 15 feet left of the start of Android to BR. Then up and right (BR) to gain Android at the PR.

45.   La Mangoustine Scatouflange   75ft   E4   ★★★
Brilliant, sustained climbing directly up the wall above the tree.
6b. Climb Android to the scoop, go up and right past a BR and make a hard move past a 2nd BR for a good hold. Pump up the fluting above, BR, to the TB at the left-hand end of the long roof.

45a.   Witherslack Flange Finish   25ft   E4   ★
A continuation finish to La Mangoustine Scatouflange that adds a little icing to the cake. E5 6b if done in a continuous run-out.
6a. From the TB on La Mangoustine, pull over the roof above and climb the wall to a BB. Exciting!

46.   Super Dupont   70ft   E5   ★★★
A hell of a route! Start at a small holly 10 feet right of Android.
6c. Climb the holly to gain a PR. A difficult sequence past 2 BRs gains a rest in the scoop. Move out left through bulges (BR) to a ledge. Climb the shallow groove above past a fourth BR to BB on Chain Reaction.

47.   Super Duper Dupont   75ft   E6   ★★★
6c. A mega route! Follow Super Dupont to the scoop then climb the exhausting right curving undercling (TR) to make a desperate lunge past BR to gain a ledge; standing on this brings an end to the difficulties, a PR and a hanging belay.

48.   Driller Killer   100ft   E5   ★★
Good climbing. Start at the right-hand end of the crag, 20 feet right of the yew.
6b. Climb directly to the TR, traverse left past a BR to a ledge behind the yew, then up left to a dubious BR. Power through the bulges above to easy ground. Either traverse left to belay or climb the rotten wall above.

49.   Videodrome   80ft   E5   ★★
Essentially a direct finish to Driller Killer.
6c. Follow Driller Killer to the first BR then move up and left to a ledge, traverse back right (BR) to small undercuts. Take 3 deep breaths, crank like a disease, and hopefully gain a flat hold and BR. Make more moves up on undercuts to enter a faint groove, BB on the left.

50.   Warm Push   25ft   E2
A short problem just right of Driller Killer.

6a. Stand on the big hold at 10 feet to gain the BR then climb the white streak to BB.

51. Cygnus X-1 215ft E2 ★
A high right to left traverse of Great Buttress. A horrible approach – walk along the base of the crag to the right-hand end, find and climb a network of yew roots on the steep ground to a second yew. Climb this tree for 10 feet until a traverse left along a painfully thorny ledge can be made to a peg and a rotting hanging rope belay.
(1) 70ft 5b. Follow the ledge left to a short corner and a tree. Move round a detached rib and reverse layback down to a traverse line at foot level, PR. An awkward move leads to a hanging belay.
(2) 70ft 5c. Go left to the top of the flake on Android and continue under a narrow roof past a hanging belay on Wargames and descend to a good footledge. Move left to a junction with Atomic Bong and reverse the traverse to belay in the niche.
(3) 50ft 5c. From the left of the ledge step down and traverse the superb horizontal break (2 old TRs) to the corner. Dead tree belay on The Rocinante.
(4) 25ft 4a. Finish up the groove above.

OTHER CLIMBS AT CHAPEL HEAD: There has been much activity in the past on the rock left of Central Gully known as **TOOL BUTTRESS** and **LOWER CRAG**. Climbing was banned on here with the access agreement; the routes have since overgrown and this area should be avoided.

HUMPHREY HEAD POINT (SD 390 740)

By Al Phizacklea

SITUATION AND CHARACTER
This crag had a reputation for being loose and horrible, but after recent activities this no longer holds true. The main wall has been transformed into an excellent climbing area by fixing bolt belays at the top of most routes thus avoiding the dangerous loose top of the crag. The rock varies from unstable blocks in some parts to the super limestone on the main wall – some of the soundest rock in the area.

Humphrey Head is a low isolated headland jutting out into Morecambe Bay, 3 miles south-east of Grange-over-Sands. It is the largest seacliff between St Bees Head and The Little Orme, but it is entirely non-tidal – this is also the place where the last wild wolf was shot in England back in the 16th century.

APPROACH
From Grange-over-Sands follow the B5277 through Allithwaite, and turn left ¼ mile past the village. After crossing the railway turn left down a track which leads to parking on the beach. It is also signposted from the square in the centre of Flookburgh.

HISTORY

The early development of the crag was largely the work of Mick Goff who, with various partners, added numerous routes during 1966-67. Al Evans visited the crag in 1976 and excavated a few new routes, all but one of which (The Decent Thing) have been reclaimed by vegetation. 1978 saw Pat McVey and Mark Danson put up the excellent Triggerfinger, a fine addition on the main crag. During the ascent, Mark was scrambling up the horrible grass slope above the route, when the block he was pulling on parted company with Mother Earth, taking him with it. Mark Plummeted the full length of the crag, but was lucky to be stopped in the branches of a friendly tree. The block, however, after destroying Ed Cleasby's sack (containing watch, Helly jacket and a new pair of Hush Puppies) went on to seek its fortune on the beach. Other routes added that year (albeit in not quite so dramatic a fashion) were Back Into The Future by Andy and Jenny Hyslop and The Left Hand Of Darkness by Danson and friends.

Iain Greenwood and Angie Widowson climbed here in January of 1981 and added the unimaginatively named January, then the crag seemed to have little to offer whilst the ethical views prevalent in Cumbria at that time remained. Al Phizacklea and Rob Knight, complete with bolt driver, paid a visit in 1984 and The Firing Squad was both the route name they used and the result of the slagging off Phizacklea received from the climbing press.

Paul Pritchard and Phil Kelly ventured up into the Blow Hole one day in 1986 with a view to looking at the aid route across its arch. Paul ended up by leading the crack above the start of the aid route, on-sight, to give The Job; a real sucker's route.

In for a penny, in for a pound; Phizacklea was back two years later, this time with John Topping, a generator and a huge drill. The primary objective was to place solid belay bolts atop the routes on the main crag, and when this admirable task was complete, Al put the drill to further use; he made first ascents of Sniffin' The Saddle and free-climbed Fusion, and then followed John up Shot By Both Sides. Paul Cornforth came over to investigate, having heard rumour of the drill whilst at Chapel Head. After accompanying the other pair on Humphrey Cushion, he borrowed the drill and proceeded to bolt the overhanging area of rock just right, which soon became Humphrey Hymen (Met A Slyman). The only route added since was Tony Brindle and Adrian Moore's free ascent of the old aid route Hammerlock in 1987.

THE CLIMBS start on the main crag which is 20 yards from the car park, and are described from LEFT to RIGHT. Leaders should be lowered from the belays back to the ground.

1. Sniffin' the Saddle   60ft E2   *
Start below a short left facing corner 10 feet left of Triggerfinger. An excellent finish.
6a. Move into the corner, swing right, PR, to easier ground which leads to a large ledge. Step left to gain a good flake, (BR), sharp pockets

enable a good hold to be reached (BR), move up to BB.

2. Fusion 50ft E3
The snaking crack above the start of Sniffin' The Saddle. Gear is good but strenuous to place.
6a. Up Sniffin' to the ledge, climb the fine crack above to BB.

3. Girdle Traverse 130ftE1
(1) 35ft 5b. As Sniffin' to the ledge.
(2) 60ft 5a. Traverse right crossing the Main Wall to a chimney bearing a fierce thorn bush: fight past this to belay on the loose pinnacle.
(3) 35ft. Move right and climb loose rock to the top.
(3a) 35ft. **The Fertility Variation**. Climb the steep wall above the belay with 2 PA and loose rock to safe ground above.

4. Triggerfinger 60ft E2   **
A very good climb up the centre of the Main Wall; a bit necky at the top. Start at a shallow scoop behind the ash which grows nearest the crag.
5c. From the scoop, swing round right to gain a small ledge (stalagtite above), move left to a PR below the little overlap and gain the ledge above by a tricky move. Climb up to a PR, then take the upper wall direct to the BB by leaps and bounds.

5. Shot by Both Sides 60ft E3   ***
A superb, well sustained climb, start up Triggerfinger.
6b. Up Triggerfinger to the stalagtite, pull directly over the roof (BR) and straight up to a PR below the overlap. Grab the flake in the middle of the upper wall and make a fingery move left for the last obvious pocket on Triggerfinger, just below the BB.

6. The Firing Squad 60ft E4   ***
A hard start and a bold finish up the curving crack high on the wall; brill!
6b. Up Triggerfinger to the stalagtite, step right on undercuts to 2 BRs. Crank up on tiny pockets to gain a jug. Easier climbing above leads to a shallow crack; pump up this to the top, BB..

7. Hammerlock 80ft E4   †
5c. The awesomely-loose left-trending grooveline is probably best left well alone.

8. Virility 80ft E1   *
Start at an obvious right-slanting gangway that leads to a niche.
5b. Cross the gangway to gain a sloping ledge below a hanging corner, BR. Step right around the arête and boldly climb the loose wall above to a BB out on the right.

9. Humphrey Cushion 60ft E2
A direct start to Virility – start directly below the hanging corner.
5c. Climb directly up the front of a pinnacle, pull into a scoop (PR) then swing left to good holds (PR). Move up to join Virility at the sloping ledge.

10. **Humphrey Hymen (Met a Sly Man)**   60ft   E5   ***
Climbs the steep grey wall just right of Humphrey Cushion.
6b. Up easily to a PR. Climb a tiny pillar and the steep wall above and
finish up the right-hand side of the vertical 'slab' to a BB. Three BRs
and strained tendons en route.

11. **Noda**   100ft   E1
A loose and vegetated climb, rather serious. Start below an oval niche
on the right end of the wall.
5a. Climb to a niche, move left using a hollow flake, then up and right
into a short groove. Follow the crack above to a loose finish by a small
bush. Cry for help or finish up loose rock. **Variation Start**: the ramp on
the left, below the gangway of Virility leads to above the niche.

12. **Sunflake**   50ft   Hard VS
Start behind the large ash tree at the right end of the buttress.
5a. Climb the wall to the obvious wide flake, up this to the top. Abseil
from something solid — if you can find it!

The shallow depression high on the hillside 40 yards right of the main
crag has been climbed on aid. The next route starts at the back of a
prominent archway 150 yards right of Main Wall. A path leads through
the arch.

13. **Back into the Future**   80ft   A2   *
A fun route. Start at the base of the hole, gain the crack on the left side
(looking out) and follow this right under the arch (many pegs and nuts)
to finish at the top with a few free moves.

14. **The Job**   25ft   E1   †
5c. The crack above the start of Back into the Future; a real sucker's
route!

15. **January**   100ft   Hard VS   **
A fingery route on good rock. Start below a right facing corner on the
buttress right of Back Into The Future.
5a. Climb the corner to a ledge then finish up the bubbly wall above
(TRs) to belay at a little outcrop above.

To the left of the Main Wall is a wide descent gully. The next route lies
just left of this near the top of the path.

16. **The Decent Thing**   40ft   Hard Sev
4a. The clean swathe that cuts up the vegetated slab. A pleasant pitch.

To the left of this route were two old routes (**Earthworm** and **Roobarb's
Corner**) which have been totally lost to vegetation. The next route lies
on an isolated buttress 150 yards left from the top of the descent route.
It is best reached from the top of the hill by scrambling down to a
brambly ledge; a machette being useful.

17. **The Left Hand of Darkness**   30ft   Hard VS
5a. Climb the prominent flake exiting left with difficulty. Thread belay
30 feet back.

There is an excellent traversing wall at the very far end of the point,
above a sloping rock platform. A sustained 6a problem.

MEATHOP QUARRY (SD 433 798)

SITUATION AND CHARACTER
The quarry has a stepped appearance due to short, steep walls separated by grassy ledges. It has some loose rock and is unpopular with local climbers.

APPROACH
To reach the quarry from the A590, drive to Meathop village, turn right, then follow this road past the hospital and park just below the obvious broken crag before the railway line. Then follow a track round to the right into the quarry,

HISTORY
Many of the routes here were climbed by Charlie Vigano, though Fat Jen and Plane Jane were named affectionately by Andy Hyslop. A couple of routes have been claimed since though lack of decent descriptions does not allow them to be located (e.g. Xanadu), but on the whole Meathop is a neglected crag with only a handful of dedicated visitors.

THE ROUTES are described from LEFT to RIGHT.

1. **Prow Face** 40ft V Diff
Takes a diagonal line from left to right across the front of the prow.

2. **Fat Jen** 50ft V Diff
Start at a detached block right of the obvious prow (The Rostrum). Follow a corner for 10 feet, then move right onto the arête and up this to the top. Various other finishes are available.

3. **Boo Boo** 90ft Diff
Start 20 feet up the descent route on the right, at a ledge and belay. Climb diagonally left over stepped rock to a tree, then up diagonally right to the top (loose).

4. **Sandwich Rib** 90ft V Diff
A direct line up the wall on the right, keeping just left of a cracked arête.

5. **Original Route** 90ft V Diff
The corner just right of Sandwich Rib. Once the recess has been gained either move left to Sandwich Rib via a projecting block on the arête, or finish direct (loose).

6. **Pedestal Route** 90ft Sev
Above and to the right of the descent route is an obvious large block with a small tree growing from its top. Gain the top of the block with difficulty to finish up broken rock.

7. **Plane Jane** 90ft Sev
Start in the centre of the bay at an obvious crack, and climb this to a ledge, then follow the blaster's groove to more ledges. Climb the steep wall for 20 feet, then easier but loose rock leads to the top.

8. **Blunt and Sharp** 80ft V Diff
The obvious arête to the right.

9. Anji's Rib 100ft Hard Sev

4a. Start as for Blunt and Sharp. Climb just left of the arête, then move right and up to a ledge on the left, and continue to a mantel onto a large ledge below a fractured arête. Step left and climb diagonally on ledges, then finish up a loose groove.

10. Synthetic Hesitations 80ft Sev

Start 30 feet right of Plane Jane and climb an easy wall to a large ledge. Then climb the obvious corner to easy ground.

11. The Barrow Line 80ft Sev

Climb the wall 40 feet left of the ruin, direct to a tree.

12. Saucy Sue 80ft Sev

Follows the cracked wall above the old ruin.

13. Loco 100ft VS

4b. Start in the next section of the quarry, 100 feet right of the ruin, at the back of a recess. Up ledges to a larger ledge and a small tree, then climb the wall and a short groove on the right to a small ledge. Move back left and over a small bulge to finish by a damson tree.

14. Arnside 90ft Hard Sev

Start at a pile of boulders 100 feet diagonally right of the ruined hut, just left of a small tree.
(1) 50ft 4a. Climb directly up to a belay.
(2) 40ft. Move right and finish as for Aperitiff.

15. Aperitiff 120ft V Diff

Start about 30 feet right, at a ramp which leads to three trees at 30 feet.
(1) 60ft Follow the ramp to the highest tree.
(2) 60ft. Move left and follow the obvious line to the top.

16. Estuary Wall 80ft Sev

Start at a white rib below the three trees.
(1) 30ft. Ascend the rib to a tree belay.
(2) 50ft. The open corner to a ledge, then left round the arête and up to the top.

17. Spring Tide 90ft Sev

Start as Estuary Wall, but follow slabby rock on the right to a ledge, then go right across a steep wall and finish past a small tree.

18. The Bore 90ft Hard VS

5a. Start at a cairn 30 feet right of Aperitiff. Ascend the steep wall, then diagonally right to a ledge. Finish up a steep wall to the right of a niche which contains a finger of rock.

19. Heatwave 120ft Sev

Start on the right at a large scoop.
(1) 40ft. Climb up and right to a good tree, then over a bulge to a belay.
(2) 80ft. Traverse left for 25 feet, then step up and climb diagonally up a steep wall to a good tree. Traverse right, then finish straight up.

20. Prickly 90ft V Diff

At the end of this section is a cracked rib.
(1) 70ft. Climb towards the rib, then left along a ledge to jungle.
(2) 20ft. Finish via a clean rib of rock.

On the beach across the railway line is a pleasant bouldering wall. Other routes have been recorded in the quarry (e.g. Xanadu), but descriptions were too sparse to allow them to be located.

MILLSIDE SCAR (SD 451 845)

By Al Phizacklea

SITUATION AND CHARACTER
The first impression from the road belies the fact that the crag is 70 feet high and is very steep in places. It has solid rock once the loose choss has been removed.

APPROACH
This small outcrop is situated high above the hamlet of Millside on the south-west corner of the Whitbarrow escarpment. From the A590 drive into the hamlet and after a couple of hundred yards turn right up a steep 'no through road' and park in a clearing after 300 yards. From here a footpath leads up through the woods, and at a clearing a second path swings back left to the crag.

HISTORY
Les Ainsworth and Dave Cronshaw opened the door to the crag, climbing Pioneers' Cave (a good place for a dump) in 1972 after a fruitless day on nearby White Scar. Two years later Al Evans put up the partly-aided Pathfinder with Dave Parker.

It wasn't until 1982 that the crag received any further interest, when Ed Cleasby and Al Phizacklea climbed Cadillac Cruiser. This name was later shortened to Cadillac after Ed realized he hadn't 'cruised' the route; in fact he had taken a spectacular 40-foot dive off it whilst attempting the route on-sight! In the same year Iain Greenwood soloed two new routes on the upper crag, Fossil Groove and Fossil Crack then in 1983 Ian Conway and D. Baker put up Enter The Neutron, the only route added that year.

To complete the crag's history, the famous Paul Ingham and the slightly famous Pete Botterill (who had made the first free ascent of Pathfinder with Steve Howe earlier in the year) climbed the steep and unrelenting piece of rock right of Cadillac to give Countach, the hardest route on the crag to date.

MAIN CRAG

1. **Pioneers' Cave** 65ft Sev
Start at the right side of the crag at a cave. Deserves a black spot after 30 feet;
(1) 35ft. Climb the cave, then move right to the start of the crag. Up to a ledge (Useful tree to abseil from).
(2) 30ft. (Don't bother with) the continuation gully!

2. **Countach** 75ft E5 **

A very strenuous route up the hanging scoop right of Cadillac.

6b. Climb the wall just right of the flake of Cadillac to the ledge. Follow the thin crack through the bulge to where you can step right to a hole (PR). Pull up left over the bulge to gain better holds and a resting place before tackling the steep flake in the scoop above. This moves right before pulling out left to finish.

3. **Cadillac** 80ft E4 **

Superb, sustained climbing up the white hanging groove 30 feet left of Pioneer's Cave.

6a. Climb the flake to a ledge. Climb up and left to a smaller ledge then move up and right to a bulge, PR. Move round this and climb the steep wall to an overhang. Get your nuts in (!) and make an awkward move right into the fine hanging groove which leads to the top.

4. **Pathfinder** 60ft E2

Thirty feet left of Cadillac is a clean groove high on the crag. Start below this.

5c. Climb a short wall to a brambly ledge (PR). Cross the gnarly wall to gain the groove; follow this to its top before finishing out right.

5. **Enter the Neutron** 90ft E1

Forty feet left of Pathfinder is a clean groove which starts halfway up the face, start 25 feet left of this, at an ash.

5b. Climb the wall left of the ash until overhanging rock bars the way. Traverse diagonally up and right to a good runner, go down and round the bulge then continue traversing to the foot of the groove. Climb this groove, exiting right at the top and then climb the wall above bearing left to a small holly.

UPPER TIER

This lies above and right of the Main Crag, and it is reached by scrambling from the path, or by the first pitch of Pioneer's Cave.

6. **Fossil Groove** 30ft E1

Start roughly in the centre of the wall.

5b. Climb a short wall to a little yew, pull onto the slab above then step right into a fine flake groove to finish.

7. **Fossil Crack** 40ft E2

5c. Climb directly up to the hanging crack 15 feet right of Enter The Neutron. Climb the flake above using a large doubtful block en-route – gently!

RAVEN LODGE CRAG (SD 463 856)

By Al Phizacklea

SITUATION AND CHARACTER

This is the small limestone crag (shrouded in trees) that lies 300 yards right of White Scar, on private land, and is somewhat dwarfed by its big brother. The pleasures of loose rock and jungle vines indicate an exciting time is to be had. The main attraction, however, is being constantly thrown off by the landowner!

APPROACH AND ACCESS
Leave the A590 as if approaching White Scar, but turn right just after the farm (before entering the quarry proper). Follow the track for about 50 yards to a lay-by on the left. The crag lies ahead on the left.

1. **Cryptic Cripple Club**   35ft   E3   *
6a. Start at the right side of the main cliff. Climb a wall, BR, and move left into a short groove, TR. Up this to B and PB, AO.

2. **Dry Grin**   35ft   E5   **
6b. Start 12 feet left of Cryptic Cripple Club; climb direct up the wall passing 2 BRs to the belay of the same, AO.

3. **Wodwo**   55ft   E5   *
6b. Start 15 feet left of Dry Grin and climb a blind flake to its end. Move left to the central groove and climb it, PR. Continue in the same line and make a hard move over the bulge (BR) to jugs. Continue to a large tree.

4. **Cain**   70ft   E4   *
6b. Start 50 feet left of Wodwo, beneath a pocket with a tiny pine, right of a small holly. Climb up to the second of 2 BRs, move right for 8 feet and climb a clean wall to a BB, AO.

5. **Cain Direct**   65ft   E5   *
6b. From the second BR of Cain, climb direct over a bulge (BR) to a PB, AO.

SCOUT SCAR (SD 486 915)

By Al Phizacklea

SITUATION AND CHARACTER
Scout Scar is the limestone escarpment 2½ miles west of Kendal, which has been known improperly as Underbarrow Scar in previous editions of the guide. The rock is fairly sound with little seepage, it is quite sheltered and provides excellent training for 'the pump'.

APPROACH
To reach Scout Scar from Kendal follow the Underbarrow road to a car park near the police radio mast on top of the hill. Cross the road to a gate and follow the scar until you are 300 yards past the mushroom-topped shelter. From here a rough path down a rake leads under the scar to the foot of the crag.

HISTORY
The crag saw its first action way back in the last century, by a local horseman called Hodgson. The story goes that he was riding back from the pub in Brigsteer (obviously drunk), when his horse committed Hari-Kari and leapt off the summit, taking poor Hodgson with him; the crag is known locally as 'Hodgson's Loupe'.

Development didn't really catch on in this mode and it wasn't until the late 1970's that the Kendal Mountaineering Club started to climb here. Bill Birkett and Iain Greenwood put up a few routes around this time; Cliff Brown was responsible for Cliff's Route, whilst Derek Jewell, Ed Cleasby and Mike Lynch added Born Free in 1975. Then the next cherry seemed to be the free-climbing of the old aid route Ivy League. Numerous parties attempted the ascent, and aid was whittled down to one point. Then Tom Walkington stepped in and cleaned up this last stubborn remainder, re-naming the route Cro-Magnon Man in the process, though local opinion suggested that the elimination of a single point of aid did not warrant the name change and it stands to this day as Ivy League.

In 1985 Paul Carling and Mark Glaister began a new wave of activity by climbing First Blood and then Jim Bird and Dave Seddon began to get acquainted with the crag, adding such routes as Born To Run, right of Born Free. 1986 saw the crag transformed, mainly by Bird; he speckled it with shiny bolts and decorated it with red, white and blue streamers (no doubt in preparation for a visit by royalty). Jim linked the lines of bolts, producing a vast crop of routes such as Sylvester Strange, A Fistful of Steroids, Crimes of Passion, Spectral Wizard and Poetry in Commotion. Dave Seddon joined in the fun and with a better ethical standpoint put up Beers for Fears and Grave New World.

Carling returned to the crag with Glaister and went away again having made the first ascent of Telegraph Road and then Tony Mitchell (complete with nice hairstyle specially for the occasion) decided to give Bird a little help in decorating the crag; Jim was obviously working just too hard and Tony's Vision Of Things Gone Wild took Jim's developments into the next dimension, being an extension of one of his earlier routes, Local Motion. Nick Conway climbed the arête left of Kathleen (the first ascent of which by Peter Short and Alan Towse made everyone sit up and think about just what gaps were left here) with two bolts; a real heart-stopper called Kathleen's Nightmare because that's what it feels like – a bad dream! Nick returned later to make a solo ascent of Bird's Spectral Wizard and put up Bar Six, an eliminate between that route and Ivy League.

On the nearby Barrowfield Buttress, Glen Sutcliffe and Paul Carling put up the well-named Crumblefoot, while Blue Screw was the work of Carling with Stew Wilson in tow. The ubiquitous Mark Liptrot then took the trouble to tramp the short distance to the buttress and made an ascent of the obvious open and heinous-looking central groove; Toirdealbach.

Bird was still busy, beavering away at the overhangs left of First Blood, which in some style and pattern became 9½ Weeks. Unfortunately the expected royal visit never happened, and Jim went home, content that his decorations were left for everyone to see and enjoy.

THE ROUTES are described from LEFT to RIGHT.

1. **Scarfoot Chimney** 50ft Diff
The obvious chimney on the left of the buttress.

The next route starts by a flake at the foot of the centre of the undercut buttress.

2. 9½ Weeks 40ft E5
6c. Attack the overhangs just left of First Blood (BRs) to gain entry to a flake-cum-groove, and finish up this.

3. First Blood 45ft E4
6b. A strenuous and gymnastic start; climb over the roof past a thin crack to a good hold, then continue up the wall to a convenient tree, passing some tied off PRs.

4. Sylvester Strange 40ft E5   ★ †
A very hard problem marked by several bolts.
6c. Power up past (or pull on!) the bolts to where it eases.

5. Telegraph Road 50ft E3   ★
Start 10 feet left of the gully of Red Rock Gully.
6b. Climb the steep groove past PR and TR to gain the easier upper wall and tree belay, AO.

Just right of this buttress is a deep, tree-filled gully with a yew tree at 35 feet, which provides the start for the next five routes.

6. Grimlin Groove 45ft Moderate
The obvious grassy left slanting break from the tree.

7. Arête Finish 40ft V Diff
The pleasant rib above the tree.

8. Red Rock Gully 60ft Severe
From the tree move right into the main gully and ascend this over several bulges.

9. Cliff's Route 100ft VS   ★
4c. Up the gully for a few feet to a clean layback crack, then climb this to reach a steep groove. Climb the right arête of the groove to gain an easy-angled slab, then cross this to the right to gain the top.

10. Brain Salad Surgery 85ft VS
4a. Start 10 feet right of the gully and climb to a tree stump below an obvious groove, then up this to finish up the top wall.

11. Born Free 105ft Hard VS   ★
A fine clean route. Start at a sound grey wall, now flecked with threads, below a mini 'Tower Of Babel'.
5b. Climb the wall right of a tiny overhang to TR. Trend left up a vague groove and then traverse right to the prominent crack on the left of the tower, which is followed to the top.

12. Born to Run 50ft E3
Only independent of Born Free if you strictly avoid using it's holds.
6a. Start at the left end of the shallow roof; pull out of this on pockets to TR, up left to PR then climb up and right past TR to the foot of the corner of Born Free. Finish up that route or abseil off the PR. **Variation**: Start up Born Free to the TR then step right into Born To Run; E2 5c.

13. A Fistfull of Steroids 100ft E3   ★
A steep start leads to an airy finish, start 10 feet right of Born Free.

6a. Climb directly over the roof, 2 TRs and PR, to a tree on a ledge. Climb left to PR on Born To Run and move up to the obvious corner crack (PRs). Up the corner a few feet then step right onto the front face of the pillar and climb this direct (avoiding loose rock out right) to a fine, sparsely protected finish.

14. **Beers for Fears** 60ft E4   ★
An awkward, strenuous route at the left end of a clean white wall.
6b. Climb through bulges to BR then up to TR. Climb the wall above towards a sapling and BR on left, then up to BB, AO.

15. **Crimes of Passion** 60ft E4
More pumpy climbing up the centre of the wall, which lacks a natural line.
6a. Climb past a BR to a jug, up left past another BR to gain flat hold above (BR), then up to BB.

16. **Grave New World** 60ft E4
Start at a very vague groove just left of the rib. Good climbing.
6b. Climb up to TR then up the wall above past a BR to a poor PR. Pull rightwards through the bulge to PB, AO.

17. **Kathleen's Nightmare** 60ft E5   †
Was the dream about the finish? Start at the toe of the rib.
6b. Climb the arête direct past PR and BR to finish up the loose groove above to belay.

18. **Kathleen** 50ft E2
Start below the much pruned corner.
6b. Awkwardly past the cave to gain the stumps, move out right to gain a porthole then finish at a tree above. AO. Usually wet.

19. **Spectral Wizard** 60ft E4   ★
Good gymnastic climbing. Start 10 feet right of Kathleen.
6b. Pull over the roof to an obvious hold then crank up left past 2 BRs to the porthole on Kathleen; finish at the tree above.

20. **Bar Six** 75ft E5
6b. Climb the wall between Spectral Wizard and Ivy League, to finish up the pillar right of the latter.

21. **Ivy League** 85ft E4   ★
Sustained climbing above the shallow cave.
6b. Climb up the obvious pockets (threads) then climb up to and over a small overhang above to gain a small corner – go to jail, do not pass go if you use the tree – up the corner for 15 feet then finish out left at a tree.

22. **A Vision of Things Gone Wild** 70ft E5   ★
Pumpy or what! Start just right of Ivy League.
6b. Climb a shallow black groove past 2BRs to a BB (The Half-Way Station). Pass this just right , then up to the small roof and PR. Pull over this and claw your way up the wall above to a tree on left. Variation: **Local Motion** (E4 6b) Up to the 1st BB.

23. **Idle Times** 60ft E4
6b. Climb the groove right of A Vision of Things Gone Wild over the bulge (TR, PR) to gain a small corner. Climb this to finish up the wall

on right to PB. AO.

24. Broken Zipper 90ft Hard Sev
4a. Climb the big right facing corner 10 yds right of Ivy League past a tree to the top — rather loose in places.

25. Steppin' Out 80ft E2
5c. Start up Broken Zipper and climb the yellow wall below the corner to a loose pinnacle. Step left and traverse left until it is possible to rattle up the steep, loose wall above on temporary holds.

26. Cross of Lorraine 140ft VS
4b. Start 10 feet right of Broken Zipper and climb the wall to a tree. Then climb the shallow groove above for 25 feet to an overhang, traverse right for 20 feet, then climb direct to the top (some loose rock). It is possible to climb directly above the overhang.

27. Poetry in Commotion 50ft E4   *
Very thin climbing directly behind the fallen tree just left of Icicle.
6c. Climb the grey wall direct to a BR, move out right to an overlap and PR. Follow this to a sapling, then up to BB above; abseil off.

28. Icicle 50ft Hard VS
5b. Climb the obvious groove just right of the fallen tree, passing a tree 10 feet below the top; better than it looks.

The next two routes start about 30 yards right of Icicle, at the second yew tree:

29. Pits Stop 30ft V Diff
Left of the yew is a wide, open groove; climb this pleasantly, exiting left at the top.

30. The Rocky Horror Show 30ft Hard Very Death!   ●
Right of the yew is a broken wall with a gnarled yew stump at 10 feet. Climb up right of this, (hopefully), to the top.

BARROWFIELD BUTTRESS (SD 487 908)

Five minutes walk south of Scout Scar is a crag directly above the farm. The descent is to the south of the crag, which is fast drying on the main wall. THE CLIMBS here are described from RIGHT to LEFT.

31. Crumblefoot 60ft E2
5c. Climb the right-hand side of the wall (bold) to an area of broken rock. Go up steeply past 2PRs to the top.

32. Blue Screw 60ft E4   *
6b. A fine, sound route. Climb the centre of the wall to the stacked PR, move left to BR, then straight up to a spike. Finish off slightly right .

33. Toirdealbach 60ft E3   †
5c. The obvious large overhung scoop/corner on the left, direct.

WHITESTONE CRAG (SD 397 849)

By Les Ainsworth

SITUATION AND CHARACTER

Whitestones is a small but pleasant crag, which is situated about 1½ miles southeast of Newby Bridge just above the A59. It can be reached in less than ten minutes walk, by taking a direct line from the lay-by which is about 300 yards on the Kendal side of the road which is signed 'Cartmel 4'.

The main crag is bounded on its left by a long broken ridge **Long Ridge** which gives many pleasant variations at around Diff. If the ridge is followed in its entirety, it gives the longest vertical route in the guide. The next routes start about halfway up this ridge, 20 feet left of two trees which grow from large broken rocks at the foot of the crag.

1. **Two Overhang Route** 55ft Hard Sev   *
4a. Climb the short, easy, right-slanting groove to the first overhang, then follow a flake crack leftwards to a large landing. Step right from this onto the slab above the first overhang, and continue right to a shallow groove. Up this to a small ledge, then follow the leftward-leading break to the arête, and finish up this.

2. **Cartmel Groove** 45ft VS
4b. From the top of the initial groove of Two Overhang Route, continue over the overlap with difficulty and then follow the continuation groove past the small ledge on Two Overhang Route, until it is possible to step left onto the arête at the top.

3. **Elk** 50ft V Diff
Above the left side of the broken rocks is a flat ledge at 10 feet. The climb takes a direct line up the wall from this ledge.

The crag now becomes a little broken, but to the right of the two trees it starts again with:

4. **Stag** 85ft Sev
(1) 40ft. Climb the obvious, short, awkward corner at the left of the wall to a tree, then continue for a few feet over grassy ledges to a spike belay below an obvious groove.
(2) 45ft. Just right of the belay is a bulging wall, which is split by two cracks. Climb this wall using the cracks to reach a slab, then continue easily to the top.

5. **Missing Words** 80ft Hard VS   *
5b. Start 3 feet right, and climb direct past two ledges to two small blocks below a short, blunt arête. Up this to the break, then ascend the overhang above on its left. Continue on pockets to the top, with an interesting move over the next overhang.

To the right the crag is dominated by a obvious overlap which splits the wall.

6. The V 80ft VS _____ *
4c. Below the right side of the overlap is a large block. Climb round the left side of this to reach the overlap, then move left for about 8 feet to a smaller block below a deep V-groove in the overlap. Ascend this on good holds to reach the slab, then finish up the wide crack above.

7. Direct Route 80ft Hard Sev
4a Follow The V to the overlap, then step up right onto the large block, and pull onto the slab above using two small grooves. Finish more easily up the slab above.

8. Jess 120ft Severe
Should get easier with traffic.
(1) 75ft. Climb Chimney Route for 15 feet then traverse left below the overlap and continue to the block below the roof of The V. Swing round this block, then continue to the blunt arête and cross a grassy bay to reach the spike belay on Stag.
(2) 45ft. Climb the obvious groove passing an awkward bulge at half height.

9. High-level Girdle 95ft Severe
Follow Chimney Route onto the slab then continue horizontally left until a rising line of small holds can be followed to reach Missing Words. Step down a little and continue past Stag to the groove on its left. Step across this, then climb diagonally left for a few feet to finish.

10. Chimney Route 85ft V Diff
Climb up to a cave in the obvious chimney, then step left onto the slab and back right into the chimney. Continue for a few feet, then either finish up the chimney, or more pleasantly up the slab on the left.

11. Wild Winds 80ft Hard VS
4c. Climbs the sharp arête right of the chimney. Follow Chimney Route to just below the chockstone above the cave, step right, then climb the arête on its right side. Easier than it might appear.

12. Moose 85ft Hard Sev _____ **
4b. An excellent route, with a bold top half. Climb the block which forms the right side of the cave on Chimney Route, to the overlap, then make an awkward step right onto the nose and finish up the steep wall.

13. Cracked Wall 75ft Hard Sev
4a. The aptly-named wall on the right. Climb to a bush just below the nose of Moose, then step up and move right up the wall. A better finish is up the groove on the left (4b).

14. Easy Chimney 45ft Diff
Start 5 feet left of the obvious Rowan tree which grows from a split block at the right side of the crag. Climb the left wall of the obvious groove, then finish right up the groove above.

15. Ridge 50ft V Diff
Climb the ridge directly behind the Rowan tree to a ledge with a small tree on it. Step right and up, then regain the ridge and follow it to the

WHITE SCAR (SD 459 853)

By Al Phizacklea, Dave Cronshaw and Phil Kelly

SITUATION AND CHARACTER

This is it, the utopia for the masochist – White Scar – the most difficult inland crag to get to in England. Known locally as 'Indian Country', this blatantly extrovert crag lies at the southern end of the Whitbarrow escarpment and scowls down at the A590 as it passes 1 mile west of Gilpin Bridge.

At the base of the crag is a horrendous slope of loose quarried scree, and several tiers of shattered rock separated by steep grass slopes prevent safe access to the top. The climbing varies from some exciting routes to some way heinous ones, and it gives a spooky and intimidating atmosphere. The day's excitement commences with an abseil that promises a greater bombardment than the Eiger while you fight off the man-eating brambles at the foot of the route. Retreat, you may notice, is highly problematical and rescue is just about out of the question. This is not the place for the wimp, but a playground for the lunatic fringe of our sport – or a Whirly Wheel Stunt! Things aren't quite as bad on Space Buttress which is provided with an abseil post at the top.

APPROACH

From the A590, follow a track which leads through a farmyard and into the quarry at the base of the crag. Drive carefully up the limestone slab (honest) to its top and park on the verge. Walk to the fringes of the forest where an ill-defined path branches off right and up the hillside. From the crest of the hill, follow paths rightwards, over hill and dale to eventually reach the top of the crag. You will have noticed by now that there is no way whatsoever of knowing where you are in relation to the routes, though help is at hand for the Space Buttress routes; a marker post points the way down to a belay stake. Finding the belay stake is hard enough, but a diagonal abseil from a tree on the top of the scarp should land on a flat grass area containing the belay stake and a tropical plant.

HISTORY

Many brave men have visited White Scar in the past, even before quarrying ceased. Al Atkinson, amongst others, is reputed to have paid a short visit in the mid-50's, and to have climbed directly up the scree slope (which was still being quarried at the time!) to gain the base of the crag proper, and then climbed a route somewhere in the vicinity of The Turin Shroud utilizing a couple of pegs for aid. He made this ascent totally on-sight and has never returned to the crag; claiming a shiver goes down his spine every time the crag is mentioned. Chris Bonnington is also rumoured to have put in a brief appearance as are an unknown pair of climbers from Vickers, who made aided ascents of Aqualung, Book of Invasions and much of Air City.

The first free routes were added by Dave Cronshaw and Les Ainsworth, hungry for adventure, when they put up Stride Pinnacle. The same pair returned a few years later and after numerous abortive attempts to gain the base of the crag via the scree slope, they finally made it, only to discover that the only means of escape was by climbing Puppy Dog Pie, the name of which reflects perfectly the non-quality of the climbing involved. Some time later Cronshaw and Ainsworth enticed some friends along and together they attempted to fix a cable along the top of the scree, to make life a little easier. Part of the cable was fixed on the Saturday, and the friends retreated. The following day they came back to complete the task, only to discover that the majority of the scree slope had avalanched overnight, taking the cable with it! Thus, development ceased for a few years until Cronshaw introduced Dave Knighton to the crag on Boxing Day 1978 when together they made the first free ascent of Aqualung.

Encouraged by this significant breakthrough, they then launched a full-frontal attack on the centrepiece of the crag, the majestic and forbidding Space Buttress. Knighton took the lead for most of the routes on Space Buttress, and in July of 1979 he made a free ascent of Book of Invasions, though retaining one point of aid to gain entry into the exit groove. A couple of months later Knighton was back with Angie Widowson to attempt a line up the smooth wall left of Book of Invasions. They only managed to complete the first pitch however, so Knighton dragged Cronshaw back screaming the following month to complete The Prometheus Crisis, which finished up the same groove as Book of Invasions and used the same point of aid. The two Daves then swung leads on T.M.A. (Tycho Magnetic Anomaly); the easiest route up Space Buttress.

Attention now changed to the Left Wing, which seemed to suit Cronshaw's style of climbing more, and so he took the lead to produce The Turin Shroud in December of 1981, which was completed in a huge blizzard, Knighton having completed Torn Curtain and The Malacia Tapestry the previous year.

Interest waned once again, only for Ed Cleasby to eradicate the mutual point of aid from The Prometheus Crisis and Book of Invasions in 1982 whilst making the second ascent of the former. Cleasby found that the aid move was in fact easier than the crux of Book of Invasions, twenty feet lower, though in a more terrifying position. The crag saw no more attention until 1987 when numerous climbers expressed an interest in developing the steep virgin walls that remained. Adrian Moore and Tony Brindle were first off the mark in November, with a long-awaited girdle traverse of Space Buttress, though the product of their efforts (Wombling Way) unfortunately ignored half a mile of rock!

Phil Kelly took the initiative and bolted the wall left of The Book of Invasions' first pitch, and attempted it over many days during 1987 though without much success. The following February Kelly relinquished all responsibility for the route and visited the crag with Dave Kenyon and Mr. Perfect – Mick Lovatt. This pair soon succeeded on the line: they both led the first pitch and Lovatt climbed a line of bolts through the bulges in the headwall to finish, offering the name Introducing The Hardline; perhaps heralding a new era of development in the crag's history.

THE ROUTES are described from LEFT to RIGHT as one faces the crag from the quarry floor.

1. **Stride Pinnacle** 230ft VS

The route takes the left side of a large pinnacle on the left of the main amphitheatre of the crag, which is almost directly below a tree which overhangs the crag. Approach by an abseil over this tree (N.B. it may be preferable to tie to a tree further back; and a sling placed round the tree at this time may later prove useful to regain terra firma). There is a large tree belay 20ft left of the foot of the route. A potential route for a black spot!

(1) 110ft 4b. Climb a short wall which leads to the deep crack which forms the left side of the pinnacle, and then climb this to a belay at the saddle.

(2) 40ft 4a. Step onto the wall behind on the left, then follow the obvious right slanting weakness to a tree.

(3) 80ft. Climb steep grass to a short friable rock band just below the top. Although this can be climbed it is very unstable and it is recommended that a sling on the tree at the top is used (if you forgot to place it earlier, then panic).

LEFT WING

The next 3 climbs are located on the left wing of the main amphitheatre.

2. **Torn Curtain** 90ft Hard VS

Approach: From the central tree of 3 which grow at the top of the crag, make a 250-foot 'hit or miss' abseil on joined ropes to hopefully arrive at the base of the route (NB). A good line.

5b. Climb delicately to the ledge, then pull over an overhang into the long flake which is followed strenuously to the top.

The next route climbs intricately up the centre of the Left Wing.

3. **The Malacia Tapestry** 170ft E2

Approach: Abseil down as for Aqualung and traverse left (as far as Turin Shroud) along a dodgy path for 100 feet. Belay at the left hand end of the obvious terrace.

(1) 40ft 5b. Move left and climb the groove over a bulge to a small stance (NB).

(2) 80ft 5c. Traverse easily right to a perched block at the foot of a steep wall. Climb this on small holds, then trend right to below an overhang. Pull round (PR on left) to a superb jug, then move right (crux) to a 'porthole'. Climb up to a horizontal break and hand-traverse left (PR – hard to clip) to a ledge around the arête. Large NB.

(3) 50ft 5c. Step right and climb a short wall to the top.

4. **The Turin Shroud** 120ft Hard VS

Approach: Descend by abseil as for Aqualung, then traverse 70 feet left along the obvious path, to a right-facing groove. Fairly overgrown.

(1) 80ft 4c. Climb the groove/corner to a small ledge below an arched overhang (situ PB).

(2) 40ft 4c. Climb the crack to the overhang and traverse right a few

WHITE SCAR Space Buttress

feet, then pull over onto a short headwall. Belay to a tree further back.

SPACE BUTTRESS
The next route takes the obvious large chimney/groove left of Space Buttress.

5. **Aqualung** 100ft VS *
Approach: Abseil down the route from a belay stake. A short route that's big on atmosphere!
4c. Climb the chimney on good holds to the cave (possible belay). Traverse right across the wall to instant exposure and move round the lip of the roof to finish easily.

6. **Wombling Way** 270ft XS †
A traverse of Space Buttress. Start 20 feet above the start of Aqualung. Thread belay.
(1) 95ft. Traverse rightwards on a vague line which apparently soon becomes obvious, and continue to the tree belay on The Book of Invasions.
(2) 25ft. Continue rightwards as for T.M.A. to a good stance and PB on the arête.
(3) 150ft. Climb to the top of the shattered pillar and escape diagonally rightwards.

7. **The Prometheus Crisis** 160ft E3 **
A superb, intricate line on the left side of Space Buttress. Approach: Abseil down Aqualung and continue for 30 feet to a small stance. A change of underwear may be useful at the top!
(1) 80ft 5b. Step right round the rib and climb a short groove to a horizontal break. Follow this right for 25 feet (PR), then move up to a shallow depression (thread) and up to a spike below the overhang on The Book of Invasions. Move right to a hanging belay.
(2) 80ft 5c. Move left past the spike for 20 feet to a thread, then pull over an overhang to a good flake. Move up for 10 feet, then traverse right round a vague rib to the junction with The Book of Invasions. Follow the thin crack above with a hard move right to finish up a groove (as Book of Invasions).

8. **Introducing the Hardline** 140ft E5 *** †
A complete contrast to the rest of the routes here, and also a good deal harder! Approach as for The Book of Invasions, BB.
(1) 70ft 6b. Surmount the archway above the belay to gain the base of a bolt ladder. Follow this steeply (crux) to the sixth bolt and enter the hanging groove above, which slants rightwards to the hanging belay on The Book of Invasions.
(2) 70ft 6a. Move up and right (PR) from the tree to a TR and pass it to gain a BR. Climb through the bulge above to a second bolt then traverse right for 6 feet and pull over a second bulge to a third bolt. Step up and right (PR on left) and finish up the right arête.

9. **The Book of Invasions** 140ft E3 **
An exciting route up the centre of Space Buttress. Approach: From the stake abseil 70 feet to a hanging stance at the top of pitch one. A second abseil leads to a platform at the foot of the route. Best to leave first rope in place, just in case!

(1) 70ft 4c. Climb the big groove which initially slants right, then directly up to a hanging stance by a holly tree.
(2) 70ft 6a. Move left to a ledge, then climb the wall and overhang to a flat hold (PR and thread), reach up left to a small hidden sidepull and climb the wall, PR, to a depression below a final bulge (poor PR). Climb the thin crack above which fades out, and make a hard move right to gain the easy groove above.

10. Air City 170ft E2
Approach as for The Book of Invasions. Rather loose in places.
(1) 90ft 5b. From the platform walk 15 feet right and climb a groove to a small ledge (PR). Continue up to a larger ledge (PB).
(2) 80ft 5a. Swing left onto the wall, then move up for 10 feet and traverse right to a shallow groove. Climb this and the steep wall above, then traverse easily left to the top.

11. T.M.A. 195ft E1
The easiest way up Space Buttress. An interesting outing.
(1) 90ft 4c. As for the first pitch of The Book of Invasions.
(2) 25ft 5a. Traverse right along a fragile break to a PB on Air City.
(3) 80ft 4c. Follow Air City for 30 feet to below the shallow groove, then traverse right across the steep wall to an easier-angled groove and follow this to the top.

12. Puppy Dog Pie 95ft VS † ●
Climbs the horrible break on the right side of the buttress. Approach by a series of abseils from a small tree, down steep grass and the route. PB (not in place) at the foot of the route.
(1) 40ft 4c. Climb up the deep crack for 25 feet, then move diagonally right to a ledge and belay.
(2) 55ft 4c. Up the corner break to the top – carefully.

YEWBARROW (SD 405 782)

By Steve Hubbard and Al Phizacklea.

APPROACH
This somewhat esoteric crag is reached from the library in the centre of Grange-over-Sands by following the Grange Fell Road towards Cartmel for about 600 yards to Eden Mount Road on the right. Turn up this to a T-junction (Charney Well Lane). From this junction a path leads diagonally right across the wooded fellside past some small outcrops, then down slightly to the foot of the main crag.

SITUATION AND CHARACTER
The crag is situated just outside Grange-over-Sands, in a small wooded area. It is a pleasant, though limited, climbing ground; the maximum height only reaching 30 feet. The crag is limestone, of average quality, unpolished and quite steep.

HISTORY
All the routes here, except for the harder problems such as Ectopic,

have all been climbed for many years. Steve Hubbard has climbed here a lot over the years and he added Ectopic early in the 80's.

THE CLIMBS are described from LEFT to RIGHT.

1. **Strategic Withdrawal II** 25ft V Diff
Straight up the chimney with a large chockstone in it.

2. **Strategic Withdrawal I** 30ft Diff
Takes the chimney a few feet right.

3. **Ivy Wall** 30ft V Diff
Follow the crack 3 feet right to a ledge and tree, then finish up the wall above.

4. **Ectopic** 30ft Hard VS
6a. The bulging wall 25 feet right, with a hard start and a loose finish.

5. **Peg Route** 30ft Hard VS
5c. The thin crack 20 feet right.

6. **Ivy Groove** 30ft Hard VS
5b. The obvious groove which cuts through the overhangs.

7. **Roll Over** 30ft Hard VS
5b. Just right is a black wall, go up this and the overhang above with a gymnastic move.
After a short gap, there is a buttress with a very large roof. The next route starts at the left side of this.

8. **Celebration Route** 30ft Sev
The undercut chimney just left of the very large roof. The roof itself remains unclimbed!

There are numerous other small outcrops close by which have a number of boulder problems.

MINOR CRAGS

BARKER SCAR (SD 334 783)
A low broken crag next to the Leven estuary just N of the railway viaduct. It is reached by turning left one mile north of Holker Hall along a road that leads to a caravan site by the sea. Walk along the beach to the crag.

Crocodile (30ft E2 6b) climbs the centre of the first big clean wall – a 'snappy' route, one bolt runner.

Further right is a conspicuous cave. An aid route – **Harry Worth Goes to Hollywood** (A2) – crosses the roof crack (big Friends). An unusual route, it finishes on the floor!

There are several boulder problems on the wall outside the cave.

BLACK YEWS SCAR (SD 439 867)
It has been agreed not to climb on this crag, which is a northward continuation of Chapel Head Scar, in order to obtain access to Chapel Head. It is mostly broken and reaches 30 feet in places.

BOW MARBLE BREAST (SD 428 938)
A steep slate crag above the hamlet of Thorneyfields, two miles north of Crosthwaite. One route of 5a has been reported up the groove high up in the centre of the diamond-shaped buttress.

BRANT FELL (SD 409 962)
Reached from Bowness on the B5284 Kendal road, the fell is the first open ground on the left, just above the steep hill. The crag is by the summit of the fell and commands the finest view of any crag in this guide. It is a popular bouldering area for local climbers, short steep slate with a sustained test-piece traverse (6b).

HIGH NEWTON CRAG (SD 404 828)
This is a small quarry situated adjacent to the A590 just south of High Newton. It contains two climbs which are well worth 20 minutes effort on the way to, or out of, The Lakes. Climbers are asked not to park on the grass verge below the crag.

The climbs lie on a steep slab at the north end of the quarry. Some doubtful holds exist due to the nature of the rock. Now overgrown.

1. **Cat O'Nine "Tales"**   40ft   Hard VS
5b. Climb the obvious right-slanting crack.

2. **The Wall**   40ft   E1
5c. Takes the wall to the left. It is easier if started from the left, rather than direct.

Some other routes include the deep groove right of Cat O'Nine Tails (V Diff), and the sharp arête just right (5a). The slab in the lower part gives routes of V Diff and Sev, and the broken arête right of this is V Diff.

KENDAL BRIDGE (SD 507 865)
This is the bridge which carries the A591 from the M6 over the River Kent. It is reached from the roundabout where the A6 meets the A591, by following the Sedgewick road. Before the bridge is reached take the right turn and follow this road until its end by the new road at the main bridge. The bridge has two tiers of climbing walls separated by a footpath/walkway. These give excellent bouldering and are always dry as they are below the roadway.

LATTERBARROW CRAG (SD 440 830)
A steep limestone outcrop 35 feet high, which is hidden in the wooded hillock opposite the Derby Arms Hotel. Ask permission from Latterbarrow Farm.

LINDALE SLABS (SD 418 817)

These clean, open, slate slabs are clearly seen from the Lindale bypass on the slopes of Newton Fell. They are reached from Lindale by taking the narrow road next to the pub at the bottom of the hill. The slabs are 50 feet high and there are several cracks running up them. These hold routes of Diff/V Diff grade, which are used by a local outdoor centre. Bolt belays at the top. In order to prevent congestion at the crag, any groups intending to visit the crag are asked to ring Castle Head Field Centre, (Grange 34300) prior to their visit. Individuals should ask permission from the farmer who lives just north of the crag.

LOW CRAG (SD 447 850)

To the north of Millside Scar and at a lower level, this crag is hidden in the woods above Beck Head. There are several buttresses up to 40 feet high, and about ten routes have been done up the gardened sections.

SLAPE SCARS (SD 448 865)

A line of short limestone crags above Chapel Head Scar on the top of Lords Seat. These extensive outcrops are over a mile long, and give varied bouldering.

IX. THE FURNESS AREA

Compiled by Al Phizacklea

Although the Furness Area does not contain any large crags, it does have a wealth of small quarries and outcrops which provide training for locals. Although the area does not merit a visit from afar, it is hoped that these notes will provide entertainment for both visitors and locals.

ABBEY ROAD BRIDGE – BARROW (SD 214 717)

This is the bridge under the A590 situated below the new hospital as the road enters Barrow. The bridge consists of sandstone blocks, the best wall is the left-hand one facing the hospital. Good traversing.

BAYCLIFF HAGGS QUARRY (SD 282 726)

By the minor road between Scales and Baycliff. Some short, hard problems, including an access problem.

BAYCLIFF NEW QUARRY (SD 287 272)

Reached from the centre of the village, which is just off the A5087. It is 200 yards on the left, along the Sunbrick cart track. The three crags are not very high, but they are long and give superb traversing.

BIRKRIGG QUARRY (SD 282 747)

The quarry is on Birkrigg Common, 2 miles south of Ulverston. The best rock is in the low quarry, below the road level just left of the main face.

Birkrigg is the centre-piece of the area, and is a popular bouldering and training area, often viewed from the 'galleries' by the public.

The usual test-piece is the low-level traverse which runs from left to right (5c). There is also a very bold upper traverse along the horizontal break near the top of the quarry, along the left and central walls (5c).

Of note are the superb boulder problems on the left wall. Use your imagination and fingers! Some of the more popular routes are indicated on the diagram, and are listed below. They are up to 30 feet long, and the rock is generally good limestone.

1. **The Slab**(V Diff)	2. **Bolt Wall**(5a)	3. **Jug Bug**(4c)
4. **Gurt Wall**(5c)	5. **Swinging Groove**(5a)	6. **Hole Wall**(5a)
7. **Pincher**(5b)	8. **Old Clem**(4c)	9. **Chopping Block**(5c)
10. **Teasy Way**(Diff)	11. **Lurcher**(5a)	12. **Searcher**(5b)
13. **Loose Bruce**(5b)	14. **Black Wall**(5b)	15. **The Corner**(Sev)

DONKEY ROCKS (SD 211 867)

This is a steep quarry, ¼ mile south of Broughton on the Foxfield road. The rock is smooth slate of a most unusual blistered architecture. There are only two routes at present.

1. **Hee Haw**   70ft   E2
5b. The widest of the cracks in the right end of the wall.

2. **Muffin' the Mule**   70ft   A2
The thin crack left of Hee Haw.

DUNNERHOLME (SD 212 797)

A curious limestone plug in the Duddon Estuary, which is visible from the A595. Approach is via Grange Marsh Farm, and care is needed with parking to prevent blocking access.

On the left are a set of short friction slabs with several hard problems marked in blue paint, as well as a delicate girdle. Around the back is a continuously overhanging low wall with a desperate monster girdle. There are some longer problems and a broken girdle down at the beach.

ELLISCALE QUARRY (SD 224 747)

By the A595 just outside Dalton. Some short, hard problems.

HOAD SLABS (SD 296 790)

Clearly seen from the A590 just north of Ulverston, these clean slate slabs are a popular practice ground. Park in the steep lane below the hill.

THE ROUTES are described from RIGHT to LEFT.

1. **Railway** 70ft Hard Sev
4a. Climb the right side of the slab, then finish right of the top arête.

2. **Devil's Armchair** 70ft Sev
Climb the central crack to the sentry box and finish direct. Classic.

3. **Armchair Variant** 70ft Hard Sev
4c. From the sentry box on Devil's Armchair, move left and finish up the slab.

4. **Hoad Road** 80ft Hard VS
5a. A straight eliminate starting midway between Devil's Armchair and Airway. Climb the slab direct via a vague crack. The thin top slab is the crux.

5. **Airway** 80ft VS
4b. Start 15 feet left of Devil's Armchair and climb the thin crack to the ledge. Move right on good holds and either, finish direct up the left arête of the top slab, or, move left and climb the short slab and overhang direct.

6. **Hoad Way** 90ft Diff
Start from the lowest point of the slab and climb up to the ledge, move right and up a groove to twin horizontal cracks, then traverse right across the slab to a sentry box. Move right round an arête and finish up a groove.

THE OLD MAN OF URSWICK (SD 249 746)

A rather grand title for a limestone block stack, halfway between Urswick and Dalton. Climb any of the 25-foot high faces to gain the summit; about VS climbing.

ORMSGILL QUARRY (SD 199 717)

Approach is along a drive 200 yards south of the Ormsgill Hotel at Barrow. The quarry is up to 60 feet high, but is composed of friable sandstone. Some ten routes have been made, mainly loose, and largely unprotected. The old tip has been reclaimed and there is a long low-level traverse as well as some shorter problems on a low top tier. The place is often frequented by glue-sniffing vandals.

STAINTON QUARRY (SD 243 727)

The quarry is near Stainton village, just south-east of Dalton-in-Furness. There are two quarries, but the new one has recently been re-opened, there was only 1 route in it, which followed the black slab on the left face (Hard VS). To reach the old quarry follow the old track on the north side of the newly-widened road. After 100 yards scramble down left of the bridge to a disused railway line. The quarry is 150 yards further along.

There are only six routes at present, although there is scope for more. They are described from LEFT to RIGHT.

1. **Broken Buttress**   60ft   V Diff
Climb the broken rocks up the centre of the buttress left of the mineshaft. Finish up blocks on the left side.

2. **The Arête**   50ft   Hard Sev   *
4a. Direct up the striking arête right of the mineshaft. Climb it just left of the rib.

3. **Fox Hole Wall**   50ft   VS
4a. Climb directly above the small cave up the wall, 20 yards right of The Arête.

4. **Evening Wall**   60ft   Hard VS
4c. Just right of the descent rake in the centre of the quarry is a steep wall, climb this to the overhanging blocks, finishing left or right. Poor protection.

5. **Stainton Crack**   30ft   VS   *
4b. The classic, steep off-width crack on the right of the quarry is climbed on improving jams. Strenuous.

6. **Girdle Traverse**   280ft   VS
4c. A poor expedition from left to right.

STOTT PARK HEIGHTS CRAG (SD 368 894)

Approach is direct through the woods from the lay-by on the Newby Bridge – Hawkshead road, just south of the south entrance of the YMCA camp. Short but pleasant.

ADDENDUM

ANGLEZARKE QUARRY

18a. I'm Spartacus E5 ★★ †
6b. Start at a short right-trending ramp about 20 feet right of Flake Out. Climb up and rightwards to a PR then up left to flakes and a second PR. Step right and finish direct.

24a. Schwarzennegger Mon Amour E5 ★★ †
6c. The capped groove and wall left of Gritstone Rain, PR. Bolt belay.

27a. If You Can't Lick 'em, Lick 'em E5 ★★ †
6c. Obvious line left of New Jerusalem, PR. Bolt belay.

32a. Kelly's 'i' E2 †
5c. Gain and climb the jamming crack round right from The Changeing.

61a. Orfice Party E5 ★ †
6a. The wall left of Gilt Complex and Helical Happiness, PR. Bolt belay.

HOGHTON QUARRY

108a. Artichoke E6 ★★ †
6b. Climb the bold wall right of The Effect Of Alcohol, to gain the flake of that route by some tricky moves (unprotected). Move right and climb the wall right of the flake to finish.

114a. Intoxicated E6 †
6c. The arête right of Maraschino, PR in that route.

TROWBARROW QUARRY

FOSSIL WALL: This is the wall above and right of Lonely Wall.

1a. Body Abuse 40ft Severe †
Climb the right arête of Fossil Wall, mostly on its right side.

1b. Shell Shock 35ft E1 ● †
4b (yes, 4b!). Climb the centre of Fossil Wall, where there is a step in the overlap, on transient holds.

YELLOW WALL

9a. Owl Surprise 70ft V Diff †
Climbs the corner between Yellow Wall and Main Wall, starting up the

pedestal and dangerous-looking flake. Finish pleasantly on Yellow Wall.

MAIN WALL

11a. Heroes 90ft E2   †
5c. Now reclimbed since the demise of a large flake. Follow Warspite Direct until above the roof then move right to the arête using a thin horizontal crack (where the flake used to be). Climb the arête (crux) and finish direct.

16a. Moondance 90ft E5   †
6a. Climb the arête just right of Touch of Class variation start and climb to the break on that route. Move right and climb to a second break and continue to Major Tom. Follow this left until it ispossible to enter a depression from the left and leave it rightwards (Rocks 2 and 3). Gain the crack of Space Oddity and follow it left to climb the left-hand of two faint cracks (just right of Jean Jeanie) moving rightwards near the top.

WARTON MAIN QUARRY

Raising the Blade E3
5c. The overhanging groove right of Karlyn Returns.

Karlyn Returns E4
6b. Starts below the roof right of Gouffle Connection and surmounts this at its widest point.

Come Here Katherine E1
6a. A resurrection of the collapsed route Karlyn Went Shopping Instead, starting just left of a stepped roof, with a small groove at its lowest point. Climb this and the wall above, moving slightly left to finish.

Beware of the Dentist E2
5b. To the right of the rampline taken by Washington, is an overhanging wall with a groove on its left side. Climb the groove (PR), with the crux just above the peg.

Two complete traverses of the quarry have been done. From left to right is **The Fragmented Tormentor** (Edsup) and takes two days, right to left is **What a Waste of a Day** (TD/TD-) and only takes one day! Obviously classics of the best kind!

NOTES

NOTES

NOTES

NOTES

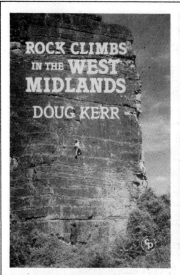

Right:
Alan Sealy on 'Cracked Actor' - Trowbarrow Quarry
Photo: Jon Sparks

TEXT PRINTED BY MARTINS OF BERWICK
COLOUR PRINTED BY CARNMOR PRINT & DESIGN, PRESTON